THE WAY THAT I WENT

R Lloyd Praeger

Robert Lloyd Praeger

The
way that
I went

an
Irishman
in
Ireland

ALLEN FIGGIS DUBLIN 1980

First published 1937
Second edition 1939
Third edition 1947
Paperbound edition 1969
This reprint 1980

Printed in Great Britain by
Richard Clay (The Chaucer Press) Ltd,
Bungay, Suffolk

PREFACE

Let my voice ring out and over the earth,
Through all the grief and strife
With a golden joy in a silver mirth:
Thank God for Life!

THESE lines of James Thomson express better than I can what has
been in my mind as I was writing this book. It is, indeed, a kind of
thank-offering, however crude, for seven decades of robust physical
health in which to walk and climb and swim and sail throughout
or around the island in which I was born, to the benefit alike of
body and soul. But lest it might appear too egotistical, my " little
human praise " is disguised as an account of the beautiful land in
which I have spent my septuagesimal holiday.

R. LLOYD PRAEGER

19 FITZWILLIAM SQUARE,
    DUBLIN

ACKNOWLEDGMENTS

I HAVE to thank A. D. Delap, A. Farrington, T. Hallissy, Dr. R. A. S. Macalister, C. B. Moffat, Prof. S. P. O'Riordan and A. W. Stelfox for furnishing or checking various details regarding topography, geology, zoology, archaeology, etc.; S. Pender for revising Irish names of places; T. H. Mason for permission to use some of his photographs of Irish places—a similar privilege was granted by R. J. Welch before his death; Miss Eileen Barnes for certain line drawings; C. W. Allen for an inspiring map; the Councils of the Royal Irish Academy and of the Royal Society of Antiquaries of Ireland, the Director of the National Museum, and the Controller of the Free State Stationery Office for permission to reproduce certain illustrations from works issued by them; Dr. Manson-Bahr for the same privilege as regards his sketch of Red-necked Phalaropes; James Stephens for allowing me to reprint his " Goat Paths " and other verses; and Messrs George Allen and Unwin, Ernest Benn, Macmillan, Sidgwick and Jackson, the Receiver of John Lane, Ltd., the Executors of Mrs Clement Shorter, and the Proprietors of *Punch* for leave to quote from poetry published by them. Also to the Clarendon Press for permission to quote from *The Shorter Poems of Robert Bridges* the lines on which I found my title, and to Mrs Rudyard Kipling and the Oxford University Press, publishers of Fletcher and Kipling's *School History of England*, for leave to reprint some lines from *The Dawn Wind*. In the case of a few other brief quotations, time or opportunity did not serve for securing the usual sanction; I hope those concerned will accept this explanation.

CONTENTS

vii

Contents

LIST OF ILLUSTRATIONS

PLATES

xi

IN·TEXT

List of Illustrations xiii

I have lain in the sun,
I have toiled as I might,
I have thought as I would,
And now it is night.

My bed full of sleep,
My heart of content,
For friends that I met
The way that I went.

ROBERT BRIDGES

THE WAY THAT I WENT

CHAPTER I

IRELAND

> He made you all fair,
>   You in purple and gold,
> You in silver and green,
> Till no eye that has seen
>   Without love can behold.
>
> DORA SIGERSON SHORTER

THE way that I went was an Irish way, with extraorbital aberrations, especially in later years, to the extent of a thousand or fifteen hundred miles.   It was from the beginning a way of flowers and stones and beasts.   When I was old enough to toddle, my father had to put a fence around a garden patch in front of the house, because I picked all the blossoms; and I knew belemnites and harebells and flint-flakes before I was five.   That obsession has remained with me throughout life, and I make no apology for the predominant place which it will occupy in what I am about to write.   For we are ourselves creations of nature, and spend our lives amid natural objects.   Who does not wish on a fine day to escape from the town into the country?   And when you get there, it adds enormously to your interest and enjoyment if you understand something about the architecture of the hills and plains, and about their teeming population of birds and butterflies and trees.   So I launch my paper ships boldly, in the desire to stimulate an interest in natural things.   I venture to hope that—

> Away down the river,
> A hundred miles or more,
> Other little children
> Shall bring my boats ashore.

1

I have traversed Ireland to and fro from end to end, and from sea to sea. Mostly on foot, for that is the only way to see and get to know intimately any country; sometimes by cycle; seldom by car, because the motor travels much too fast for the serious observer. Used as one uses the train, for rapid transit to some desired spot, it is often a boon beyond price: it can take the town-dweller rapidly beyond the zone of bungalows, and the less sturdy far afield. But for the nature-lover, and for the mind jaded with the meaningless noise and hurry of modern life, with " the rush and glare of the interminable hours ", quiet wandering on foot along brown streams and among the windy hills can bring a solace and a joy that is akin only to the peace of God that passeth understanding.

But, finite and worldly creatures that we are, we cannot exist long on that high plane. Hunger and a westering sun soon drive us back towards the abodes of men, and in the evening the bus or clattering tram is often a godsend as great as was the welcome freedom of the heather in the forenoon. And so the following chapters, built up chiefly of impressions gained in many years' wayfaring in Ireland, must recognize the interest of the populous places as well as those of the country-side. But this is not a guide-book—heaven forfend! Rather have I, in memory, wandered over the country, picking out places and things that have interested me, and which I have hoped may interest others. Nor is the Ireland I describe, like that of many recent writings, the Ireland of the motorist, who, like the " wind-borne mirroring soul " of Matthew Arnold's *Empedocles*,

> A thousand glances wins,
> And never sees a whole;
> Looks once, and drives elsewhere, and leaves its last employ.

There are plenty of books for him. It is rather the Ireland of the man who goes with reverent feet through the hills and valleys, accompanied by neither noise nor dust to scare away wild creatures; stopping often, watching closely, listening carefully. Only thus can he, if he is fortunate, make friends by degrees with the birds and flowers and rocks, learn all the signs and sounds of the country-side, and at length feel at one with what is, after all, his natural environment. And I hold that in this mood he will also be better fitted for due appraisement of the many monuments of man's industry and faith that he will meet in this Ireland of ours, be it a cairn of the Bronze Age, a medieval church, or some marvel of modern science.

There is no need to begin with any general description of Ireland; that has been done over and over again, and by hands more skilled than mine. But it may be desirable to recall a few topographical features which have affected and still affect much that is within the country. There is, first of all, its unique position—an island out in the North Atlantic, doubly cut off from direct continental influences by intervening seas. At the same time, it lies, along with the adjoining and larger island of Great Britain, on a shallow shelf, projecting into the ocean between Spain and Norway, so that a slightly higher level of the land, by spilling the water off this shelf, would allow, and has allowed at certain periods in the past, free immigration from the Continent. These times were too long ago to have affected human affairs as we know them, but they had a considerable influence as regards the peopling of the land with the animals and plants which still occupy it, and possibly as regards movements of the earlier races of man.

Next, there is the unusual nature of the surface. Ancient crumplings of the Earth's crust have resulted in the formation of mountain ranges in the coastal regions, leaving a broad low plain in the centre. Easy access to the interior has consequently been limited to gaps in the high rim, thus fixing trade routes and the position of coastal towns; but free dispersal over the central parts has been possible once the coastal barrier was passed or evaded. This has profoundly influenced the effect of the various human invasions which Ireland has endured, tending to push pre-existing cultures not into an inaccessible centre, as in most islands, but into the mountain-fringe:

witness the present and recent distribution of the native Irish tongue. Again, geological vicissitudes have produced an astonishing variety of rocks, as compared with most areas of similar size: this has given us delightfully varied scenery, and also different kinds of soils, with obvious repercussions on human life. The wholesale mixing-up of superficial deposits caused by the moving ice of the Glacial Period has tended to more uniform and also better soil conditions than would otherwise have been the case. Climate also intrudes itself strikingly in Ireland. The position of the island relative to the warm Atlantic results in high rainfall, cool summers, mild winters, and much wind; these factors influence all life within the island, from man down to mosses. This peculiar position is also at the root of that most delightful of Irish climatic phenomena, its ever-changing cloud-effects, so different from the monotonous and more settled skies—whether cloudy or cloudless—that characterize continental areas. The western hills and the clouds which are their legitimate accompaniment are inseparable; the eye is carried upward from the hill-tops for thousands of feet into the infinite blue. The cloudland is indeed so wonderful a creation that Ireland would be a dull place without it: here it is almost always with us, as vital to our enjoyment as the landscape itself. And if frequent condensation and consequent precipitation is the necessary corollary to the frequent temperature-changes which give us our snowy cumulus and colourful cloud-curtains, we can afford to take with grateful hearts whatever comes. As J. W. Riley sings:

> It ain't no use to grumble and complain;
> 　It's jest as cheap and easy to rejoice;
> When God sorts out the weather and sends rain,
> 　W'y, rain's my choice.

Perhaps the most marked effect of the wet climate is the vast development of peat-bog on the plains, which has rendered one-seventeenth of the lowlands of Ireland useless for purposes of agriculture, but has provided the people with a widespread and almost inexhaustible supply of fuel. It is curious to speculate what would have been the

PLATE I

T. H. Mason: photo

SUN AND SHADOW ON CARAGH LAKE

history of the treeless, coal-less rainy western areas had peat not been present almost everywhere.

A marked result of the marginal distribution of high ground is seen if the river-courses are studied. The streams which rise on the seaward slope of the mountains are short and rapid, while those whose sources lie on the inland side have mostly long and devious courses, and their mouths often lie many times further away from their springs than does the nearest sea. The Shannon, whose " basin " occupies over one-seventh of the whole of Ireland, is a case in point. Its source is distant 24 miles from Donegal Bay; the river is 214 miles long, and its mouth is on the confines of Kerry. The Bann, whose length is 97 miles, rises within 7 miles of Dundrum Bay in Down.

Ireland does not extend through a sufficient range of latitude to show a marked difference between north and south, and there is actually a greater amount of divergence between east and west. The combination of maximum rainfall, maximum exposure and minimum range of temperature which one encounters along the Atlantic seaboard produces effects, especially as regards vegetation, which are very noticeable, and of much importance to agriculturists, horticulturists, botanists and zoologists.

If we imagine Ireland as it was until some couple of thousand years ago, before drainage and peat-cutting had affected the surface, we get a striking picture. The central area in particular was little more than an archipelago—ridges and knolls of firm ground set in a sea of shallow lakes, deep swamps, and wide peat-bogs. Traffic within this region must have been much constricted, and no doubt the frequent coincidence of esker-ridges with present-day roads gives a hint of past conditions.

The former prevalence of lake, marsh and bog has a bearing on the question of past forests. We know that within the period of deposition of our peat-bogs drier spells permitted of the growth over immense areas of the Scotch Fir, and that the slightly warmer climate that prevailed during Neolithic times allowed such forests to spread even to the exposed islands of the west coast. By the way, Caleb Threlkeld in his *Synopsis Stirpium Hibernicarum* (see p. 269) puts forward an explanation of the presence of these now buried pine-forests which has at least the charm of novelty: " But whether the Firr-wood taken out of Mosses or Bogges, which being split into small Sticks do burn like a Torch, or Link, be of this Tree [Scotch Fir] or the *Abies mas* in Irish *Crann Giumnais*, planted by the Danes and after their expulsion cut down, and left to be burryed in the Earth by the Natives to extinguish the Badges of their Servitude, is not to be determined by me ".

When Oak began to replace Pine, the forests tended to become increasingly restricted to the better drained and more sheltered ground. At present the extensive woods of Oak in the Wicklow and Kerry valleys, and of Oak mixed with Birch, Holly, Arbutus, etc., about Killarney, are the best representatives of the ancient woodlands. Wherever the ground was fit for pasture or tillage, the forests have been destroyed long since. Our existing native woods, whether of Oak or of mixed species, are delightful, for they are not so dense as to exclude a rich ground-vegetation of flowers and ferns.

The recent complete disappearance of the Pine as a native is the most notable event in the history of Irish trees. In comparatively recent times there were several species of tall Conifers in Ireland: now the only representatives of that great and ancient family are the Yew and the Juniper. We have none of the grand forests of Central Europe, where the Pine stems rise like gigantic columns into a canopy which the sun cannot penetrate, where the silence is complete,

And the gloom divine is all around,
And underneath is the mossy ground.

But I do not think, having traversed them in Switzerland and Germany and Bulgaria and Scandinavia, that I mourn the absence from Ireland of the dense dark gnome-haunted forests of the Continent. You soon get too much of them, and long for open glades and tree-free hill-sides where you can have sun and wind and a wide prospect.

When you are in Switzerland or Tyrol, the reason for your steady climbing through the two or three thousand feet of forest zone is, after all, your desire to get out of it! The mind does not work at its best there; and the shadow and restriction of the imprisoning trees produce at length a feeling of depression and in some minds even of fear. So you hurry upward towards the crags, and there if anywhere, with the round earth below you and the sky above, you may achieve freedom of spirit.

I can claim a fairly extensive knowledge of every county in Ireland—particularly as regards its topography and botany—otherwise this book would not be written; and in order that the reader may understand the kind of information which I mean (which is a very small portion of what might be acquired) and which it shall be my endeavour in some measure to transmit to him, it will simplify matters if I indicate briefly the sources of both my knowledge and my ignorance: to do this I am compelled to be briefly autobiographical.

My scientific life began in the field, and has continued there. When I was promoted from a small private school to the " Inst." in Belfast I knew a good deal about local plants—where they grew, when they flowered, what their roots and seeds were like as well as their blossoms; and I eagerly joined the small group of boys who attended a bi-weekly botanical class. But when I found that botany consisted in drawing a series of adnate parallelograms and entering in the blank spaces such terms as " monochlamydeous " and " gamo-sepalous " I fled in terror, and later, at college, I did not venture again to approach my favourite subject as seen through the eyes of a teacher of Victoria's glorious days. Indeed, Queen's College, as it was then, was a rather forbidding and comfortless place. The professors for the most part arrived five minutes before lecture-time, talked for an hour, and departed again to the fastnesses of University Street or the Lisburn Road. There were no laboratories or practical work except in chemistry—and for the medical students, of course, anatomy. In each of the three Colleges that constituted the Queen's (later the Royal) University there was a chair of Natural History, the unfortunate occupant of which had to diffuse light on zoology, botany, geology and palaeontology—" Professors of Creation ", as A. C. Haddon used to call them. This is much too wide a field for any man, and it is not surprising that some of the subjects were treated in a rather perfunctory manner. If you were adrift between lectures, the only place where you could even sit down was on a wooden bench in a small severe room off the main hall, where a silent man with a white beard, as uncommunicative as the Professor of Metaphysics, served plump buns and weak coffee at a reasonable charge. I took geology lectures, necessary for the engineering course, but never handled a rock-specimen or a fossil, though I was allowed to peer at some through the dusty glass of museum cases. But all the time I was fast learning geology and zoology and botany of another kind through the Belfast Naturalists' Field Club. I had joined the Club at the age of eleven, and after a short lapse during school days, rejoined with added enthusiasm. The Club had been founded in 1863 as a consequence of the stimulating lectures given under the Science and Art Department by Ralph Tate, afterwards Professor of Geology at Adelaide, and some of his pupils were still leading members. It was an association of enthusiastic amateurs, remarkably well versed in local geology and biology, eager to impart knowledge: and under this stimulating influence I probed wonderingly into the fairyland of nature. Experience gained on the field excursions stood me in good stead. I remember a *viva voce* in geology in Dublin at the old Royal University building in Earlsfort Terrace. " Can you name that rock? " " Granite." " Can you say what part of Ireland it comes from? " " Dublin " (the wall in front of the building was of granite, and I had noticed in passing how it differed from the Mourne rock, the only granite I knew). " Quite right: now point out the constituent minerals." I could have done this at six years old. " Do you see any other mineral there? " Horrors! What was there besides quartz, felspar and mica? " Tourmaline " I said at a venture. " Right: now show me the tourmaline." I chose an almost microscopic black speck, which might be anything, so far as I knew. " Yes—but you might have selected a larger crystal, like *that*. Now show me another." Not difficult, once one knew! Then presently, " Have you any ideas about this fossil? " " *Gryphaea incurva*, a mollusc from the Lower Lias, allied to the oyster "—I could have named almost any Irish Liassic shell, thanks to Field Club excursions to Barney's Point, and the friendly instruction of Swanston, Stewart and Bulla. Full marks. A bit of Old Red conglomerate was equally easy, for had I not played about the caves at Cushendun, and read Miller's *Old Red Sandstone* ? So the Field Club did for me what R. O. Cunningham's lectures might have failed to do. All the same, I have felt continually the want of the laboratory training in the natural sciences which I never got: that is a bad handicap in modern scientific work of whatever kind: but it was not to be had in Belfast fifty years ago, and as I always preferred the field as a laboratory, I have continued to have a wonderfully good time without it.

I owe a very great deal of the interest and pleasure of which my life has been full to those early associations with the sturdy workers of the Belfast Field Club. Foremost among them was that remarkable man S. A. Stewart, trunk-maker, botanist and geologist (p. 92); then there were Wm. Swanston, linen manufacturer and geologist; F. J. Bigger, solicitor and archaeologist; Joseph Wright, grocer and specialist in the Foraminifera; Wm. Gray, Inspector under the Office of Works, and in science jack-of-all-trades; Charles Bulla, commercial traveller and palaeontologist; S. M. Malcolmson, physician and microscopist; Robert Bell, shipyard worker and geologist; R. J. Welch, photographer and fanatical crusader in the interests of Irish natural history; Canon Lett, botanist; W. J. Knowles, insurance agent and prehistorian; and others—men of all sorts brought together by a common interest. It is noteworthy that in those times no member of the staff of the future university took part in the work of this enthusiastic and democratic society; in that respect things are different nowadays. With this Field Club group, men who knew all there was to know about local birds and insects and flowers and rocks and fossils, I foraged all over Ulster and beyond, picking up the field lore that is not found in any book, but passes from hand to hand, and so from generation to generation.

When I left the north in 1893 I exchanged the Belfast Club and Ulster for the Dublin Club and Leinster, Connaught and Munster. The Dublin Field Club had been founded in 1885 by A. C. Haddon and others; and the same pleasant scientific camaraderie existed as in Belfast—though of a more professional kind.   There was no need to mourn a change that brought one into contact with R. M. Barrington, R. F. Scharff, G. H. Carpenter, C. B. Moffat, G. A. J. Cole, W. J. Sollas, T. Johnson, A. C. Haddon, E. J. McWeeney, de Vismes Kane, Greenwood Pim, and later many more.   The presence of a number of other scientific societies in Dublin never allowed of the Field Club there attaining the local importance long held by its elder sister in Belfast, but since its inception it has fulfilled a fruitful rôle in popularizing scientific study, and has proved a useful training-ground for young people who later pass on to the larger societies.   Field Clubs were started, too, in the nineties in Limerick and Cork.   We established a joint committee which arranged triennial meetings of a week's duration in Kerry, Cork, Galway, Sligo, Donegal, in which all the clubs as well as members of kindred societies across the channel took part; these were especially useful in promoting inter-club intimacy of a fruitful kind.   The latest phase of Field Club activity has been the formation in several provincial centres in Ulster of similar societies, affiliated to the Belfast Club and drawing from it much of their inspiration.   My own heavy debt of gratitude for help in former days has led me to be ever a strong supporter of the Field Club movement, and in spite of the many alternative facilities now available for the acquisition of a knowledge of natural history, I do not find that the usefulness of the Field Clubs has in any way diminished.   Especially among the younger folk, whose lives tend in these days to be so dominated by cinemas, dancing and motoring, the little antidote offered by the Field Clubs, the " back to the land " attitude which is theirs, is I think salutary. It certainly leads to a better understanding of our country, which is an asset of no small value.

It was my Field Club training that led to a deep interest in all natural phenomena which Ireland affords, and to raids into every portion of it: but a special piece of work which I undertook forty years ago brought about a much more detailed acquaintance; it arose thus. Since 1866 our knowledge of the distribution of plants in Ireland was based on *Cybele Hibernica*, a work compiled by David Moore and A. G. More, and issued in that year. In it, the authors divided Ireland into twelve "districts", and the range of each species in the country was shown by reference to them. While this constituted a great advance on previous works, such as Mackay's *Flora Hibernica* (1836), it became obvious as years went on that for purposes of phytogeographical study a finer division was required, so that the distribution of each plant might be shown in greater detail. It was true that my friends Colgan and Scully were engaged on a new edition of *Cybele*, but this did not meet the case, as the twelve-fold partition was being adhered to. So in 1894 I put forward a scheme for the partition of Ireland into forty "divisions", county boundaries being for convenience used as much as possible. The problem was then to work out the range of every Irish flowering plant within this new framework: in other words to compile forty county lists. The total flora of an average division (about 800 square miles) I reckoned as being about 700 species, using the word "species" in a conservative sense. I thought that publication would be justified if I could show at least 500 species for each. The present state of knowledge indicated that, thanks to the work of many botanists, both past and contemporary, the flora of eleven of the forty divisions was already well known, while of seven more the flora was about half worked out—say 200 to 400 species. Of the remaining twenty-two divisions, an average of 100 species each would have been a high estimate of the amount of our information concerning them; of some the flora was almost totally unknown. Again, the best-worked counties were naturally those which had the greatest botanical or physical attractions—such as Kerry and Wicklow, West Galway, Antrim—or those which adjoined the larger centres of population, like Dublin and Down. The area where, as an exhaustive stock-taking showed, work was most required, was the great inland region, largely occupied by the Central Plain, and extending from Limerick and Kilkenny northward to Tyrone. While welcome assistance came from many sides, the survey of this central region—one-half of Ireland—fell almost entirely to myself, with frequent raids into the half-worked counties in addition. Not only each division, but every kind of ground included in each—mountains, rivers, lakes, bogs and marshes, gravelly ground, seashore (where present), had to be visited not once, but so far as possible in spring, summer and autumn, so that no plant might be missed. The planning, with the aid of maps, lists and time-tables, of expeditions designed to fulfil these conditions was fascinating, and was always carried out well in advance. I had reckoned that with a well-thought-out campaign of this kind, fifty days in the field in each of five consecutive years (1896-1900) ought to yield the results desired, a day's work consisting of twelve hours in the field, during which twenty to twenty-five miles of diverse ground would usually be covered. This estimate proved more than justified; in 1901, when *Irish Topographical Botany* was issued by the Royal Irish Academy, it showed an average of not 500, but 628 species for each of the forty Irish divisions. But the point I wish to make concerns not these botanical results, but the extensive and intimate knowledge which this campaign gave me of all those parts of Ireland which, being reckoned uninteresting, are to the majority of people unknown. The more immediately attractive areas one can hardly help knowing if one lives in this island, and I was already intimate with them. This special work, involving some five thousand miles of tramping—mostly across country—over the less familiar parts, equalized one's knowledge, and gave a uniform and much truer impression of the country as a whole. Since that period of special activity I have travelled continually over Ireland, especially in its more remote regions, on quests botanical or zoological or geological or archaeological, but the field-work of 1896-1900 provided a solid basis of knowledge that I do not think I could have acquired otherwise.

Field botany seems a pursuit particularly adapted to this purpose. The lover of walking makes instinctively for the more picturesque districts: the artist does the same, and is sedentary besides. The golfer sticks to his links, the sailor to the sea. The field geologist and zoologist get a more extended acquaintance with the country, but their work tends to keep them on certain selected ground. But the field botanist ranges far and wide over hill and dale: though there is good ground and bad ground, he never knows where an interesting or rare plant may not be concealed: and often his best find is made at the close of a long day in some quite unexpected spot.

Nor is his day's work over when he gets home. Plants cannot all be named on the ground; they often need study, which involves the collecting and drying of specimens; and a full vasculum—as his tin case is called—means a couple of hours' evening work. This botanical case, the botanist's oriflamme, is often an object of sore puzzledom to the country folk. I remember going into a roadside public-house in County Waterford on a hot day to get some cider; they make—or made—good cider down there. The only other customer was a broad man with a face like a cow: I didn't fancy him. Like a certain Cabinet Minister in one of P. G. Wodehouse's stories, he looked as if he had been poured into his clothes and had forgotten to say " When! "; nor did I like the bovine stare which accompanied his absence of greeting when I said good-day. After an interval his curiosity was too much for him; the queer tin had to be accounted for. "Will they be gettin' the new road in Ballybeg finished before the winter? " he enquired (evidently the vasculum was some engineering instrument, and I must be the County Surveyor). " I don't know," I answered. A pause. Then, " The fishin' is bad the year " (the tin case must surely be a receptacle for trout or salmon). " Is it? " Another pause. Then in a more hearty tone, " The people hereabouts is very slow in partin' with

their money. What are you sellin', sir? " " I'm not selling anything." Complete mystification and rising indignation. Then at
last, with a bang of his fist on the counter that made the tumblers
jump—" Ah! What the divil are ye at all? "

A more amiable speech was that of an ancient lady fiddler with
whom I had tea in a little back room in Killala—a village consisting
of a round tower and many public-houses—when I paid her modest
reckoning along with my own: " Faith, an' I didn't know, acushla,
what the divil I was to say to Mrs Casey, for sorra a pinny I had on
me barrin' three-ha'pence, an' the half of that owed already; but the
Lord has sint a holy man from the dear knows where with a tin drum
on his broad back, who has relieved me of all my dishtress; and may
all the blissin's," etc. etc. etc.

Ireland is an unusually convenient land for cross-country walking,
which is what I have always loved. There is little, especially in the
agricultural and hill regions that make up most of the country, to
prevent your wandering where you please, and you are welcome
everywhere. Gamekeepers and other deterrent elements such as
notices concerning trespass are rare and local phenomena, and
generally of perfunctory significance. " Sure and nobody here
takes any notice of notices! " A difficulty sometimes arises owing
to the superfluity of water in Ireland, which results, in certain areas,
in a plethora of broad ditches or anastomosing swamps or lakes.
There is a curious flat region by the Shannon near Roosky that was
troublesome in this way—lakelets connected by silent swift-flowing
streams full of long submerged water-weeds—two feet of water and
three feet of soft muddy bottom, impossible either to wade or swim.
I hesitated on the edge, and then, remembering the cow in *Punch*
that (if my memory serves me)

> gently whispered " Dammit,
> If other beasts have swum it, I can swim it "—and she swam it,

I stepped in. One could only flounder across, using both arms and
legs, wishing that coiling pond-weeds did not lead to such Laocoon-
like struggling. Or as you hesitate on the edge of a twenty-foot

drain, a friendly hay-maker in the next meadow will hail you: " Ye'll fin' a foot-stick down beyant the fince", and you weather five formidable " finces " to reach a wobbly fir-trunk thrown across from bank to bank, so slippery that it would puzzle a tight-rope walker to negotiate it.

It is certainly a matter for regret that the climate of these northern regions makes it so uncomfortable to get wet and so difficult to get dry. The clothes which the prevailing temperature compels us to wear are even in summer of a thickness which renders them capable of absorbing a vast amount of water, and the air is of a dampness which slows up evaporation, and so keeps them wet. Not but that I think Ireland has a worse reputation as regards weather than she deserves. Rain is frequent, especially in the west, but seldom lasts long. A whole wet day is rare. A wet morning mostly means a fine afternoon, and if the early morning has been very bright the reverse is often true. But even in Kerry I have several times had botanical work interfered with by drought: and when that moist greenhouse-like atmosphere remains dry for a spell, it is mere disaster to all the mosses and liverworts and Filmy Ferns which by their abundance and luxuriance lend so special a charm to the south-west. The whole west coast indeed is a country redolent of wind and rain, with an atmosphere that recalls blue eyes with tears in them: the only conditions under which it can look simply un-attractive is in dry weather, with an east wind and that peculiar dispiriting grey haze that mostly accompanies it. Better than that, honest rain sweeping in from the Atlantic, and the sea shouting on the rocks.

But to return to the vexed question of suitable clothes. Apart from being rained on, there is the problem previously mentioned of rivers to be crossed and lakes to be explored. How you may envy your dog which, after swimming, gives himself a shake and carries on as before! Up to the knees in water is all right: you soon dry again, especially if you wear shoes with holes in them to let the water out; but waist deep or more is distinctly inconvenient. And to

take off clothes is a loss of time, and makes work difficult except in
open ground. To get your clothes across a stream, carrying them
while swimming, is more troublesome than you might imagine.
For a while, when working rivery and lakey country, I bore a rubber
bag which could be closed tightly at the mouth, and which could
safely be towed; but it proved hardly worth while, and if the sun
was shining swimming in one's clothes was good enough for the few
occasions which demanded it. For work on the islets and rocks off
the west coast such a rubber bag would be useful, for occasionally it
is very difficult to regain your boat if the sea gets up, while it would
be easy to plunge in and swim to her: but to sit in a boat in wet
clothes for hours is not pleasant. If only the weather is warm,
overalls *pro toto indumento* for land and water alike save a lot of
trouble. Ireland, especially in the west, is an amphibious kind of
land; if you want to probe effectually into the corners, some sort
of amphibious costume becomes necessary. And both here and elsewhere, I doubt if naturalists realize how much they miss by having,
according to the code, to keep dry and reasonably clean, instead of
poking their enquiring noses, like terriers, into every hole, be it dry
or wet. These domestic details bearing on field-work in Ireland
may seem trivial, but they are not so, for little good work is done
under conditions of discomfort. Proper provision for eventualities
is as important to the nature-lover or to the exploring archaeologist
as is fine weather.

Owing chiefly to her past geological history and present climate,
Ireland has a facies of her own. A different rural economy, akin to
that of Scotland rather than of England, gives a characteristic touch
to the country-side: and the towns also have a distinctive aspect.
Though in times both prehistoric and historic the country has
experienced wave after wave of human invasion, these have made
themselves permanently felt in only a limited degree, and an independent note has been maintained. And though much has been
imported, Ireland has in some notable instances evolved her own
methods and manners. We may take at random a few instances,

ancient and modern. The gold ornaments of the Bronze Age stand out conspicuously, not only on account of their number, but of their form. Perhaps the most characteristic is the lunula, a flat crescent-shaped plate of gold, up to eleven inches across, and intended for wearing round the neck. They are mostly ornamented, sometimes richly, with finely cut chevrons, triangles, lozenges or cross-hatchings, akin to those characteristic of axes of the early Bronze Age—say 1200 to 1400 B.C. Their distribution shows that they were an entirely Irish production, which got spread sparingly over Great Britain and the western edge of the Continent owing to raids or to commerce. It is impossible to estimate how many of these golden collars may once have been in Ireland, for ancient Irish gold has been melted down for centuries. About seventy are in existence or known to have existed here; nine are recorded from Scotland, Wales or Corn-wall, six from western France, one from Belgium and two from Denmark—a highly significant distribution. A collection of over thirty-five of them is preserved in the National Museum in Dublin, and George Coffey has summed up in 1909 our knowledge con-cerning the provenance of this peculiar and striking form of personal decoration.[1]

In the early centuries of the Christian era the Ogham alphabet made its appearance—an interesting though clumsy mode of writing. It remained current only a few hundred years, for the almost simul-taneous introduction of the Roman script soon ousted it: but it lingered long in the knowledge of the people, as is shown by the startling fact that so late as the early nineteenth century a farmer called Collins, living near the Old Head of Kinsale, was prosecuted by the police for not having his name duly inscribed on his cart: but it *was* there—in Ogham. It is recorded (*Windele Letters*) that the Rev. Daniel O'Sullivan procured his discharge, but he was recommended by the magistrate to add a translation on the cart shaft, to avoid future trouble! Like the lunula, the Ogham writ-

[1] " The Distribution of Gold Lunulae in Ireland and North-western Europe", *Proc. Royal Irish Acad.*, vol. xxvii., sect. C, pp. 257-258, plates 9-12. 1909.

ing originated in Ireland, and spread only sparingly beyond it (see p. 274).

(see p. 274).

Then there is the *clochteac* or round tower, so characteristic of early Irish ecclesiastic establishments—a fine subject of controversy among the earlier archaeologists, some of whom insisted on regarding it as of pagan origin, but now known to represent a happy combination of bell-tower and refuge and beacon of early Christian times, well suited to a country sparsely populated, and liable to sudden raids from the dreaded Norsemen. In its characteristic form, with elevated doorway for purposes of defence, and belfry under the conical roof, the round tower is a native product, unknown outside Ireland save for a few Scottish examples clearly derived from ours. " As architectural objects ", writes Fergusson,[1] " these towers are singularly pleasing. Their outline is always graceful, and the simplicity of their form is such as to give the utmost value to their dimensions. . . . In a town or amid the busy haunts of men, they would lose half their charm; situated as they are, they are among the most interesting of the antiquities of Europe."

Again, during the eighteenth and nineteenth centuries Ireland evolved several types of vehicles which appear to have been unique. There is some difficulty in making out the histories of these, as they do not seem ever to have been " written up " by any enthusiastic delver into the more recent past. First there was the Noddy. I do not know when or how it was born, but it was in full blast in 1764, as shown by the following extract from Bush's *Hibernia Curiosa*:[2] " But they have an odd kind of hacknies here, that is called the *Noddy*, which is nothing more that an old cast off one horse chaise or chair, with a kind of stool fixed upon the shafts just before the seat, on which the driver sits, just over the rump of his horse, and drives you from one part of the town to another at stated rates for a *set-down*; and a damn'd set-down it is sometimes, for you are well off if you are not set down in a kennel by the breaking of the wheels,

---

[1] James Fergusson, *History of Architecture*, p. 925. 1855.
[2] The book is dated 1767, but describes a tour in 1764.

on an overset-down, nor can you see anything before you but your nod-nod-nodding charioteer, whose situation on the shafts obliges his motion to be conformed to that of the horse, from whence, I suppose, they have obtained the name of the Noddy; I assure you the case of the fare is not much consulted in the construction of these nodding vehicles.   However, they are convenient for single persons, the fare being not more than half that of a coach, and are taken to any part of the Kingdom, on terms as you can agree."   Pictures of the noddy show a small open two-wheeled vehicle rather like an arm-chair with shafts, the driver perched close in front of the passenger, as described.

The noddy was apparently ousted by the inside car or jingle, which seems to have slightly preceded the familiar outside car. Both arrived early in the nineteenth century, and both were every-where by 1830.   The jingle, as represented in Dublin, seems to have impressed the visitor even less favourably than the noddy: " At the Pigeon-house ", writes Gregory Greendrake,[1] " were collected a number of vehicles, of which you can form no idea; they are called *gingles* from the gingling or rumbling noise produced by their motion, consequent of their crazy and wretched condition. The Irish seem particularly fond of the application of *nick-names*; the gingle has four [2] wheels, the body like a sociable or berlin, it is drawn by one miserable half starved spectre of a horse, and the driver, or *gingleman*, seated in front, exhibits, in his person, a most disgusting combination of nudity, dirt, and rags."   One suspects that Master Gregory had been very sea-sick, for there follows more violent abuse of the " gingleman "; but he recovers soon, and admits that Dublin is a fine city.   Though now nearly extinct, the jingle was for a long time widespread in Ireland—a two-wheeled four-passenger covered affair entered from behind, with seats facing each other, the driver outside in front, and the back, which mostly sagged

[1] J. Coad (pseud. Gregory Greendrake), *The Angling Adventures of Gregory Greendrake* (Dublin, 4th ed.), p. 11.   1832.

[2] Surely a mistake.

distressingly, closed by a flapping curtain. Fifty years ago they were still in Dublin, and I can remember one at Holywood near Belfast, with a driver as ancient as itself; they remained common in and around Cork until lately. But except in the south, the jingle seems to have succumbed early to the onslaught of the outside car. The *Irish Penny Journal* writes in 1832: " Almost every citizen who can afford it keeps a car ", and clearly the outside car is intended. Since the beginning of the present century, the motor-car has been steadily supplanting that characteristic Irish vehicle—the " jaunting car " of the English tourist, but never, so far as I know, of the Irishman. This is to be regretted, for there was no vehicle—except the dog-cart —which was so ideal for viewing the country. For the naturalist it had a value beyond price: you saw everything by the road-side and far away; you could hop on and off as you liked; and it could go almost everywhere. Many a rare plant did I " spot " from an " outside ", which I would never have detected from a saloon car even if going at a staid eight miles an hour instead of the usual thirty or forty: and even still I regret its approaching extinction. But partiality to this national vehicle was not universal. Thus in Murray's *Handbook*, last edition (now nearly thirty years old) the editor strikes a note almost as pensive as those which previous writers indulged in when on the subject of noddies and jingles: " To all but Irishmen, or those who have lived long enough in Ireland to have become educated in the art of adhering to the seat of the popular ' outside car ', any machine is preferable to it, owing to its swinging motion and other inconveniences ". It is curious that the outside car should have arisen under an Irish sky, for there never was a vehicle which provided passengers with so complete a soaking in wet weather.

The " Bianconi " or long-car was clearly developed from the short outside car. Lengthen your outside car so as to allow half a dozen passengers on each side, with a glorified ' well ' between the two rows of seats for the reception of a vast amount of luggage, put it on four wheels, raise and widen the driver's perch till it looks like

PLATE II

R. Welch: photo

THE LONG CAR, 1894.   (The Author's first incursion into Connemara)

a triple throne, place two plodding horses in front—or four for a heavy load—and you have the long-car which antedated the motor bus as a necessary and ubiquitous supplement to the railways (Plate II). The inventor, a Milanese picture-dealer of Clonmel, little dreamed how familiar his type of vehicle would become, when he started his first public long-car between Clonmel and Caher in 1815. I presume it ousted entirely the stage-coach, which had been the main public conveyance previously for the carriage of mails and passengers between town and town prior to the advent of the railway. Or was it the railways that " did for " the stage-coaches, so far as the main routes were concerned? I feel hazy on the subject. But the days of the long-car are over also; I wonder is there one left in service in Ireland today.

To these few odd things especially characteristic of Ireland perhaps the Orange drum should be added by way of a stirring finale. I do not refer to " The Drums "—half a dozen of these instruments, of astonishing power, which, manned by a stalwart crew and accompanied by one fife, are paraded at funeral pace through the streets of the northern towns; words fail to convey any idea of the impression which that amazing rite leaves on the mind of the innocent stranger who inadvertently encounters it. Rather I refer to the drum of Ulster and all that it implies, as may be gathered from the impassioned speeches of orators on the 12th of July. It is, among other things, an emblem of an ineradicable characteristic of Irish people—that of looking backward rather than forward. We can never let the dead past bury its dead. Finn M'Coul and Brian Boru are still with us; and I should not blame the friendly Saxon who carries away with him the impression that Catholic emancipation happened yesterday, that the Battle of the Boyne was fought last Thursday week, and that Cromwell trampled and slaughtered in Ireland towards the latter end of the preceding month.

CHAPTER II

DONEGAL

THERE is no logical or natural sequence which we can follow in our peregrination through Ireland. To begin in the north and end in the south is as good as any, so let us start in Ulster. And by Ulster I mean not the mutilated area which Belfast now calls by that name, but the old nine-county Ulster, that politicians cannot expunge from the map. Being myself a native of Down, I sympathize with the desire for a crisper designation for the " Six Counties " than " Northern Ireland ". That is an awkward term, and incorrect geographically; but to use " Ulster " for the area is even more misleading.

If you ask what is the best county in Ireland to walk in, I reply, Donegal (or Tirconnell (*Tír Conaill*, Connell's country), to give it its ancient name); the best region to cycle in, Connemara and its natural adjunct West Mayo, or alternatively Kerry. I express no opinion as regards motoring, for if one can traverse a county from end to end in a couple of hours, it is countries (or at least provinces) not counties, that should be the unit. But for the wise motorist who can restrain his ardour, and uses his car in order to *see* the country instead of to leave it behind, the walking choice holds good, and Donegal comes first. I choose it because there is nowhere else where the beauties of hill and dale, lake and rock, sea and bog, pasture and tillage, are so intimately and closely interwoven, so that every turn of the road opens new prospects, and every hill-crest fresh combinations of these delightful elements. But the best kind of car for Donegal would be one whose maximum speed is ten miles an hour, and which needs to rest at frequent intervals.

22

Donegal (*Dún na nGall*, fort of the foreigner) owes its topography to very ancient happenings. In times so remote that scarcely any portion of the present Ireland was in existence, the rocks of this area were crumpled together and thrown into ridges and hollows running north-east and south-west; the features thus impressed upon the region millions of years ago still persist. Look at a geological map and at a map showing elevation, and you will see how intimately related are the rocks with the modelling of the county; compare these with a general map, and you will note how human movement within the area, as demonstrated by the trend of roads and railways, obeys the ancient disposition. Communication is easy along the lines of folding, but railways and highways achieve a north-west direction with difficulty, and to the accompaniment of much clambering and twisting. Londonderry and Strabane, the natural centres of distribution, transmit their merchandise—human or otherwise—to the Atlantic coast only by devious meanderings among mountain ridges.

In the inland portions of Donegal the hills are lower, the old foldings less pronounced, and there is much fertile land and some fine streams; this region has many pleasing prospects, but little of the charm of rock and bog and lake which characterizes the remainder. A maritime zone fifteen miles wide, embracing about half the county, includes all the places which make Donegal beloved by the tourist and the naturalist; the landward part, drained mostly by the Foyle and its tributary streams, is welcome mainly as a means of passage to the wilder country beyond. A further glance at a geological map shows a prevalence of quartzite—a hard and intractable rock—in the north-western half of Donegal: and mountain-climbing there confirms the deduction that most of the higher hills—Slieve Snacht, Muckish, the beautiful white cone of Errigal, Slievatooey, Slieve League, for example—are great humps of this resistant material, which have remained while the softer rocks around them have slowly crumbled under the attacks of rain and wind, and for a while of ice. The great area of schists which occupies the south-eastern half of Donegal and extends far across Derry and Tyrone shows no outlines equally bold, though the Sperrin Mountains rise to over 2000 feet. This wilder north-western region, which gives Donegal its fame, is extensive, measuring over eighty miles from Inishowen Head to Malinmore Head (which has nothing to do with Malin Head), fronting the ocean all the way; and not a mile of it is dull. It is sown with mountains, gashed by deep rocky inlets of the sea, studded with lakes; where neither sea nor lake nor mountain holds possession, little fields struggle for mastery with rock and heather. Of the features that go to make a region lovely, woodland alone is rare in Donegal: exposure to Atlantic storms inhibits natural tree-growth save where shelter is found. In such places vegetation is luxuriant; not only native trees but half-hardy exotic shrubs flourish here in a manner recalling the wonderful gardens of Kerry. Indeed, the two hundred miles or more that separate these two extremities of Ireland cause very little change so far as climate is concerned. Both Kerry and Donegal have over-abundance of rain and wind, and there is surprisingly little difference as regards temperature. The January isotherm of 42° Fahrenheit, which crosses Donegal, crosses also the northern end of Kerry; and Kerry is only one degree warmer in July than is the most northerly county in Ireland. This mildness is reflected in the fact that some of the native southern plants—of Spain and the Mediterranean—which add so much interest to the Kerry flora, extend along the west coast into Donegal. Such are the co-called " London Pride " (which we ought to call Fox's Cabbage (*Cabáiste Mhadaidh Ruaidh*) now, for it is not the true London Pride, and needs an English name), and the Irish Spurge. But up here their numbers are sadly diminished, while on the other hand certain characteristically northern or arctic plants make their appearance—the Scottish Lovage and the Oyster-plant for example; and the Hiberno-American group, which is also of northern type, is well represented in Donegal by the Blue-eyed Grass, the Slender Naiad and the Pipewort. These interesting plant-groups will be further referred to later (p. 360).

Let us begin then with Inishowen, that mountainous peninsula lying between Lough Swilly and Lough Foyle, which terminates in Malin Head, the most northerly point of the Irish mainland. This is a diversified area full of natural history and antiquarian interest, and an ideal place for the walker. The straightish Lough Foyle shore follows the north-easterly trend of the ancient folding, and is backed by a continuous chain of hills, from Scalp (1589 feet) to the cliffs at Inishowen Head. A choice place to stay is Greencastle, where the strange sand-triangle of Magilligan protrudes from the base of Benevenagh in Derry to within a mile of the Donegal shore. The narrows here were long guarded by Richard de Burgo's great stronghold of Northburg, later New Castle, later Greencastle, beside the ruins of which a much more modern fort now forms a pleasant hotel. Carndonagh (the carn of Donagh (parish)) and Ballyliffan (*Baile lia finn*, the town of the white stone) are well situated for exploring central Inishowen, and one can stay also at Malin in the most northerly hotel in Ireland, and clamber along the wild coast-line about Malin Head, and the gigantic cliffs towards Glengad. Buncrana in the west, on Lough Swilly (*Súileach*, abounding in eyes (whirlpools), from the River Swilly), is the place to sojourn if you want to explore by boat that loveliest of Irish sea-loughs. Inishowen rises to 2019 feet in Slieve Snacht, near the centre, and mountainous ground extends thence far to east, west and south. In view of the large amount of heath and rock and hill, and the poor soils that prevail, it is a surprise to find that this has always been a well-peopled area. That no doubt accounts for its unexpected richness in ancient remains. Nowhere in Ireland is there a greater variety of memorial crosses of various date; these include an interesting very early one, the Donagh Cross, near Carndonagh, which is accompanied by two small pillar-stones, all three being covered with sculpture, some of which recalls strikingly work of the La Tène period. Mademoiselle Henry, in her elaborate study of early Irish sculpture, places the Carndonagh monument as the earliest of Irish crosses, dating from the latter part of the seventh century.[1] The free flowing lines of its low-relief sculpture strike the eye as very pleasing in contrast with the stiff square panelling of more imposing high crosses of later date. Its beauty is marred only by the solid metal bars with which the Board of Works has so tightly and safely enclosed it.

On an isolated swelling hill half-way between Londonderry and Lough Swilly stands the most imposing monument of prehistoric times found in the Inishowen region—the great cashel or stone fort known as the Grianan of Aileach. *Grianán* means sunny place, and *Aileach* a stone house; the exact significance of the name seems uncertain. Here a sub-circular enclosure about seventy-seven feet across is surrounded by a formidable dry-built wall seventeen feet in height, nearly vertical on the outer face, stepped on the inner, so that two platforms intervene between ground-level and the flat top; flights of steps lead from one level to the next. In structure it approximates closely to Staigue Fort in Kerry, the great cliff forts of the Aran Islands, and the cashel in Doon Lough near Narin: and one may safely postulate the same race of builders and similar date for all of them. The Grianan was surrounded by three concentric rings of earth and stone, now but faintly marked: and in the wall of each side of the doorway—a passage with slightly sloping jambs and heavy lintels through the thirteen-foot rampart—though not connected with it, there is a creep-passage down the centre of the base of the wall, as in the Narin cashel (p. 40). Its builders are unknown, but it was a residence of the O'Neills, kings of Ulster, until demolished by Murkertagh O'Brien, king of Munster, in 1101, and remained in a completely ruined condition till restored by Dr. Bernard of Londonderry in 1874-78. The restoration was carefully carried out, and a line of tar on the masonry separates the original wall from the replaced stonework. The monument is most impressive, and from its walls a very lovely prospect of Lough Swilly, the Donegal mountains and the Foyle valley is obtained.

---

[1] Françoise Henry, *La Sculpture irlandaise pendant les douze premiers siècles de l'ère chrétienne*. Paris, 1933.

An " antiquity " of a different and puzzling sort is the Picture Rock, as it is called locally, which stands a mile north-east of Glenalla House, on the other side of Lough Swilly. It shows a steeply inclined face covered over much of its surface with strange markings on a bold scale—hemispherical bosses set in " deep, roughly rectangular box-like hollows " placed close together; the bosses are half a foot or more across. Local ingenuity sees in these curious markings footprints of animals and what-not, but they have nothing to do with beasts either living or extinct. The rock and its sculpture is a purely geological phenomenon, which has been dealt with learnedly by Grenville Cole in a paper read before the Royal Irish Academy.[1]

The most interesting plant of Inishowen is the Irish Spurge, an essentially " Atlantic " species, which has here, by the Dunree River, its most northerly known station. It inhabits Spain and western France, Devon and Somerset, and the south and west of Ireland. In this country it is abundant in Cork and Kerry, spreading eastward into Waterford, and northward into Limerick, with outlying colonies on Slieve Aughty in Galway, Inishturk in Mayo, and this single station in Donegal, for its reported occurrence in the Poisoned Glen near Errigal has never been verified. It is a beautiful plant in spring, forming tall clumps of golden-green flowers and leaves. Otherwise the Inishowen flora is, as one might expect, northern rather than southern, and boreal plants such as the Scottish Lovage and the Sea Gromwell or Oyster-plant are frequent on its exposed shores.

The visitor to Inishowen intent on seeing the best of its scenery may concentrate on the area lying between Buncrana (*Bun crannóige*, mouth of River Crana) and Clonmany (*Cúil Maine*, Mainy's angle (of land)) on the western side, and that lying north of Culdaff (*Cúil daibhche*, corner of the flax-dam) and Trawbreaga Bay (*Traigh brega*,

---

[1] G. A. J. Cole, " The Picture-Rock or Scribed Rock near Rathmullan, in the County of Donegal ", *Proc. Roy. Irish Acad.*, vol. xxviii., sect. B, pp. 113-119. 1910.

treacherous strand) on the eastern.   Go from Buncrana by Dunree (*Dún fhraoigh*, fort of the heather) and through Mamore Gap (*Mádhm mór*, great gap, a steep and bad way for motorists), round Dunree Head to Clonmany, and back over the summit of Slieve Snacht (*Sliabh snechta*, mountain of snows) and you will have had two very fine days' walking.   For the Malin area, walk north from Malin village along the west side to Malin Head (where you can sleep) and back along the cliffs to Glengad Head, and again you will have seen a splendid stretch of precipitous coast.   If you want more cliff-walking, push northward from Inishowen Head to Culdaff, and you will be well satisfied.

Inishowen takes its name from Eoghan or Owen, son of Niall of the Nine Hostages, who lived in the fifth century: *Inis Eoghain*, Owen's Island.   But whether the peninsula over which he ruled was actually an island within the historical period appears doubtful, despite statements that it was.   The highest point of the narrow low isthmus which runs from Lough Swilly by Burnfoot to Lough Foyle is too much above tide-level to have been submerged during the depression of Neolithic times which has left so many traces (in the way of raised beaches and so on) around the north-eastern shores; and certainly there has been no depression since then approaching this in amount.   Nor can the designation *Inis* be put forward as evidence of an insular existence when that name was bestowed, for the word is frequently used to signify a peninsula or even an area only half surrounded by water.   Undoubtedly Inishowen was an island in recent times—speaking geologically—as was also the hill on which Londonderry stands, and the higher ground north-west of this: but the dates of all these islands is still uncertain.   Inch (*Inis*), on the other hand, was an actual island in Lough Swilly until embankments were built in the middle of last century to exclude the sea.

It is sixty miles from Fanet Head (*Fanad*, sloping ground) to Glencolumkille, and all of it is lovely.   It is a region of mountain and valley, lake and bog, with a wild, fretted coast-line; there is no special centre or centres, no town that is much more than a village. Everywhere there is beauty and interest, and in many places hotels —unpretentious pleasant hostelries, where you are welcome at all hours, and dinner has an amazing way of turning up at any time from one till eleven as may be needed. There are a few others, too, as at Portsalon, Rosapenna, Gweedore—five-to-seven-guinea, Rolls-Roicey, auction-bridgy places, beloved of many, but evaded by humble-minded naturalists like myself, as suiting neither our pockets nor our temperament. Personally, I like a homely small hotel, where there are no gongs or waiters or pygmy coffee-cups; where your host is full of information about local matters, and the son of the house wants to sail you out to foamy skerries to see the seals and the sea-birds, or to take you over the hills to hidden loughs, where otters abound and a plant is found which grows nowhere else in Ireland (it is always some common thing), and the maid puts her head round the door at intervals to enquire " Is the tea holdin' out? ", and your hostess sews up your torn clothes, to the accompaniment of a good scolding for being so careless.

To deal with this large area *seriatim*, place by place, would be too guide-bookish, and in any case this has been done again and again: but for those who do not know the country a few hints may be useful. Stay somewhere between Lough Swilly and Sheep Haven for the lovely district that lies around Mulroy Bay (*Maol ruadh*, red bald hill)—that extensive, land-locked, most complicated piece of water. If on the Lough Swilly side—which is the more varied and to my mind the more interesting—you are jammed between the two firths; plenty of room for walking, but circumscribed for motoring: if on the Sheep Haven side of Mulroy, you have all western Donegal open to you. If you are intent on the grand cliffs of Horn Head, you will stay at Dunfanaghy (*Dún Fionna chon*, fort of Finn chu (great hound), a chieftain's name); and somewhere between that place and Bunbeg (*Bun beg*, little river-mouth) or Gweedore (*Gaith Doír*, Doir's inlet) should lie your camp for Muckish (*Muc ais*, pig's back, 2197 feet), Errigal (*Aireagal*, an oratory, 2466 feet), the stern scenery about the Poisoned Glen, and the wild ground between. The lovely quartzite cone of Errigal gleams white from all the country round, for it is the highest hill in Donegal, and stands somewhat isolated. Undoubtedly its vicinity, with Altan Lough (*Altán*, little cliff) and Lough Nacung (*Loch na cunga*, the lake of the narrow neck) and Dunlewy Lough, is the finest thing in Donegal. Errigal ought to be a holy mountain, like Croaghpatrick; but it needs no association with a saint to make it an object of worship to all lovers of beauty. For one delightful week I watched it from Arranmore, where it rose gleaming over the low hummocky brown plain of The Rosses. The eye sought it continually, an absolutely satisfying thing, ever changing as the sun slowly encircled it, and as the clouds came and went. But as for ascending it, you must " watch your step ". Around much of its periphery, the summit is guarded by great screes of sharp quartzite lying at a steep angle, to be avoided at all cost. But ascend from the south, from near the inn at Dunlewy (*Dún Lughaidh*, Ludaidh's fort), and there will be no trouble. The view from the summit is very extensive and lovely, embracing on a clear day an immense extent of mountain and coast and ocean. The botanist will be disappointed to find scarcely an alpine plant on this lofty northern mountain. The reason lies in the rock of which it is composed. Quartzite is the most inhospitable of materials, and the Dwarf Willow and Rigid Sedge are the only members of the alpine group that can endure the conditions of starvation that prevail on the summit of Errigal. If you want to see the mountain flora of Donegal at its best, you must go to a lower hill away to the south-west, Slieve League (1972 feet), where on the northern face, overlooking Lough Agh, a delightful colony of alpine plants occupies the precipitous slope (p. 41).

The Poisoned Glen is an impressive place, a valley in which the ice has dug deeply into granite mountains, resulting in a steep-walled hollow as remarkable as Glendalough. The meaning of its forbidding designation is not clear: but there is an old record from here of the Irish Spurge, a highly toxic plant: and though it has not been seen recently, a former colony of it may have been the origin of the name. The Irish Spurge still grows by the Dunree River on Lough Swilly twenty-five miles to the north-west—its only Irish station north of Mayo—so its occurrence in the Poisoned Glen is not unlikely. Its refinding there would be very welcome to botanists.

But we must return to " The Horn ", perhaps the finest headland in Ireland. It rises sheer out of the ocean to over 600 feet, a great mass of hard quartzite with a conspicuous sill of diorite forming a dark band across the face of the cliff. To elaborate for the benefit of non-geologists:—a great deposit of quartz sand, representing waste from an old land area, accumulated here, and became in time consolidated into sandstone. Subsequently, molten igneous matter invaded the sandstone series, and at Horn Head forced its way along a bedding plane of the sandstone, where it solidified to form a dark band, a hundred feet or so in thickness. During a later epoch of earth-movements the series was folded, and alteration of the rocks also took place, the sandstone passing into quartzite, and the igneous rock into diorite. It is the massive architecture of Horn Head that both produces so imposing an effect, and at the same time makes it difficult to realize the scale on which it is built—a similar impression is sometimes produced by a well-proportioned building of great size. The quartzite forms solid bastions rising from base to summit, separated by deep vertical rifts, the whole being tilted over at an angle. The ledges are a breeding-place for tens of thousands of sea-fowl, and as one passes in a boat the air is thick with Razorbills, Guillemots, Puffins, gulls of several kinds, and other species in smaller numbers. By land, one approaches Horn Head through Dunfanaghy, situated on the low narrow neck of the peninsula on which the headland rises. About Dunfanaghy blowing sand has long proved a serious menace, as it has done also near Rosapenna. At the latter place, in 1784, it finally overwhelmed Lord Boyne's house, demesne and garden, as well as sixteen farms, burying some of them to a depth of twenty feet. This catastrophe is stated to have been due to the killing of the foxes, which preyed on the rabbits inhabiting the dunes. The latter increased greatly in numbers, and burrowed into and destroyed the turf to such an extent that, during a dry stormy winter, the dunes were themselves destroyed, the material being blown inland and deposited to the amount of thousands of tons on the demesne and farm-land.

Away out to the north-west, across seven miles of open Atlantic, rises Tory (*Toraigh*, towery, abounding in tors), the most remote and most exposed of inhabited Irish islands. It is utterly windswept, with a rocky coast mostly low, but precipitous at the eastern end. It is strange to find that so desolate and tempestuous a place has been long inhabited, and even fortified. At the cliff-bound end formidable ramparts built across a narrow neck show a prehistoric fortress of great strength. According to legend, this was the stronghold of Balor of the Mighty Blows, chief of the Fomorians, who held the island twelve centuries before Christ. Some seventeen hundred years later, St. Columba founded a monastery in this remote spot: the remains of two early churches may still be seen, as well as the lower portion of a round tower; also a cross of the curious " tau " class, which has arms but no head, and some other relics of bygone days. In spite of the fact that every available sod of peat or semi-peat has been cut for fuel or roofing, so that much of the surface is mere desert, there is a population of several hundred, living by fishing and by the product of small fields of barley, rye and potatoes. Fuel (peat) comes from the mainland, a precarious passage even in summer. The tall lighthouse, the chapel and school, and the excellent boats by which the Congested Districts Board replaced the local canvas curraghs, impart a touch of modernity to this primitive place.

Mention of Tory recalls a strange day and night which, with half a hundred members of Irish Naturalists' Field Clubs, I spent in July, 1910. We were staying at Rosapenna for a week, and the *pièce de résistance* of the trip was to be a visit to Tory. It began inauspiciously, for the steamer which was to have conveyed us ran on the rocks at Ramore Head a few days previously. At the last

The population of Tory in 1966 was 243. C.M.

moment a substitute was secured—the *Cynthia* from Lough Foyle, with a captain who was not familiar with the North Donegal coast. We went off with flags flying on a bright calm morning with a smooth sea. Out beyond Horn Head a thin driving mist came down, hiding both land and ocean, and gradually thickening. We crept on and on, slowly and more slowly, sounding our siren. Then suddenly human voices, coming apparently from the sky, hailed us. We saw a dark cliff above us, and the white gleam of breaking waves ahead. The engines were reversed, and invisible pilots guided us to a safe anchorage. A boat came alongside. We found we had struck not West Town, for which we aimed, but Port Doon, at the extreme eastern end of Tory. We got ashore in open boats, and for four hours gropingly ransacked the fog-wrapped island for animals, plants, antiquities and what-not, while a fleet of lost destroyers wailed unceasingly round us, and the fog-horn on the tall lighthouse at the west end roared out with monotonous regularity. By five o'clock we had all groped our way back to Port Doon, and we steamed off into the smother. Presently we were feeling for the entrance to Sheep Haven—and found it, as was judged from the cessation of the slight roll from the west. We crept on—still no land: then an increasing clamour of birds to starboard, and suddenly white foam around a conical stack of rock, followed by a long line of white along the base of a range of cliffs: then more breaking water to right and left. Where were we? There was nothing for it but to down anchor and wait. It was dead calm and quite still save for the endless clamour of the sea-birds—the musical cries of hundreds of Kitti-wakes, the hoarse notes of Guillemots and Razorbills and the shrill piping of their young, the calling of the Herring Gulls: and all the time flying shapes flickered out of the mist and vanished again. Time passed slowly. Gradually it got dark. Then a large white fishing-boat loomed up, its crew greatly surprised at the encounter. From them we learned where we were—under the Little Horn, south-east of Horn Head. But what with fog, darkness and rocks the captain wisely refused to move. So we resigned ourselves to a

night at sea.   At 10.30 we dined—a cup of black tea and one sandwich for each, the remnants of our afternoon meal.   A few cushions
and rugs were found, life-belts and other things were commandeered
as pillows, and we were settling down when a tenor voice piped up
from the bridge:

> Will you come?   Will you come?
> Will you come to my wedding, will you come?
>   Bring your own cup and saucer,
>   Bring your own tea and sugar

.   .   .   .   .

It was our energetic conductor summoning us to a smoking-concert.
That finished, we stretched ourselves on deck, and by one o'clock
all was quiet.   But I found a coil of rope for head-rest uncomfortable, and lay listening to all the mysterious night-whispers that come
whether on sea or land.   At three o'clock the birds again took up
their chorus, and a new day began.   At four our indomitable
waiter went round with lump-sugar in a saucer—the last of the
provisions.   At seven, the fog seemed a trifle thinner, and the captain
warily crept away eastward, and presently land was seen, which was
recognized as the Black Rock off Rosguill.   The end came with
startling abruptness.   The fog vanished: the sea and headlands were
suddenly revealed sparkling with colour;   and at eight o'clock the
Cynthia came alongside Downings Pier in full sunlight, with the mist
rolling in sheets of snowy white off the surrounding hills.   And
there was the whole hotel population assembled to meet us.   We
had endured without anxiety: but those ashore, visitors and staff
alike, had waited up all night hoping for our return and fearing
accident at the same time.   Rosapenna Hotel had never to supply a
larger breakfast than the one we consumed that morning.

At Gweedore we are fairly in the main mountain-region of
Donegal.   The hills follow in a very marked way the old N.E.–S.W.
folding of the country.   The ridge nearest the coast is pre-eminent
in possessing both Errigal and Muckish.   The next ridge contains
Slieve Snacht West (2240 feet), and the Derryveagh Mountains

(*Doire bheathach*, birch wood). Then comes the most pronounced valley in all Donegal, which runs south-west almost from sea to sea, forming the beautiful Glen Veagh (*Gleann bheathach*, birch glen) in its eastern part, and the long valley of the Barra River in its western portion. There is another ridge behind that again, containing the Glendowan Mountains (*Gleann domhain*, deep glen) and other hills. These parallel high ridges and deep valleys tend to make roads at right angles to them few and steep, and indeed for fifteen miles no highway crosses the Derryveagh ridge at all—circumstances which limit the efficacy of the cycle or car in this region, but in which the walker can rejoice.

South of the bold promontory of the Bloody Foreland stretches an indented coast with many outlying islands, of which Gola and Owey are specially attractive. One can stay at Middleton or Bunbeg or Burton Port, and have fine sailing hereabouts, and exploring among the bays and peninsulas. The rock is a handsome red granite, contrasting finely with yellow sand and green pastures and bright sea: and I know of no place that is more inspiriting when the wind is coming in from the ocean and the sun is shining—and it should be noted that rainfall, which is high in the mountainous parts of Donegal, is less on these lower coastal grounds. Here we are in the extensive low hummocky region called The Rosses (*Ros*, a promontory), a land of innumerable lakelets, a windswept heathery region, with small peaty fields grudgingly yielding difficult crops of potatoes and oats and turnips, and roads meandering through granite hillocks.

To the westward, opposite Burton Port, the large island of Arranmore or North Aran (*Arainn mór*, big Aran) forms a conspicuous feature, for over the greater part of its area it far overtops The Rosses, presenting a kind of tableland of 500 to 700 feet. This is a delightful place. You stay at the little hotel, so sheltered that it is actually surrounded by trees—which you have scarcely seen anywhere in the Rosses—facing eastward across the narrow island-strewn channel towards Burton Port, with the white cone of Errigal

rising surprisingly beyond the wide brown lowland.   The island is
four miles long by three miles wide, so there is plenty of room for
playing about.   Beyond the heathery central plateau, the western
coast is all wild cliffs, which rise near the lighthouse to 535 feet: and
in the centre are several little lakes, harbouring Water Lobelia and
Quillwort.   But although there are some rare plants, Arranmore is
poor ground for the botanist, on account of the excessive grazing.
On none of the many Irish islands which I have explored is the flora
so mercilessly eaten down.   To find plants which normally grow
half a foot high you must lie flat and get your eyes close to the ground
to discover a tiny leaf or two; and you are always on the look-out
for some little thicket or crevice into which the sheep and goats have
not been able to push their voracious jaws.   With the aid of per-
severance and wanderings all over the island I made a list of 304
species of wild plants.[1]   It is interesting to compare this with the
flora of some other Atlantic Irish islands, taking into account size,
elevation and distance from the mainland.   The following have
been thoroughly searched for plants, and the figures given will not
be much increased by future work:

	Area in Sq. Miles	Max. Height (in Feet)	Minimum Width of Channel (in Miles)	Flora *
Tory Island. . .	$1\frac{1}{4}$	282	$6\frac{1}{2}$	147
Arranmore . . .	7	750	1	317
Achill Island . .	57	2204	$\frac{1}{4}$	414
Clare Island . .	$6\frac{1}{8}$	1520	$2\frac{1}{2}$	393
Inishturk . . .	$2\frac{1}{4}$	629	7	327
Inishbofin . . .	$4\frac{1}{2}$	292	$3\frac{1}{2}$	379

* Flowering Plants and Higher Cryptogams, according to the standard of *Irish Topographical Botany*.

It will be seen that increase of area in itself does not materially
increase the flora of the islands: Achill hangs back badly, and Bofin
is far ahead: these discrepancies mean that variety of habitat, not
size, is the important thing.   Also it is evident that distance from

[1] H. C. Hart, who explored the island in 1879, found 14 others not seen by me.
I found 85 not seen by him.

land is in no way an important factor: either the flora arrived on the islands before they became separated, or else the plants succeeded in the course of time in crossing the intervening channels. It is the small size of Tory, the uniformity of surface, and the way it has been " skinned " for fuel, that give it so poor a variety of plants—not the width of stormy water which lies between it and the mainland.

The wild life on Arranmore is a source of delight. Seabirds of many sorts breed on the savage cliffs in the north and west, and others haunt the sheltered eastern shores. And then there are the Great Grey Seals. While I was there a few years ago a mighty hunter arrived, pledged to the destruction of these attractive creatures. And indeed with good reason, for the fishermen had a piteous tale to tell of a new net, value £80, spread at night for the capture of salmon; and in the morning torn to pieces, and the heads—the heads only—of half a hundred fish left in the meshes. So vengeance followed, as is narrated by Monk Gibbon in his book *The Seals*. I was glad to have no part in this, for no one who, like myself, has watched these beautiful animals on the coasts of half the counties of Ireland could wish them ill; but then I am not dependent on the capture of salmon for my daily bread. I remember a deep clear calm gully, cliff-encircled, on Inishkea; and in it a seven-foot seal at play—now resting on the surface, now diving to the bottom and groping fish-like among the long sea-weeds, clearly visible since the opposite cliff cut off the sky's reflection—a very beautiful sight: and I thought of this when I saw a full-grown seal and a very young one laid out on the boat-slip on Arranmore.

I confess that a shrinking from the taking of life in any of its myriad manifestations has grown on me with the passage of the years. Not that I was ever a " sportsman ". I remember a pleasant month spent at Ambleside when I was fourteen years of age. Almost all the people we happened to meet indulged either in trout-fishing or fern-hunting. I tried both, and after a fortnight plumped for the ferns—and studied them with such growing interest and enthusiasm that even still I feel that I know more about those verdant plants than

the majority of botanists.   As for the trout and the snipe and the
hare, it seems to me more " sporting " to let my fellow-creatures
live their lives—often tragic enough—than to want to kill them.
Not that if the postman delivers a brace of grouse at the door they
are not welcome, nor that thanks are not duly tendered to the donor.
I do not feel moved to progress towards the logical goal of vege-
tarianism: but at my hungriest I could prefer to say even to a mackerel
as Lady Anne said to Richard of Gloucester—" Though I wish thy
death I will not be the executioner ".

But self-defence is a plea that carries much weight all through this
world of ours.   I wonder did even St. Francis—

> He that in his catholic wholeness used to call the very flowers
> Sisters, brothers—and the beasts—whose pains are hardly less
>   than ours

—suffer *Pulex irritans* to browse unmolested.   Among the lower
animals, especially the insects and arachnids, there are many against
which we are compelled to wage war.   Though I have not fought
with beasts at Ephesus, I have battled with bugs in the Orient
Express, sand-flies on Fuerteventura, and mosquitoes in Lapland,
undismayed by their numbers, and glorying in the slaughter.   But I
never wish, for instance, to kill a wasp (unless, indeed, it has stung
me first!).   Wasps are dainty creatures, intent on their own affairs,
though with an inordinate love of sugar that brings them into
competition with ourselves: but they never attack us except in self-
defence—mostly when we have unwittingly come into too close
contact with them—and fair play demands that we should do no
less.   Of course I might feel differently were I the owner of a valuable garden of fruit, but I am not discussing hypothetical cases.   I do
not think, however, that even if I owned the Garden of Eden I could
wish to execute Blue Tits or Bullfinches because they desired to share
its riches with me.   But we are all a bit illogical in these matters—
like a friend of mine who sent a rat to Kingdom Come with a
devastating wallop from a blackthorn, and then exclaimed " poor
thing! "   Our assured position in the astonishing crowd of God's

creatures among which we live, our confident assumption of superiority, are not so very clear to anyone who thinks a bit. At least, we cannot afford to be twentieth-century dictators. " Other existences there are which clash with ours ", and the courtesy of the road, wherever that road may lead to, or whatever fellow-travellers we may encounter, demands that in our brief passage through life St. Francis should not find cause to frown on us too heavily. But perhaps this is all twaddle. In these murdering motoring days, when in one small country we kill some thousands of our fellow-men each year only because we want to go a little faster than we have any need to, what matter the lives of a few of the " lower animals " like innocent deer and white gulls and flickering butterflies?

South of the long narrow estuary of the Gweebarra River we come at once to the wild Dawros promontory (*Damh ros*, headland of the oxen), not lofty, but full of little heathery hills and lakes, with a sandy or cliffy shore—a particularly attractive area, as is borne out by the existence of hotels at Narin, Portnoo and Dawros, all near its ocean-washed extremity. I shall take Portnoo as exemplifying what the visitor will find in this region. Facing north, with a hill to westward, it is sheltered from the direct ocean blasts, and wind-torn trees can grow here and there. You look out across Gweebarra Bay to a high promontory ending in Crohy Head and its old watch-tower, beyond which lies Arranmore with the high stack of Illanaran off its seaward end. West of that all is ocean. Below the scattered line of houses of Portnoo, green fields, white with Pignut instead of Daisies, slope steeply to a rocky shore, but to the right this gives way to a great beach of yellow sand, which at low tide connects with Inishkeel, where you will find the relics of a bygone ecclesiastical settlement, with two early churches, and some incised crosses of primitive type. Down by the little harbour you cannot but be struck by the great variety of rocks, and the evidence they bear of intense crushing and twisting. There are slates, highly contorted, with veins of yellowish granite injected into them, and black crystalline limestone, which you will know by its smooth surface

and little undercut pool-hollows with drainage channels like miniature cañons leading from them—effects of the eating away of this
soluble rock by rain and spray. Above the grassy slope of Portnoo,
the scene changes abruptly, for everywhere there is rock and heather
and lakelet, stretching southward to Loughros More Bay (*Loch ros
mór*, lake of the great wood, or promontory). Eastward, this country
stretches away to Glenties; westward it ends close by in a wild line
of great cliffs, which decrease as one goes towards Dawros Head.
The heathland is dotted with granite boulders instead of bushes, and
Juniper replaces the familiar Gorse. This is a late place, and in early
June it is still spring; the slope to the sea full of Primroses, Wild
Hyacinths and even Wood Anemones; and in the little lakes the
Water Lobelia and American Pipewort are yet hardly stirring.

You see about Portnoo few of the birds which are associated with
the inland country-side—Rooks, Jackdaws, Sparrows, and so on.
Instead there are more attractive species characteristic of the moor-
land—Yellow-hammers, Stonechats, Wheatears, Linnets, Reed-
Sparrows; on the lakes are plenty of Teal and Coot, Water-hens and
Dabchicks; and " sauntering hither on listless wings ", are the Gulls.
Red-beaked Choughs are everywhere, playing in the air and calling
to each other. From the sea-rocks you watch Gannets fishing, Divers
of different kinds, Shell-Duck, and all the Puffin fraternity; and
Great Grey Seals watch you with their brown dog-like eyes.

By far the most interesting relic of past times hereabouts is the
great cashel built on a small island in Doon Lough, which lies behind
Narin. It closely resembles in structure the famous Staigue Fort in
Kerry, and the Grianan of Aileach near Londonderry, but it has not
been restored like these, and all that is now standing—about half the
circumference of the wall—is original work, beautifully dry-built
of the local slaty rock, and densely covered with a shaggy coat of
grey lichen. The structure is oval, not circular as in the other cases,
and encloses a grassy space some 150 feet long by 100 feet broad.
The wall, 12 feet high, is battered on the outside, stepped on the
inside, 12 feet thick at base, 8 feet at top, and there is a creep-passage

down the middle at ground level. (I give these particulars since this monument appears to be scarcely known even to archaeologists.) On the top of the wall and around its base, Common Gulls (by no means common birds despite their name) are nesting: and the mysterious grey ruin in the blue-brown lake deserted save for its white-winged colonists, makes a remarkable picture. It may well have been this cashel which inspired William Larminie in *The Nameless Doon*:

> Who were the builders? Question not the silence
> That settles on the lake for evermore,
> Save when the sea-bird screams and to the islands
> The echo answers from the steep-cliffed shore.

The north-south road from Ardara (*Ard a'raith*, the height of the rath) to Killybegs (*Cealla beaga*, the little churches) forms the baseline of the grandest mountain-promontory in Donegal, which projects thence westward for over thirty miles, filled with hills. The shore-line is so broken and precipitous that it can be reached at most points only by roads coming from inland. One can stay at Ardara or Killybegs or Carrick (*Carraig*, a rock), and the simple accommodation to be obtained at Malinmore and Glencolumkille (*Gleann Choluim chille*, St. Columba's glen), right out at the point, and approached by many miles of mountain-road, has now lost the primitive character which it possessed formerly. A friend of mine, staying there years ago, was puzzled to find the chicken which was served at dinner-time trussed up with hairpins: but honours were even when it was observed that the parlour-maid's hair was kept in position by means of wooden skewers. Those days are fortunately —or unfortunately—past.

The glory of this promontory is Slieve League (*Sliabh leic*, mountain of flagstones), on the southern shore. A tall mountain, of nearly 2000 feet, precipitous on its northern side, has been devoured by the sea till the southern face forms a precipice likewise, descending on this side right into the Atlantic from the long knife-edge which forms the summit. The traverse of this ridge, the "One Man's

Path ", is one of the most remarkable walks to be found in Ireland—
not actually dangerous, but needing a good head and careful progress on a stormy day.   To see the full beauty of Slieve League you
start at the lovely land-locked bay of Teelin, and cross to the outer
shore at Carrigan Head.   Thence along the coast to Bunglass (I
assume the reader, if he is in Donegal, or proposes going there, has
a good map at hand) where an astonishing view bursts on him.   The
gigantic cliff is concave towards the sea, so that the whole of it is
visible, stretching away for miles in a grand curve (Plate III).   The
quartzite and gneiss of which it is composed is singularly variegated,
and on a bright day the kaleidoscope of colour—yellow, red, white,
gold—which it displays is wonderful against the blue of sea and sky.
Thence you climb steadily, with the steep cliff falling directly to right
and left, past the highest point (1972 feet), by Traban to Malinbeg
and Malinmore, where, unless you are a strong walker, you will have
a car to meet you—I assume you are staying at Carrick, the best
perch from which to make a swoop on this grand hill.

H. C. Hart, who made the plants of Donegal his special study,
writing in 1885, narrates an incident which befell on the gigantic cliff
of Slieve League.   " There is a track to the sea at one place between
the Eagle's Nest and the One Man's Path.   While scrambling along
the sea face I came on this track amongst the steep heather, bracken,
and bear-berry, and a bare-foot print induced me to follow it to the
water's edge.   Considerably above the sea the track had disappeared,
but I could still notice footholds on the almost vertical rock, and
finally appeared an old man and a little boy emerging from the ocean
brink.   They were loaded with samphire, which they ate as they
rested, and were vastly surprised at my appearance—the only
stranger they had ever seen there, and they besought me to go no
further with my boots on!   I have never before found the peasants
using raw samphire as food.   Boiled with milk it is supposed to cure
a cough.   This track is called Thone-na-calliagh." [1]

[1] H. C. Hart, " Report on the Flora of South-west Donegal ", *Proc. Roy.*
Irish Acad., vol. xiv., p. 446. 1885.

Plate III

T. H. Mason: photo

Slieve League (1975 feet) from Bunglass

The northern precipice, which drops 1500 feet into the coomb surrounding the little Lough Agh, harbours the majority of the alpine plants of Slieve League, the most varied group of alpines to be found anywhere in Donegal. There are here twenty-one species of H. C. Watson's "Highland" type; these include Alpine Meadow-rue, Mountain Avens, Purple Saxifrage, Yellow Mountain Saxifrage, Bear-berry, Holly Fern, Green Spleenwort. But the ground is steep, and only an alpinist can hope to see them all.

If you want to visit one of the finest stretches of coast in Ireland, stay at Glencolumkille, and explore not only the Slieve League side, but also the northern shore towards and past Slieveatooey. Glencolumkille itself is a lonely and lovely spot, with interesting associations, for hither, in the sixth century, St. Columba journeyed over miles of moorland with a band of disciples, to find in this sequestered valley, shut in between the mountains and the ocean, a spot meet for meditation and prayer. The place is still full of relics of subsequent religious occupation, with some of earlier date—mounds of stone, gallauns, inscribed crosses, a souterrain; and the saint's house, bed, chair and well are pointed out.

If you walk north from Glencolumkille—walk you must, for there are no roads—you traverse a wonderfully broken stretch of coast. First you climb Glen Head, with its ancient tower perched on the summit of a sheer cliff 745 feet high. Downhill to Port, and then up again over Port Hill, with the huge stack of Tormore rising off shore. Now you are under Slieveatooey, the highest point of which (1692 feet) is out to the east over Lough Croagh. You traverse for five miles the steep seaward slope, with gigantic cliffs below you; at Loughros Beg Bay (*Loch ros beag*, lake of the little promontory) the ground drops, and you skirt the sandy estuary for six miles more to Ardara.

Ardara, Glenties and Killybegs are all good centres for much picturesque country. The last-named lies on a small deep inlet of the sea, well sheltered and, excepting the steep road by Glengesh, it stands on the only entrance to the Slieve League–Glencolumkille area. From Killybegs also you can visit St. John's Point, which forms the extremity of a narrow five-mile promontory, jutting far into Donegal Bay, and differing from all the land to the westward in that it is made of limestone. It is indeed the last outpost of the Carboniferous limestone which extends southward across Sligo and over the whole Central Plain of Ireland: and it is interesting to note that a few of the characteristic plants of the limestone, such as the Bloody Crane's-bill, the Northern Bedstraw and the Blue Moor-grass, have followed their favourite rock to this remote spot.

The name of Killybegs recalls an expedition—in two chapters—which was at the same time one of the most uncomfortable, most pleasant, and most interesting experiences that I have had during an uneventful life—the Royal Irish Academy expedition to Rockall, which took place in June, 1896. Rockall is a name known to few, familiar to none: how many are aware what or where it is? Steer west into the Atlantic from North Uist in the Hebrides for forty miles, and you will strike lonely St. Kilda, till lately inhabited, now derelict: a precipitous island, the home of thousands of Gannets, which in old days supplied the people with both food and clothing. Keep on west for another 200 miles, and with luck you will sight Rockall—a tiny cone of granite, like a haycock bent over by the wind, only seventy feet in height, and described by Captain Basil Hall, one of the few who have visited it, as " the most isolated speck of rock in the world ". Or go from Donegal 250 miles north-west, and there, one-third of the way to Iceland, you may find the dangerous reef on which it stands. Rockall was unknown to the earlier geographers; the first reference to it that Professor T. Rupert Jones [1] was able to find is in 1698, in M. Martin's *A Late Voyage to St. Kilda*: " Rokal, a small rock, sixty leagues to the westward of St. Kilda, the inhabitants of which call it Rokabarra ". It was not till 1810 that close acquaintance was made with it, and its exact position

[1] " On Rockall and its Previous History ". In "Notes on Rockall Island and Bank", *Trans. Roy. Irish Acad.*, vol. xxxi. 1897.

determined, as narrated by Captain Hall.[1] He tells how H.M.S. *Endymion* chased what was thought to be a brig, with white sails aloft, while the lower sails were dark: which proved to be Rockall, its top snow-white from the droppings of innumerable birds. The ocean being exceptionally calm, two boats were lowered and a landing was effected with difficulty, and with greater difficulty the venturesome invaders were got off again, only to find that their ship had vanished in a fog: and it was not till night that she was found. Apparently the only other landing which has been recorded was in 1862, when a boatswain of H.M.S. *Porcupine* succeeded in getting a footing on the rock despite a heavy sea, and broke off a few fragments with a sounding-lead, which, still in existence, furnish all we know as to the structure and geological history of Rockall. These specimens are very important, for soundings show that this speck of rock is all that remains of a once extensive island. This is now represented by a bank of shallow water (less than 200 fathoms) about 150 miles long and 50 miles broad, having nothing to link it to Scotland or Ireland, from which it is separated by an abyss of water of oceanic depth.

Several considerations made it seem desirable that Rockall should be further investigated—the establishment there, if possible, of a meteorological station would be of great importance; was there any possibility that this was the home of the Great Shearwater, whose breeding-place had never been found,[2] and which was known to frequent the Rockall Bank in numbers? What other birds frequented the rock? Were there any plants on it? And what animals lived in the shallow water surrounding it? The energy of W. S. Green and R. M. Barrington overcame the many difficulties of arranging an expedition. The Congested Districts Board steamer *Granuaile*, gross tonnage 380, was obtained after negotiation; the Meteorological Office advised as to the most likely date for good weather; and at

[1] *Fragments of Voyages and Travels*, ser. I, vol. iii., pp. 178-196. 1831.
[2] It is now known to breed on Inaccessible Island in the Tristan da Cunha group, far away in the South Atlantic.

midnight on 3rd June, 1896, the adventure began. On board were our three leaders—W. S. Green, R. M. Barrington, and J. A. Harvie-Brown; W. F. de Vismes Kane, H. L. Jameson and myself to note and preserve specimens of biological or geological interest; and Charles Green as photographer. We had on board trawls and dredges, sounding-machine, wire rope, a harpoon gun which fired a small grapnel, by means of which and a rope ladder we hoped to scale the rock: and the usual naturalist's outfit of jars, bottles, boxes and cameras; so we left Killybegs well prepared.

The following brief account of our experiences is condensed from W. S. Green's narrative in the *Transactions of the Royal Irish Academy* (*loc. cit.*) and my own diary. On Thursday morning the sun rose red, and soon disappeared behind a bank of cloud, to be seen no more for four days. All day we steamed N.W.; by evening the weather was very thick and dirty, with a heavy sea. Next morning we sounded at 6.30, getting bottom at 130 fathoms: so we had crossed the ocean abyss which separates Rockall from the European plateau, and were well on Rockall bank. A high sea and driving rain; no chance of finding our position—or Rockall. Then we got 80 fathoms, then 130. We had evidently passed the rock. " There was nothing to do for it but to ' lie to ' until the weather should clear. The ship's head was therefore brought round to the north, and we dodged slowly ahead, taking the big seas on our starboard bow, rolling and pitching heavily. It was now blowing a whole gale, which sent the spindrift flying from the sea." We tried to shoot the trawl, but only got it torn to pieces. " At 6 P.M. we sighted a ketch-rigged fishing-smack ' head reaching ' under close-reefed canvas; and steaming up as close as we could with safety, we asked how the rock bore from us. ' South-west ' was the answer, but the distance in miles escaped our ears." We ran down in the direction indicated, but saw nothing, and an attempt to sound resulted only in the smashing of the steam steering-gear. Eventually we put out a sea-anchor, and drifted to leeward all night, pitching and rolling. Next morning at 3.45 we were awakened by a cry of " Rockall at

PLATE IV

ROCKALL, LOOKING E.N.E.
From a water-colour sketch by W. S. Green

last ". We rushed on deck in all sorts of costume or absence of costume. And there it was, half a mile to windward, a solitary speck of rock amid that wilderness of foam-flecked billows. Near by, the low Hasselwood Rock showed black between the waves, and further away the seas were breaking heavily on Helen's Reef, where the brigantine *Helen* was wrecked in 1824. All day we hung about the rock, coming at intervals as close as we dared. The top was thick with birds, chiefly Guillemots. In the sea to the lee of the rock was an enormous flock—a thousand or so—chiefly Manx Shearwaters, with a good many Great Shearwaters among them. Puffins, Gannets, Kittiwakes, Fulmars, Pomatorrhine Skuas, Buffon's Skuas and Razorbills were also about. The sea roared round the rock, often enveloping it in foam two-thirds way up—close on fifty feet: and in the hollows of the waves we could see that the base was hung with long bright brown seaweed. The illustration here (Plate IV), is from a water-colour sketch by W. S. Green, painted rapidly as he crouched in the deck-house door out of the wind and spray. Having studied the rock as far as was possible, we fell away to leeward. We sounded and dredged, but only lost our gear. In the evening we had watery gleams of sunlight, and the last we saw of Rockall was at 10 P.M., a black conical speck against a dark sky, on the edge of the darker water. On Sunday morning the weather was as bad as ever. We tried trawling; the net was torn to ribbons on the rocky bottom, but a few interesting animals were taken. Then, on a report that coal was running low, we had to abandon our quest, and ran for Killybegs through a heavy and rising beam sea. And so ended the first chapter.

But all was not over yet. It was agreed that should conditions promise better success, we should try again in a week's time, and the Meteorological Office arranged to send daily reports to us from Tory and Shetland. These were favourable, and Saturday, 14th June, saw us again on board and off into the North Atlantic. The run to Rockall was made in calm weather, but when we reached the rock conditions were again very bad—high wind and sea, and a sky dark with rain. The second trip was a repetition of the first: landing quite impossible, though twice the dinghy was lowered and the rock inspected at close quarters by Mr Green. " It was only now ", he writes, " we could appreciate the height of the swell, the ship going completely out of sight to the top of the masts when the first sea rose between her and us." He and his crew of two men were got on board with nothing worse than a drenching and a bumping against the side of the *Granuaile*: also, dredging was more successful, in spite of some loss of gear. At the end of two weary days of rolling and pitching we were compelled to abandon all hope of a nearer acquaintance with Rockall, and ran east to St. Kilda, where we explored the cliffs and great bird colonies in mist and pouring rain in company with the Kearton brothers, and then started for Ireland. But the ocean had not quite done with us yet. A sudden gale came up, so bad that we turned and ran for Barra Head, at the southern end of the Outer Hebrides, and spent the night in shelter under huge cliffs of basalt: then, at last under a clear sky, we got away at daybreak, and reached Derry the same evening.

As to the results of these rather tempestuous ventures (I can still remember my extravagances of sea-sickness!). Though landing on Rockall was impracticable, we learned a good deal about it—that its small size and great exposure made it no possible site for a meteorological station; that there were no rare birds breeding there—it provided a nesting-place at most for some Guillemots and possibly a few Puffins; and no possible habitat for any land plant. More interesting were the results of our very difficult dredging. Quite a good list of the inhabitants of the Rockall bank was secured, including three sponges new to science: but specially noteworthy was the occurrence of dead shells of a number of molluscs which live in shallow water. " How, under present conditions," writes Mr Green, " such shells could be found living anywhere on the bank was difficult to understand. It would seem to afford the strongest confirmation to the theory that the time is not so very long distant when there was more land, with a shallow coast-line, and possibly extensive sand-banks where now the pinnacle of Rockall is the only speck, acting as a memorial stone to what tradition has called the ' Sunken Land of Buss '." " It is highly probable ", writes Professor Grenville Cole, " that the relics of a basaltic plateau lie submerged at Rockall bank, and that the material of the rock itself represents another phase of igneous activity." " Rockall ", concludes Professor T. Rupert Jones, " must be the relic of a mountainous island near the north-eastern border of the Atlantic before it was connected with the Arctic."

I shall never see again that desolate and lonely rock: but I feel a deep affection for it, because it brought me a fortnight's intimate fellowship with some of the best companions it has been my privilege to know.

From Killybegs, road and railway take you eastward along the indented shore of Donegal Bay to Donegal town, lying at the mouth of the Eask River, which flows out through a sandy archipelago. Lying far from the open ocean, there is shelter here, and tall trees grow, in striking contrast to the exposed coasts we have been traversing. Walk down the southern bank of the tidal stream to the little quay, and you reach the unimposing ruins of the Franciscan Abbey of Donegal. The site is still often given—erroneously, as is claimed—as the place where Michael O'Clery and his three collaborators compiled the remarkable chronology known as the *Annals of the Four Masters*—a name given to it by Colgan, whose *Acta Sanctorum* is equally famous. The scheme of the *Annals* was an ambitious one—the setting down in order of all happenings in Ireland from the earliest times down to the date of writing, as recorded in available manuscripts and books. Michael O'Clery dedicated the work to Ferall O'Gara, Lord of Moy O'Gara and Coolavin (in the county of Sligo), " who set the antiquarians to work, and most liberally paid them for their labour, in arranging and transcribing the documents before them, in the convent of Dunagall, where the Fathers of the house supplied them with the necessary refreshments ". For four and a half years Michael O'Clery, Conary O'Clery, Cucogry

O'Clery and Ferfeasa O'Mulconry worked at the compilation, which was finished on 10th August, 1636. The monastery on the river-edge at Donegal had been destroyed and abandoned in the opening years of the seventeenth century. The brotherhood moved down the coast to Bundrowes, close to Bundoran, and it was there, in a new Abbey of Donegal on the banks of the river that comes down from Lough Melvin, that the great compilation was made.[1] The leader, Michael O'Clery, was a lay brother of the order, and he and Ferfeasa O'Mulconry, in undertaking this work for Ferall O'Gara, were practising their profession of hereditary antiquaries and historians. The *Annals*, which were written in the Irish language, begin with Anno Mundi 2242 (2958 B.C.) and come down to the year A.D. 1616. The manuscript remained with the O'Gara family. The first portion of it (to the latter part of the twelfth century) eventually found a home in the Duke of Buckingham's library at Stowe, and on the break-up of that famous collection was purchased by the British Government and deposited in the library of the Royal Irish Academy. The second and final portion was given by an O'Gara of the day to Charles O'Connor of Ballinagare; from him it passed to Colonel Burton Conyngham, from whom it was purchased by George Petrie and presented to the same institution: so the whole of the original manuscript has again come together in a very appropriate home.

The first part, up to 1171, was translated into Latin and published along with the Irish text by Rev. Dr. Charles O'Connor in 1826 (*Rerum Hibernicarum Scriptores*, vol. iii.), the MS. source being the Stowe original, but his work contained many errors. It was John O'Donovan who, in 1851, published the whole of the Irish text, the first part from two copies of the autograph original (since he had not access to the original itself), the remainder from the autograph original already in the Royal Irish Academy. He added an English translation and voluminous notes dealing with historical and geographical questions, place-names, and so on, also a full index of people

[1] See *e.g.* Pól Breathnach in *Irish Book Lover*, vol. xxiii., pp. 109-115. 1935.

and places; and where the *Annals of the Four Masters* is referred to it is always O'Donovan's exhaustive work that is intended.

The entries begin with a date forty years before the Deluge, and relate the coming to Ireland of Noah's granddaughter. But even among early historians this interesting immigration received little credence. " I cannot conceive ", says Keating gravely, " how the Irish antiquaries could have obtained the accounts of those who arrived in Ireland before the Flood, unless they were communicated by those aerial demons or familiar sprites, who waited on them in times of paganism, or that they found them engraved on stones after the Deluge had subsided."

Then under Anno Mundi 2520 it is recorded that Parthalon came to Ireland, and ten years later the first battle that Ireland had known was fought between the invading Fomorians and Parthalon's people —would it had been the last! Under these early dates we find mention of the " eruption " of many of the Irish lakes, which were formed, according to the views of the time, by the bursting forth of waters, which filled hollows in the land—whether pre-existing or not is a nice question. However, we are told that in this way not only the principal Irish lakes were formed—Lough Conn, L. Gara, L. Mask, and a little later L. Derevaragh, L. Ennell, etc. etc.—but also arms of the sea, called *Loch* like the lakes (" lough " is a meaningless corruption of spelling). Then there are plagues, battles, and the arrival of the Firbolgs. Later, and for a long time, the records are concerned chiefly with battles and abbots—for ecclesiastical history is always to the fore. The entries increase in length as the centuries pass, and for the later times are largely histori-cal, but history and fighting are mostly synonymous terms. The last entry records the death of Hugh O'Neill in 1616, and the record ends with a panegyric on that " powerful and mighty lord ". The work, it should be remembered, is not original, but a compilation from pre-existing sources which are given. As most of the older records are found in widely scattered unique manuscripts in the Irish language, the *Annals of the Four Masters*, as translated and printed, bring these records within the reach of everybody: and no matter what may be one's interest, the seven volumes will ever be a mine of information, traditional or historical.

The River Eask, which enters the sea at Donegal, traverses a valley of much beauty. The stream rises at Barnesmore Gap, but most of its water comes from Lough Eask, lying on its northern bank three miles above Donegal. " Barnesmore " means the big gap, an appropriate name. It is a deep pass, a glacial overflow channel, utilized by both road and railway, the only way through the hills for many miles in either direction: on both sides of the high boggy gorge the hills rise steeply for a thousand feet, stony and bare. Lough Eask (*Loch eisc*, lake of the fish) offers a softer type of scenery, for, though surrounded by hills on three sides, its sheltered position allows rich woodland to clothe its western shores (Plate V). It is indeed a very beautiful lake, seen to best advantage from the southern end, where the rounded summits of the naked Blue Stack Mountains (2219 feet) are seen rising behind the lower heathery hills that surround the lake. Blue Stack, otherwise Croaghgorm (meaning the same thing) is a wild group of hills, with several points rising well over 2000 feet, formed partly of slaty rocks, partly of granite.

Follow the Eask river for two miles through the hills from the upper end of Lough Eask to Lough Belshade, a wild and picturesque sheet of water, and you will be at the foot of Croaghgorm, which offers some fine walking, with deep glens and rocky mountainsides. Lough Belshade has a picturesque name, *Loch bél séad*, the lake with the jewel mouth, and a picturesque ancient story is attached to it which Eugene O'Curry [1] has thus translated from the *Leabhar Breac*: " *Coerabar boeth*, the daughter of Etal Anbuail of the fairy mansions of Connacht, was a beautiful and powerfully gifted maiden. She had three times fifty ladies in her train. They were all transformed every year into three times fifty beautiful birds and restored to their natural shape the next year. These birds were chained in couples by chains of silver. One bird among them was the most

[1] *Lectures on the MS. Material of Ancient Irish History*, pp. 426-427. 1861.

Plate V

R. Welch: photo

Lough Eask, Donegal

beautiful of the world's birds, having a necklace of red gold on her neck, with three times fifty chains depending from it, each chain terminating in a ball of gold. During their transformation into birds they always remained on *Loch Crotta Cliath* [that is, the lake of Cliath's harps], wherefore the people who saw them were in the habit of saying: ' Many is the *Séad* [that is, a gem; a jewel, or other precious article] at the mouth of *Loch Crotta* this day '. And hence it is called *Loch Bél Séad* [or the Lake of the Jewel Mouth]."

The most interesting plant of the Lough Eask area is the Whorled Caraway, a species with a limited and " Atlantic " distribution on the Continent and in Britain, and a peculiar range in Ireland—north end of Lough Eask, heathy ground in central Derry and northern Antrim, and banks of the Bann, and no more till you get away down into the south-west, where it is locally abundant in Cork and Kerry. The moist shade prevailing about Lough Eask is shown by the occurrence there of Killarney Fern and both Filmy Ferns.

At Lough Eask you bid goodbye to the wilder parts of Donegal, which, if you have followed my rambling paragraphs, you have traversed from Lough Foyle round to the Eask river; for south of Donegal town you are on undulating country, with many drumlins, underlain by Carboniferous limestone, giving a different type of scenery and of surface. But out among bleak peat-covered hills to the eastward lies Lough Derg (*Loch dearg*, the red lake), dreariest of Donegal waters, one of the most famous places of pilgrimage in the country. To St. Daveog, a disciple of Patrick, is attributed the foundation of a monastery here, and for centuries the place was famous throughout Europe. Destroyed by the Danes, and later by order of Pope Alexander VI; restored by Pope Pius III; destroyed again by order of the Lords Justices of Ireland; prohibited by Act of Parliament in 1704, the place has had a very chequered history; but the faith of the people has conquered, and today St. Patrick's Purgatory is a loadstone attracting thousands of pilgrims between 1st June and 15th August. The penitential exercises which they perform on Station Island during the three to six days of their stay are of a very severe nature, and a test of both devotion and endurance. The situation of the place is striking. One road only, starting from Pettigoe, leads to Lough Derg. You ascend steadily; cultivation gives away to poor pasture and that to heather: and abruptly you are on the shore of a large desolate lake, surrounded by miles of peat-covered desolate hills on which no house or trace of human industry is seen: and in the middle of the lake, strangely striking and incongruous, the tall crowded ornate buildings—churches and hostels—which cover the little island.

The extreme southern corner of Donegal, between the town of that name and Bundoran, offers some interesting country—the bare limestones and accompanying caves about Brown Hall, the picturesque gorge of the Erne, the sands and rocks about the watering-place of Bundoran (*Bun Dobhráin*, mouth of river Doran). The clear rock-pools in the level beds of limestone at the last-mentioned spot are fascinating, as they are spread out on flat rocks as if intended for display. Covering the bottom and sides of the pools is a pink crust of the calcareous seaweed called *Lithothamnion*, thickly dotted with the dark round spiny shells of the Purple Sea-urchin, *Paracentrotus lividus*. This is a very interesting animal. It excavates for itself a circular hollow in which it lives, apparently never using, for purposes of locomotion, the tube-feet with which it is liberally endowed. These organs, which are characteristic of sea-urchins and star-fishes, are finger-like liquid-filled processes which it can push out at will through small openings arranged in rows on the test, and they can be used for walking or for seizing food by a process of suction. The animal has a ridiculous way besides of decorating its spiny top with empty shells of limpets, whelks and so on, which rest on the spines—a habit difficult to explain. This is a rare creature, for though it is common in many places along the western and southern coasts of Ireland, from Donegal to Cork, it is absent from Great Britain, and to see it again we have to go to the Channel Islands. The Purple Sea-urchin, at Bundoran as elsewhere, has a habit of almost monopolizing the rock-pools; it and the *Lithothamnion* make such a delightful and unusual duet of pink and dark purple that one does not grudge this: and a little search reveals all sorts of other creatures—small fishes, crabs, sea-slugs, sea-anemones, hydroids, tube-building worms, and what-not: an assemblage of creatures which it would need a chapter to describe or discuss.

The gorge of the River Erne, which runs from Lough Erne to Ballyshannon (*Beal atha Seanaigh*, the mouth of Seanach's ford) exemplifies a peculiar feature of almost all the rivers of the West Coast, of which the meaning is, I believe, still uncertain—a sudden final plunge downward to sea-level following a long placid course. The Erne, the Garvogue, the Corrib and the Shannon behave thus as they emerge from Lower Lough Erne, Lough Gill, Lough Corrib and Lough Derg respectively. The Ballysadare River and the Moy do the same, following on miles of level reaches. In the case of the Ballysadare River and the Shannon the rapids coincide with a barrier of older and non-soluble rocks, whose slower wasting may have acted as an obstruction; but in the other cases the basin lies entirely in limestone, and one is puzzled by the bar of rock just above their estuaries. A recent slight tilting of the coast would account for it: but this must be considered with reference to other coastal phenomena before it can be advanced as an explanation.

Near Ballintra (*Baile an tsratha*, the town of the river-meadow), north of Ballyshannon, there are low rounded hills where the Carboniferous limestone is bare of soil. On one of these, in the middle of an extensive tract which has never at any time supported habitations or cultivation, there is a little patch of the Common Rock-rose, without question indigenous. The few tufts which grow there are all that is known of this plant in Ireland. In Britain, on the other hand, it is a very familiar wild-flower, widely spread in England, Wales and Scotland. How does one explain the presence of so isolated a colony?

This question of what we may call single-station plants—and there are animals to match—is one of great interest, and raises curious problems. They cannot have been so for long; nature does not stand still. " Nothing that is can pause or stay." Migration and increase and decrease are slow processes, but continuous. The plant that occupies a single area among its crowd of competitors must either advance or retreat: in other words it is a new-comer which has succeeded in effecting a foothold and will presumably spread, or it is an old inhabitant now decreasing in the face of competition, and on the way to extinction. The compelling force behind these fluctuations is mostly slight change of climate, which alters the suitability of this or that area for the plants which are contending for it. Now we know that not so long ago—at a period to be measured by not many tens of thousands of years—a cold spell or spells—the Glacial Epoch—played havoc with the pre-existing vegetation (which was on the whole very like the present one), and allowed the immigration of a number of hardier species, capable of resisting a much lower temperature. As milder conditions were resumed, these retreated to the mountains: and there seems little doubt that the frequency of one-station or few-station plants in our alpine flora indicates that these are relics of the cold time, now maintaining themselves under uncongenial conditions, and heading for early extinction. But then the rising temperature-curve between the Glacial Period and our day has a kink in it. In Neolithic times—say 3000 years ago—a rather warmer climate prevailed for a while. This had repercussions on the distribution of both the fauna and the flora. It sent some animals—certain molluscs found fossil in the clays which underlie Belfast and Larne for instance—scurrying northward, only to be driven south again when the temperature fell back to its former level; and likewise it allowed some plants to extend to new territory—the Scotch Fir, for example, climbed up the hills high above its former or present limit, and spread to exposed western islands where it cannot grow now. Can we trace any effect of this mild phase among our one-station plants? It is probable that it gave the *coup de grâce* to some of the Glacial relics, which would still be lingering on but for its onset. And it must have helped the migration northward of more tender plants, which possibly reached here then, and still hold on in spite of the return of more unfavourable conditions. So it is conceivable that among the one-station or few-station plants there are both relict and incipient northern species, and also both relict and incipient southerners. Of all these, the relict northerners are the only obvious ones. The Fringed Sandwort on Ben Bulben, the Cloud-berry on the Sperrin Mountains, and the Round-leaved Winter-green in Westmeath may safely be looked on as the last survivors of northern species formerly more widely spread in Ireland. As for the Rock-rose in south Donegal, it furnishes a double puzzle—if in Ireland at all, why should it be so rare? And if in Ireland at all, why should it be in this remote spot, not in some of the many suitable habitats which it could find in eastern Ireland, where climate, soil and proximity to its British headquarters would all seem to invite its presence?

To botanists the flora of Donegal will always be associated with the name of Henry Chichester Hart. He was a man of many parts—a skilled botanist and zoologist, a profound Shakespearean scholar, a remarkable athlete. He was born in 1847, and before he entered Trinity College, Dublin, was hard at work botanizing in his native county of Donegal. His floral studies went further afield also. He was appointed naturalist on the polar expedition of 1875, serving on the *Alert* under Nares, while Colonel Fielden was his biological colleague on the sister ship *Discovery*. Eight years later he took part in an expedition organized by the Palestine Exploration fund to explore the geology of the Jordan valley and western Palestine, when Professor Edward Hull was in command, and Major (afterwards Viscount) Kitchener was one of his colleagues. Irish naturalists will remember him by his work in his native country. He was one of the excellent band of botanists whom A. G. More brought together for the systematic exploration of Ireland. Full advantage was taken of Hart's endurance and skill as a climber and walker, and many of the mountain groups and less accessible areas fell to his share—the Reeks, Galtees, Comeraghs, Twelve Bens, Brandon, Croaghpatrick, Mweelrea; the courses of the Barrow, Suir, Nore, Blackwater, Slaney:

and the lonely shore-line of Wexford and Waterford. But he never abandoned the survey of his own county, and at length published, in 1898, his *Flora of the County Donegal* (now out of print) a very complete account of the vegetation of one of the most interesting areas in Ireland. He died ten years later. Of his remarkable athletic powers his life-long friend R. M. Barrington narrates some examples. " In 1889, in company with the writer, Hart ascended the Weisshorn (14,800 feet) and the Dent Blanche (14,300 feet), in Switzerland. The days were fine and five or six other parties were climbing the same peaks independently. Hart proposed to give them all at least an hour's start, and, notwithstanding these tremendous odds, the Irishmen on each occasion reached the summit first." For a wager with the same friend, Hart walked from Dublin to the summit of Lugnaquilla, the highest of the Wicklow mountains, and back, some seventy-five miles, in less than twenty-four hours, keeping to the hills most of the way. The following episode, also told by Barrington, is so characteristic of both men that I cannot help quoting it: " By appointment he [Hart] turned up at Fassaroe one dreadful day to botanize on the cliffs around Powerscourt Waterfall, and to hear, if possible, the Wood-Wren. Well knowing that if the expedition failed the incident would for years be a theme for ridicule, a few slices of bread were hastily wrapped up, and we started in torrents of rain, absolute silence being observed regarding the atmospheric conditions. Both wet to the skin ' in no time ', Hart deliberately kept walking among the scrub, briars, and long grass by the river's edge, so as to discourage his companion. To prove utter indifference to moisture, the writer walked into the river and sat down on a submerged stone and began to eat lunch. Hart, with the utmost nonchalance and without saying a word, did likewise. Saturation was soon complete. All rivalry ceased, and friendship prevailed during the remainder of the day." [1]

[1] *Irish Naturalist*, vol. xvii., pp. 249-254, portrait. 1908.

CHAPTER III

THE VOLCANIC NORTH

In bestowing the title which heads this chapter I have in my mind no social or political *arrière-pensée*. It is true that the words have a historical implication: but that history did not begin—or end—with the Battle of the Boyne, which to so many worthy Belfast-men is the alpha and omega of historical conceptions. The vulcanism to which I refer is many millions of years older than that: but it also is of great importance to the dwellers by the Blackstaff—of whom I may reasonably claim to be one—for it gave them their fertile soil, their glorious scenery, their " largest lake in the British Isles " (for Belfast, like the United States, loves to have the largest of things), their rim of heathery mountains sweeping in a semicircle from Colin Top to Mullaghmore, and the rich valley of the Bann.

But there is, after all, a sociological parallel to the geological contrast as between Antrim and Donegal: for may we not compare life in that old land of the North-west, with its primitive rocks, its worn-down hills, its mild dreamy atmosphere, and its people of ancient race still harbouring old legends and traditions, with the newer erupted land of the basaltic area, its traces of ancient life all burnt and buried far beneath, and now crowded with a stalwart race largely projected into it in recent times by eruptions from Scotland and England, and vigorous in the bracing air of Antrim?

The story of this plutonic episode in the history of the North-east, which took place long before man was heard of, in the period which geologists call Eocene, is familiar to most readers—how as a consequence of internal stresses portions of the earth's surface cracked, molten lavas welled and spread far and wide in level sheets, till they

59

attained a thickness of a thousand feet and more. Though fissure-eruption was frequent, there were also typical volcanoes here and there—Slemish, Scawt Hill, Tiveragh, for example, are the stumps of well-marked vents of this kind; and in the cliffs at Carrick-a-Rede you can see the bombs and blocks that were shot out of a crater to fall back into it again, and along with volcanic ash to be eventually cemented into solid rock. The outpourings were not continuous. A bright red band, rich in iron, which is a conspicuous feature in the median part of the basalt cliffs along the Antrim coast, points to a long pause, during which the volcanic rocks on the surface were disintegrated, and soils formed on which forests flourished. The trees which composed these woods, of which fragments are preserved in the ancient clays, were mostly of genera which still grow in Ireland, though the species were different; they included Pines, Willows, Poplars, Maples, Oaks, and so on. Not only have leaves and cones been found, but thin beds of lignite occur—half wood, half coal—composed of ancient vegetable matter, and sometimes yielding trunks of the trees that then flourished.

The evacuation of so great a mass of material had after-effects of a startling nature. The high plateau collapsed down the centre from north to south, forming a long trough but little above sea-level, while the edges remained elevated. One area, west of where Belfast now stands, sank throughout a long period and formed the basin of Lough Neagh, of which more anon (p. 95).

The waters which collected in the ancient Lough Neagh found an outlet down the valley in the centre of the broken-backed plateau, and formed the Lower Bann. Since then the edges of the lava area have been attacked by sea or by rivers or by weather, and the plateau has become boldly scarped almost the whole way from Belfast round the coast to Dungiven.

This volcanic episode did more than give us the fine scenery of the Antrim and Derry coasts. Previous to its arrival, a series of rocks of different kinds had been laid down through an immense period of time known to geologists as the Mesozoic. First came the

New Red Sandstone, thick beds deposited in lakes or under desert conditions. Then a series composed largely of blue clays, some of which have never consolidated into hard rock, was laid down in seas full of life of many kinds, so that the Lias, as it is called, is rich in fossil bones and teeth and shells of bygone creatures. After an interval, this was followed by the Chalk, a deposit of almost pure carbonate of lime formed in warm quiet seas, which still preserves the white colour of the original limy mud, produced by the decay of the shells of millions of minute creatures. In some other areas these beds attain a great thickness, but in Ireland they are comparatively thin. What their former extension here may have been cannot now be determined, but they were worn away in the course of time by denudative agents except in the North-east. There the outpourings of basalt covered them deeply, and cover them still, so that they are preserved to us, appearing chiefly as a fringe round the basalt area, where its edge has been scarped so as to expose them. Thus we have to thank the eruptions of Eocene times for the presence in Antrim of the white Chalk and ruddy New Red Sandstone which lend so much colour to local scenery. The grey Lias, too, plays an important part in some places such as Garron Point and Benevenagh: for its plastic clays have failed to withstand the pressure of the hundreds of feet of rock piled above them, and have oozed forward, bringing down in ruin the Chalk and basalt, and causing the gigantic land-slips which give so remarkable a profile to those places. On both sides of Glenarm slipping is actively in progress, and the Coast Road, once straight and level, undulates and twists across a kind of glacier of jumbled Lias, Chalk and basalt, mixed together in confusion.

From the geological point of view—and consequently the agricultural and economic—the boundary between Donegal and Derry lies not along the Foyle, but in the valley of the Roe (*Ruadh*, red) fifteen miles to the eastward. There the ancient rocks of the North-west give way abruptly to the great lava-flows of the North-east. In the country between Derry and the Roe the scenery has none of the boldness that characterizes the further parts of Donegal: it is a pleasant undulating region, watered by the Faughan and the Roe, and largely agricultural. Guarding its western edge, where the Free State impinges on Northern Ireland, the City of Londonderry occupies a commanding position on a hill round the base of which the tidal Foyle sweeps in a broad curve. Its name has always been associated with the Oak (*Dair*); its ancient designation was *Daire Calgaith*: then it became *Daire Columchille* (St. Columba's oak-wood); and it obtained its present title when the Irish Society of London received grants of land in the time of James I. A deep valley on the inland side of the city, only slightly above tide-level, completes the magic circle of its virginity. With its defiant walls still intact, decorated with " Roaring Meg " and other ancient pieces of ordnance, its Protestant Cathedral set high on the hill-top, with soaring spire and chapter-house full of keys and cannon-balls and letters of Schomberg, it seems to typify its history: the very street names—Artillery Street, Magazine Street, Lundy's Lane, Mountjoy Street, are redolent of 1699; while Cowards' Bastion and Hang-man's Bastion are full of grim suggestion. There is a grimness, too, about the squatting skeleton on the city's coat of arms; but that commemorates a much earlier episode. As is characteristic of Ire-land, the dead past is not allowed to bury its dead: and Derry's Prentice Boys and Closing of the Gates and drumming and marching seem natural there. But the memory of the siege and of the gallant resistance of its burghers appears to satisfy it: Derry shows none of the desire to perpetuate political and religious warfare or intolerance to the extent of outrage and murder such as has so frequently in Belfast aroused the reprobation of all right-thinking people. In the working-class areas, which now spread across the valley and far up the opposite slope, the distribution of the emblematic signs placed on the doors at the time of the Eucharistic Congress in Dublin shows that an intimate mixing of creeds and politics need not of necessity con-stitute an explosive compound. At the same time, the establishment of a " frontier " a couple of miles out, where the Free State begins,

PLATE VI

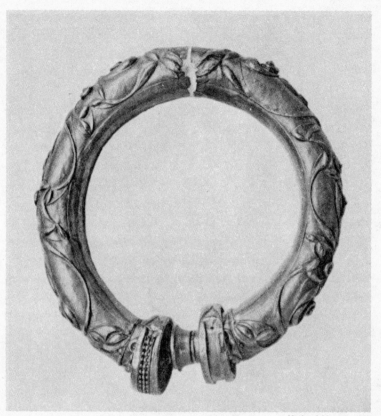

THE BROIGHTER GOLD COLLAR
About one-half natural size

is wholly deplored, for it causes heavy loss equally to the city traders and to the Donegal farmers to whom Derry is an essential market. The city lies on the Donegal side of the Foyle, it should be noted; but the " Liberties of Londonderry ", some twenty-five square miles of land surrounding the town, push back the Free State border. For the purpose of the present book, we need not delay over Derry, except to say that many interesting spots lie around it, and that it is a pleasant place in which to sojourn.

Fifteen miles to the east, across the undulating area of " Dalradian " rocks aforesaid, the edge of the basaltic plateau of the Northeast rises abruptly from the wooded valley of the Roe, where the little towns of Limavady (*Léim an mhadaidh*, the dog's leap) and Dungiven (*Dún Geimhin*, Geimhin's (Given's) fort) nestle by the stream. The mention of Limavady recalls the Gold Ornaments Trial of 1893, which was a remarkable and indeed unique legal episode. The circumstances will be still within the memory of many. A man ploughing at Broighter, situated on the flat ground near the tidal Roe, in a field the surface of which was about four feet above high-water, turned up some rare and beautiful objects of gold —a collar richly ornamented with repoussé designs of the Celtic Period (Plate VI); a little boat, with oars, etc., complete; a bowl, a torc, a necklace, and so on. He parted with them to his employer for a few pounds; the latter sold them to that active collector Robert Day of Cork for a greatly enhanced sum; and Mr Day disposed of them to the British Museum for £600. It was only after the conclusion of these transactions that the Royal Irish Academy heard of the discovery, and through the State Solicitor they claimed them as treasure trove, the Academy being the body appointed to represent the Crown in such matters. Roughly stated, the law of treasure trove amounts to this: if precious objects such as these are found under circumstances which point to their having been lost or abandoned, then it is a case of " finders keepers "; but if there is evidence that they were concealed or deposited with the intention of ultimate recovery, then the Crown claims them on behalf of the unknown next of kin. The Trustees of the British Museum refused to deliver up the objects, on the ground that they were not treasure trove: and so the issue was joined, and the Irish Government requested the English law officers to take action for their recovery. When the line of argument for the defence became known, it appeared that the British Museum contention was that at the time of the deposition of the articles the waters of Lough Foyle, which adjoins, flowed over the lands in question, so that the objects could not have been deposited there with a view to recovery: the Museum suggested that they had been cast overboard from a ship as a votive offering, and were therefore abandoned. Involved questions were also raised regarding the law of treasure trove. Matters of the latter kind were for the lawyers, but the question of submergence and date of uplift were for the geologist and antiquary—for the latter because these latest fluctuations of the sea-level in north-east Ireland are intimately connected with early human industry, as in the case of Larne raised beach (p. 79). George Coffey and I, who had worked, both together and separately, on the raised beaches and their associated flint implements, were called in, and asked by the solicitor to the Treasury to demonstrate if possible that the site where the ornaments had been ploughed up had been actually dry land at the time of their deposit there (the objects dated from about the beginning of the Christian era). Geologists had no doubt on this point, since the flat on which the ploughing was done, now only four feet above high tide-level, clearly formed part of the uplift of the much older Neolithic times, but to satisfy a court of law on the point might not be so easy. Especially, it was necessary to prove that the movement of elevation was completed before the objects could have been manufactured. Coffey and I visited various sites in search of convincing evidence on this point, and finally obtained it by excavation in hollows of the dunes at Portstewart, where undisturbed Neolithic land-surfaces, with implements and pottery, were found to go down to two feet above present storm-level of high-water. This showed that in Neolithic times here the land stood quite as high as at

present, and that it had not been submerged since, for submergence
on that exposed coast would have destroyed the human occupation
sites with their " black layers " and implements.   What was true of
Portstewart must have been true of Broighter only thirteen miles
away.   Armed with these facts, we were prepared to face the trial
with equanimity, and hoped to " do our bit " successfully.   The
case was heard before Mr Justice Farwell at the Royal Courts of
Justice in June, 1903.   There was an imposing array of counsel.   On
our side were the Attorney-General (Sir R. B. Finlay), the Solicitor-
General (Sir Edward (afterwards Lord) Carson), H. Sutton (afterwards Sir Henry, Judge in the King's Bench Division) and R. J.
Parker.   The British Museum defence was led by Mr Warmington,
K.C. (afterwards a Baronet); with him were R. B. Haldane (afterwards Lord Chancellor and 1st Viscount) and E. Beaumont.   First
we heard the evidence of the ploughman: how the gold hoard was
about fifteen inches below the surface, and " one part catched on the
nose of the plough and it turned out of line ".   After that J. L.
Myres, then Lecturer in Classical Archaeology at Oxford, and A. J.
Evans, keeper of the Ashmolean Museum, were called, and during
a lengthy examination and cross-examination we heard a mass of
interesting information concerning the practice of votive offerings:
the period ranged from the time of Xerxes to modern days, the *locus*
from Finland to the Malay archipelago.   Mananaan MacLir was
dragged in as an Irish sea god, and Frazer's *Golden Bough* was well
to the fore.   The judge got restive over this wealth of folk-lore
and legend, and protested once or twice.   Professor Edward Hull,
Robert Munro and Robert Cochrane brought us to some extent back
to earth, and Professor Cole and J. R. Kilroe of the Irish Geological
Survey completed the process.   George Coffey and I were in turn
examined by Carson and cross-examined by Haldane—if you must
appear in a court of law it is well to do so in good company.   Mr
Warmington for the defence had a lot more to say about treasure
trove: but by the end of the third day the flood of oratory and
question and answer had spent itself, and there remained only the

Court's judgment on the case. This followed a week later. Mr Justice Farwell had no doubts on the matter, and he expressed himself emphatically. Leaving out learned decisions concerning the treasure trove plea, I give the latter portion of his finding. " I must express my opinion that the Court has been occupied for a considerable time in listening to fanciful suggestions more suited to the poem of a Celtic bard than the prose of an English Law Report. The defendants' suggestion is that the articles were thrown into the sea, which they suggest then covered the spot in question, as a votive offering by some Irish sea king or chief to some Irish sea god at some period between 300 B.C. and A.D. 100, and for this purpose they ask the Court to infer the existence of the sea on the spot in question, the existence of an Irish sea god, the existence of a custom to make votive offerings in Ireland during the period suggested, and the existence of kings or chiefs who would be likely to make such votive offerings. The whole of their evidence (if I may so describe it) on these points is of the vaguest description, and I find as follows: [A judgment as to treasure trove succeeds.] It was perhaps natural that the defendants should grasp at theories which, in justice to them, I may say were not invented for the purpose of the defence; but it is really little short of extravagant to ask the Court to assume the existence of a votive offering of a sort hitherto unknown, in a land where such offerings are hitherto unknown, in a sea not known to have existed for 2000 years, and possibly for 4000 years, to a sea god by a chieftain both equally unknown, and to prefer this to the commonplace but natural inference that these articles were a hoard hidden for safety in a land disturbed by frequent raids, and forgotten by reason of the death or slavery of the depositor. . . . The result is that I will make a declaration that the articles in question are treasure trove, belonging to His Majesty by reason of the Prerogative Royal, and order the delivery up of the same accordingly."

And so we won by two goals (or more) to nil. I was present at the closing scene when, at a meeting of the Royal Irish Academy on 11th November, 1903, these beautiful objects were placed on the table, and George Coffey narrated their adventures. Since then they have occupied a place of honour in the Academy's unique collection of Irish prehistoric gold in the National Museum.[1]

Benevenagh, the north-west angle of the basaltic plateau, is a striking hill as seen from the low grounds over which the railway and road pass towards Derry, though from the plateau itself it is but the uptilted corner of a large area of flattish heathery moorland. The great land-slips, already mentioned, here have brought the basalt down, down, in a series of steps, from 1100 feet to sea-level. Below the lofty precipice which now impends over the wreck of the former cliff-face, all is chaos and confusion; but so slow is the slipping movement that woods and fields and streams remain unchanged or nearly so through generation after generation of men. Benevenagh is famous for harbouring a large colony of alpine plants, here growing at unusually low level—Mountain Avens, Purple Saxifrage, Cushion Pink, Twisted Whitlow-grass, and others. In May, the flowering masses of Cushion Pink, of every tint from white to crimson, are a delightful sight. From the summit of the hill we get a bird's-eye view of the remarkable flat sandy triangle with five-mile sides, known as Magilligan, which almost blocks the entrance of Lough Foyle. If we descend the hill and walk over its sandy surface we can study the successive ridges, parallel with the outer shore, which show its growth mile after mile towards the open sea, nor does this process appear yet to have ceased. As to *why* it was so formed one may well puzzle; as to *when*, it is of course comparatively new—post-Glacial at least; but where did such a prodigious quantity of sand come from? The question of water-supply in an area raised only a few feet above high tide has been solved by capturing the small streams that come down from the basaltic highlands and leading them in parallel courses across the triangle, so that each of the many farms may get a due supply.

Benbradagh (*Beann bradach*, the peak of robbers, 1536 feet), twelve miles south of Benevenagh, commands an interesting view,

[1] There is a sequel to the story, but it cannot be told yet.
The hoard was the subject of a parliamentary enquiry which pronounced it to be Treasure Trove and it remains on exhibit in the National Museum in Dublin. The date of the burial has never been established. C.M.

on account of the sharp contrast of rock and of surface to east and west. Looking eastward, almost the whole of the broken-backed basaltic plateau is in sight, the ground sloping gently down into the valley of the Bann, beyond which the opposite rim (the Antrim hills), forms a long line from Knocklayd overlooking the northern ocean right down to Belfast. Northward, Lough Foyle lies like a great lake, and the highlands of Inishowen rise behind it. Further west, Donegal spreads, with all its familiar hills—Muckish, Errigal, Croaghgorm—away far into the south-west. Below us is the broad wooded valley of the Roe, and to the left the imposing mass of the Sperrin Mountains, where the Roe has its source. It is a noble prospect, extending right across Ulster almost from coast to coast. No wonder that the summit was chosen as the burial-place of some old chieftain of the Bronze Age, whose sepulchral cist, large blocks of basalt, still stands there in ruins.

The Sperrin Mountains (*Cnoc speirín*) form a broad ridge of high hills, smothered in peat, their flanks gashed by deep wooded glens, which are their most attractive feature. There are few roads, and fewer places where one may stay. I remember coming down with a friend to Plumb Bridge after a long day's traverse of the ridge, spent in searching (unsuccessfully) for the Cloud-berry, which has here its only Irish station. We were successful, however, in securing a lodging for the night—a room measuring six feet by five, with a single bed set the five-foot way. Now my length between perpendiculars, when in an attitude of repose, is six feet, and Dr. Donnan's is six foot three. Fortunately, there was a small window at the bottom of the bed, and by taking out the sash we could project our superfluous length into the yard beyond. In the morning, the hens had discovered a new and comfortable perching-place.

This Cloud-berry, well known to dwellers in more northern climes, is a little herbaceous Blackberry, an inhabitant of bogs. I remember a far-stretching road on the Lofoten Islands, which, as we drove along, was edged mile after mile with its large orange fruits, while the moors on either side were full of people gathering them—for they make an excellent preserve. The plant is frequent on the Scottish hills, but in Ireland only a single small patch of it exists, high on the dreary bogs of the Sperrins. No doubt it was common in Ireland before the cold of the Glacial Period passed away: but in the uncongenial warmth of today it has come to its final flicker, like half a dozen other Irish plants which belong to the Arctic, and in a little while it will join other former inhabitants of Ireland now known only from their remains entombed at the bottom of our bogs.

The broad Sperrin highland, prolonged to the northern sea by the basalts of the Benbradagh range, cuts Londonderry off from Belfast, seventy-five miles away, and compels a railway journey of 100 miles. The Great Northern route keeps to the southward, and climbs across the ridge above Dungannon (*Dún Geanainn*, Gannon's fort), taking advantage of Glacial drainage channels now abandoned by former streams. The Northern Counties line passes along the Derry coast, tunnelling where the basaltic uplands descend in cliffs into the sea at Downhill. The distance by road is less, owing to the use of heathery passes through the hills from the valley of the Roe.

Except for the low lands that front the sand-banks of Lough Foyle (*Loch Feabhaill*), the coast of Londonderry is varied and picturesque. East of the great sand-flat of Magilligan, the sea resumes its ancient place along the base of high basaltic cliffs. The presence of a raised beach of Neolithic age allows the railway and road from Magilligan to Coleraine to squeeze along between the waves and the precipice as far as Downhill, which, with its splendid broad beach of gleaming sand, and its dunes plastered up against the dark basalt or the underlying " white limestone ", is a remarkable place, especially when after rain streams discharge veils of yellow water over the cliff.

The irregular band of red clay and flints that separates the surface of the Chalk from the overlying basalt, and with which I have been familiar since childhood, has always had a fascination for me, it provides such a vivid fragment of ancient history. We begin with the picture conjured up by the Chalk itself—a quiet clear sea in which lived myriads of animals with calcareous or silicious coverings or skeletons—molluscs and sea-urchins and numberless others, including especially the minute and lovely organisms called Foraminifera. Generation after generation, these shed their solid parts on the sea-floor till a great depth of limy mud accumulated. This became consolidated by degrees, and by a curious process familiar to geologists the silicious particles drew together, often around the skeletons of sponges, till they formed lumps of flint in the chalky rock. Later came a period of elevation, and the hardened sea-bottom emerged and became dry land. Now it was exposed to the ravages of rain and wind, and as carbonate of lime is readily soluble the surface was vigorously attacked by the elements. As it became washed away, the flints scattered through the rock were left behind, as they are hard and insoluble. Also the small quantities of clay and sand which the Chalk contained collected slowly on the denuded rock-surface, which became by exposure fissured and irregular. Then came a catastrophic change. Volcanic activity set in. The earth's surface cracked, molten rock welled up from below through fissures or vents and spread far and wide, submerging the old Chalk surface under glowing lava, and finally burying it deeply under perhaps a thousand or more feet of black volcanic rock. The flinty soil, bright red from staining by iron compounds, was left as a narrow band between the white Chalk and the black basalt. But the special interest of this layer is that here is an actual old land-surface, on which many millions of years ago the sun shone and the rain fell, flowers grew and beasts grazed, and over which butterflies and birds, all of kinds long extinct, hovered and darted. The boiling lava has effectually destroyed all trace of the life which once pulsated there, save that fragments of carbonized trees still remain to tell of forests over-whelmed. But from contemporaneous deposits elsewhere, in which organic remains have been preserved, the life of the time can be reconstructed. We find ourselves transported back to a momentous period in the history of both animals and plants. On the one hand, this is the close of the epoch which saw the rise and complete domination over the Earth of the great Reptile empire. In every form and size—fish-like, crocodile-like, toad-like, dragon-like, as large as whales or as small as sparrows—reptiles had been for long the undisputed masters of land and water and air alike, but now their sway had collapsed with a crash, and the rise to power of the Mammals, which remain still the lords of the Earth, was imminent. In the vegetable world, on the other hand, the flowering plants, late-comers in the history of vegetation, had just achieved their pheno-menal rise to power, while the former masters of the Earth—the club-mosses and horsetails and cycads and so on—were dwindling or had dwindled, to hold henceforth subordinate places in the scheme of nature. And what were the animals which we must conjure up when we try in imagination to repeople these ancient Chalk Downs? There were strange quadrupeds, of the group to which elephants and tapirs and pigs belong, and in the air were bats and primitive birds; in the seas or rivers turtles, sea-snakes and crocodile-like creatures disported themselves: but most of our modern animal groups were still to come. Among the plants, cycads and palms, remnants of older and warmer times, still flourished; but the advent of the modern flora was shown by the presence of Birches and Beeches and Oaks, Planes, Maples, Hollies, Ivies, though all of species different from those which now inhabit the Earth. This modern aspect of the flora seems strange when we remember that Europe as we know it was still largely non-existent, that its mountain ranges—the Alps, the Pyrenees, the Carpathians and even the gigantic Himalayas and Andes of other continents—were still undreamed-of, though the period of stress which resulted in their formation was now close at hand.

At Downhill the cliff advances to meet the sea, and the railway has to tunnel for the better part of a mile to emerge again at Castlerock, whence a broad sandy beach backed by dunes sweeps away to Portstewart, scarcely interrupted by the deep narrow entrance of the River Bann—" the fishy fruitfull Bann ", as Spenser calls it.

Castlerock, a couple of furlongs of scattered villas facing the sea, has changed but little in the last half-century. For this I am grateful, for it is bound up with many of my happiest childish recollections. Hither, away back in the seventies and eighties, we used to have a family migration in August. Here we learned to swim without fear in rough water; here we found Hare-bells and Gentians, and white and yellow Water-lilies difficult to gather without a wetting; and the sand-dunes, now thronged with golfers, were lonely and exciting places, ideal for the hunting of Red Indians and for expeditions through untrodden mountain passes. And they yielded wild strawberries too, in profusion, a gift beyond price for starving explorers. Then there was "the Churn", a little bay where the rim of cliff curved in like a parabola so that in a northerly wind each wave became piled up, and broke, with a clap like thunder, against the apex, sending a great fountain of spray fifty feet into the air. There were zeolites, too, and other crystals to be found in what had once been bubbles in the lava, and on the shore half a hundred kinds of shells, of which the rarest and most prized were the "blue snail" (*Ianthina*), and the delicate watch-spring *Spirula*, which belongs to a kind of cuttle-fish. The former, a pelagic mollusc, often came ashore with its curious bubbly float still attached; but of the *Spirula*, brought from the West Indies to our shores by the Gulf Stream, we never got anything but the curious coiled internal shell. And there were Sea-mice, with iridescent bristles, and the transparent *Velella*, which we called Sea-sundial. When the tide was low there were rock-pools lined with pink corallines, inhabited by coiling brown sea-weeds, small fishes darting about, red sea-anemones that clung to your fingers, and green crabs that wanted to fight you. On the strand, in the shallow water, were quantities of shrimps, very difficult to see, and an occasional sting-fish or "gowdy", a vindictive little white creature with a poisonous black dorsal fin, that sent you to the sofa for a couple of days if you had the bad luck to step on him. And there were rabbits, brown and black, to be watched and stalked, and an occasional exciting seal or porpoise out beyond the breakers, and in the dusk the flashing light on distant Inishtrahull away to the northward, and a mysterious long snake-like goods train that crept in after we ought to be in bed, and shunted in a fascinating way. Port Vantage, too, was a place of delight—a cliffy gorge running down to the railway and the sea between the two tunnels, full of rocks and Lady Ferns, with a pond in which Waterhens and Dab-chicks dodged in and out among the reeds, where their discarded nests might still be found. I wandered over these places last summer. They have all grown very small now, and are less exciting than they once were: but is it any wonder that I retain in my heart a very warm corner for Castlerock? And the Bog Myrtle still grows in an unexpected marshy place by the roadside among the houses, where I was thrilled at ten years old to find it for the first time.

A short mile east of Castlerock the River Bann, at that time unencumbered by training walls, poured out between steep banks of sand to meet the northern sea. This was an exciting place, with green water racing past as the tide rose and brown water as the tide sank; and towards ebb the river water would push its way far out to sea in a great loop, with a fringe of white foam curving round between the brown and green. And there was an old song we heard concerning the Bann and the delectable product of the distilleries of Coleraine (*Cúil rathain*, corner of the ferns), of which I remember only one verse and the chorus:

> Cleopatra once gave a great banquet,
> And sent for her wines off to Spain;
> But knowing Mark Antony's weakness
> She smuggled a cask of Coleraine.
>
> Then here's to the gay little river
> That smiles as it flows to the main;
> For its water will banish all sorrows
> When mixed with a drop of Coleraine.

And the last syllable of the second and fourth lines was prolonged into a long drone—Spai-ai-ain, as they do in country singing in Ireland—and equally in Bulgaria, at the other end of Europe. I wonder is that song still sung?

Portstewart, unlike Castlerock, has grown almost out of recognition in the last thirty years, and makes a good second to the populous resort of Portrush (*Port ruis*, the landing place of the peninsula) three miles further east; indeed, it will soon be the western end of Portrush if the intervening tract continues to be built over—and no doubt it will do so, for this rocky coast, all open Atlantic in front, is an extraordinarily invigorating place. Therefore Portrush is especially beloved of the people of Belfast, and thither they troop in thousands in July and August. When I first came to Dublin from the north, over forty years ago, I remember being struck by the different conception in the two cities as to the venue for the annual holiday. Belfast people turned out *en masse* to Portrush and Newcastle, where they bathed and played golf and tennis with all the people with whom they consorted at home. Dublin folk, on the other hand, got their passports into order and bolted to Switzerland or Tyrol or Italy or Germany. It is true that Dublin has attractive places around it, but they have remained to some extent undeveloped —with the exception of Bray, which is to Dublin merely what Bangor is to Belfast—and probably that is to some extent accountable for the difference in procedure: but it is no doubt mainly due to the fact that Dublin was a capital city with many cosmopolitan interests while Belfast was still to all intents a market-town. It has still a weekly market-day like the little towns around it, and until a few years ago a flock of leisurely geese waddled among the parked motors in Cromac Square, and camped on its barren concrete—possibly a survival of the days when grass grew there; two of them are there even yet. Belfast is now a city, larger I believe than Dublin: yet I am inclined to think that this difference as to holidays persists to a great extent, and that many more foreign travel tickets are issued in the southern capital than in the northern. Which is a pity, for the great business community of Belfast, absorbed in office work for forty-eight or fifty weeks out of each fifty-two, stands to gain more from a complete change of environment—new people, new language, new ideas, new customs—than the more varied, more professional and more leisurely groups that make up the same class in Dublin.

Before we leave Portrush mention may be made of the occurrence there of a lithological feature which recalls one of the great scientific controversies of the past. Towards the end of the eighteenth century geology was still in its infancy, but it received a notable impetus when Werner was appointed to the geological chair at the School of Mines at Freyburg in Saxony in 1775. He was a brilliant and dogmatic teacher, and under him an enthusiastic and equally dogmatic school sprang up which for a while dominated geological thought in Europe. Among other things, Werner and his disciples did not admit that any rocks except recent lavas were of volcanic origin. Volcanoes were modern phenomena; and the basalts of various ages were chemical precipitates from water. The " Neptunists " as they were called, poured ridicule and scorn on the " Vulcanists ", who found what they considered to be igneous rocks in even very ancient deposits; the latter replied in kind, and a war characterized by extraordinary bitterness and vindictiveness went on. Questions of religious belief were by no means excluded, for those who would not admit that all rocks were sedimentary were accused of attempting to undermine Holy Writ, in that their tenets were incompatible with belief in the universality of the Flood. The feud spread to these western isles, and Hutton, Playfair and finally William Smith, whose names bear honourable places in the history of geology, raised their voices in support of the " Vulcanists ", and were in consequence bitterly attacked both abroad and at home. Hutton's blunt statement, " In the economy of the world I can find no trace of a beginning, no prospect of an end", was regarded as nothing short of blasphemy, for even scientific minds had not yet fully grasped the enormous periods of time which are now freely admitted as necessary for the transaction of geological processes; and fossils, those essential keys to the history of the globe, were still looked on as traces of one universal deluge. In Ireland, Kirwan, President of the Royal Irish Academy, was insistent on the aqueous origin of all

rocks, and proclaimed that " sound geology graduates into religion "
—religion including and indeed signifying literal belief in the teach-
ing of the Old Testament. So "Neptunism" became associated with
the orthodoxy of the day, and " Vulcanism " with heterodoxy, and
eminent divines as well as laymen thundered forth their condemna-
tion. " We cannot estimate ", writes Lyell,[1] " the malevolence of
such a persecution, by the pain which similar insinuations might now
inflict; for although charges of infidelity and atheism must always
be odious, they were injurious in the extreme at that moment of
political excitement [about 1790]; and it was better, perhaps, for a
man's good reception in society, that his moral character should have
been traduced, than that he should become a mark of these poisoned
weapons." In the end, the violence of the dispute brought such
discredit on both sides that a strictly neutral school of geologists
arose, who directed their energy to observing instead of disputing:
and with that wiser method of discovering the truth, the foundations
of modern geology were laid.

And what has all this to do with Portrush? For answer you must
examine the indurated Lias for which the place has long been famous
among geologists, and which was first observed by Dr. Richardson
about 1799. The Lias which, mostly in the form of grey shales and
clays, underlies the white Chalk in Antrim, represents silts deposited
in shallow seas full of animal life, and as a consequence it is often
highly fossiliferous. At Portrush an intrusion of molten lava, of the
long subsequent date of the overlying basalts, so baked the Lias that
it became a hard dark flinty rock, which was mistaken for one of the
volcanic series: and the inclusion in it of numerous fossils was hailed
with delight by the " Neptunists " as proof that the basalt itself was
of aqueous origin, as contended by Werner and his followers.
Local geologists disputed hotly as to the origin of what appeared to
be a fossiliferous basalt, and partisans of both sides came across channel
to view this startling piece of evidence and to join in the fray. It
was not till about 1835 that there was any general agreement as to

[1] Sir Charles Lyell, *Principles of Geology*, 6th ed., vol. i., p. 99. 1840.

the true nature of this disconcerting rock. It still outcrops boldly on the beach at Portrush, a monument to a famous battle.

Now we come to one of the most delightful playgrounds in Ireland, one that I have known and loved since childhood—the Antrim coast (Antrim = Óentrebh, one tribe). It is quite true that, like all other places of whatever kind, its delights are not for all. If you want to motor a couple of hundred miles a day, Antrim's possibilities will be exhausted in no time. If you want to bathe among crowds of people and of rubber porpoises don't go to Cushendall or Cushendun—nor if you yearn to spend the fine afternoons in playing bridge in a crowded smoke-room. But if you love rocks and cliffs, deep glens, sparkling sea, air like champagne, great stretches of brown moorland (with a sufficiency of tennis and golf and sailing and fishing)—then the Antrim coast is the place for you. Best of all are the surprising colour-contrasts supplied by its cliffs and scarps—black basalt, white Chalk, red Trias—and the changing views of the Scottish headlands and islands across the North Channel, from Ayrshire up to Islay, and the grand run of tide which twice daily sweeps down the narrows between Kintyre and Fair Head, and around Rathlin, and twice back again. And what cold water it is!— the coldest to be found on all the coasts of Ireland. Why? for one thing, you are here well beyond Malin Head, which marks the end of the warm drift that comes up along the west coast; for another, there is very deep water close by—135 fathoms at Rathlin to the north, and 150 fathoms off Belfast Lough to the south. I well remember a cold wet July at Glenarm in my student days, and courageous headers off a rock with James and Eoin MacNeill, and the scramble to get out of the icy water as quickly as arms and legs could accomplish it.

I got to know the Antrim coast intimately in early youth. During three summers especially, every cliff and glen and moor was explored, from Larne to Portrush, and I could have taken a much better degree in local topography, geology and botany than I eventually did after three years of engineering at " Queen's ". Is there any place in western Europe where there is so great a variety of rocks as in Antrim, or where the rocks take so prominent a part in the production of varied scenery? Over much of the north of Ireland the newer rocks have all been stripped off, exposing the very ancient schist and gneiss which give us the scenery of Donegal and western Derry; but things are different in Antrim. From Cushendall to Cushendun Old Red Sandstone forms a rocky coast; from Murlough Bay to Ballycastle are Carboniferous sandstones and shales, with bands of coal, and fossil trunks of the strange trees of that period. All round the coast the Secondary rocks form a broken ribbon—Trias, Lias, Chalk—red, blue-grey, white—and capping them all the solid beds of black volcanic rock which we know so well. Then comes the Boulder-clay, generally bright red, and finally the black peat of the mountains and the northern inland parts, and along the coast raised beaches full of the flints that Neolithic man worked into weapons and domestic implements. What a twelve-course feast for a hungry geologist!

For the botanist also there are attractions—a large and varied flora (Antrim can claim as large a flora as any county in Ireland) which, as one might expect from the narrowness of the North Channel, has a special Scottish flavour about it in the occurrence here, and in Ireland only on this basaltic plateau, of some plants characteristic of North Britain, such as the Wood Crane's-bill, the Wood Cowwheat, the Tea-leaved Willow, and the Few-flowered Sedge. But it is the glorious abundance on the coast and in the glens of commoner wild-flowers, rather than the presence of these and other rarities, that make Antrim a garden, especially in spring.

To the ancient peoples, much the most important natural local production was the nodules of flint that are found in the white Chalk, where the contained silica has segregated out from its calcareous matrix. Being insoluble, and much harder than the Chalk, it has remained when the latter was destroyed, and the ice of the Glacial Period has scattered it all over the country as a common ingredient of the Boulder-clay which the ice left behind. Round the coast, the

Boulder-clay itself has been in turn attacked, especially by the sea during the low land-level that occurred in Neolithic times. Then the stony materials in the Boulder-clay were sorted into gravel-beds, the clayey part being carried out into deeper water: and these gravel-beds, subsequently raised above tide-level, bequeathed to the early people abundance of flint to fashion into implements—for flint, from its very hard glassy nature, gave especially sharp cutting edges to the skilled worker, and all over the world was highly valued by Stone Age people. So it comes about that the raised beaches are full of worked flints, the debris of the implement-makers' trade, mixed with scrapers, knives, axes, spears and what-not, which were imperfect, or which got lost. The most extensive of these raised beaches is that which forms the Curran at Larne—a sickle-shaped spit a mile in length, composed of twenty feet of stratified gravel, full of marine shells to attest its origin.

The main ice-sheet, coming down channel from Scotland, has scattered Antrim flint everywhere to the southward—across Belfast Lough into Down, and away on to Dublin and Wexford. When we were children at Holywood, a great event was the arrival of a load of shore gravel and its spreading on the avenue. We were inveterate collectors—to the great inconvenience of our mother— and the gravel was in a few minutes cleared of its worked flints. We got to know well the different types of implements, and more than one well-formed axe or arrow-head was with pride placed in the box which served as a museum. That and pieces of the riebeckite-granophyre of Ailsa Craig—a granite-like rock with green crystals in it, brought south by the ice—were the principal spoils yielded by the local gravel.

Years afterwards a vexed question agitated the Belfast Naturalists' Field Club as to whether the worked flints were found at all depths in the Larne gravels—which would show that their manufacture was as old as or older than even the lowest layer—or only at or near the surface, implying a later date. We—a committee of the Club— made two excavations in consecutive years to elucidate this point, and found that the implements occur at all depths, though they are most plentiful near the surface—an important fact that has been confirmed by subsequent investigations.

Good wine needs no bush, and I need not exhaust the reader's patience—and my own—by going into a detailed itinerary of the Antrim coast. From Portrush all the way to Ballycastle bold cliffs prevail, with outlying stacks—of which Carrick-a-rede with its precarious bridge and salmon fishery is the most picturesque—and occasional sandy stretches as at Bushfoot and Whitepark Bay. The finest cliffs are those about Bengore Head (*Beann gabhar*, peak of the goats), just east of the Giant's Causeway. Unlike the cliffs to the east and west, these are of basalt from top to bottom, and display to perfection the sequence of the successive lava-flows, with the red band in the middle that marks a long pause in volcanic activity, and the formation of fertile plains and shallow lakes: above, the black rock supervenes, bed upon bed, showing the resumption of the reign of terror and the local extirpation of fauna and flora alike. At Whitepark Bay, on the other hand, the Chalk stands much higher, and it, not basalt, forms the cliffs which enclose this lovely spot: but out at sea, at *lower* levels, stacks of black rock rise from the water, showing how the Earth's surface has cracked and portions have been dropped down hundreds of feet as a result of deep-seated disturbance. Here and there along this north coast are ruined castles perched on the edge of the cliff, mostly on isolated projections where they had natural defences in the form of precipices which almost encircled them. Here MacNeills and MacQuillans and O'Cahans fought and wrestled for spoil in old days, and raided each other's cow-pens. And the names of these strongholds—Dunluce (*Dún lios* or *Dur lios*, strong fort), Dunseverick (*Dún Sobairche*, Sobairche's fort), Dunanynie—suggest that they were in occupation long before the days of castles, and formed the " promontory forts " of older peoples, the neck which joined the headland with the mainland being fortified by a deep fosse, such as is found on other parts of the coast. The sandy stretch between the sea and the encircling cliff at Whitepark

Bay was a populous settlement in Neolithic and Bronze Age times, as is shown by the abundance of bones, charcoal, and implements which occur there, especially in the " black layers " which mark old surfaces. The most interesting of the animal remains are bones of the Great Auk (see p. 331) which are found mixed with those of Red Deer and domestic creatures, showing that this extinct bird was in those days an article of food.

Rathlin Island or Raghery (*Rachra*, genitive *Rachran*; *Rikina* of Ptolemy) lying a few miles off Ballycastle, continues the Chalk and basalt area out to sea. The intervening gap, which now forms a deep and turbulent strait, probably arose from a collapse of the surface during the many and extensive earth-movements resulting from the disturbances which led to the great volcanic outpourings. The island, shaped like a letter L, is mostly cliff-bound, but low at the part which is nearest to Fair Head; the surface is heathy, with cultivation on shallow soil and lakelets or marshes in the hollows. There is now no fuel, which has to be brought from Ballycastle. At the west end the cliffs, which the White-tailed Sea-Eagle used to haunt, run up to over 400 feet, with high outlying stacks, and here there are vast colonies of breeding sea-birds, which include Manx Shearwaters and Fulmar Petrels. The whole island is a delightful open breezy place, inspiring and invigorating, and one can now stay there in as much comfort as a lover of nature needs. Before the advent of the motor-boat the passage was a precarious undertaking, on account of the powerful currents: if you missed the tide you might go joy-riding away round Fair Head or towards Inishowen, and a high wind might make the passage impossible for days at a time; but now, at least in summer, there is seldom difficulty. A ruined tower on the north-eastern cliffs, still known as Bruce's Castle, is the scene, according to tradition, of the famous episode of the persevering spider: but S. A. Stewart, who was an acute observer of animal life, has reported gravely that he could detect no greater intelligence among the spiders of Rathlin than among any other spiders.

One of the finest promontories on the Irish coast is Benmore

(*Beann mór*, great headland) or Fair Head, which looks across to Rathlin and to Kintyre a few miles east of Ballycastle (Plate VII). Others are loftier, but none has a more imposing or clean-cut profile—a tip-tilted promontory of 636 feet falling in a straight vertical line to a talus of huge blocks sloping to deep water. Here again, as in so many places in Antrim, the geological structure will excite the interest even of one who does not know—nor care to know—the difference between granite and slate. What happened is this. Lower Carboniferous sandstones, lying in nearly horizontal beds, were invaded by a mass of molten lava, which squeezed its way in between the strata, forming a solid bed of basalt (dolerite) some 300 feet thick. The sandstones can be seen peeping out under the mass—softish rocks with thin beds of coal—above which the dolerite " sill " rises as a sheer cliff. Having cooled slowly between two cold surfaces, it has assumed a columnar structure at right angles to the planes of cooling, after the manner of such rocks (as is seen in the Giant's Causeway). But here the columns are some fifty feet in girth and hundreds of feet high. The sandstones which originally formed the cover of the sill have been removed by denudation; only traces of them remain, and the wide heathy area on the top of the head is the upper surface of the volcanic intrusion.

Immediately behind the pleasant watering-place of Ballycastle, Knocklayd (*Cnoc leithid*, the broad hill) rises to 1695 feet, a massive dome-shaped outlier of the Antrim plateau. The upper part is basalt, below which the white Chalk peeps out, resting on an ancient floor of schist. One does not associate this well-behaved and decorous hill with recent volcanic gymnastics, such as the newspapers of 1788 would have us believe. If we turn to *Faulkner's Dublin Journal* of 31st May of that year we read, in an " Extract from a letter from Ballycastle to a gentleman in this city ", of a violent thunderstorm which did damage there: but worse was to follow: " Our fears were very much increased in the evening by a most uncommon noise from Knocklade, the top of which burst, and the discharge of burning matter and hot stones from it was truly

PLATE VII

R. Welch: photo

FAIR HEAD FROM THE WEST

alarming, killing several cattle in the adjacent fields, many cabbins
were thrown down, and several people are missing (among whom
are the dissenting minister and parish priest of this place) supposed to
have been overtaken by the burning matter, which was thirty
perches in breadth, and ran near a mile and a half ". This was followed by a letter in the *Morning Post or Dublin Courant* of 9th June
signed " Pliny the Younger " and also emanating from Ballycastle.
The writer states that the published accounts of the affair have been
so unsatisfactory that he is induced to supplement them: " A shower
of ashes and stones extending for a quarter of a mile all round the hill
was followed by a stream of lava which rushed in a sheet of liquid
fire into the village of Ballyowen, where everyone perished except
Richard Mulholland, his wife and two children, who fled into a
neighbouring field. Father Magennis and his niece, who was a very
fine young woman, are among the lost. Twenty-seven persons in
all perished. The lava continued to flow for 39 hours, finally entering
the sea near Fair Head" [it must have run up-hill for some hundreds
of feet to get there!]. On 12th June " Pliny the Younger " sends
a further communication. The lava has destroyed four villages;
many fields are covered with ashes. The people are manuring their
fields with the heaps of dead fish killed when the lava entered the
sea. Yesterday he ventured up Knocklade with Dr. Hamilton of
Portrush and others. Great quantities of smoke were still issuing
from the crater, which was seen to be about 100 yards in diameter,
but could not be approached on account of the intense heat: and
thrilling details are added. So far as I know this was the end of
direct evidence, but reverberations of these remarkable statements
continued for a long time—in the *Hibernian Gazetteer* for 1789, in
Seward's *Topographia Hibernica* (1795), in Thomas Beggs' long-
winded *Rathlin, a Descriptive Poem* (1820), and finally as a footnote
in Connellan's edition of the *Annals of the Four Masters*, p. 559 (1846).
Only then, apparently, was this volcanic episode finally concluded.
It is strange, as Professor Cole has noted,[1] that William Hamilton,

[1] *Irish Naturalist*, 1922, p. 86.

the author of the *Letters concerning the Northern Coast of the County of Antrim*, of which the second edition appeared in 1790, should say not a word about the business, considering the details into which he enters on geological and other matters. One suspects that he must have known, but chose to be silent—why? It is clear now that the whole business was an elaborate hoax: and I suspect that the same person wrote the letters which appeared in both the Dublin newspapers. Grenville Cole points out that at this time the controversy between the "Neptunists" and the "Vulcanists" ran high (see p. 75); any sort of skit dealing with igneous and sedimentary rocks might be expected. It may be significant that Beggs in his poem writes:

> Lands o'erwhelmed with watery peat
> From Black *Knock-laida's* bursting breast.

May we assume that a small bog-slide on Knocklayd was the origin of the whole thing: and that some wag, inspired by statements as to the volcanic origin of the rocks of Knocklayd, gave a local setting to some account of an eruption of perhaps Vesuvius or Etna, and thus produced this wonderful story?

Immediately south of Fair Head is Murlough Bay (*Murbholg*, a sea-inlet), a place of singular charm. An 800-foot slope descends steeply to the sea, clothed with wood to the water's edge. Once again, it is the great variety of rocks which the bay contains that forms its most remarkable feature. To the north is Fair Head, with its gigantic columns resting on Carboniferous sandstone, shale and beds of coal. In the centre there are elevated cliffs of white Chalk, overlying bright red Triassic sandstone. And the southern horn of the bay is formed of ancient mica-schists, an outlying fragment of the rocks of Donegal. The wet surface of the red sandstone is the home of the Yellow Mountain Saxifrage, which makes here a brave show in July, descending to the level of the sea. In spring the extraordinary profusion of Primroses and Wild Hyacinths, Red Campion and ferns, under the fresh leaves of the sloping woods, with the open sea immediately below, provides a delightful picture.

Next we have Torr Head (*Tor*, a tower, hence tall rock), a few miles to the south, a knob of ancient slaty rocks, in a kind of amphitheatre of high green slopes, where the bright grassy covering betrays the presence of the Chalk. The roads here are metalled with the " white limestone " and form winding lines of dead white against the hills, where Primroses, Wild Hyacinths and Early Purple Orchis linger almost till July. After an interval comes Cushendun (*Cois abhann Duine*, mouth of the river Dun), with its sheltered bay and curious series of caves cut in the " pudding-stones " of the Old Red Sandstone; south of that again Cushendall (*Cois abhann Dhalla*, mouth of the river Dall) nestles among its trees—an excellent and popular centre: and beyond Red Bay and the flat that forms the end of the cliff-walled Glenariff, Garron Point (*Garrán*, a shrubbery) stands boldly out, a high and massive promontory. Its remarkable outline is due to a series of extensive landslides. The treacherous slippery clays of the Lias underlie solid beds of Chalk and basalt, which cover them to a depth of close on a thousand feet, and these beds have slid forward and downward, producing a series of gigantic steps descending to the sea, with rocky faces of·white or black, and grassy sheltered tops sloping inwards: on one of these steps Garron Tower Hotel stands. Above the cliffs and land-slips the top of the headland, about 1000 feet above the sea, forms the most unfrequented and remote portion of the basaltic plateau. For ten miles in a south-westerly direction, and a breadth of several miles, this elevated table-land extends, roadless, houseless, covered with deep soaking bog, with little lakes here and there, and tenanted only by gulls and moorland birds and hares. Its wild flowers, too, are interesting. Here grow two sedges, *Carex pauciflora* and *C. magellanica*, unknown elsewhere in Ireland, and also the rare Yellow Marsh Saxifrage. Thence you descend east to Carnlough (*Carn locha*, the carn of the lough) and its pretty bay, and you pass on to Straidkilly, where the Lias clays are flowing slowly down like a glacier, bearing on their surface the wreck of the Chalk and basalt, as well as a village, and for ever striving to overwhelm the Coast Road or to carry it with them into the sea. Beyond the little village of Glenarm we pass below lofty cliffs of Chalk, and a dozen miles more takes us to Larne and the railway, and thence by Larne Lough and Carrickfergus to Belfast.

This whole coast is so full of beauty and interest that, knowing it so well as I do, I find it hard to select, as I have tried to do, a few spots for special mention; I feel that I have by no means done justice to Cushendun and Cushendall, two places of high attraction. One generalization may be ventured—the scenery and varied interest increase northward. You begin at Larne (*Inver an Latharna*, river-mouth of Lathair, son of Hugony the Great) with primrose-starred slopes dropping to the raised beach on which the Coast Road runs: and thence the ground gets more broken and more beautiful all the way to Fair Head, which, with Murlough Bay, must stand as the special jewel in the Antrim crown: along the northern shore other jewels, such as Whitepark Bay and the cliffs of Bengore, are not far behind it in lustre. Weather is an important factor here: to see the coast at its best you must have a keen clear north wind, bringing in a sparkling sea that edges the rocks with snowy foam, and makes the high line of the Scottish coast—Islay, and the Paps of Jura, and the frowning projection of Kintyre—seem scarcely more than a stone-throw away.

I have said little about the Antrim glens, that cut deep into the high scarp that fronts the North Channel; but it is they, rather than the narrow coastal fringe, that maintain the prosperous farming population, and make " The Glens of Antrim ", or simply " The Glynns ", a well-known geographical expression, like the Kyles of Bute. For the basalt weathers into a heavy rich soil, and the narrow sheltered valley-bottoms have much good agricultural land, though on the slopes it soon gives way to Gorse and then to Heather. The most picturesque of the nine glens (as they are mostly counted) is Glenariff (*Gleann garbh*, rough glen), cliff-walled, flat-bottomed in its lower part where it debouches to the sea in half a mile of sandy shore; narrowing above into branching wooded gorges, full of ferns and wild-flowers. Glendun (Glen of the Dun (river)) is likewise wide below, from Cushendun up to the viaduct which carries the main road on its way northward towards Ballycastle: above that it forms a fine V-shaped valley, running up into wide moorlands. Glenshesk (*Gleann seisg*, glen of the coarse grass ?), behind Ballycastle, contains a more divided river-system, receiving tributary streams from right and left—a broad beautiful valley, with Knocklayd towering over it on the west. All the glens contain good roads, highways by which the coastal region is connected with the interior of Antrim behind the high basaltic fringe, so that despite the prevalence of elevated moorland one can walk or drive across at frequent intervals, or on foot strike north or south over the heather from glen to glen. The glensmen, too, are well worth meeting—a fine hardy hearty race, closely akin in descent and in language to their Scottish neighbours, shrewd, friendly and hospitable.

When in the course of our peregrination we pass Black Head, we come within the sphere of influence of Belfast—that great busy place, not quite a *mushroom* city—there is nothing fungoid about it—but one of growth so fast and vigorous that the more deliberate higher races of plants supply no suitable parallel. How far the rapid extension of Belfast (*Béal feirste*, the ford of the sand-bank) is due to natural advantages, and how far to the vigorous blend in the blood of its inhabitants, I am not qualified to enquire: but if we glance at local geological history we unearth some facts which, if they afford no clue to this riddle, at least explain some of the natural aids and also difficulties which have accompanied its development. Belfast Lough, a fine harbour of refuge, twelve miles long and three to four wide, at the head of which the city stands, represents the long-sunken termination of the valley of the Lagan. It is also a marked geological boundary, for the elevated basaltic area ceases abruptly on its northern shore, though the underlying red sandstones of the Trias edge the lough on both sides, giving way on the County Down coast almost at once to the much older Ordovician and Silurian slaty rocks which cover most of the latter county. Belfast Lough and the Lagan valley above it have in fact been excavated in the Triassic sandstones. During the Ice Age these soft rocks suffered severely, and the bright colour of the Boulder-clay about here shows how the red material of the marls and sandstones has been ground up and scattered. When the ice was in process of withdrawal, the Lagan valley was left clear, while the adjoining lough and the sea outside were still choked. This ice formed a dam, behind which, over and around the site of Belfast, a great lake was formed. Into this lake turbid streams brought much sediment, which settled as red sand or fine red clay. Thus are derived the sands of Malone and Knock, which form a dry and excellent foundation in those suburbs, and also the brick-clays out of which most of Belfast is built. In later times, when Neolithic man roamed the country, the land around Belfast stood lower than at present; the sea lay over the site of the future city, and the tide flowed far up the valley. In the calm waters, sediments accumulated. Deep excavations in Belfast Harbour give us glimpses of this post-Glacial history. Overlying the red sands, and now no less than twenty-seven feet below high-water mark, is a bed of peat, pointing to a much higher land-level than at present, and a surface on which woods of Scotch Fir, Oak, Alder, Willow and Hazel grew, and in these woods Red Deer, Wild Boar and other large animals roamed at will, while insects crawled among the herbage or flitted among the trees. The forerunner of the Belfast-man was no doubt present in those days, but his traces have not as yet been found in this deposit. Then the land began to sink, and this continued till the old land-surface was buried fifty or sixty feet under the sea, which covered the site of the future city and flowed up the valley as far as Balmoral. While Neolithic man was busy with his flint-implement factories at Larne and Kilroot, deposits of fine grey mud accumulated in Belfast Lough and elsewhere, burying deeply the old peat-bed. Then at last the land rose again, leaving a flat plain of soft clay from which the sea had retreated, and around it the scarps that told of the old land-edge on which the waves had beaten, and which still stand out boldly, as in the steep bluff at Tillysburn and the sudden little hill

at the back of York Street and Royal Avenue in Belfast. Old
Belfast, as around High Street, arose on the former sea-bottom, and
it was only as the town spread that buildings began to be erected on
the firmer foundations furnished by the red Glacial clays and sands
—the deltas and sediments of "Lake Belfast". Below, on the flat,
light buildings were possible; but when taller structures were
planned, a firm foundation was necessary, which could only be
obtained by piling—by hammering long balks of timber down
through the soft silts to the red sands or hard clays far below. So
the Belfast of today is essentially a city on stilts. How quaint it
would be if some new kind of X-ray would allow us to see the city
as it really is—all standing up on sticks thirty or forty feet above its
true foundation, just as the dwellings of certain primitive peoples,
past or present, were or are built on piles in lakes or rivers. I have
vague visions of the blue clay—sleech, to use the local term—all dissolved away, and a busy prehistoric community living on the old
forest surface amid a modern forest of piles, far below the roaring
streets of the present city. Perhaps the souls of certain northern
stalwarts might be sent down there, to learn that there are other
things in the world besides politics. Cannot you imagine —— receiving lessons in the art of fashioning ineffectual knives out of flint,
and —— peacefully grinding corn in a sandstone quern in further-
ance of the domestic policy of his household, with Custom-house
steps and Ulster Hall platform alike forgotten. I do not think I
should mind being there myself later on, if I were allowed to work
out the flora of the peat, as compensation for neglected opportunities
of nearly fifty years ago.

Belfast has always been a centre of biological research, and even
in its younger days, when it was a smaller place than Cork, Galway
or Limerick, Belfast men were working actively at local natural
history. In this field, which alone I can touch on here, three names
stand out pre-eminently—Templeton (1766–1825), Thompson (1805–
1852) and Stewart (1826–1910). John Templeton was a gentleman of leisure, living at Cranmore near the "Bog Meadows".

From boyhood he was interested in zoology and botany, especially the latter, and throughout his life this interest retained the form of investigations of a purely local character. Wicklow and Scotland appear to be the farthest points afield that he reached during an active life, and there is no record even of a visit to London, though he was in touch with botanical and zoological leaders resident there. But the flora and fauna of the Belfast region, till then almost unknown, he investigated thoroughly. He was the first to find (on the Cave Hill) the Red Broom-rape, which Sir J. E. Smith described as new from specimens which Templeton sent him; and his critical faculty was shown by his recognition as something novel of *Rosa hibernica*, then looked on as a new species, afterwards shown to be a hybrid hitherto unknown. His main work, his *Hibernian Flora*, remained unfinished and unpublished, but the manuscripts which he left may fairly be said to form the foundation on which our present knowledge of the flora of north-east Ireland has been built.[1]

William Thompson was the son of a Belfast linen merchant, and in his younger days showed no inclination towards natural history. When he was an apprentice to a firm engaged in the linen industry, he came again in contact with an old school friend, William Sinclaire, who was interested in ornithology; that proved the begining of a lifelong devotion to zoology, for in 1831, when he was twenty-six years of age, he gave up business and thenceforth spent his time in investigation of the local fauna (especially birds) and to a lesser extent of the flora. He soon amassed a large body of notes relating to both terrestrial and aquatic species, from mammals down to rotifers, and the idea of a work on the Irish fauna began to take shape. Much local assistance was forthcoming from energetic zoological friends such as Robert Patterson and G. C. Hyndman; correspondence was maintained with naturalists in other parts of Ireland regarding local animals and with the leading British zoologists of the day: and in 1850, when Thompson was forty-five years

[1] See *Magazine of Nat. Hist.*, vols. i.-ii. 1828–29; and *Flora of the North-east of Ireland*, ed. 2. 1928.

old, the first volume of his *Natural History of Ireland* appeared. A second and a third were published in the two years succeeding. These three volumes dealt with and completed the Irish birds, and give an idea of the elaborate scale on which his plans were made. But Thompson's work was destined to go no further. He was seized with illness while on a brief visit to London, and died within two days, at the age of forty-seven years. Under his will, Robert Patterson and James R. Garrett were entrusted with the task of editing and publishing the remainder of the work. The material relating to the rest of the vertebrate animals, and to the mollusca, was fairly full, but for the many other sections of the animal kingdom a mere skeleton was all that existed: a fourth volume, which appeared in 1856, was found sufficient for the publication of the whole of the existing material. Garrett died in 1855, and the volume was seen through the press by my grandfather, Robert Patterson, F.R.S., whose own books on zoology attained a wide vogue in their day. Until the publication of Ussher and Warren's *Birds of Ireland* in 1900, Thompson's work remained the court of appeal on all matters relating to this, the most popular branch of zoology: and even now the material which it contains relative to the whole fauna is of the highest value. Thompson believed he had found a new species of rat in the North of Ireland which he described as *Mus hibernicus*. This creature seemed most nearly allied to the old Black Rat, which occupied the British Isles before it was driven out by the Norway Rat, the brown species which is so common nowadays. The " Irish Rat " (which is now known to be widely spread, and not confined to Ireland) differs from the Black Rat by having a triangular white spot on the breast and shorter tail and ears, and it seemed distinct; but later it was shown to be a melanic or dark-coloured form of the Norway Rat: indeed a case is recorded of typical Norway Rats and Irish Rats being produced in the same litter. This phenomenon of melanism is found in many creatures, and is especially well known among some of the insects, such as moths; it is in Great Britain and Ireland associated with the western coasts; but no definite connection appears to have been established between it and the climatic factors which probably affect it, such as high rainfall or limited insolation.

Samuel Alexander Stewart was a man of type quite different from Templeton and Thompson. He began life by working in a Belfast distillery on a wage of two shillings a week. Later he joined his father, who was a trunk-maker, and as a maker of trunks he passed most of his life, in his shop in North Street. Eventually, in 1891, he became curator of the Museum of the Belfast Natural History and Philosophical Society at a salary of £65. So it will be seen that few worldly advantages came his way. But let us consider what he did. As a youth his evenings were spent at a night school, and later he progressed so well in self-education that he became a court of appeal among scientific friends on many subjects—even on points of English grammar and composition. Always inclined towards nature study, his opportunity came when the Science and Art Department established lecture courses in Belfast in 1860. Under J. Beete Jukes and Ralph Tate he eagerly drank in the principles of geology and botany, and was quick to apply to local phenomena all that he learned. Already in 1863, when Tate published his *Flora Belfastiensis*, localities for a number of the rarer plants were supplied by Stewart, and many further notes were contributed to *Cybele Hibernica*, 1866. He steadily pursued local botanical exploration, and despite strict limitations of both time and means, accomplished this so thoroughly that when in 1888 the Belfast Naturalists' Field Club published his *Flora of the North-east of Ireland*,[1] the completeness of the account given of the distribution of the Flowering Plants, Mosses and Liverworts was largely the result of his own unaided work. The Field Club referred to had been established in 1863 by Tate and his pupils as a direct result of the lectures aforesaid. From the beginning, Stewart was a leading member, and as his studies spread from botany into geology and

[1] His colleague in this work, Thomas Hughes Corry, perished in a boating accident on Lough Gill before he had opportunity for carrying out more than a small amount of local field-work.

zoology, he became a referee in all these subjects both within and without the Club. In Quaternary geology he did especially valuable work. He was the first to show that the clays underlying Belfast and other local estuaries furnish evidence of a depression and subsequent re-elevation of the land of a considerable amount—the " Neolithic depression " so familiar to present-day local geologists; and in a valuable paper he listed all the known fossils of the northern Boulder-clay. Nor was his work confined to the Belfast region. A. G. More was not slow to see in Stewart a valuable ally in the working-up of the Irish flora for the second edition of *Cybele Hibernica*. His museum appointment having made occasional absences possible, he explored, under grants from the Royal Irish Academy, western Fermanagh, Rathlin Island, the Lough Allen and Slieveanieran area, and the Shannon estuary; and I joined him in 1889–90 in a thorough examination of the Mourne Mountains. But it was Stewart's successful fight against heavy odds all through life, and his sterling character, that especially deserve recognition. Of the former enough has been hinted. His intuitive thoroughness and accuracy, his clearness of vision and caution in scientific questions, his modesty and his courage, made him respected and loved. Of " the strife for triumph more than truth " he was incapable; and the only thing towards which he showed intolerance in scientific matters was slipshod work or self-praise. As to his own considerable achievements he was depreciative, and the award of the Honorary Fellowship of the Botanical Society of Edinburgh, the Associateship of the Linnean Society, and eventually a pension from the Civil List, were to him more than ample recognition of his work.

I am proud to pay this brief tribute to the memory of S. A. Stewart, for I cannot say how much I owe to him. Ever ready to help, he befriended me when I was still at school, and was tireless in naming specimens and in imparting all that lore relating to botanical and geological field-work that is not to be found in any book, but which passes from mouth to mouth among those who keep the torch of knowledge burning. No young naturalist ever had a better or more patient teacher, or a more delightful friend when in after years we tramped the hills of Down together.[1]

" Away, away, from men and towns." From the modern city of Belfast, with its modern history and modern buildings and modern factories and shipyards, we turn to the beautiful and attractive area which surrounds it. Not that any slight to Belfast is implied. For what does the Belfast business-man himself do (and in Belfast almost every man is a business-man) but get away from it as soon as ever his business is done—to Balmoral or Knock or Bangor: and I may claim the same privilege, and leave the guide-book to do justice to Belfast. Dublin is beautifully situated, with mountains rising only a few miles beyond its southern suburbs, and the richly wooded Liffey vale, the bold headlands of Howth and Bray, and the broad sands of Dublin Bay. Cork can make a good bid too: but to my mind Belfast stands pre-eminent in Ireland for the beauty and variety of its environment. To north and west the high scarp of the basalts rises nobly. The City Hall, standing at sea-level, is distant only two and a half miles from the thousand-foot contour-line; and the lofty cliffs of the Cave Hill are a conspicuous feature from Castle Junction, the central point of the city. On a volcanic vent at Carrickfergus (*Carraig Fhearghusa*, Fergus's rock) ten miles down the lough, the great castle which John de Courcy built in 1177 stands intact, now a local museum, its stirring military days long past. A significant feature near by is the pit-heads of the Duncrue salt-mines—one of the very few of the many Irish mining enterprises that is not now abandoned. Beds of salt up to eighty-eight feet in thickness occur here among the marls of the New Red Sandstone. In mining, half of the bed is left to form a roof, and the other half is cut away except for massive pillars left to support the overlying strata. The mineral is often very pure, containing up to 98 per cent of salt. Beyond, where the coast turns northward, are the Chalk and basalt cliffs of White Head and Black Head. South-west of Belfast lies the valley

[1] See *Irish Naturalist*, vol. xix., pp. 201-209, portrait. 1910.
Mining ceased for some years but in 1967 the Eden Mine at Carrickfergus was reopened and there are good prospects for future developments. C.M.

of the Lagan, richly wooded. South-east, the undulating lands of County Down stretch far—fertile and smiling, but supplying less variety than any other part of Belfast's environment. The Down side of Belfast Lough, however, compensates for this, being well-wooded, varied, with a rocky shore. Then a little further off is the long island-studded lough of Strangford, anciently *Loch Cuan*, the *Strang Fiord* of the Norsemen, full of archaeological and natural history interest. Only twelve miles west of Belfast, across the hills, lies Lough Neagh, the largest sheet of water in Ireland and larger also than any in Great Britain; and beyond White Head is Larne Lough. So delightful a combination of land and water within a few miles of a great city is surely unique; and the variety of rocks which occurs also is striking, representing a remarkable span of world history.

Lough Neagh (*Loch nEchach*, Eochy's lake) demands special consideration, for from many points of view it is a very interesting place. First as to its origin. You may take your choice between a legend a few thousand years old or the much more ancient story which present-day geologists have to tell. According to the legend, the source of the lake was a magic well that sprang up when Angus MacIndoc's great horse was allowed to stand still, contrary to the owner's warnings. Ecca, who was the leader of the party to whom the horse had been lent, was troubled about this well, and had a house built around it, and placed a woman in charge. But one day she forgot to close the door of the house, whereupon the water burst forth and formed Lough Neagh. For the surprising adventures of Liban, the daughter of Ecca, and her lap-dog, the reader must turn to the original tale in the *Leabhar na hUidre* (or Book of the Dun Cow), compiled about the end of the eleventh century, and preserved in the library of the Royal Irish Academy; or to Dr. Joyce's free translation of it, in his delightful *Old Celtic Romances*.

The geological explanation of the formation of Lough Neagh is almost more surprising. When the centre of the basaltic plateau collapsed owing to the evacuation of vast quantities of liquid rock, and a great north-south valley was in consequence formed, the area in which Lough Neagh now lies continued to sink, a roughly rectangular portion of the Earth's surface of about 400 square miles going down and down until its surface was some 1200 feet below sea-level; and all the time, in the lake which resulted, sediment derived from the surrounding land continued to be deposited by rivers, slowly filling up the deep depression. These clays now underlie the present lake, which is quite shallow, and they extend for some distance over what is former lake-bottom, especially towards the south-west. Fossils found in the deposits—trees, including a *Sequoia* (a genus to which the " big trees " of California belong) and fresh-water shells—show that their date is not much later than the upper beds of the basalts.

Next, the subaqueous topography of the lake is peculiar. The shore slopes gently till a depth of a few feet is reached, when there is a kind of cliff, at the base of which the lake deepens to a curiously uniform depth of 40 to 50 feet save in the north-west corner where there is a narrow gut which descends to 102 feet below water-level. These features are difficult to explain.

The "Water-guns " of Lough Neagh are another curious local phenomenon. Not infrequently, and according to W. S. Smith (who spent most of his life beside the lake), in all conditions of weather and season, booming sounds are heard—" dull, heavy, explosive sounds "—appearing to come sometimes from this, sometimes from that portion of the lake; but no cause is ever discoverable. Mostly they sound distant and muffled, but sometimes very loud. "When the lake was covered with ice, as it was in February, 1895 [an extremely rare occurrence], on a very calm sunny afternoon," writes Mr Smith, " there were regular boomings at distant intervals, and lasting perhaps a couple of hours, apparently far away in the south-west, the writer being engaged skating near the Massereene and Shane's Castle demesnes at the time. On another occasion, but during the same protracted frost and when the ice was about breaking up, there were terrific boomings, apparently about half a mile, or less, from the shore nearest Antrim. Skaters were momentarily alarmed, and stopped to look round to see what had happened; but there were no visible effects." Loud noises in connection with frozen lakes are not unknown, but the "lough shootings" as the local fishermen call them, occur equally in summer. It was at that season, on a hot day, that I heard them for the only time. Then they seemed close by—indeed, all around—a strange roaring noise which was accompanied by a little whirlwind which crossed the meadow where I was. It tore down a haycock and carried the hay high into the air, where it spread out and slowly came down over a wide area. Then calm was resumed. These mysterious sounds seem never to be heard at night. They are not accompanied by any disturbance of the water of the lake, nor by flashes of lightning. Similar mysterious sounds have been reported from across water in several parts of the world, but no satisfactory explanation appears to be forthcoming.

Lough Neagh yields certain animals and plants which might suggest former connection with the sea, but their presence is now more usually thought to be explicable in other ways. Shells of the Common Mussel, a familiar marine mollusc, in a Glacial deposit on the lake-shore, are believed to have been brought hither by ice from the north. The Pollan or "Fresh-water Herring," and the small shrimp *Mysis relicta*, though they have marine relations, do not necessarily point to invasion of the sea; and the occurrence on the shores of half a dozen maritime plants is held to be the result of the open conditions or sandy shores which prevail where they occur.

Another unusual feature in connection with the lake is the far-spreading deposits of diatom-earth or kieselguhr which occur at the north end, around Lough Beg, and on down the Bann for some distance. About Toome, where this material is extensively cut like turf and dried, to be used mainly as an insulator, it may be seen lying under a bed of peat, and resting again on peat, a white layer three to six feet deep between two black ones. It is composed almost solely of the flinty skeletons of the microscopic fresh-water algae known as diatoms, minute plants which abound in all lakes as well as in the sea.

The beautiful and varied forms which characterize these lowly and tiny forms of life may be seen from the figure (Fig. 1), taken from Messrs West's report on the present diatom-flora of Lough Neagh.[1] When alive, the flinty skeleton is combined with a speck of jelly-like material with green colouring-matter: this last is chlorophyll, the

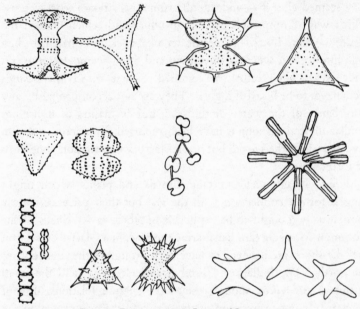

FIG. 1.—DIATOMS FROM LOUGH NEAGH, ETC.
Magnified 340 times

mysterious substance through whose agency the energy of sunlight is used by all green plants to build up their bodies out of water and air. What led to so vast a development of these organisms in and about the lake is not clear. They must have been thrown ashore in countless millions for a long period, but no such accumulations are known to be forming at present. The occurrence in the lower part of the diatom bed of numerous flint implements of Neolithic type [2]

[1] *Trans. Roy. Irish Acad.*, vol. xxxii., sect. B, pp. 1-96, plates 1-3.

[2] H. L. Movius, " A Neolithic Site on the River Bann ", *Proc. Roy. Irish Acad.*, vol. xliii. sect. C, pp. 17-40, plates 4-9. 1936.

allows us to fix its age, though the date of the topmost layer is still uncertain; but it is clear that the whole deposit is of recent formation, though in some places it is covered by peat to a depth of a couple of yards.

In old days petrifying properties were assigned to the waters of Lough Neagh. Pieces of silicified wood are found on the shores which were supposed until comparatively lately to have been fossilized by lying in the lake. The older writers on Lough Neagh— Gerard Boate, Walter Harris, and Dr. Barton—have much startling information to give about this and other local curiosities. To show the state of scientific knowledge in Harris's time (1744), the following extract from his *Antient and Present State of the County of Down* will serve: " As it is now a determined Point among Naturalists, that *Stones Vegetate as well as Plants*; it seems not impossible, but there may be a peculiar Stone, which though in the manner of their Growth they may resemble Wood, and especially Holly, yet are not from that resemblance necessarily to be admitted such, any more that those Representations of the Shells of Cockles, Oysters, and Escalops, some forming, and some formed, frequently observed in Lime-stone in the Peak of *Derbyshire*, are to be supposed ever to have been real Shells, or those exact Representations of the Branches, of a Lion couchant, of a human Corps laid out, nay of several artificial Things, as Chairs, a Set of Organs, and innumerable other Sportings of Nature in the vegetating Lime-stone, are to be imagined to have been ever the real things they resemble ".

The pieces of silicified wood were efficient for sharpening tools, and in the old days the cry

> Lough Neagh hones! Lough Neagh hones!
> You put 'em in sticks, and you take 'em out stones.

might be heard in the streets of Belfast: but these fragments, which also occur in the Boulder-clay of the district, formerly supposed to have been recent material changed into stone by the action of the lake water, were in reality derived from the lake-clays referred to.

They represent branches and trunks carried into the lake by ancient rivers, and gradually converted into flinty rock. Plenty of vegetable material appears to have got included in the clays of the lake-bottom, and, now half converted into coal (lignite), it forms beds which may attain a thickness of twenty-five feet.

The present flora of Lough Neagh also offers points of interest. Its shores harbour a whole group of plants which are regarded locally, and some generally, as confined to sea-side places. Others, which in the district are of extreme rarity, find a refuge here, though the artificial lowering of the lake about 1855 has affected some of them adversely. The most interesting plant of Lough Neagh is an orchid, a rare species of Lady's-Tresses (Plate VIII) which is widely spread around the lake and down the River Bann. It is an American plant, unknown elsewhere in Europe till a few years ago, when it was found on the island of Colonsay in western Scotland.

The very size of Lough Neagh, and the fact that on every side its shores are low, lessen its attractions from a scenic point of view; but the matters referred to above, and others that might be mentioned, are indications that high interest attaches to the lake. As it is now, it presents a wide expanse of water usually empty of boats as of islands, with wide flat lonely shores of which cattle and birds are the prevailing inhabitants.

PLATE VIII

Andrews: photo

SPIRANTHES STRICTA, A NORTH AMERICAN LADY'S-TRESSES,
FROM LOUGH NEAGH

CHAPTER IV

MID-ULSTER

THIS is the shortest chapter in the book: a blunt statement that recalls Owen Seaman's shortest verse in his delightful skit on Richard Le Gallienne in *The Battle of the Bays*:

> And O the stars! I cannot say
> I see a star just now,
> Not at this time of day;
> But anyway
> The stars are all my brothers;
> (This verse is shorter than the others).
>
> O Constitution Hill!
> (This verse is shorter still).

The reason of its brevity is that the predominant partner of the region—Tyrone—though a large and pleasing area, is lacking somewhat in special interests, topographical, biological or archaeological. Fermanagh, also included here, is a much more varied and attractive county.

Tyrone (*Tír Eóghain*, Owen's territory), like Inishowen, takes its name from Eóghan or Owen, son of Niall of the Nine Hostages, a great man of the fifth century. As now defined, it forms a large area, mostly hilly but with broad fertile valleys watered by the tributaries of the Foyle. Now that I wish to write about it, I find it a curiously negative tract, with a paucity of outstanding features when its size and variety of surface are considered, for it stretches from Lough Neagh to within ten miles of the western sea at Donegal Bay. On its north-eastern frontier stand the Sperrin Mountains, raising broad peat-covered domes of schist and quartzite to over

2000 feet (Sawel, 2240 feet). These hills have been referred to already (p. 68): they are among the least inspiring of Irish mountains, though on the Derry side some fine glens are found. The only lake to be mentioned in connection with Tyrone is Lough Neagh, also dealt with previously (p. 95): for fifteen miles it forms the eastern boundary. Here the broad flat shore characteristic of this great lake prevails, and there are bays, and low dunes of sharp silicious sand, much prized for building in Belfast. A minor excitement is provided by the occurrence in this neighbourhood of a small coal-field; the coal is of good quality, but the strata have been so much disturbed by earth-movements that the seams are broken up by faulting, tending to make mining difficult and expensive.

The most interesting prehistoric monument in Tyrone stands on the summit of Knockmany (*Cnoc manaigh*, hill of the monk), an eminence that rises abruptly north of Clogher; it consists of an oblong chamber formed of large stones still or once upright. Four of the stones bear complicated incised markings—series of concentric circles, cup-hollows, and others difficult to describe, all belonging to the Bronze Age. The chamber was once covered by a large cairn, the periphery of which can still be traced. Clogher (*Clochar*, stony spot), now an unimportant place, is the seat of what was probably the earliest bishopric in Ireland, claiming to have been founded by St. Patrick: beyond a few interesting crosses in the graveyard around the small cathedral, there is now nothing to indicate antiquity.

When we pass out of Tyrone into the adjoining area of Fermanagh (*Fir Mhanach*, the men of the Managh (Menapii)), we find ourselves in a district which is more picturesque and from many points of view more interesting. This is due chiefly to the presence of great lakes and of steep limestone hills. Fermanagh is in fact the broad valley of the Erne, carved mainly out of the Carboniferous limestone by the dissolving action of water. The Erne (in Irish *Samhair*, the Morning Star) is the most curious river in Ireland. It

PLATE IX

ENNISKILLEN FROM PORTORA

rises in Lough Gowna (*Loch gamhna*, lake of the calf) in Cavan, to enter the sea at Ballyshannon in Donegal after a course of over seventy miles. Lough Gowna is a large mazy lake, a network of land and water. It is a piece of half-submerged drumlin country, drumlins being whale-backed ridges of Glacial drift, which are often well developed over the Silurian rocks such as prevail here. Thence it flows a few miles north into Lough Oughter (*Loch Úachtar*, upper lake), a larger and still more complicated archipelago, but quite different in origin, for it lies in a limestone basin, and its formation and shape are due to irregular solution of the rock by water. From there its course is entirely over the latter formation. Soon it enters Upper Lough Erne, another maze, which is almost continuous with Lower Lough Erne. Between them they present a stretch of nearly forty miles of water, all except the lower half of the Lower Lake full of islands and points, and lakelets connected by channels with the main waterway. The middle part has more land and less water, and divides the Upper from the Lower Lake. Here, on an island, stands Enniskillen (*Inis Ceitleann*, Ceitle's island), the county town of Fermanagh (Plate IX). This place was, and still is, the main crossing-place of the Erne for a long distance, and its single winding street, climbing over the island-ridge and down again between two bridges, is a busy place, for the town serves a large area. It has a stirring military history, and its name is associated with two famous regiments, the Inniskilling Dragoons and the Royal Inniskilling Fusiliers: but the fort-like buildings to right and left of the western bridge have no historical associations. Its chief merit for the visitor is its excellence as a centre for the cyclist or motorist, and especially for excursions by boat: there is plenty of attractive ground around, but it cannot be explored conveniently by the walker without some such adventitious aid, as the district is a large one.

Along the western side of its course, many other lakes of various sizes drain into the Erne, so that the river with its branches presents a surprising area of water. Though there are high hills not far away, especially to the west, the shores are low till the seaward end of the Lower Lake is reached, when picturesque hills of limestone, capped with yellow sandstone, impend directly over the lake to a height of more than 1000 feet, dropping in a tall cliff with grey talus at its base. With a boat and a tent one can have wonderful water trips from Enniskillen right up to Lough Oughter, but the bolder scenery and more open views which obtain on the Lower Lake make it the more attractive. If you row down from Enniskillen (where boats are more numerous, better and cheaper than anywhere else I know) you pass the hill on which stands Portora House, a handsome eighteenth-century building erected to accommodate the Royal School founded in 1626 by Charles I. Below it on the water's edge is all that remains of Oldcastle, once a fortress, later a bishop's palace. Thence the river begins to expand, throwing out lake-like arms to right and left. Soon the large island of Devenish comes into view, with its round tower standing up grey behind the green grassy curve of its skyline. This is one of the most interesting of the round towers of Ireland, on account of the superior style of the masonry (grey limestone), and the very unusual feature of a cornice of rich Romanesque scroll-work just below the conical apex. Immediately below are four windows, above each of which is a well-sculptured human head. Around are the ruins of the Abbey, of the " Great Church ", of the House of St. Molaise, and in the graveyard some ornate early crosses, all of which possess features of interest to the archaeologist. Beyond Devenish the lake continues to widen, with islands, often densely wooded, of whale-backed form (for they are mounds of Glacial drift) stretching away in a long vista, and you will need more than a row-boat if you wish to go further, especially as the lake gets more and more open. The islands are interesting—some of them, especially about Ely Lodge, have been planted, others have been cleared of timber and are grazed, but many are occupied by dense native wood which has never been interfered with; these harbour a purely indigenous flora and fauna, and are consequently of great attraction to the naturalist, as they tell us what the country-side was iike before ever man began to cut or burn down trees or to graze herds of cows and sheep, or to break up the land for tillage.   The largest native trees are Oak and Ash, of which Oak is much the commoner; then come Birch, Alder, Aspen, Holly, Mountain-ash, Crab-apple, Hazel, Hawthorn, with bushes of Spindle-tree, Buckthorn, Guelder-rose, Blackthorn, and several willows; there is also a remarkably fine bramble, of which I do not know the name, with pinkish flowers two and a half inches across.   Underneath the tree canopy a dense vegetation occupies the ground, largely of showy wild-flowers such as Primroses, Wood Anemones, and Wild Hyacinths, mixed with abundance of ferns.   The stony shores have a different vegetation: they are more exposed, are liable to floods, and are more limy.   Here are groves of Purple Loosestrife, Mint, Hemp-Agrimony, Hare-bell, Golden Rod, and carpets of Creeping Jenny.   Some of the plants of the shore grow extraordinarily luxuriantly—imagine a tuft of Milkwort bearing a hundred stems a foot high, crowned with deep-blue flowers, or Golden Rod like a torch up to four feet in height.   The most delightful time on Lough Erne is May or early June, for then the trees are at their freshest, the wild-flowers are in full blow, and the bird population of the lake at its busiest.   The breeding birds alone, as on most Irish lakes in late spring, would make the place worth a visit, though none of them is a rarity.   There are populous colonies of Terns and of Lesser Black-backed and Black-headed Gulls: Tufted Duck breed in numbers, and there are also Mergansers, Sheldrake and Mallard, all very busy; but Robert Warren has commented on the curious scarcity of birds on the wooded islands, as observed when he went there to see the breeding-place of the Sandwich Tern. Peregrines and Ravens haunt the high cliffs of Poulaphuca, as they do in similar ground all over Ireland (see p. 197).   I once spent a delightful spell in June camping on one of the small islands with Frank Bigger.   We would steal forth between three and four in the morning, before the sun was up, to watch the birds.   Reassured by the still lingering quiet of the night, they were very tame, and we could stalk them and watch them as we never could during the

It is unlikely that the Shelduck still breeds on Lough Erne. An interesting nesting duck, not on Praeger's list, is the Common Scoter. c.m.

day; the ducks of several kinds swam along quite close to us, and the Cormorants would hardly trouble to fly away from their perches on rocky points: not to be treated as an enemy gave a delightful feeling of kinship with fellow-creatures.

The antiquary visiting Lower Lough Erne will make a pilgrimage to White Island, south of Kesh, to see the remarkable carved human effigies of which Lady Dorothy Lowry-Corry has made a special study. These were discovered and built into their present position when the ancient church was restored by Canon M'Kenna and others in 1928–30. Additional similar grotesque carvings have since been found in the neighbourhood, and their very peculiar style seems to indicate a strange local form of art. They are usually assigned to the ninth or tenth century A.D.

We now turn to the hills which impend over the southern shore of Lower Lough Erne at its broadest part, opposite Boa Island (*Inis Badhbha*, Badhbh's island). Here also the lake attains its greatest depth—200 feet, which makes its bed 50 feet below sea-level. The geological structure of the country is the cause of its peculiar topography. All the strata are slightly tilted up towards the north. Ten miles south of the lake, you are standing on thick beds of Yoredale sandstone, whose stratigraphical position is above the limestone. Looking northward, you see a long slope, which is the natural tilt of the sandstone strata. As you walk up this slope the sandstone beds give out one by one, each ceasing in a straight line of low cliff often with a lakelet at its foot, so that you climb down before continuing the slow ascent over the bed next below. Finally you drop over the edge of the lowest layer of sandstone and find yourself on the bare limestone, a thousand feet up: but the limestone almost at once breaks away in a great cliff, subtended by a high talus, which slopes down into Lough Erne. This high furrowed table-land is a grand breezy place, all heather, with a wide view over mountain and lake. On the limestone, on the other hand, grass prevails, and to the east, where this simple topography gets broken up and moundy limestone hills and deep hollows prevail, the char-

acteristic greenness makes a striking contrast to the brown heathland. The limestone area around Carrick Lake (*Carraig*, a rock) and
Bunnahone Lake (*Bun na hAbhna*, the river foot) near Church Hill
is highly picturesque, like a kind of condensed Switzerland—barring
the snow: instead of that, great shelter and moisture prevail, as is
shown by the luxuriance of the vegetation. Correl Glen is a ravine
choked with huge blocks of sandstone, covered by a canopy of
gnarled Birch trees; boulders and tree-trunks alike are smothered
in mosses and Filmy Ferns—Cow-berry also, unexpectedly—making
a sort of strange fairyland. Further up, Carrick Lake is romantically
situated, with grassy limestone hills rising from one shore and
heathery sandstones from the other. The limestones and sandstones
between them yield a galaxy of rare plants, those of the elevated
sandstones especially being of a distinctly northern or Scottish type.
All three species of Wintergreen are here, including abundance of
the rare " One-sided " *Pyrola secunda*; also Welsh Poppy, Mountain
Avens (on Knockmore), Mossy and Yellow Mountain Saxifrage,
Blue Moor-grass, Green Spleenwort and so on. To visit this
delightful ground you must stay at Enniskillen or Belleek, for there
is no place between.

It was when exploring this region that I struck the worst streak
of weather that I have ever encountered in Ireland during the
botanizing season—three and a half very wet days out of five. As
the negro " Spiritual " says:

> Didn't it rain, didn't it rain,
> Tell me, Noah, didn't it rain!

But the area was so interesting that I worked right through with
the exception of one half-day; on that occasion I was on the hills
around Carrick Lake; the downpour and wind became so violent
that I sought shelter in a lonely poverty-stricken cottage, where an
old woman comforted me with tea. Then unconcernedly she threw
a shawl over her head and went up the mountain to look for her
heifer, leaving me in the charge of a cat and an Aspidistra. Cats

have had their praises—and other things—sung since the days of the Pharaohs, but their vegetable companion in so many humble dwellings still lacks a champion. I must confess to a sincere admiration for the Aspidistra. It will consent to grow under conditions where almost all plant-life would be impossible—in a room where it never sees the sun, in a potful of sour worn-out soil, occasionally drenched, with dire desiccation between—in semi-darkness, semi-drought, semi-starvation; and it will even flourish there, adding a pathetic touch of greenery to a dreary environment, and if encouraged will bloom, with humble little brownish flowers of strange form set in the brown soil. How many women are there among the narrow streets to whom an Aspidistra and a cat are the only intimate things amid the glorious exuberance of plant and animal life that the world offers?

If you travel from Enniskillen to Poulaphuca (*Poll a' púca*, the sprite's hole), as the slope between the great cliff and Lough Erne is called (the name seems somewhat indefinite in its topographical application), you will pass a bit of interesting ground at Carrick-reagh (*Carraig ríabhach*, grey rock), seven miles out from the former place. Here also the limestone impends over the lake, and has been quarried extensively by the roadside. Bare rock, densely wooded, rises steeply and then extends more or less level over a wide area. The vegetation is entirely native, and under tall Oaks there is a remarkable profusion of the Broad-leaved Helleborine, growing up to four feet high, and large beds of luxuriant Beech Fern. The place ought to furnish good hunting for the zoologist.

Belleek (*Béal leice*, river-mouth of the flagstone), on the Erne a little below the termination of Lower Lough Erne, is a pleasant village well known to fishermen, and a good centre, for here you are within easy striking distance of the hilly ground just described, and also of Lough Melvin a few miles to the southward. At Belleek the Erne suddenly abandons its placid lake-like character, and plunges into a fine limestone gorge. It falls 150 feet in less than five miles, and finds sea-level at Ballyshannon, where it broadens

In 1946 work began on the damming of the River Erne for electricity generating. Most of the lower river, as here described, has been flooded. C.M.

into a sandy estuary, to enter the sea between great stretches of dunes.

Lough Melvin (*Loch meilghe*), just mentioned, is a pretty lake, eight miles in length, partly in Fermanagh but mainly in Leitrim, with hills rising all along the Leitrim shore. There is good fishing here, so the little inn at Garrison is often a cheerful place. To naturalists the lake is as yet but little known, but it has at least one plant of interest and beauty—the Globe Flower, which is abundant on one of the small islands; elsewhere in Ireland it is found only in the Lough Gartan district of Donegal, while in Britain it is characteristic of Scotland and Wales, and in general is northern and arctic in its range. Lough Melvin runs south-east, and if you follow in that direction the depression in which it lies you will pass between long heathery slopes to right and left and reach Lough Macnean (*Loch mhic an éin*, the lake of the bird's son), Upper and Lower, separated by a very short placid stream on which stand the villages of Belcoo (*Béal cobha?*) and Blacklion, now in different countries owing to the imposition of that absurd frontier between Leitrim and Fermanagh. Here we get into a region of limestone caves, of which the best known are those of the Marble Arch, at Florence-court, nine miles south-west of Enniskillen. Some three miles south of Florencecourt, the high ridge of Cuilcagh (2188 feet) dominates all the country around. The Millstone Grit, which forms the summit, gives way to Yoredale rocks as one descends, and this in turn to limestone. Several streams, coming down the northern face of the mountain, vanish underground as soon as they strike the soluble rock. Their further courses are betrayed by occasional collapses of the roofs of the caves through which they flow, resulting in deep tree-filled depressions in the undulating ground; at the bottom of some of these you can see the stream emerging from a cave on one side and re-entering the rock at the other. The underground topo-graphy cannot be exactly explored, since in places the roof descends below the level of the water, but apparently all the branches combine to make their exit at the Marble Arch, whence the stream flows down a fine glen to enter the Arney River near Lough Macnean. The Marble Arch itself is a lofty bridge of limestone just below the exit of the stream. Above this " Arch " the river forms an underground lake, but a little further up large pot-holes caused by the collapse of the roof allow of entrance into a rather complicated cave, through one branch of which the stream runs. These caves were explored by Mons. Martel in 1897, and much more thoroughly by C. A. Hill, H. Brodrick and some others, including E. A. Baker and myself, in 1907-8. I have elsewhere (p. 323) dealt with the delights and difficulties of cave exploration. The experiences mentioned in connection with the Mitchelstown cavern were all encountered here, with the addition that—until we discovered a new entrance further up the stream—the underground lake had to be swum (Martel used a collapsible boat). If you want an unusual experience, try cave-lake swimming. The water is cold and as black as ink, the candle stuck in your hat is inclined to be extinguished if the roof gets low or if owing to a blunder your head goes under, parts may be too narrow for swimming with the arms, and from the unplumbed bottom knife-edges of limestone may rise, so that legs must be used with extreme caution. Fortunately, when you land, the stillness and saturation of the air are such that you do not feel cold, and can proceed with mapping without inconvenience —if you have managed to keep your note-book dry. The Marble Arch glen is very beautiful, and the caves and pot-holes form a most interesting series, with some fine displays of stalactitic incrustation: but it is difficult ground on which to find your way, and it will be well to consult first the map and account of our exploration published at the time.[1]

[1] H. Brodrick, " The Marble Arch Caves, Co. Fermanagh: Main Stream Series ", *Proc. Roy. Irish Acad.*, vol. xxvii., sect. B, pp. 183-192, plate 12, map. 1909.

CHAPTER V

THE SILURIAN REGION

(DOWN, ARMAGH, LOUTH, MONAGHAN, CAVAN)

THE grouping together of Down, Armagh, Louth, Monaghan and Cavan in one chapter may not accord with present political divisions. So much the worse for politics, for it is a natural grouping, being a geological one. Soils are dependent on the rocks, agriculture is dependent on the soil, and many human conditions both in country and town are based on agriculture: so no excuse is required for founding our subdivision on geology, whether our interests are zoological or botanical or archaeological, or concerned with modern human problems. A broad wedge of Silurian and Ordovician rocks—slates and grits—intrudes from the east coast of Ireland to the centre, its base extending from Belfast Lough to the Boyne, its apex lying on the Shannon at Longford; the only serious interruption to its continuity being the granite masses lying around Carlingford Lough. In certain other places in Ireland rocks of the same age rise into high mountains, but here the characteristic surface is low and undulating, with many Glacial drumlins and inconsiderable hills, small lakes, and a light soil through which the slaty rocks often protrude. There is a large amount of excellent agricultural land, and if you compare a one-inch map of Down or Monaghan with one of most other Irish areas, you will be struck with the great number of farmhouses and roads. Peat-bog never achieved extensive development in this region, and as a consequence almost all there was has been cut away for fuel. Much flax used to be grown for the local linen mills, and after having suffered a severe decline, this beautiful crop is again on the increase—but unfortunately for its picturesqueness, a white-flowered form is now usually planted instead of the lovely blue of old days. Nowhere in Ireland does one see better farming, or a more prosperous country-side, than say in eastern Down. The people here are a hard-headed, thrifty, hearty race, closely akin to the lowland Scotch, with a dialect also akin, while those of Antrim, adjoining on the north, savour more of the Highlands. The language of both counties is characterized by the large element which it contains of Elizabethan English on the one hand, and of translated Gaelic on the other. The dialect and strong northern accent, indeed, are sometimes bewildering to the stranger. If you think you hear " ace won ", the reference is not to any game of cards, but to the fact that the wind is in the east; and " key of hell " has nothing to do with the infernal regions, but signifies the Cave Hill near Belfast. And can you translate the following, supplied by my sister: " Ther a lock o' carryons an' blethers goin' wi' them gorsoons that's hoakin a wheen o' whuns out o' the sheugh down thonder forninst the boor tree "?[1] And here is a contribution sent by Rev. W. R. Magaw: " Ere yesterday at dayligone he begood to the banterin' and starts jundyin' our Jamie and him on his hunkers at the bing there, walin' a wheen o' clarty pritas ".[2]

The county of Down (*Dún*, from the great fortress of Down-patrick) is the most attractive portion of this Silurian area, for several reasons. It has an extensive coast-line, curving round from Belfast to Newry, and including the large island-studded lough of Strang-ford, as well as the border of Carlingford Lough and Belfast Lough. It has high mountains, for at two widely separated epochs there have been volcanic outbursts, the first giving us the picturesque hills west of Carlingford Lough (just beyond the Down boundary) and Slieve Croob, the second the adjoining fine group of the Mourne Moun-

---

[1] There is a deal of larking and nonsense going on among those boys who are digging gorse-bushes out of the ditch down there opposite the elder-tree.

[2] Only yesterday at dusk he began bantering, and started pushing our James while he was squatting at the pit there, sorting a lot of muddy potatoes. Artificial fibres have replaced linen to such an extent that the flax crop is again becoming rare. C.M.

tains. In the north is the fertile and richly wooded valley of the Lagan, beyond which the high scarp of the basaltic plateau rises abruptly. About one-fourth of the growing city of Belfast lies on the Down side of the river, and the whole southern shore of Belfast Lough, including Bangor, is practically suburban Belfast. The fifteen-mile strip of land that intervenes between Strangford Lough and the Irish Sea shows Down at its best—all tilled fields and white cottages and little winding roads, and a low flowery coast-line with alternating points of sharp upturned slates and bays of fine grey sand. My sister, who has lived in Down all her life, has sketched excellently its characteristics as seen by a nature-lover:

A CHILD'S SONG IN COUNTY DOWN

In County Down—where I live—
Are cornfields and heather,
Low hills and high hills
Sitting down together.
Rainbows and dewdrops,
And mosses everywhere—
Oh! County Down is beautiful,
And I live there.

In County Down—where I live—
The sea sweeps by.
Far above the ploughlands
The white gulls fly.
Bees in the clover,
Honey in the air—
Oh! County Down is beautiful,
And I live there.

In County Down—where I live—
The dear daisies grow.
They hide their little faces
When the sun sinks low.
When the sun is rising
They lift their heads—and stare!
For County Down is beautiful,
And I live there.

There are relics of the past too—prehistoric duns, and Dundrum Castle upon its hill, and the tall ruins of Grey Abbey. The last was one of the amenities which Down owed to John de Courcy, its Norman conqueror, for it was founded by his wife Affreca, daughter of Godred, King of Man, in 1193, and was occupied by Cistercian monks whom she brought over from the abbey of Holm Cultram in Cumberland. Here the foundress died, and her recumbent effigy may be seen in the chancel. The buildings, of grey sandstone from Scrabo Hill a few miles off, though much ruined, still form the most imposing group of monastic remains in the North-east.

One cannot mention local ecclesiastical history without reference to the earlier and much more famous monastery of Bangor (*Beann-chor*, the pointed horns, *i.e.* hills). Its foundation about the year 559 was due to St. Comgall, a native of Magheramorne, on the opposite shore of Belfast Lough. Under Comgall and his successor Carthagus the monastery and the schools attached to it flourished exceedingly, becoming, according to St. Bernard, "a noble institution, the parent of many thousands of monks, the head of many monasteries. A place it was truly sanctified, and so fruitful in saints, which brought forth fruit most abundantly to the glory of God, insomuch that one of the sons of that holy congregation, Luanus by name, is alone reputed to be the founder of one hundred monasteries." For eight centuries this great institution maintained a European reputation, and sent forth missionaries to many lands. Among these was Gallus, after whom the Swiss canton of St. Gall is named, and the great Columbanus, who founded the abbeys of Luxeuil and Bobbio. Twice it was burned down, and twice it arose from its ruins to minister again to the crowds of students who thronged its schools. But the ravages of the Norsemen, who plundered it over and over again from the ninth to the eleventh century, led at length to its decline. When St. Malachy came to Bangor in 1121 he found the great monastery a wreck. "Now he gladly took possession of it," writes St. Bernard, "resolved on planting a second paradise on the spot, partly through respect for its ancient dignity, and partly because of the many bodies

PLATE X

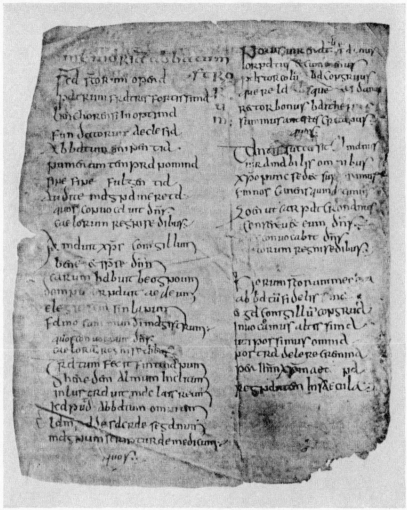

THE ANTIPHONARY OF BANGOR

Folio 36 verso, showing the reference to Abbot Cronan. ½ natural size

of saints which slept there. For not to mention those who were buried in peace, it is related that nine hundred perished on one day, massacred by pirates." He rebuilt it in part, and when he died there twenty-seven years later he had done much to restore its fallen fortunes; but in spite of the patronage of King John it never recovered its former greatness. A single fragment of a wall, supposed to have belonged to Malachy's church, alone remains as a monument of one of the greatest monastic institutions that the world has known. But one priceless relic of the abbey is preserved in the Ambrosian Library at Milan—the *Antiphonarium Benchorense*, or Antiphonary of Bangor, written in the seventh century for the use of the abbey clergy. This is a document of extraordinary interest, on account of its early date, its contents, and the fact that the time and place of its compilation are exactly fixed, in this way: its contents include prayers for the abbots who ruled at Bangor from the foundation till the time of writing—from St. Comgall onwards. The deaths of these abbots are recorded in other historical documents, and in the *Antiphonarium* they are mentioned in the past tense till the last, Abbot Cronan, is reached: then the present tense is used. It is known that Cronan became abbot in 680, and died in 691, so within that period the manuscript was written. The page reproduced here (Plate X) is the one (fol. 36, v.) on which this vital information is given:

> Tantis successit Colmanus
> Vir amabilis omnibus
> Christo nunc sedet supprimus (= supremus)
> Ymnos canens. Quindecimus
> Zoen ut carpat Cronanus
> Conservat eum Dominus
>   Quos conuocabit Dominus
>   Caelorum regni sedibus

> (To such a one did Colman succeed,
> A man friendly to all:
> Now he sitteth on high, to Christ
> Singing hymns. The fifteenth [abbot]

May Cronanus lay hold on life:
May the Lord preserve him.
[These they are] whom the Lord shall summon
To the seats of the kingdom of the heavens.)

The contents of the manuscript consist of a large number o collects and anthems, the creed and paternoster, and some canticles and religious poems.   Had the book remained at Bangor it would almost certainly have been lost in the ruin of the monastery, but fortunately it was taken to Bobbio, very possibly by one Dungal in the ninth century, and it was subsequently transferred to the famous Ambrosian Library, where it is treasured along with other early Irish manuscripts of great importance.   It was reproduced in facsimile in 1890 by the Henry Bradshaw Society—appropriately enough, for Henry Bradshaw was himself a County Down man, and spent his early years only a few miles away, where Bradshaw's Brae above Newtownards still commemorates his family.

The modern Bangor, with its hundreds of villas, its Marine Gardens and bathing-pools and tennis clubs and buses and swarming motor cars, offers a strange contrast to the great religious establishment among its woods which the Northmen harried a thousand years ago, and of which no vestige now remains, unless the single fragment of old wall, already referred to, belongs, as is reputed, to St. Malachy's restoration.

A monument of another kind, of interest to the geologist, is seen in Scrabo Hill (*Scrath bó*, the sward of the cows), which rises steeply to the west of Newtownards, for here we may read again the ancient history that the Antrim uplands have to tell us, though some of the middle chapters are missing, being replaced by older ones.   The story begins with a floor of folded Silurian slaty rocks, the same as prevail over much of Down.   Over this the Carboniferous sea laid down limestones, such as still cover the Central Plain.   Uplifted and exposed to atmospheric denudation, these have been destroyed locally except for a patch lying in a hollow of the Silurians at Castle Espie (*Easpoc*, a bishop) near Comber (*Cómhar*, a confluence), where

till lately they were quarried, a valuable source of lime. A long
subsequent period allowed Triassic rocks—first red Bunter sandstones
and then pink Keuper sandstones and marls—to be spread over a
wide area, but these have in their turn suffered great erosion. They
still fill the hollow between Belfast and Scrabo and beyond, and the
Lagan valley from Lurgan to Carrickfergus, but are gone from the
rest of Down. They were probably subsequently covered by beds
of Lias and Chalk as in Antrim, but if so, these were worn away
before the next episode occurred. At Scrabo the volcanic history
of Antrim was then repeated. Lava welled up locally through pipes

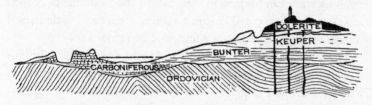

FIG. 2.—DIAGRAMMATIC SECTION OF SCRABO HILL AND CASTLE ESPIE

and narrow cracks. In many places it forced its way horizontally
between the beds of sandstone, and pushing on upwards it eventually
flowed out over the surface to form thick beds of basalt. These now
cap Scrabo Hill, and indeed are the reason of its present existence;
and in the extensive quarries in the pink sandstone which the basalt
has protected we may read what is quite a geological fairy-tale. We
see that these beds were deposited as sand or mud in shallow water,
for if we split the blocks lying about in the quarries we find ripple-
marks produced by little waves exactly like those of sheltered
existing beaches. Furthermore, the tide ebbed and left the beds
exposed to the weather, for often they are covered with a network
of sun-cracks, such as are seen in a dried-up muddy pond, and others
are pitted with the marks of rain-drops. In those ancient days the
tide flowed and the waves danced, the sun shone and the rain fell,
exactly as they do today, but we have to imagine the sea filled with
strange fishes, and on the land fantastic reptiles, all now long extinct.

And in contrast to this picture of a peaceful lagoon and its vicinity we have the vision of molten lavas bursting through the surface and spreading destruction far and wide. The summit of the hill is now crowned with a lofty quadrangular turreted tower erected in 1858 to commemorate General Charles William Stewart-Vane, 3rd Marquess of Londonderry, which appropriately, in view of its situation, is built of black volcanic rock. It has replaced a cairn of Bronze Age date in which were found an urn and calcined bones, the last resting-place of some long-forgotten chieftain.

Down is rich in human monuments of all periods, and a very interesting week can be spent in their examination—dolmens, horned cairns, stone circles, raths, Norman mottes, castles and ecclesiastical establishments; but here only a few need be referred to.

On Mahee Island (*Inis Mochaoi*, St. Mochoe's island), in Strangford Lough, stand the remains of the Celtic monastery of Nendrum (*Nóendruim*, the nine ridges). This was once a considerable establishment, with church, round tower, school, living rooms and so on, all within the outermost ring of a cashel of three concentric walls of dry stone, of earlier and probably pre-Christian date. Its very name had been lost when Bishop Reeves with difficulty discovered the site, an " old lime-kiln " to which he was directed proving to be the base of the round tower. Nendrum was thoroughly excavated and restored under the superintendence of H. C. Lawlor by the Belfast Natural History and Philosophical Society in 1922-24. The name Mahee, which the island still bears, commemorates Saint Mochoe, the first abbot.

Built into the wall of a modest house in Killyleagh (*Coillidh liath*, grey wood) is a block of Castle Espie limestone bearing the inscription " 1637. G.S. M.W." This marks the birthplace (1660) of Sir Hans Sloane, famous collector and physician. He studied medicine abroad, and took his degree of M.D. at the University of Orange. Two years later, in 1685, he was elected a Fellow of the Royal Society on the proposal of Martin Lister. After amassing a large collection of the plants of Jamaica, whither he went as physician to the Governor, the Duke of Albemarle, he returned to London and soon achieved fame in the medical profession. For nine years he was secretary of the Royal Society, and in 1727, on the death of Sir Isaac Newton, he was elected president. He published in two folio volumes *A Voyage to the Islands of Madera, Barbadoes, Nieves, St. Christopher's, and Jamaica, with the Natural History of the last* (1707-25), a work still of much scientific value. His medical practice included most of the great people of the day; he was consulted by Queen Anne, and became first physician to George II. He founded the Botanic Garden at Chelsea. By his will his great collections of specimens, books and manuscripts were bequeathed to the nation. These, together with the Cottonian and Harleian libraries, were placed by the Government under the administration of trustees, and were the nucleus around which the vast collections of the British Museum have grown up. His daughter Elizabeth married Colonel Charles (afterwards 2nd Baron) Cadogan, and carried much of the Sloane property into that family. Such names on the Cadogan estate in London as Sloane Square, Sloane Street, Hans place and Hans Road perpetuate his memory.

Strangford Lough, we are told by the ancient annalists, was formed Anno Mundi 2546 (1654 B.C.) by an inundation of the sea over the lands of Brena, and the flooded land became *Loch Cuan*. This, or the bursting out of a spring, was the usual way in early days of accounting for lakes and enclosed arms of the sea. The geographer sees in this lough a slight north-south depression which left most of the surface a little below sea-level, with the tops of many drumlins (rounded hillocks of Glacial drift) rising above the water, and forming a multitude of islets. As in the case of some other Irish loughs, local tradition fixes their number at 366—one for each day of the year and two for Easter Sunday. The Norsemen named the place *Strang Fiord*, the violent inlet, from the rushing tide that sweeps up and down the deep narrow channel which connects it with the Irish Sea. But above this, where it expands to a width of two or three miles, and especially along the western shore, which is a kind of archipelago, it is a placid and pleasing sheet of water, with many grassy islets fringed at low tide with a broad band of brown and yellow Bladder-wrack and Tangle, and tenanted in summer by innumerable birds. These haunt mostly the smallest islets, mere ridges of gravel or clay raised a few feet above tide-level, and covered with coarse grass and seaside flowers. The most abundant are the Arctic and Common Terns, which nest together in great colonies, laying their eggs on the shingle or the grass, and especially on the fringe of seaweed which marks spring tide; they raise a tremendous din when one lands, swooping down on the intruder with determination enough to occasionally knock off a hat or inflict a scratch. Oyster-catchers are there, nesting always on a gravelly point, never on a straight beach, and Ringed Plovers, often with a few bright yellow shells (*Littorina obtusata*) placed among their eggs. Shelduck are frequent, concealing their nests in holes, and Red-breasted Mergansers, their eggs hidden under a covering of down among the long grass. There are Lesser Terns also in small numbers. A visit to the lough when this great bird population is at its busiest is a delightful experience. Then there are many monuments, pagan and Christian, scattered along the shores or on the larger islands, so that an interesting holiday may with the aid of a boat be spent on Strangford Lough.

When we reach the Quoile (*Cuaille*, a pole), which flows into Strangford Lough below Killyleagh through an island-studded estuary, we enter St. Patrick's country. Here in Lecale (*Leth Cathail*, Cathal's portion) he landed with a few disciples in the year 432; here at Saul he preached and made his first convert to Christianity—Dicho, the lord of the territory; here arose the first church in Ireland, named after the humble building in which the first Christian service was held (Saul = *sabhal*, a barn); here to Saul he frequently returned to rest from his missionary labours, and here he died in 493: and close by, at Downpatrick, he was interred. Of the monastery of Saul which subsequently arose, built in the twelfth century by the famous St. Malachy—Malachi O'Morgair, Bishop of

Down—very little remains: fragments of buildings and some old crosses amid a crowd of more recent graves. The present church, standing on the ancient site and approached between rows of Irish Yew, is a white-washed building so plain that it not inaptly bears the name of *Sabhal*. The site of the first Christian edifice in Ireland is a not unworthy one. It stands high, commanding a very fine prospect to the northward—the winding Quoile and island-decked Lough of Strangford; the rolling hillocks of Down stretching away to the hill of Scrabo, the higher ridge of Slieve Croob (*Sliabh crúb*, mountain of the hoof), and in the distance the mountains which overlook Belfast. A couple of miles to the eastward is a second very early church, that of Raholp (*Rath cholpa*, fort of the heifer) built like several other early local edifices with yellow clay instead of mortar, consequently dilapidated, and more recently restored. Raholp church also is ascribed to St. Patrick, and at the hand of its first bishop, St. Tassach (according to the hymn written by St. Fiach, Bishop of Sletty, and a disciple of Patrick, in the sixth century), he received communion before he died. A little south of Saul, and once a great place of pilgrimage though now deserted and ruinous, are St. Patrick's wells at Struell, " to which ", writes Walter Harris in 1744, " vast throngs of rich and poor resort on Midsummer Eve and the Friday before Lammas, some in hopes of obtaining health, and others to perform penance ".

Downpatrick itself stands a few miles westward of the places just mentioned, on the edge of the former estuary of the Quoile, which lock-gates have transformed into pasture and extensive swamps. This was an important place long before the coming of Patrick. On a hillock almost surrounded by the Quoile marshes some unknown leader erected an earthen fort of great dimensions, known as early as 1031 B.C. as *Árus Cealtchair*, the habitation of Celtchar, and later as *Dún Cealtchair*. Celtchar was one of the heroes of the Red Branch, and a companion of Conor MacNessa, King of Ulster. It was also known as *Dún da leth glas* (the meaning is obscure) and this, shortened into *Dún*, became its familiar designation, and gave its name to

The white-washed church at Saul was replaced in 1932 by a neat stone building in Romanesque style. C.M.

County Down besides. When in 1177 John de Courcy marched from Dublin to subjugate the north, he made Downpatrick his objective. Here he defeated Rury MacDonlevy, King of Ulster, and here he established his headquarters. Its connection with St. Patrick is not clear, but it would appear that he was interred here in the little church built by himself or one of his disciples. The place waxed in ecclesiastical importance: John de Courcy dispossessed the Canons Regular and founded a Benedictine Abbey instead; and to Downpatrick he conveyed, with much pomp, the remains of St. Brigid and St. Columba, two of the most famous of St. Patrick's followers, that all might rest together. The subsequent checkered history of Downpatrick need not be told, as it is easily accessible: it is a story of rapine and plunder, and of faithful rebuilding. The final restoration of the cathedral began only in 1790, and was completed in 1826. It is a plain and not imposing building, but on account of its commanding position it dominates the little town (Plate XI). The reputed burial-place of St. Patrick is marked by a large block of rough granite brought from the Mourne Mountains to replace a gaping hole excavated by pious pilgrims, who wished to carry away some of the sacred soil. The long line of bishops of Down includes some notable names—St. Malachy, Jeremy Taylor, Thomas Percy (editor of the *Reliques of Ancient English Poetry*); Richard Mant, theologian, poet and historian; and William Reeves, foremost of local antiquaries. Downpatrick was apparently the birthplace of Duns Scotus, the philosopher.

The great dun, which the Normans altered considerably to suit their own military requirements, still stands imposingly on the low ground close to the town; and on the opposite side of the Quoile are the ruins of Inch Abbey on what was formerly an island (*inis*). An early church once stood here, which John de Courcy replaced by a monastery conducted by Cistercian monks whom he brought across from Furness Abbey in Cumberland. In addition to all these Christian relics there are around Downpatrick a number of older monuments to occupy the attention of the antiquary—stone circles,

PLATE XI

R. Welch: photo

DOWNPATRICK FROM GALLOWS HILL

dolmens and so on; and for the student of the past this area is one of the most interesting in Ireland.

Down by the sea, south-east of Downpatrick, is the little town and harbour of Ardglass (*Árd glas*, green height), a port of importance in early days, as testified by its numerous small castles; now a busy centre of the herring fishery and, being a breezy and picturesque place, a rising favourite with holiday-makers. This is the place to stay if you are exploring the district, for it is cheerful, and offers plenty of accommodation; Downpatrick, on the other hand, long the centre of the area, has declined since the advent of the railway has allowed people easily to do their shopping and other business in Belfast.

Seven miles south-west of Downpatrick, overlooking the little village of Dundrum (*Dún droma*, the fort of the ridge) and the curious hammer-headed sandy sea-inlet called the Inner Bay, stands the imposing ruin of the great castle which John de Courcy built for the Knights Templars about the end of the twelfth century. It replaced an earthen fort known as *Dún Rudhraidhe*—Rury's fort—a place which figures in the ancient annals. This was one of the main fortresses of the Anglo-Normans. "I assure your lordeship", wrote Lord Deputy Grey to Thomas Crumwell, Lord Privy Seal, in 1539, "as yt standeth, [it]ys one of the strongyst holtes that ever I sawe in Irelande, and moost commodios for defence in the hole countre of Lecayll, both by see and lande." The great barbican is now much wrecked, but the donjon still towers imposingly to fifty feet, and the ruin conveys an idea of great strength in former days.

At Dundrum we have the lofty group of the Mourne Mountains beckoning us from a distance of a few miles, and by road or rail we slip down the back of the extensive dunes that fringe Dundrum Bay to Newcastle. This picturesque range has, from its compactness, the advantage of having on all sides, close to the hills, places where the visitor can stay comfortably: from Newcastle, Kilkeel, Rostrevor and Hilltown every part of the Mournes is within easy reach. There is, moreover, a road which crosses the range from Kilkeel to Hilltown, rising to over 1200 feet at the Deer's Meadow, beside the source of the Bann.

The mountains of south Down and the adjoining parts of Louth belong to two widely separated periods of geological disturbance. From Slieve Croob in central Down south-westward to Slieve Gullion (*Sliabh Cuilinn*, mountain of holly) in Armagh and then south-eastward to Carlingford Mountain are granite and other rocks that belong to the time of the ancient Caledonian folding that determined once for all the main features of the surface of Ireland. The Mourne highlands are very much newer, and consist of a granite mass that pushed up through Silurian rocks at about the same period as that which witnessed the outpouring of the Antrim basalts. These two areas of granite are close together, but are separated by a belt of the Silurian slates. It is the recent origin of the Mourne Mountains that gives them their steep sides, deep valleys and occasional cliffs. Their topography is " immature ", and time has not yet worn them down as it has, for instance, the once loftier older ridge of Wicklow. And it is this immaturity which makes the Mournes so delightful a region for the walker. These hills were my favourite and frequent playground during twenty of my most vigorous years, and I may fairly claim to have traversed every acre of them. There were summer months at Newcastle, with rambles in many directions. Later my old teachers E. A. Letts and Maurice FitzGerald, of Queen's College (as it was then) used to come camping at the Hare's Gap, amusing themselves in searching for beryl and topaz, and I often tramped across the hills to join them at breakfast and go hunting in their company; and later again, S. A Stewart and I spent two summers in an exhaustive botanical examination of the range. So any tips I can give to the visitor come from an old hand. First, a glance at a map will show you that the higher peaks, the few lakes, and the deeper valleys all lie east of the Hilltown–Kilkeel road. West of it, the fine cliff on Eagle Mountain alone is well worth the exertion of getting there—but it must not be forgotten that the views obtained from the rather tame hills over Rostrevor, of Carlingford

Lough and Carlingford Mountain, are among the loveliest things that Ireland has to offer. Newcastle forms the best centre of all. Thence you can either ascend the Glen River, climb over the 1900-foot col between Slieve Donard (*Sliabh Domhanghairt*, mountain of St. Domangard) and Slieve Commedagh (*Sliabh coimhéada*, mountain of watching) into the heart of the hills, or you can work by road along their northern or eastern flanks, in the former case ascending the Trassey Burn to the cliff-bound Hare's Gap, which leads you into the heart of the mountains; or in the latter case following the granite-workers' road up the Annalong River (*Ath na long*, the ford of the ships) for the ascent of Slieve Bingian (*Sliabh binneann*, the mountain of the sharp peak, 2449 feet) the largest and most picturesque, though not the highest, of the group. A striking feature of the Mournes is the great granite crags that crown some of the summits, notably Slieve Bingian, Slieve Bearnagh (*Sliabh bernach*, gapped mountain, 2394 feet), and the less lofty Doan. As seen from the main road a few miles west of Kilkeel (*Cill chaol*, narrow church), these great crags, standing in a row against the sky, form a remarkable picture; the long crested ridge of Slieve Bingian is especially conspicuous, resembling the back of a two-mile *Diplodacus*. The name of Slieve Bingian recalls a day when I saw—and felt—weather at its very worst: and it is not often that one does that, even as regards summer weather. The occasion was an excursion of the Belfast Naturalists' Field Club, and the programme was to drive to the entrance of the Happy Valley (which the Belfast Waterworks engineers renamed Silent Valley when they began to build their great reservoir there), climb Slieve Bingian, and walk through the mountains to Newcastle—a tough menu for a mixed party. In those hardy days it was a rule that excursions started regardless of weather, and were carried through unless that proved impracticable. We reached the Happy Valley to encounter a south-easterly gale howling in from the Irish Sea, and a sky that meant mischief. Half the party decided to stay with the wagonettes (no buses in those days!) and the other half started up the valley. The weather worsened rapidly; heavy rain began. When we got to the point where we should turn to the right up the steep slope of Slieve Bingian there were only three of us left, and half-way up two more gave out. The Secretary (myself), left alone, decided to maintain the Club tradition and put the programme through. There was comparative shelter till the vicinity of the crowning crags was reached; then the furious gusts compelled me to hands and knees, and even so I was twice rolled over. I wormed my way in to the topmost crags, among which the gale shrieked and yelled; one would have been afraid to venture had not everything around been solid granite. As it was, the rocks seemed to sway and cower under the furious buffets. I could not show my face, for every drop of rain stung as if it had been a flying pebble: it was an exhilarating and almost terrifying struggle, and an interesting lesson in what exposure really means. When I dropped back behind the crest, my rain-coat was in ribbons, and my hat was gone; I was drenched and battered, and sorely out of breath—but I had done it! Then of course came the reward of virtue. The wind dropped as quickly as it had risen, the clouds broke, and three hours later I swung into Newcastle in bright sunshine, ahead of time. Those were the days!

Botanically, the Mournes offer no special points of interest. Like the other eastern mountains of Ireland, they are poor in alpine plants, but there are some rare hawkweeds. The geologist will find various features to catch his attention—the Silurian rocks at 2000 feet on the summit of Slieve Muck, pushed up by the granite when it broke through the slaty covering; the beautiful little curved embankment-like moraine under the fine cliff of Eagle Mountain; the drusy cavities—crystal-filled bubbles—in the granite at the Diamond Rocks near the Hare's Gap, into which minerals have infiltrated to form crystals of smoky quartz, orthoclase, black mica, topaz, beryl; and there are interesting intrusion phenomena and others of a similarly technical nature.

If you go to Newcastle for mountain-climbing, first ascend Slieve Donard (2796 feet, the highest point in the group) in order to

PLATE XII

GRANITE PILLARS ON SLIEVE COMMEDAGH

R. Welch: photo

get a general view of the ground, and then arrange your walks so as
to include the eastern faces of Cove Mountain and Slieve Lamagan,
ascend Slieve Bingian by way of the Blue Lough and Lough Bingian,
and Slieve Bearnagh by way of the Hare's Gap; traverse the ridge
from Slieve Meel-more to Slieve Muck, and drop down on Lough
Shannagh (*Loch sionnach*, the foxes' lake) and Doan (*Dubhán*, a hook)
from Ott Mountain; if to these you add the cliffs on the east side of
Eagle Mountain and of Pigeon Rock Mountain, you will have seen
all that is best. The valley bottoms are often filled with deep bog,
sometimes dissected by anastomosing channels full of soft peat and
boulders, so keep to the hill-slopes and especially to the ridges as
much as you can. If you are lazy, push on to Rostrevor and stay
there, and I think you will feel that nowhere have you seen anything
lovelier than the land-locked lough of Carlingford, with the cloud-
shadows chasing each other along the rugged slopes of Carlingford
Mountain.

Hilltown, half-way along the range on the northern side, is high
and breezy—a tiny, silent village where one can dawdle and watch
the changing colours on the mountains, and forget the hurry and
noise of the towns. Half a century ago, when I knew it first, it was
a " backward " place—one might still hear Irish spoken by the old
people, who were full of old tales. Here is one of them, concerning
the fairies: " There was a girl called Shusie M'Kee was tuk away
by thim. They tuk her first to a dance, an' siz they: ' Who'll
dance the reel? Who but Shusie M'Kee! An' who'll dance the jig?
Who but Shusie M'Kee!' An' when she had danced the reel an' the
jig, they tuk her away to a funeral, an' siz they: ' Who'll dig the
grave? Who but Shusie M'Kee! An' who'll carry the corp?
Who but Shusie M'Kee!' An wid that she tuk to her heels an' ran."

" And did she get home again?"

" Oh, aye, she got home right enough. She did that."

Newry (*Iubhar cinntragh*, the Yew-tree at the head of the strand)
is the most important town in this area, a busy and rather restless
place, divided in its allegiance between north and south. It is not

a spot at which one tarries, especially after Rostrevor or Newcastle. It might be lovely, wedged in as it is with rocky ground rising on either hand: and as seen from Goraghwood, a few miles north, its setting is very beautiful. But the river which traverses it recalls the notorious Irwell. Its canal and the space on either side, which should be picturesque, are a grave of derelict barges and abandoned motors, with roofless factories rising as tombstones. There is one busy business street, rather narrow and cramped. Though there is much waste space, the Town Hall and railway station, curiously enough, can only find standing room by straddling across the stream. At its north end alone does Newry cheer up, with some fine old houses and a welcome splash of colour from flowering shrubs. But when mellow evening light falls along the canal with its battered hulks and jumble of old buildings it can become transfigured into something very lovely.

When will Ireland waken up to the advantages of having a clean and smiling face? There are indeed here and there signs of an awakening in this direction, but it is still feeble and local. In the larger towns, especially those to which the tourist traffic is of importance, much has indeed been done: but these form a very small portion of Ireland. It is of the villages rather that I am thinking. Some there are gay with flowers, and with whitewash and paint performing their allotted tasks: but especially over the Central Plain how many do we see that consist of something like this—ten public houses, ten private houses and ten roofless houses, with only a bit of blank wall and two tattered trees by way of relief? The melancholy ruins in our villages are their most depressing feature. I wish we had an organization of break-down gangs—desperadoes who would swoop down on a village, raze the ruins to the ground, and plant a few common flowering shrubs—Lilac and Laburnum and Fuchsia and Dorothy Perkins—to hide the nakedness until such time as the ground is needed for some useful purpose.

Having devoted a good many pages to Down, which for several reasons—its varied history, its extensive shore-line, its high moun-

PLATE XIII

R. Welch: photo

KING JOHN'S CASTLE AND CARLINGFORD MOUNTAIN

tains—is a particularly attractive area, the rest of the Silurian-Ordovician region may be passed over somewhat rapidly, for only here and there can it compare with Down in general interest.   Louth claims attention chiefly on account of the fine scenery in the north, around Carlingford (Fiord of Cairlinn (Danish)), already alluded to. Carlingford Mountain (1935 feet) is a beautiful rugged hill, descending steeply into the water, and the old town of the same name, nestling at its base, is dominated by the great Norman stronghold known as King John's Castle (Plate XIII).   Carlingford Lough is itself interesting because it is a true fiord, deep within and shallow at the entrance, owing this peculiar form to deepening by the grinding ice-masses of the Glacial Period.   It was well described by Gerard Boate two hundred years ago, in his *Natural History of Ireland*:

" This haven is some three or four miles long, and nigh of the same breadth, being every where very deep, so as the biggest ships may come there to anchor; and so inviron'd with high land and mountains on allsides, that the ships do lye defended off all winds; so that this would be one of the best havens of the world, if it were not for the difficulty and danger of the entrance, the mouth being full of rocks, both blind ones and others, betwixt which the passages are very narrow: whereby it cometh that this harbour is very little frequented by any great ships."

Except for Carlingford Mountain, the surrounding hills, including the massive Slieve Gullion (1893 feet) to the northward, have little biological interest.   But there are plenty of problems here for the geologist in the intricate series of ancient volcanic rocks, and the archaeologist will find much to examine—the great dolmen of Ballymascanlan, the pagan-Christian stone called Kilnasaggart, and so on.

One of the many legends referring to Finn MacCoul ends on the shore of the little lake on the top of Slieve Gullion, where, on the site where a magic drinking-horn had disappeared, " a growth of slender twigs " grew up, gifted with the virtue that any one who looks on it in the morning fasting will know in a moment all things that are

to happen that day.[1]   When I first climbed Slieve Gullion I took the
precaution of bringing breakfast with me in my pocket, but unfortunately failed to find anything which resembled the description of
the plant.   Historically the region is important, for these hills form
the ancient as well as the present frontier of Ulster, and at the Moyry
Pass (*Maigh Tréa*, Trea's Plain) south of Slieve Gullion (*Sliabh
cuillinn*, holly mountain), many a battle was fought between English
and Irish, and no doubt by others long before the English came.
From Dundalk, road and railway climb for 400 feet in order to win
through to County Down.   The hills slope southward to Dundalk
Bay, and more level ground extends thence to Dublin.   Several
small square castles remain, visible from the railway and main road
as one passes under the shadow of Slieve Gullion, to tell of troubled
times: but more interesting and imposing are the earthworks, dating,
it is believed, from the second or third century of our era, which tell
of much more ancient fortification of the boundary of Ulster.   On
the western spurs of Slieve Gullion stand the remains of " The
Dorsey " (*Dorus*, a door or pass), an immense fortified camp of
peculiar shape—an irregular oblong a mile and a quarter long by
600 yards wide.   The enclosure is encircled by a great earthen
rampart, with a fosse on either side still about twenty-three feet
deep, twelve feet or more wide at bottom: and external to these
fosses are lesser ramparts.   This great fortress was presumably
associated with the imposing ditches known in different portions of
their length as " The Black Pig's Dyke ", " The Dane's Cast " and
" The Worm Ditch ", of which fragments exist in many counties on
either side of the boundary of Ulster, belonging apparently to three
contemporary or more likely successive lines of defence.   The most
northern of them runs from Bundoran on the Atlantic by way of
Lough Allen to the neighbourhood of Newry: it is upon this line
that " The Dorsey " is seated.   The most southern stretches from
Athlone on the Shannon to Drogheda.   The intermediate ditch,
more fragmentary and difficult to understand, lies roughly between

[1] P. W. Joyce, *Ancient Celtic Romances*, p. 361.

the two. W. F. de V. Kane spent much time in tracing and mapping what is left of these ancient fortifications, but historically very little is known about them.[1] The fact that no tradition remains among the people concerning them, and that supernatural agencies embodied in fantastic stories are brought in to account for them, points to an early date of construction.

Armagh (*Árd Macha*, Macha's height) is a fine county, its fertility increased by the presence of limestone in the north, where also the Eocene clays of Lough Neagh cover the portion of the area which approaches that sheet of water. Much of the surface resembles Down, save that lakelets are almost absent. For all purposes the most interesting centre is the ancient city of Armagh. It was founded by St. Patrick about the year 444, but the great earthwork now called Navan Fort, the ancient Emania, carries its history back at least eight hundred years further. Emania was the seat of Ulster sovereignty during six centuries, ending in A.D. 332, when Fergus Fogha was defeated, and Emania burnt and pillaged. As in the case of Tara, little but uninspiring earthworks remain to tell of former greatness. Armagh is a small and pleasant town, a place of importance ever since its foundation, for it is the seat of government of both the Roman Catholic and the Protestant Episcopal churches in Ireland. It boasts two cathedrals and other buildings of note, such as the Public Library, which houses many valuable old books and early records, and the fine Archbishop's palace. The handsome red marble with which the city is paved is obtained locally from a limited area of Carboniferous beds which intervene between the New Red and the Silurian rocks. One wishes that many other towns in Ireland were so well kept, and presented an appearance of equal prosperity and general well-being.

The county of Monaghan (*Muineachán*, little shrubbery), which succeeds on the west, is a rather dull area. The north shows a

---

[1] See Kane, " The Black Pig's Dyke: the Ancient Boundary Fortification of Uladh ", *Proc. Roy. Irish Acad.*, vol. xxvii., sect. C, pp. 301-328, plate 16. 1909. *Ibid.*, vol. xxxiii., sect. C, pp. 539-563, plate 48. 1917.

succession from Millstone Grit on the summit of the desolate bog-covered hills of Slieve Beagh (*Sliabh Beatha*, Bith's mountain, 1196 feet) through Yoredale rocks and Carboniferous limestone to Ordovician and Silurian slates, the last, as in Armagh, covering the south of the area. I have botanized a good deal in Monaghan, with despair in my heart at the monotony and lack of interest which its flora displays; and of its zoology and archaeology one can say nothing better. Monaghan contains much pleasant country, and some pretty lakes, but it is not an area inviting much expenditure of time.

Cavan (*Cabhán*, a hollow), which lies close to the extremity of the great wedge of Silurian rocks, includes much besides, for it is a large and sprawling county, with a long arm running in an absurd way far to the north-west, and not stopping till it reaches Lough Macnean. The main portion of Cavan is undulating country formed of Ordovician and Silurian slates, with lakes of all sizes in profusion, and these give the landscape a picturesqueness and interest that otherwise it would not possess. On the southern border Lough Ramor (*Loch Muinreamhair*, lough of Fatneck (man's name)) island-studded and beautifully wooded, is well worth visiting. Westward, the larger and more open Lough Sheelin (*Lough sighleann*) covers about eight square miles—a pretty lake, set in diversified fertile country. In contrast to this, Lough Gowna, on the western margin, and Lough Oughter to the north of it, are maze-like—especially the latter, which is a complicated tangle of land and water. These two lakes, which lie on the upper course of the Erne, have been referred to already when that strange river was dealt with on an earlier page (p. 103). One can stay comfortably at Cavan for the exploration of this curious water-logged region.

The long north-western arm of Cavan from the Erne to Belcoo (*Béal cobha?*) is a remote region, little known to visitors whether scientific or otherwise, full of lakes in the Erne watershed, rather grim and lonely towards the north-west. Up here also it gets mountainous, marching with Fermanagh over the summit of Cuilcagh (*Cuilceach*, reeds?, 2188 feet) and with Leitrim over Slievenakilla (*Sliabh na cille*, church mountain, 1793 feet). It can claim also the head-waters of the Shannon, the source of which is by tradition assigned not to the origin of the Owenmore (*Abha mhór*, great river), as one might expect, but to a round pool on a short feeder of the same, the pool being known as Lugnashinna or the Shannon Pot. This is the exit of an underground river, presumably coming from either east or north-east, in both of which directions, a few miles away, streams sink underground in a suggestive way. There is a good deal of limestone here, riddled with subterranean passages, as notably displayed in the Marble Arch area (p. 109).

CHAPTER VI

THE LIMESTONE PLATEAU

(LEITRIM AND SLIGO)

LOUGH ALLEN (*Loch aininn*), into which the infant Shannon descends from its source among the Cavan hills, is not so attractive a lake as its mountainous setting might suggest. High brown hills rise from both its eastern and western shores, Slieveanieran attaining 1922 feet. A certain monotony and barrenness, a prevalence of peat-bog on barren clays and shales and sandstones, is caused by the presence here of Upper Carboniferous rocks. Yoredales are succeeded as one ascends by the Millstone Grit series, and the hills are topped with Coal-measures; these and the Millstone Grit actually contain some workable coal—a phenomenon unusual in Ireland. When first I tramped these hills, many years ago, I stumbled on one of the " mines "—a heading driven horizontally into a steep scarp. A rough narrow path led up the cliff to it, and a man was descending leading a donkey carrying two panniers of the precious mineral. Scrambling down to the adit, I found one man hewing coal inside. A fairly primitive coal-mine! Previous working on a much larger scale had come to this, for the narrowness of the seams and the poor quality of the coal make mining here a precarious business. Lately an attempt on the grand scale has again been made to wring riches from these stubborn hills, to the tune of £30,000 of government money, but no success has crowned it. Slieveanieran, as its name implies (*Sliabh an iarainn*, the mountain of iron), contains iron as well as coal. This occurs as bands and nodules in shales underlying the coal-bearing beds. But so far the iron-ore has not been found in

The Arigna coalfield at Lough Allen yields sufficient coal for local industrial use. It supplies a small electricity generating station. C.M.

sufficient quantity to ensure permanent successful working. Smelting used to be carried on with charcoal, and when trees got rare the local coal was used: but nothing now remains but slag-heaps and weeds. If Ireland has not proved a land of mines, whether of coal, iron, lead, copper, zinc, sulphur, or gold, it has not been for want of trying. Hardly a county in the island but has somewhere its ruined mine-heads and desolate spoil-banks; the amount of money expended must have been prodigious, and the amount lost has been large. But still there is a pathetic belief everywhere in the country that Ireland is teeming with mineral wealth, only waiting to be exploited. One does not observe, all the same, an overwhelming desire to invest in mining ventures when, occasionally, opportunity offers, which shows that people are wiser than they know. So we need not linger over Lough Allen and its bleak hills, nor over southern Leitrim, a flattish rather water-logged area, with slow streams and many lake-lets, but push on to the much more interesting regions lying on the limestone to west and north.

If you halt at Boyle you will find yourself in a very pretty district quite unknown to the tourist. The town lies on a rushing river which, emerging as a broad slow stream from the large bog-fringed Lough Gara, breaks away suddenly just above Boyle to enter Lough Key. This stream flows along the southern edge of a line of heathery hills known as the Curlew Mountains—a pretty designation, but nothing to do with Curlews, for the name is *Coirr Shliabh*, rough mountain, and the highest point is only 863 feet. These hills are a crumple in the Earth's crust, owing to which the Old Red Sandstone and Silurian rocks have been forced up. Their former cover of limestone having been worn off them, they now rise as a dark heathery ridge. At their base, just below Boyle, lies the lovely Lough Key (*Loch cé*, lake of night?), richly wooded—quite one of the prettiest lakes in Ireland, with indented shores and a variety of islands; on one of these stands the remains of the Abbey of the Trinity, in which was compiled the important manuscript work known as the *Annals of Loch Cé*, a chronicle of events from 1014 to

1590, which has now found a home in Trinity College, Dublin. On another island rise the ruins of a castle of the M'Dermots. From Lough Key the Boyle River emerges to flow in a curious half-lake, half-river form past Cootehall to join the Shannon—here a much less imposing stream than itself—near Carrick. With a small boat one can do plenty of interesting exploring in this neighbourhood. Boyle itself is a pleasant little town, with trees and bridges, and several good buildings. Down by the river, overlooked by steep wooded slopes, is the ancient Cistercian abbey founded by Maurice O'Duffy in 1161. It had the usual disturbed history of Irish monasteries, but much that is beautiful remains—the fine west front, and a number of delightful arches. The ruins cover a considerable area, pointing to an establishment of importance.

Take the Collooney road from Boyle, which rises at once to cross the Curlew Hills. You get lovely views of Lough Key and the lakey country to the south-east, and on passing the summit, a fine panorama opens on the opposite direction—Lough Arrow (*Loch Arbhach*, Arbhu's lake), five miles long, broken up by promontories and islands; out to the north-east, the long dark ridge of Bralieve (*Breágh shliabh* (?), fine mountain) and the Arigna hills (*Arigne* (?), desolating—referring to the rapidity of the river); and rising directly from the western shore of the lake, the strange flat-topped limestone hill of Carrowkeel (*An cheathramha chaol*, narrow quarter, 1029 feet), with the higher limestone dome of Keshcorran (*Céis Chorainn*, the wicker bridge of Corrann, 1183 feet) beyond it. These two hills have during the last thirty years yielded much information concerning the past—the first in relation to life and burial customs in the Bronze Age, the other as regards the wild animals which roamed Ireland during that and preceding periods. Carrowkeel is a hill of peculiar and unusual construction, for the large flat top, a square mile or so in extent, is cut up by parallel rifts—straight gorge-like hollows running N.N.W. and S.S.E.—which intersect the plateau. And on almost all of the little promontories in which the portions of the plateau terminate, stands a stone cairn. I happened on this curious place when engaged on field-work for *Irish Topographical Botany* in 1896, and was greatly struck by the curious topography, and by the number of cairns, some of which had clearly never been opened. Fifteen years later, when R. A. S. Macalister, E. C. R. Armstrong and I planned a campaign of archaeological digging, the queer cairn-topped ridges of Carrowkeel came back to my mind, and a visit to it decided us to make it the site of our first excavation. It was a fortunate choice, for the place proved to be one of high interest. A survey of the hill showed us that the flat rifted top had on it fourteen burial cairns, two ruined dolmens, and a group of some fifty circular stone foundations, the remains of a prehistoric village. The cairns were built entirely of the local limestone, and under the action of the weather the outer blocks had broken up into material resembling road-metal. Examination showed that the peat which now covers the hill was formed subsequent to the building of the cairns: this accounted for the great amount of stone, often in the form of large blocks, used in the structures; for when they were built the hill was bare of covering, and no doubt thickly strewn with the wreckage of the limestone, as in similar areas in Clare, Galway and other places. The exploration of the monuments, which occupied three visits, was of the greatest interest, and gave abundant results. On the very first day we discovered the hidden entrances to two of the intact cairns, which proved to contain not simple cists as we had expected, but beautiful cruciform chambers, eight to ten feet high, like that of New Grange, but smaller. Ground-plans of two of them, taken from our report, are reproduced here (Fig. 3). In the first opened (G) there was an entrance passage, a polygonal central chamber, and three polygonal cells around it, evenly disposed. Several sill-stones divided up the entrance-passage, and a sill separated the central chamber from each of the side chambers. Between the sill-stones, each section of the floor was paved with a large slab. The roof was formed of large overlapping slabs, sloping outwards. It was a most symmetrical and beautiful piece of architecture. I had the privilege of being the first to crawl down the entrance-passage, and I did so with no little awe. I lit three candles and stood awhile, to let my eyes accustom themselves to the dim light. There was everything just as the last Bronze Age man had left it, three to four thousand years before. A light brownish dust covered all. The central chamber was empty, but each of the three recesses opening from it contained much burnt bone debris, with flat stones on which

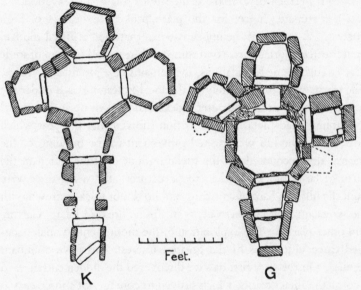

K   Feet.   G

FIG. 3.—PLANS OF CHAMBERS OF BRONZE AGE CAIRNS ON CARROWKEEL
MOUNTAIN

evidently the bones had been carried in, after the bodies had been cremated in strong fires outside. There were also beads of stone, bone implements made from Red Deer antlers, and many fragments of much decayed pottery. On little raised recesses in the wall were flat stones on which reposed the calcined bones of young children. This brief description gives a sample of the construction and contents of the more complete cairns. We also got implements made from bones of Bear, Wild Boar and Ox, and two complete urns of food-vessel type. The other cairns showed much variety—some with no chamber or burial at all, some with a single small cist, and one, to be mentioned immediately, of quite unique design. There were burnt interments and also unburnt; there were many white stones such as are constantly associated with Bronze Age burials, beads and pendants of jasper, steatite, serpentine; a sea-shell, a pebble bored by sea-animals.

But the gem of this great cemetery was the cairn which we called F. This contained a magnificent chamber of unique and complicated design. It consisted of a well-built entrance passage, a polygonal chamber with recesses cut off by sills, and a second larger chamber beyond with three separated recesses, and in this, most remarkable of all, a slender pillar-stone in the centre-line, 5 feet in height, and $7\frac{1}{2}$ by 9 inches in section. Over this the roof rose to its greatest height, some 16 feet above the floor. The unfortunate fracture of a large slab at some bygone time had brought about a great collapse, and we had to remove tons of stuff to clear the chamber. Another accident had snapped the standing stone across, near its base, but had not impaired the sanctity which apparently was attached to it, for we found the ashes of a burnt human body laid on the butt end of the prostrate part. The architecture of this monument was of most massive character, slabs up to four tons in weight being used in its construction; and its design, and especially its inner sanctuary with the standing-stone, is without parallel.

In general interest the Bronze Age cemetery of Carrowkeel is equalled only by the more famous ones of Brugh-na-Boinne and Lough Crew. None of its sepulchral chambers approaches the regal proportions of New Grange, and the rock-scribings that form so remarkable a feature of both the great Meath monuments are entirely absent at Carrowkeel. On the other hand, the Carrowkeel group displays a greater variety of design: but the main interest of its exploration lay in the fact that there was no evidence that its cairns had been opened and ransacked long since, as in the other places: most of them appeared to be intact, even when ruined, and they gave an important insight into the burial customs of the Bronze Age people. Assuming that the apparent absence of any disturbance means that at no time subsequent to the period of interment have these chambers been robbed, their contents tended to explode the popular idea that at least the more elaborate of the Irish cairns contained, along with the human remains, golden torcs or lunulae, or other contemporary treasure belonging to those who were buried in these imposing mausoleums. The monuments are grand, and there may have been elaborate funeral rites, but a few trinkets alone appear to have accompanied the actual sepulture. (But see also p. 288.)

I have been tempted to prolong these notes on Carrowkeel because they formed the first important archaeological " dig " in which I was privileged to take part, and because I still recall the thrill of successive discoveries. Macalister, Armstrong and I subsequently carried out other excavations—a crannog near Tuam, a curious Bronze Age interment in the form of a ring-fort with a small central sepulchral cist guarded by a slender pillar-stone seventeen and a half feet high near Naas; and after the Great War, and Armstrong's lamented death, the very curious settlements of Uisneach and Togherstown (see p. 241) and the cemetery of Killeen Cormac with its wealth of Ogham stones (p. 273); but none of them had the fascination of Carrowkeel, and none yielded more important results.[1]

The hill of Keshcorran (*Céis Chorainn*, the wicker bridge of Corrann, 1183 feet) which adjoins Carrowkeel on the north-west, though formed of the same limestone, is of different appearance, being a rounded hump, which on the west rises steeply from the undulating plain across which the railway runs towards Sligo. Its most conspicuous feature is a low cliff half-way up this face, pierced by a row of caves. These have been the site of a good deal of digging, and have yielded great abundance of bones of animals which in past times lived in them—including Bears and Wolves and Foxes, which in their turn dragged in their prey, so that a whole museum

---

[1] See Macalister, Armstrong and Praeger: " The Exploration of Bronze Age Cairns on Carrowkeel Mountain, County Sligo ", *Proc. Roy. Irish Acad.*, vol. xxix., sect. C, pp. 311-347, plates 10-25. 1911.

of bones was unearthed, including those of Reindeer and Arctic Lemming, which like the Bear and Wolf are now extinct in Ireland. Altogether, remains of some seventy kinds of animals were identified, ranging from snails and fishes up to man, the bulk belonging to birds and mammals.[1]

Keshcorran and Carrowkeel are cut off from the main mass of the limestone mountains of Sligo, which we now approach, by an ancient ridge around and over which limestone was originally deposited in the Carboniferous sea, but which denudation has now left bare. This ridge belongs to the Caledonian period of folding, and, following the usual direction of this crumpling, extends from Clew Bay north-eastward for seventy miles to beyond Manor-hamilton. The western part, of granite and gneiss, is broad and high, forming the dark heathery ridge of the Ox Mountains (*Sliabh ghamh*, stony mountain, misrendered *S. dhamh*, mountain of the oxen, 1780 feet). Quartzite comes in further eastward, forming the peculiar bare rocky knobby hills about Collooney (*Cúil Mhúine*, corner of Múine?); and then a high narrow wedge of gneiss continues, rising over the southern shore of Lough Gill and penetrating among the cliffy limestone hills, providing interesting contrasts. The Ox Mountains do not offer much to the visitor—broad wet heathery slopes and a broad flat boggy top are the leading features, and only about some of the little lakes is the range attractive. Lough Talt (*Loch Tailt*, Talt's lake), towards the west, is very pretty, with diversified scenery and some good plants: approachable moreover, as is the less picturesque Easky Lough (*Loch Iascach*, fish-abounding lake), since a good road (as mountain roads go) borders each, on its way to cross the main ridge. Collooney, east of the Ox Mountains, is an important pass, for here the ancient ridge sinks almost to sea-level, and in the narrow gap—the only one between Ballina and Ballyshannon—river, road and railways jostle each other in their passage from the Central Plain to Sligo Bay and Sligo town. The

[1] R. F. Scharff and others, " The Exploration of the Caves of Kesh, County Sligo ", *Trans. Roy. Irish Acad.*, vol. xxxii., sect. B, pp. 171-214, plates 9-11. 1903.

rushing stream and the tumbled country of gneiss, limestone and quartzite, with woods and bald hills, make Collooney a picturesque place, and interesting to the topographer and geologist. The river which escapes through the gap meanders for a couple of miles to Ballysadare (*Baile easa dara*, the town of the waterfall of the oak)— an appropriate name, for the picturesque rapids by which the stream reaches the sea and the adjoining oak-woods are the principal features here, in addition to the little abbey founded by St. Fechin about 645, and a large flour-mill.

Sligo Bay (*Cuan sligig*: *sligeach*, shelly place), which enters the land between Roskeeragh Point and Aughris Head, breaks at once into three long fingers of complicated outline, with points and islands, making an extensive shallow area of calm water invading the limestone country, with miles of bare sand at low tide. The southern finger runs up to Ballysadare. On the promontory to the north of this, giving character to the whole area, the massive cliff-walled hill of Knocknarea (*Ard na riaghadh*, hill of the executions, 1078 feet) looks down on the broad golden beach at Strandhill. On the summit, a huge flat-topped cairn of stones, 34 feet high and 600 feet in circumference is, according to tradition, the burial-place of the famous Queen Maev of Connacht (Queen Mab of English folk-lore), who reigned in the first century A.D. It would appear, how-ever, that she was more probably interred at Rathcroghan, so the huge Knocknarea cairn may have been a cenotaph. It is certainly a noble monument, placed on one of the finest sites in Ireland. The view from Miscan Maeve, as the cairn is called, is one which for beauty and variety has few equals, embracing a great extent of mountain and plain, headland and ocean, between Mayo on the west and Donegal on the north. The nearer view also is full of interest—the complicated network of Sligo Bay, Sligo town on its river, and the woods that embosom lovely Lough Gill.

While the huge cairn of Knocknarea is the most conspicuous and striking prehistoric monument in Sligo, it is but one of a large number which remain to attest the importance of the district in

prehistoric times. Between Knocknarea and Sligo is situated the
Bronze Age cemetery of Carrowmore (*An cheathramha mór*, the
great quarter). Here, within a limited space, is a group of monuments no less than sixty-four in number—dolmens (especially), stone
circles, cairns. Tradition associates this imposing array of megalithic structures with the Battle of Northern Moytura, recorded in
the early annals as having been fought in Anno Mundi 3303 between
the Fomorians and the Tuatha-dé-Danann. At least two hundred
sepulchral monuments are stated to have existed at Carrowmore
until comparatively lately: but now many have been destroyed.

On the hill between Sligo and Lough Gill is a large flat-topped
cairn of the type of Miscan Maeve; in the " Deerpark " over the
north end of that lake stands a megalithic monument of complicated and unusual design; and around are many cairns, etc., the
series not ceasing till we get to the Curlew Hills. For those interested in antiquities of the Christian era, there are here the Dominican
abbey of Sligo, founded by Maurice Fitzgerald in 1252, with its
pretty cloisters; the round tower and high cross at Drumcliff (*Druim
chliabh*, hill-ridge of baskets) to the north; the little early abbey of
Ballysadare, and at the pleasant village of Dromahaire (a picturesque
name—*Druim dá eithiar*, the ridge of the two air-demons) the Franciscan abbey of Creevelea (*Craebh liath*, grey branch) looking down
on the rapids of the Bonet River (*An Bhuanaid*, lasting river).

Sligo is a port capable of receiving vessels of large tonnage, and
is a bright and busy place. It arose at a ford across the Garvogue
River (*An gharbhóg*, the little rough thing) of strategic importance,
for to the west is the sea, and to the east and south the slow deep
stream, then Lough Gill, and beyond that a rough mountain area.
It is the centre of a district of high interest and beauty, and whether
one's tastes are archaeological or biological or aesthetic, there is
much to be seen and done. Even were Lough Gill alone the
attraction, Sligo ought to be a resort for the holiday-maker, for it
is one of the loveliest lakes in Ireland, and one of the most accessible.
From Sligo you row for two miles up the slow-flowing Garvogue

River, through woods and pastures, to the lake, which stretches for five miles more, its winding banks and islands mostly richly timbered. Hills rise on every side; while those on the north are of grey limestone, mostly steep and naked, and often of fantastic form, those on the south are of ancient gneiss and schist, and above the tree-limit are shaggy with brown heather. The smaller islands have a native woodland vegetation of Yew, Arbutus, White Beam, etc., exactly as at Killarney; elsewhere Oak and Birch are the dominant indigenous trees, and many others have been planted. Uncommon woodland plants grow beneath them, like the Bird's-nest Orchis and the Yellow Bird's-nest: and in Slish Wood on the southern shore the abundance and profusion of ferns and mosses is remarkable. Near the south-east corner one can row up the Bonet River to within a mile of Dromahaire, and visit the ancient abbey mentioned above. The eastern extremity of the lake, where the main road runs along the edge of the water, is especially picturesque. Spend a couple of days boating from Sligo and a couple more from Dromahaire, and you will have the most delightful lake holiday to be found short of Westmorland. The ground immediately adjoining the north side of Lough Gill is full of surprises: there are little cliff-walled flat-topped limestone hills with unexpected lakelets among them, and deep ferny glens; the queer bare limestone mountains rise on one side and the tree-embosomed lake stretches on the other.

Six miles due north of Sligo, Ben Bulben (*Beann Gulban*, the peak of Gulba) dominates the landscape—a level-topped mountain running westward till it drops in a 1500-foot cliff and talus to the low grounds that fringe the Atlantic. It and its name are symbols of what is quite one of the most picturesque as well as interesting areas in Ireland; for it is a token—a kind of sign-board to the cliff-walled valley-gashed limestone plateau that lies behind it, and its name stands for the whole region. Here, for a considerable area, the upper beds of the Carboniferous limestone, which over much of the Central Plain have been worn away, stand up in a high plateau, 1000 to 1500 feet above the surrounding country. The edges, as is frequent when horizontal strata are exposed to long-continued denudation, form lofty cliffs. The high ground is intersected by two great rifts—Glencar (*Gleann chairthe*, the glen of Garthe or ?pillar-stone), running from above Sligo eastward to Manorhamilton, and Glenade (*Gleann éatha*, glen of jealousy), running thence north-westward to debouch between Bundoran and Mullaghmore. The Manorhamilton end of each of these valleys is pretty, but tame compared with the other portions, which in each case have lofty grey cliff-walls looking down on a lake of considerable size. It is the combination of cliff, wood and water that make Glencar and Glenade so singularly attractive. The outer (north-western) edge, facing the Atlantic, is almost continuously cliff-walled, and offers much diversity of outline, as rather deep valleys penetrate into it. The highest parts of the plateau lie behind this scarp, between it and Glencar and Glenade; the most elevated point, Truskmore (2113 feet), is formed of a patch of Yoredale rocks overlying the limestone. The Yoredales continue to cap the limestone over much of the upland area which extends away to Lough Allen and Lough Erne.

While this Ben Bulben region is beloved of all seekers of the picturesque, it is to the botanist a special place of pilgrimage, on account of the profusion of alpine plants which cling to the grey cliff-walls, and the presence among them of some of extreme rarity. The Fringed Sandwort, rather widespread about Glenade and Gleniff, grows nowhere else in Ireland, nor is it found in Britain, while the Clustered Alpine Saxifrage and Chickweed-leaved Willow-herb have no other Irish station; the rocks are decked with Mountain Avens, Cushion Pink, Yellow Mountain Saxifrage, Green Spleen-wort, Holly Fern, and many other plants of the hills. The Canadian Blue-eyed Grass occurs on the lower grounds; the Maidenhair fern in limestone chinks both on the cliffs and down by the sea.

An interesting feature of both Glencar and Glenade is the great land-slips which in places form miniature mountains below the cliffs. They are not conspicuous when one looks at them across the valley, as they merge with the talus which subtends the cliff: but when you climb to them, you will be surprised at their size, and at the deep rifts that now intervene between them and the precipice formed by their breaking away. One of the largest is that which is called the " Swiss Valley ", in Glencar. You get to it by turning to the north into the wood at the east end of Glencar Lake; a rough track takes you steeply up and to the left, till you find yourself in a sheltered defile with a huge cliff of grey limestone on the right and a slope crowned with a wood of Silver Fir on the left—a spot that can be best described as romantic (Plate XIV). Beyond the far (west) end of it, if the weather has been wet, you will see a couple of fine waterfalls which leap over the cliff from the plateau above; the streams disappear on reaching the talus on which you stand, to re-appear down by the lake. You can ascend here by a turf-track to the cliff-top, where you will find miles of heather stretching far. Other great slips may be seen in Glenade, with strange pinnacles of limestone crowning the edge of the portions that have broken away. The origin of these land-slides is interesting. During the Glacial Period the valleys were filled with ice, whose scooping action deepened them materially, the sides becoming nearly perpendicular. When the climate mitigated, these gigantic walls, deprived of their ice-supports, broke down, and huge slices slipped forward and slid slowly, some as far as the valley-bottom. They form a remarkable feature of local topography.

If you want to visit the best of the unusual and very striking scenery of the Ben Bulben area you will traverse Glencar, seeing the lake and the Swiss Valley, and then Glenade, spending some time climbing under the great cliffs west of the lake: and on the outer (seaward) face of the plateau you will ascend Gleniff and climb to the cavern known (like many other spots in Ireland) as Dermot and Grania's Bed. And if you want a heathery walk over the high ground, climb one of the turf tracks which lead up, and cross from Glencar to Glenade or *vice versa*, or from either to Gleniff: but it is not easy to find your way exactly across the flat top except by com-

PLATE XIV

THE SWISS VALLEY, GLENCAR

pass and map, and you may have to skirt the cliff-edge for up to a mile before you find a grassy slope to descend: do not take any risks with the limestone cliffs, for the rock is splintery, and there are often perpendicular parts that you cannot see from above. Good roads pass through both Glencar and Glenade, leading from Sligo and Bundoran to Manorhamilton.

The actual coast of Sligo is uniformly low, in contrast to that of Donegal which adjoins on the north, and Mayo, which is Sligo's western neighbour. The stretch from Bundoran to Sligo Bay is a rather lonely and unknown region, save at Mullaghmore (*Mullach mór*, great summit), where a projecting knoll provides a sheltered nook with a little harbour and a couple of hotels. This is a choice spot, quite sheltered though the outer shore of the small promontory faces deep water and the open Atlantic. South of this there is much sand, with islets and rocky points—a pleasant place in summer, but bare and inhospitable in bad weather, as Captain Cuellar found when he was washed ashore here after the wreck of the Spanish Judge Advocate's ship at the time of the Armada (see p. 154). Right opposite to Mullaghmore, four miles out, lies Inismurray (*Inis Muireadhaigh*, the island of Muireadhach, who was first bishop of Killala in the eleventh century). It is a low islet a couple of hundred acres in area, much exposed to Atlantic storms; yet the place is full of early Christian antiquities, pointing to considerable importance in old days; and it still has a population numerous in relation to its size and agricultural possibilities, largely dependent on fishing for its livelihood. The fine cashel, or circular stone fort, is the oldest structure, being pre-Christian in date. Inside it are three bee-hive huts and three small early churches, of which the one known as *Tech Molaise*, St. Molaise's house, measuring only nine feet by eight, has remarkably thick walls sustaining a stone roof; also within the cashel are three altars; there are several pillar-stones, early inscribed slabs, holy wells, and so on. One of the altars, strangely enough, was till comparatively recently used for cursing, the medium being some curious stones, which were turned according to the ancient practice. On account of its open position, Inismurray is not always approachable even in summer; but with good weather it makes an interesting trip from Rosses Point or Mullaghmore. In its ocean setting, its group of primitive monuments forms an impressive picture.

CHAPTER VII

CONNEMARA AND THE HILLS OF MAYO

Now with the coming in of the spring the days will stretch a bit,
And after the feast of Brigid I shall hoist my flag and go,
For since the thought got into my head I can neither stand nor sit
Until I find myself in the middle of the County of Mayo.
JAMES STEPHENS (from the Irish of Raftery).

NOTE the accent on the last syllable of the last word: that is correct, for Mayo is *Muigh eó*, the Plain of the Yew-tree—one of the numerous place-names with *eó* or *ure* which testify to the former wide distribution of the Yew in Ireland, a special cause of its subsequent disappearance from many areas being its use as " palm " on Palm Sunday. This question of the pronunciation of Irish names is a puzzling one for the visitor who, misled by the fact that English is the common language of the Irish country-side, would pronounce place-names according to English standards: not realizing that in these names he is dealing not only with a different language, but with a language belonging to a group quite different from any of the main sources of the English tongue. Irish place-names are interesting, for they are mostly descriptive or commemorative, referring in many cases to some bygone feature or event; but their study is a difficult one, for the names are often now misspelled or mispronounced or corrupted in one way or another. I remember Dr. P. W. Joyce, author of the *Irish Names of Places*, when I asked him as to the meaning of what seemed a very simple Irish designation, replying that he would never venture to translate a place-name till he had heard it pronounced by the people of the locality, and even then—and he raised his hands in a way that meant much. So we need not be surprised to find that " Ballyshannon " (see p. 108) has nothing to do with either the common word " Bally " (*Baile*, a town) or with " Shannon ", and that " Silentia " does not refer to an absence of sound, but is corrupted from *Lios na Loingsigh*, the fort of the Lynches. But Joyce's own fascinating book, Father Hogan's *Onomasticon* and other sources are a mine of information, and help to keep us from floundering.

That little terminal syllable, which seems insignificant, is often vital, and must be fully recognized. Athy, for instance, has the accent on the second syllable, not the first, for it is *Áth-Í*, the ford of Ae, a Munster chieftain. Athenry is not At-henry, as one may hear it pronounced by visitors in the train on their first visit to Connemara, but Athen*ry*, *Áth-na-ríogh*, the ford of the kings. Clones is Clon-*es*, *Cluainn-Eóis*, Eos's meadow, and Thurles is Thur-*les*, *Dúr-les*, strong fort. Ardara is not Ar*d*ara, but Arda*ra*, *Árd-a'-raith*, the height of the rath. It is all difficult, and full of pitfalls even for those who know Irish, but Joyce and Hogan assist greatly.

The west coast of Ireland is a fascinating place from many points of view, as the extreme edge of a continental land-mass is sure to be. It is the farthest west—the *Ultima Thule*—of all Eurasia. Thither come strange silent messengers—floating seeds and so on—from tropical lands across the ocean. Out beyond the sunset are legendary islands—Hy Brasil and the rest—and the shoals that mark the grave of the " sunken land of Buss ". Along this wild coast staggered the ill-fated ships of the great Armada, many to meet their doom on the rocks of Clare or Kerry. And from south to north in the late spring of each year the greatest fish that swims the sea passes in leisurely migration, coming from the unknown and vanishing again into the unknown; nor can we yet be sure that stranger wonders of animal life may not be hidden in the deep waters that lie beyond the edge of the Continental Shelf—in

> the green hells of the sea,
> Where fallen skies and evil hues and eyeless creatures be.

And here also we find the people venturing forth into the roughest waters of the coasts of the British Islands in the frailest craft to be found within the same area. I feel that this paragraph will endure expansion.

First as to those who go down to the sea in ships. I must sing the praises of the *curach* or curragh, the canvas boat used everywhere along the western coast of Ireland for inshore fishing, lobster work, and as the usual means of communication in the island regions (Plate XV). Originally the covering was of hide; nowadays tarred canvas has replaced this. The framework is sometimes still made of rough hazel saplings, spaced a few inches apart; but light sawn slats like slating-laths are now often seen. The solid gunwale has thole-pins, on which the oars, with blades only three inches wide, are fixed. The bow rises high, like a pointed spoon; the stern is broad and square; and there is no keel at all, the boat being semi-circular in section. Each man—and there are one-man, two-man and three-man curraghs—wields two oars. If a novice attempts to row one of these boats, it merely spins round, even in the absence of wind, until he gets the hang of it: and he barks his knuckles in addition, since the oars overlap, and must be kept one above the other. But the extreme lightness of these curraghs and the raised bow make them extraordinarily seaworthy in the hands of the men of the west, who will put to sea in them when the crew of many a larger boat might hesitate. They dance over the waves like corks, with a motion which is surprisingly rapid. I remember landing with George Francis Fitzgerald from an egg-shell curragh on the great boulder-beach at Fisherstreet in Clare when the Atlantic waves were dashing over it incessantly: our men backed the boat so skilfully that we stepped ashore without even getting splashed. On Clare Island one day, when some heavier boats were anchored close in against the sand in the sheltered bay by the castle, a sudden violent squall came in from the east, raising a sea which threatened to drive them ashore and smash them to pieces. The islanders dashed out from the little harbour in curraghs, and through the breaking waves to the boats, which they towed out to safety. It looked a crazy and dare-devil performance, but to them it was all in the day's work. These boats are not left at anchor, but are brought ashore, overturned, and two or three men, according to the size of the curragh, carry them on their heads to some place of safety, a hollow well out of the wind. Such cavalcades, looking surprisingly like crawling black beetles, are one of the most characteristic sights of the west coast. The curragh serves as a tent also, for the lobster-men often spend a night on houseless islands, sleeping comfortably under the overturned boat whatever the weather may be. One of these temporary campings saved T. J. Westropp, George Fogerty, A. W. Stelfox and myself from spending an uncomfortable night on Caher Island near Inishturk in 1910. We were working in connection with the Clare Island Survey; the first two had come to inspect the cashel, early church, crosses and stations on that lonely and interesting islet, Stelfox and I to collect animals and plants. In the evening the wind and sea suddenly got up; our boat after many attempts failed to get alongside the rock at the landing-place; some of the party could not swim, or we might have reached her that way. Rain was clearly not far away, and the wind increased as we wandered round the little island, looking before it got dark for a sheltered corner for sleeping. We found one—already occupied. The sight of an overturned curragh and a face peeping in amazement from underneath it was as welcome as it was unexpected: in a few moments two lobster-men had their boat in the water, and one by one we were safely ferried to our tossing hooker.

Its very liveliness makes the curragh a delightful boat to be in. Returning once from Clare Island it fell dead calm. There had been a blow, and the sea was still high. We were towing a curragh astern, and I got into it and rowed ahead to Roonah Quay. To be alone on those big rollers in that dancing cockle-shell was singularly exhilarating, with the high mountains around rising and vanishing, to be replaced by green mountains of sparkling water as the curragh sank into each trough, for she responded like a live thing to every ripple that touched her canvas sides.

PLATE XV

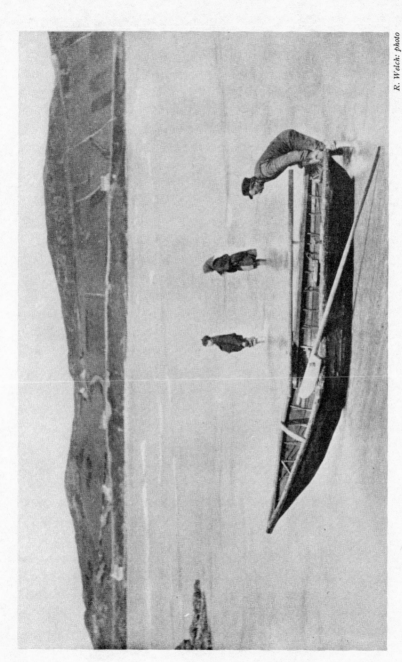

R. Welch: photo

A TWO-MAN CURRAGH, CO. DONEGAL

As to the Basking Shark, which is in fact the largest fish in the world. It ought from its relationship and size to be the most terrible monster in the sea: but actually it is one of the most harmless—thirty to forty feet in length, big enough to devour a buffalo, and yet living not on its fellow-fish of many kinds, like most sharks, nor even on the larger invertebrates that haunt the middle waters and the bottom, but on tiny copepods—cousins of the crabs—that swarm in or near the surface. These last are seasonal creatures, and reach a maximum off the west coast during May; the Basking Sharks follow this to us unexpected food-supply, moving slowly northward to vanish again into the ocean—for their further movements are still unknown. Huge lazy creatures, they loll on or about the surface, without fear and without guile, showing above water their high dorsal fin as they open their shark jaws and scoop in ten thousand copepods at a gulp. Before the days of petroleum, the islanders of the west coast hunted them for the sake of the oil contained in the liver, which furnished many a house with its only source of light—a practice resurrected by Robert Flaherty to add picturesqueness to his film *Man of Aran* a few years ago, but belonging in fact to a bygone time. Now peace reigns again, and the Basking Sharks drift along the coast in the bright spring sunlight, doing no hurt and receiving none. But occasionally one of them blunders into trouble. A few years ago I watched from where I sat in a hotel on the cliff at Ballycottin a great commotion in the sea close below. A Basking Shark had blundered into a salmon net, and got himself thoroughly tangled up. The fishermen had tried for hours to shoot him, but bullets did not seem to incommode him in the least, and there he wallowed in a rather leisurely way, showing sometimes a huge fin, sometimes a great tail. In the end he got away, leaving behind a net so torn as to be beyond repair.

The tropical jetsam that is not infrequent on the west coast is interesting. It consists mainly of seeds of large beans, the biggest being no less than two and a half inches in diameter. The origin of these was long a mystery, and some early observers believed that

There is now a fishery for the Basking Shark on Achill Island where the fish are captured in nets and killed with lances. The liver oil is exported and the flesh is used for fishmeal. C.M.

they were a product of the sea. It was Sir Hans Sloane, the County Down man who founded the British Museum, and was well acquainted with the flora of Jamaica, who in 1696 identified three of the beans as belonging to plants which grew in that island; later several other similar large seeds were recognized as also belonging to West Indian species. Another question that vexed the minds of botanists was whether these seeds had floated right across the Atlantic, or had been brought by sailors (for they are handsome and striking things); the ultimate decision was wholly in favour of natural transportation. Many facts support this view: for instance, the similar washing-up on the west coast of various oceanic or tropical animals—the "Blue Snail" (*Ianthina*), *Velella*, *Salpa*, and the "Portuguese Man-of-War" (*Physalia*); also the fact that two seeds of *Entada*, the largest of the "sea-beans", have been found sub-fossil in a low-lying bog in south Sweden. The seeds that come to us, carried down into the Gulf of Mexico by rivers, are all highly buoyant and hard-coated; experiments have shown that not only can they float in water for a year or more, but that some are actually still capable of germination on reaching the shores of Europe. Sir Joseph Banks, who went round the world with Captain Cook, actually identified one of the drift-seeds as belonging to *Guilandina Bonduc* from a plant grown from a bean which was washed ashore in the west of Ireland. In all, the seeds of eight West Indian plants have been identified from the Irish coast;[1] six of them belong to the Pea family, one to the Convolvulus family, and one to a less familiar group. Other seeds, and also stems and leaves, as of palms and bamboos, are known to have been occasionally washed ashore, but they have not been preserved or identified; and no doubt smaller and less conspicuous seeds await discovery.

Jetsam of a different kind came ashore on the Irish coast in 1588, when remnants of the Spanish Armada staggered southward, having rounded Scotland in an endeavour to regain their home ports in

[1] N. Colgan, "On the Occurrence of Tropical Drift Seeds on the Irish Atlantic Coasts", *Proc. Roy. Irish Acad.*, vol. xxxv., sect. B, pp. 29-54, plate 10.

Plate XVI

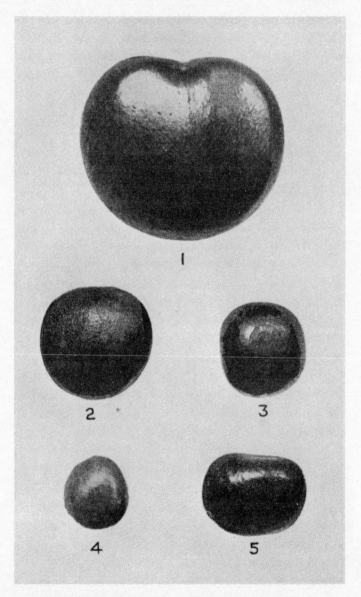

Tropical Drift Seeds from the Irish Atlantic Coast

1. *Entada scandens*, Donegal.   2. *Mucuna ?altissima*, Kerry.   3. *Ipomœa tuberosa*, Donegal.   4. *Guilandina Bonducella*, Donegal.   5. *Dioclea reflexa*, Donegal. All slightly reduced

Spain. The coasts of Scotland, Ireland and England all saw ship-wreck and disaster at that time. As regards Ireland, some vivid accounts of adventure are extant. The narrative of Captain Cuellar, translated and published several times,[1] is well known: how the writer, Don Francesco Cuellar, commanding the *San Pedro*, a galleon of twenty-four guns, was placed under open arrest, ap-parently owing to misunderstanding, during the fight with the English fleet, and, narrowly escaping hanging, was transferred to the larger vessel of the Judge Advocate; how this ship was wrecked along with two others on Streedagh strand in Sligo, with appalling loss of life, Cuellar being one of the few survivors; how he reached the little abbey of Staad (of which remains may still be seen) to find it recently sacked and burned by the English, and seven Spaniards hanging there to show the welcome that awaited him if captured; how after many adventures he found friendly people in Glenade, and subsequently obtained refuge with the chief MacClancy in his castle of Rossclogher on an islet on the south shore of Lough Melvin (where its ruins still stand); how MacClancy, hearing that the English under Lord Deputy Fitzwilliam were about to descend on him, withdrew with his people to the hills, leaving Cuellar and a small party of other Spanish refugees to defend the castle and their lives as best they could; how the castle was unsuccessfully besieged for seventeen days by the English, who then withdrew; how MacClancy returned and as a reward offered Cuellar the hand of his daughter (had he accepted, there might have been Cuellars still in Leitrim); how, anxious to get home, Cuellar, with four Spanish soldiers, marched venturously across northern Ireland to Dunluce, where he was welcomed by Sir James MacDonnell; how he journeyed thence to Scotland, and eventually reached Antwerp and got back to Spain. It is a wonderful tale, as exciting and romantic as any to be found in the pages of fiction, and the refugee's description of the country and of the people whom he met are of high interest. A less-known

[1] For instance, by Hugh Allingham and Robert Crawford in 1897, with copious geographical notes.

account of Armada adventures in Ireland, by sea rather than by land, was published some years ago by W. S. Green.[1]   The author is Don Marcos de Aramburu, of the *San Juan Bautista*, twenty-four guns. His was another of the many ships scattered by gales along the west coast of Scotland after the break-up of the Spanish fleet.   From the neighbourhood of Rockall (see p. 44 *ante*) the vessel made land-fall at the Blaskets (p. 380), after sighting and losing in the incessant gales several other ships.   She staggered in through those dangerous rocks and found anchorage in Blasket Sound, between the Great Blasket and Inishbeg, in a pitiable condition.   English soldiers are on the shore, and they cannot get water or help.   The *Santa Maria de la Rosa* comes in, her sails blown to ribbons.   The single anchor left to her does not hold; she drifts, and in sight of her comrade ship goes down with all on board (but according to the English State Papers one escaped death—the pilot's son, who was captured and sent with other Spanish prisoners to Dingle).   Other wounded ships straggle in. The *San Juan Bautista* tries to get away to sea, but gales, blowing now from one direction, now another, keep her around this death-trap, till at length she gets clear, only to be driven hither and thither by terrible storms; but at last she rounds Dursey Head, better weather enables the crew to repair damage and to get some rest, and finally she reaches home.   The ill-fated *Santa Maria*, it would appear, had on board 50,000 ducats in gold and an equal amount in silver, besides a quantity of gold and silver plate.   Some ninety years ago, Mr Green adds, Blasket islanders fished up near the place where she went down a small brass cannon with a coat of arms upon it bearing the device of an uprooted tree; this is now preserved in Clonskeagh Castle near Dublin, the sole remaining relic of the tragedy.

I watched that dangerous place in a harmless summer storm, when the Atlantic combers were breaking heavily on the sunken reefs, and leaping a hundred feet up the island-cliffs; it was tragic to think of those helpless unhandy vessels, with sails and anchors mostly lost,

[1] W. S. Green, " Armada Ships on the Kerry Coast ", *Proc. Roy. Irish Acad.*, vol. xxvii., sect. C, pp. 263-269, plate 15.

their crews worn out, fighting gale after gale in this fatal spot, but still clinging to the hope of a safe return to the land of their birth.

Lastly, a word as to Hy Brasil. Ever since the time of Plato there have been reports and legends concerning unknown lands out in the western ocean; writers of various periods have not failed to make the most of them, and islands have grown even into continents, now sunk beneath the waves. Geologists and zoologists, too, have pointed out features which led them to suppose that " land-bridges " had once existed joining Europe and America. Wegener's now famous hypothesis taught that the American continent once lay alongside and in contact with Europe and Africa, from which it had drifted west into its present position. There is an extensive literature dealing with these matters, with which we are not at present concerned. But Hy Brasil, along with St. Brendan's Isle and Buss, are our own particular property, islands lying only a few hundred miles west of Ireland and intimately concerned with the maps of the early geographers and with Irish legend. More than that, Brasil even appears on maps of comparatively recent date. On a MS. map of about the middle of the seventeenth century, of unknown authorship, excellently and correctly drawn, which was unearthed by Dr. William Frazer, Hy Brasil and Rockall (see p. 44) are both shown—Rockall in its correct place, Hy Brasil to the south of it and about 300 miles west of Galway. A Dutch map of about 1655 shows a large island at Rockall, and Brasil in about the position of the Porcupine Bank. Brasil indeed survives well into the nineteenth century. In J. Purdy's *General Chart of the Atlantic*, " corrected to 1830 ", " Brasil Rock " is plainly marked in lat. 51° 10' north, long. 15° 50' west— much the same place as in the last. It is important to note that Brasil mostly appears in the vicinity of the Porcupine Bank, which is an isolated shoal where the ocean bottom abruptly rises to only eighty-two fathoms below the surface. Is it possible that within the period of ocean navigation there actually was an island there? Probably there *once* was one, and presumably it was a volcanic island, to judge from the prevalence of gabbro among the many rock-specimens that have been dredged up. The shallow-water shells dredged at the Porcupine Bank and at Rockall indicate islands with shoal water around them in comparatively recent times. But the fact that Rockall appears to be no smaller now than when it was first accurately observed about a hundred years ago makes it difficult to believe that in the few centuries that have elapsed since man first ventured forth into the Atlantic even a small island could have completely disappeared from the Porcupine Bank, and its very roots removed by wave-action to a depth of 500 feet. Of other conceivable causes—a recent sinking of the sea-floor, for instance—there is no direct evidence: so Hy Brasil, St. Brendan's Isle, Tir-na-n'Og, and all Maildun's wonderful islands, must remain in the sea of imagination and of legend—where possibly they will last as long as if they were real islands exposed to the tempestuous billows of the North Atlantic. With the aid of mirage alone can they be seen in these degenerate days: and under certain atmospheric conditions a fairy isle may still be observed off the West Coast. " I myself", says T. J. Westropp, " have seen the illusion some three times in my boyhood, and even made a rough coloured sketch after the last event, in the summer of 1872. It was a clear evening, with a fine golden sunset, when, just as the sun went down, a dark island suddenly appeared far out to sea, but not on the horizon. It had two hills, one wooded; between these, from a low plain, rose towers and curls of smoke. My mother, brother, Ralph Hugh Westropp, and several friends saw it at the same time." [1] It and the rest are gone, but Rockall is still actually with us for a little while, a speck in the wide ocean where once a considerable island certainly existed, to remind us that " There rolls the deep where grew the tree ".

It is not only in regard to mythical islands that the West Coast is rich in legend. In every domain one can still elicit from the people interesting folk-lore. For instance, while collecting the Irish names

[1] T. J. Westropp, " Brasil and the legendary Islands of the North Atlantic ", *Proc. Roy. Irish Acad.*, vol. xxx., sect. C, pp. 223-260, plates 20-22. 1912.

of plants and animals on Clare Island, Colgan[1] took down from the lips of the islanders some very curious tales relating to these, of which I transcribe the following both for its own sake and because his exact rendering of the boatman's words provide a sample of the picturesque Irish-English of the west (though the characteristic western pronunciation is not rendered phonetically). The legend refers to the common small marine univalve *Gibbula umbilicata*, called in Irish *Faochán Mhuire* (the Virgin Mary's Fweecawn), and the origin of its operculum.

"One time the Jews were chasing St. Patrick all over Ireland to kill him, and at last they caught him and buried him deep in the ground. And then the Jews went off with themselves and came into a house to get their supper. It was a cock they put into the pot, and, as they were sitting there waiting for it to be cooked, says one of them: 'I don't know, is there any fear of the saint rising up again on us?' And another of them made answer with a laugh—' Ay is there, just as much fear as there is of that cock there in the pot rising up and crowing twelve times'. And lo and behold you, the words were hardly out of his mouth when up the cock rose in the pot and let twelve crows out of him. And when the Jews heard that, it was real mad they got, for well they knew by it that the saint had made a miracle and rose up on them. So away they went to hunt for him; and the first thing they met on the road was the *Primpeallán* (the Dung Beetle, *Geotrupes stercorarius*), and says the Jews to the *Primpeallán*, ' Did you see Patrick passing this way? ' ' Ay did I,' says the *Primpeallán*, ' I seen him *indé*,' meaning yesterday, for you see the *Primpeallán* wasn't wishing to give the Jews any help at all, at all. So away they went; and the next thing they met was the *Ciaróg* (the black beetle *Calathus cysteloides*), and he walking along the road: and they up and axed the *Ciaróg* if he seen the saint. And the *Ciaróg* made answer that he seen the saint sure enough; and that it's hiding himself behind a *Faochán* he was that was creeping over the rocks and putting a cap on the *Faochán* when it drew back into its shell

[1] See *Proc. Roy. Irish Acad.*, vol. xxxi., part 4. 1911.

with him. So off them Jews set hot foot down to the seashore to hunt for that *Faochán* with the saint in it and the cap on it. But it's well St. Patrick knew what they were after; so what does he do but put a cap on every one of them *Faocháns*, and so sorrow bit of them Jews could ever find the one he was hid in. And that's how them *Faocháns* came to have caps (*i.e.* opercula) on them, for ne'er a one of them had a cap on it before that."

Connemara or Cunnamara (which I once saw rhymed with camera in a poem in a local English journal, the accent being put on the second syllable) is *Conmaicne mara*, the Conmaicne (*i.e.* descendants of Conmac) by the sea: Conmac's descendants formed several colonies, and the sea-side one in West Galway was distinguished from the others in this way.

There are two Connemaras. South of the Galway–Clifden road a vast bog-mantled granite moorland extends, undulating or flattish, sown with innumerable brown lakelets, and with a low indented coast-line which is a mere labyrinth of land and sea. Immediately north of the same road, from Oughterard westward, the tall bare quartzite domes and cones of Maam Turk and the Twelve Bens (one should avoid the meaningless corruption " Pins ") rise steeply, and other mountains formed of schist and gneiss continue the highlands northward to the beautiful fiord of Killery, where Mayo replaces Galway. Both regions of Connemara have their charm, but I am not sure that of the two I do not prefer the great brown bogland to the grey naked hills. There is something infinitely satisfying about these wide, treeless, houseless undulations, clothed with heather and Purple Moor-grass, so filled with lakes and so intersected by arms of the Atlantic that water entangled in a network of land becomes almost imperceptibly land entangled in a network of water, and only the presence or absence of the mauve Lobelia or of brown seaweed tells whether one is on a lake-shore or on a seashore. On a day of bright sky, when the hills are of that intoxicating misty blue that belongs especially to the west, the bogland is a lovely far-reaching expanse of purple and rich brown: and the lakelets take on the quite indescribable colour that comes from clear sky reflected in bog-water, while the sea-inlets glow with an intense but rather greener blue. On such a day the wanderer will thank his lucky star that it has brought him to Connemara.

There are not over-many places where one can stay in this strange, lonely region—Roundstone, Cashel (*Caiseal*, stone fort), and Carna in the middle part, Oughterard (*Uachtar árd*, high upper land) on the eastern edge, Clifden on the western, and here and there a hospitable single house. The fine hotel with which the railway company replaced the old hostelry at Recess, in the centre of the loveliest scenery, was burned down during the troubled times of twenty years ago, and accommodation there is very limited now. Of the places named, I have no hesitation in awarding the palm to Roundstone, though it is not the goal of the majority of pilgrims to Connemara; many make for Cashel or Carna, intent on fishing or shooting. At Roundstone, thank goodness, the killing of animals is a subordinate pursuit—not that one does not appreciate fully the delicious lobsters and fresh mackerel and trout which turn up with a frequency which their excellence makes never monotonous. The street of white-washed two-storeyed houses which constitutes Roundstone lies along the edge of a deep, narrow, sheltered inlet, widening a mile or so down into the open ocean. In the opposite direction, looking northward up the village street and across the little harbour, with its " hookers " and " pookauns " alongside the quay, the peaks of the Twelve Bens, rising eight miles away, form an arresting and ever-changing spectacle. Ever-changing: that is the peculiar quality—and the best, for most people, but for the artist the most tantalizing—of this Connemara scenery. A painter friend of mine, accustomed to southern England, returned to London from Roundstone in a state of mixed exaltation and exasperation that was quite in keeping with Connemara atmosphere and climate and scenery. The confounded thing—whatever he tried to sketch— would not " stay put ": but like a chameleon or a kaleidoscope it changed incessantly, reducing him to impotence—not that he did not return with many delightful studies of sea and bog and hill.

Immediately behind the village—to the west, that is—a dark rocky serrated ridge, Urrisbeg, rises to nearly 1000 feet, and provides much protection from the ocean winds. A marked change of colour, especially noticeable from the south, shows where the pale granite of the low grounds is replaced by the rugged faulted dyke-sown gabbro which makes up the mass of the hill, and which contrasts in its dark colour with the grey of the quartzite mountains to the northward. From its summit we may obtain what is quite one of the most remarkable prospects in Ireland. For, stretching westward from Urrisbeg away to Clifden, there extends a vast flattish bogland so strewn with little lakes that it appears half land, half water—not an archipelago, but an archigeo (what a word!—my own invention too). The lakes all lie in rock-basins, and the peat which stretches between rests directly on the granite. Only in the Outer Hebrides is there, in Great Britain, any parallel to so strange an area. But the view from Urrisbeg yields much more. Northward a sea of mountains extends. At the extreme western end, we note far away the great hill of Croaghaun on Achill Island, and the jagged outline of Achill Head below it. We see Clare Island, Inishturk, Inishbofin, while to the right the mountains continue— the Nephin Beg group, the high shoulder of Mweelrea, and then the nearer ranges of the Twelve Bens and Maam Turk stretching to Oughterard. Eastward all is undulating bogland and tessellated coast-line, where Iar Connacht fades in the distance towards Galway; and southward lies a vast expanse of ocean, across which, on a clear day, the high ridge of Brandon in Kerry rises like a grey cloud. To the south-east we see the long ridges of the Aran Islands, and beyond them, the Cliffs of Moher make a fine background. Directly below us are the lovely shining sands of Dog's Bay (abominable corruption of a beautiful Irish place-name, of which more anon).

That great bogland behind Urrisbeg recalls a quaint scene on a very wet day in August, 1935. A number of botanists had foregathered at Roundstone, and the particular occasion was a kind of symposium on bogs, held in the middle of one of the wettest of them. There were A. G. Tansley from Oxford, H. E. Godwin from Cambridge, Hugo Osvald from Stockholm, Knud Jessen and H. Jonassen from Copenhagen, G. F. Mitchell from Dublin, Margaret Dunlop from Manchester. We stood in a ring in that shelterless expanse while discussion raged on the application of the terms soligenous, topogenous and ombrogenous; the rain and wind, like the discussion, waxed in intensity, and under the unusual superincumbent weight, whether of mere flesh and bone or of intellect, the floating surface of the bog slowly sank till we were all half-way up to our knees in water. The only pause in the flow of argument was when Jessen or Osvald, in an endeavour to solve the question of the origin of the peat, would chew some of the mud brought up by the boring tool from the bottom of the bog, to test the presence or absence of gritty material in the vegetable mass. But out of such occasions does knowledge come, and I think that that aqueous discussion has borne and will bear fruit. For the bogs and what they can teach us of the past history of our country are yet to a great extent a sealed book, though they will not remain so much longer. It is now many years since in my pet subject of plant distribution I found progress held up owing to absence of knowledge of the history of our flora: which history, or at least that fragment of it which we can hope ever to elucidate, lies buried in and under our bogs and other superficial deposits. More recently, finding that in the domain of archaeology Dr. Mahr was similarly handicapped, I joined forces with him. We persuaded Knud Jessen, a foremost worker in Glacial and post-Glacial floras, to undertake researches in Ireland: a strong committee was formed, the Government and various learned institutions gave grants of money, and for two seasons Jessen dug and explored in many parts of the country, and also trained Irish workers to continue the investigations which he initiated. Results are only just beginning to appear, but the researches already carried out, when published, will cast a flood of light on the history of both our fauna and flora, on Irish archaeology, and on cognate subjects.[1]

Dog's Bay (Plate XVII) is one of the greatest attractions that Roundstone offers. A narrow mile-long granite island set half a mile off shore has got joined to the mainland by a sand-spit, which forms two curving bays—Dog's Bay and Gorteen Bay—set back to back, and filled with the clearest of Atlantic water. The sand, excessively white, is in itself remarkable, for it is formed not of quartz grains, as is usual, but of shells—mostly the tiny perfect tests of Foraminifera (of which no less than 124 species and varieties have been found here), the rest being the comminuted shells of the more familiar Mollusca. To lie down on one's face on the beach and examine this sand with a strong lens is a revelation to those un-acquainted with the Foraminifera, for their almost microscopic shells are of great beauty and display remarkable variety of design. Some are curled spirally, some appear plaited, some are shaped like a lemonade bottle, some are spherical, some flat, many most delicately sculptured. A sample brought home and examined under a microscope shows an astonishing range of beautiful forms, which these tiny creatures—mere specks of translucent jelly—have evolved in their protective covering (Fig. 4). W. B. Carpenter, one of the leading authorities on the group, wrote of them: " There is nothing more wonderful in nature than the building up of these elaborate and symmetrical structures by mere jelly-specks, presenting no traces whatever of that definite organization which we are accus-tomed to regard as necessary to the manifestations of conscious life. . . . The tests (shells) they construct, when highly magnified, bear comparison with the most skilful masonry of man. From the same sandy bottom one species picks up the coarsest quartz-grains, unites them together with a ferruginous cement, and thus constructs a flask-shaped test, having a short neck and a single large orifice. Another picks up the finer grains, and puts them together with the

[1] See *Irish Naturalists' Journal*, vol. v., no. 6, November 1934 (Quaternary Research Number).

Dr. Jessen's work was published by the Royal Irish Academy in 1949: *Studies in Late Quaternary Deposits and Flora-History of Ireland.* C.M.

PLATE XVII

R. Welch: photo

DOG'S BAY AND URRISBEG, CONNEMARA

same cement into perfectly spherical tests of the most extraordinary finish, perforated with numerous small pores disposed at pretty regular intervals." Some go indeed still further in the choice of materials: one, for instance, selects needle-shaped crystals of a mineral by no means abundant on the sea-floor, and will use nothing else. A large number use no ready-made substances at all, but secrete limy material present in solution in sea-water, and out of this build up beautiful and amazing symmetrical shells as clear as glass. The microscopic blob of jelly which constitutes the body is not entirely enclosed, but protrudes from the end of the test, or through the minute pores, as wide-spreading and anastomosing threads (pseudopodia), by means of which the creatures catch their food—minute particles of organic matter. The Foraminifera can be separated into genera and species only by their shells, which present an extraordinary range of form: how the particle of jelly knows its own identity, and exactly what kind of shell it is expected to build up, is a mystery of mysteries. Miss Barnes has figured (Fig. 4) a few of these tiny shells, from the rich collections made by Heron-Allen and Earland in connection with the Clare Island Survey. Their elaborate report, dealing with 300 species and varieties, of which a dozen species were new to science, and more than twice that number new to the British Isles, forms a notable contribution to the study of the Foraminifera.[1]

I had the privilege of an early introduction to these fascinating minimosities (if I may coin the word) because from childhood I had known Joseph Wright, that cheerful Cork quaker, who for years had made a special study of the group, and published many papers dealing with it. He loved to get out his old-fashioned microscope and show and discuss his latest finds—and marvellous things some of them were. Many an evening I spent in his house in Alfred Street, Belfast, listening spell-bound to his demonstrations, and his yarns about dredging and about his finding of Foraminifera in the Boulder-clay high on the Belfast hills; and I am glad that I was with

[1] *Proc. Roy. Irish Acad.*, vol. xxxi., part 64. 1913.

him when he achieved one of his great ambitions by dredging up the Globigerina ooze of the ocean depths (see p. 342). A more kindly enthusiast than Joseph Wright never lived. I remember one occasion on which his self-restraint and benevolence were put to a severe test. In a dredging sent to him from—I forget where—he

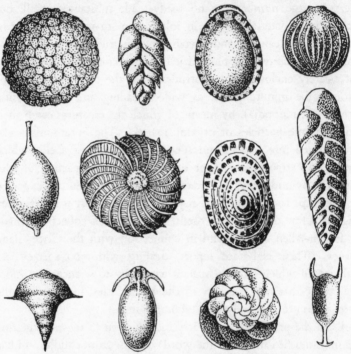

FIG. 4.—FORAMINIFERA FROM THE CLARE ISLAND AREA
Magnified 30 to 130 times

discovered a single specimen of remarkable novelty—the type of a new genus of Foraminifera. He mounted it temporarily on a slide —neglecting to put on a protective cover-glass, for he was a careless manipulator—and at a conversazione of the Belfast Naturalists' Field Club held immediately afterwards he showed it to J. H. Davies and others. Davies was a fellow-quaker, an ardent bryologist, a man of singular courtesy, a neat and skilful microscopical expert. Seeing that the slide was dusty, and not noticing the absence of the usual cover-glass, Davies leisurely produced a silk pocket-handkerchief and, before the horrified eyes of the owner, in a moment ground the specimen to powder! But Wright's self-restraint stood even that test. He gasped, and his face went white; but he uttered no word of reproach. " It couldn't be helped "—and that was an end of it.

The stretch of blown sand that lies between the before-mentioned two curving bays is an ancient habitation of man. The numerous stones which are scattered about are all broken, and reddened or blackened by fire. We see the gatherings of larger stones which once formed huts or shelters; and where the wind has not yet scattered them there are solid deposits of limpets, periwinkles and dog whelks (*Purpura*), showing that shell-fish was the attraction which brought the Bronze Age folk here. The distribution of the shells calls for notice. In some places the layers are purely of limpets, in others of periwinkles, in others of these two combined: but the deposits of dog whelks are separate, and while the other shells are perfect, the *Purpura* shells are always broken for the extraction of the animal (which yields a purple dye, and may have been used for this purpose, not as food). In spite of the great amount of shells and of burnt stones, little else has been found—bones of horse, cow and sheep, scraps of charcoal, a few bronze pins, and some hammers and knives of stone: perhaps the place was used only as a summer camp, or in times of stress alone. Similar settlements occur near Slyne Head to the westward, where the remains include the circular foundations of a stone hut; and on many sands round the Irish coast the story is repeated.

As has been hinted already, some of the picturesque Irish place-names down here have had a severe mauling. Roundstone is *Clogh róinte* (pronounced roanty) the seal's rock: and the incorrect translation, due to a similarity of sound, is falsely confirmed by a Glacial boulder on the shore which has been called " The Round Stone ", and is so marked on the Ordnance Map—a crystallizing of error comparable to the phoenix erected in the " Phoenix " Park by a viceroy with more zeal than knowledge. Nor is the " Round Stone " even remarkably round—but it stands up, a useful landmark if you approach *Clogh róinte* by water, and makes a convenient eyrie for the Great Black-backed Gull. Dog's Bay is really *Port na feadóige*, the plover's shore, a delightful name, with no canine association at all. Clifden is *Clochán*, the bee-hive-shaped house, commemorating the primitive stone dwellings still to be seen, especially in Kerry. Urrisbeg (*Iorras beg*, little promontory) and Cregduff Lough (*Loch na creige duibhe*, the lake of the black rocky land) have fortunately escaped mutilation.

Irish place-names are of special interest because they are so often descriptive of the spots to which they are applied, or commemorative of some event which long ago happened there. But since, as I have pointed out, Irish is a language belonging to a group different from any of those which have given us the English tongue—Latin, German, French—one can seldom, in the absence of knowledge of Irish, make even a guess at their meaning. Besides, as I have said already, they have often got so corrupted that in their present dress even an Irish scholar is puzzled. I have always reproached myself for the mental laziness that prevented my getting a working knowledge of that distressful language (for it certainly *is* difficult, and I have no gift of tongues), if even for the sake of place-names alone. The running of the words together into one, as for instance on the maps of the Ordnance Survey, certainly often makes the longer names look formidable, but spaced out they are more understandable, and translated they are often charming, or suggestive—Cahernashilleevy (*cáthair na silinidhe*), the caher (stone fort) of the cherries; Gortnagusetaul (*Gort na giustala*), the field of the athletics; Cnockannamaurnach (*Cnocán na mbáirneach*), the little hill of the limpets; Attinaskollia (*Áit tighe na scoile*), the site of the school-house; Drummeennavaddoge (*Druimín na bhfeadóg*), the little ridge of the plovers; and so on—so when we meet with even larger ones like Fiddauncrindarree or Shannaghcloontippen or Cuskeannatinny, we need not blanch, but turn with hope to Joyce's *Irish Names of Places*.

PLATE XVIII

R. Welch: *photo*

THE PIPEWORT, *Eriocaulon septangulare*

Roundstone is a kind of botanical Mecca, for in its vicinity, and especially about Craiggamore a few miles to the northward, may be found a whole galaxy of the peculiar Pyrenean and American plants whose presence makes the flora of western Ireland so interesting (see p. 360).   The Mediterranean Heath (so-called, though it does not grow by the Mediterranean), Mackay's Heath, and the beautiful St. Dabeoc's Heath with purple bells half an inch long, as well as some rare hybrids and varieties of these, are here.   The lakelets are full of the curious Pipewort (Plate XVIII), and another American water-plant, the Slender Naiad, is near Roundstone and Slyne Head. It has recently been found, too, that the presence of calcareous sea-sands has allowed some of the peculiar plants of the limestone pave-ments of Clare and East Galway to spread to this remote region— notably the Close-flowered Orchis, which hails from the Mediter-ranean, and the Salzburg Eyebright, on the Continent a plant of the mountains.   To many people, the unexpected abundance about Roundstone of a number of commoner wild-flowers will appeal more than the presence of these rarities.   Walk down from the village to Dog's Bay in August—the time when Roundstone is most frequently visited—and you will be astonished at the profusion of blossom which occupies the little boggy fields set among bosses of glaciated pinkish granite—masses of white Ox-eye Daisies, of yellow Water Ragwort, and sheets of Purple Loosestrife and Marsh Wound-wort; while on drier or more exposed ground rounded bushes of the smaller Furze, *Ulex Gallii*, covered with golden blossom, are almost overwhelmed by the purple profusion of Heather and of St. Dabeoc's Heath (Plate XIX).   Down by the sea, where the limy sand, scattered far by winter gales, has turned the heath vegetation into short green grass, the sward is gay with Hare-bells and Squinancywort, and the air fragrant with the delicious scent of the Autumnal Lady's-tresses.

I have dwelt long on Roundstone, because there is at that spot a kind of concentration of interests, as well as a delightful combination of hill and moor, sea and lake, rock and sand: but let not the reader think that other places in the great bogland area may not appeal to him as much, or perhaps more.   Thus, Cashel nestles with a thousand-foot hill rising directly behind it, the head of Bertraghboy Bay immediately in front, and on either hand miles of bog and rock, with lakelets and sea-inlets.   Carna, further south, has no impending hill, but otherwise has similar and equal attractions.   Oughterard, far to the east, lies on the boundary of the limestone with its characteristic grass and tillage and bare grey pavements, and the older Connemara rocks with their accompanying peat and heather.   It is the proximity of Lough Corrib and its excellent fishing that provides the principal attraction of Oughterard.

Clifden forms the western outpost of Connemara, sheltered from the open Atlantic by rising ground about Ardbear.   Do not be disheartened if, approaching it by the Roundstone road, you are confronted with the shabby backs of a row of tall houses on the top of an untidy slope.   In Irish country towns the backs of the houses are seldom presentable, and Clifden is no exception; it is its misfortune that the Roundstone road takes it in the rear.   It is a pleasant, quiet little place, and an excellent centre for motorist or cyclist. You can penetrate westward by Aughrus or Cleggan or Rinvyle over increasingly storm-swept stony moor till there is no land between you and Labrador.   Or you can go south, towards Slyne Head; or more probably you will choose to enter the great mountain region that begins at once on the north-east—of which more immediately.   But before leaving Clifden, the naturalist in me compels mention of an unusual feature to be seen well at Mannin Bay, close by.   This is the " Coral Strand " so called.   Examine the uniform cream-coloured coarsely granular material that here forms a piled-up beach; it is certainly very coral-like, but despite its chalky branching nature, it is in reality not an animal product, like all true corals, but vegetable—a novel kind of seaweed which, instead of building up a filamentous or leathery body, constructs one of lime derived from the water in which it lives.   High up on the beach the material is broken into small fragments, but try down near low-water mark and you will find the complete organism, a much-

PLATE XIX

St. Dabeoc's Heath growing through Dwarf Gorse, Connemara

branched rounded mass a few inches across (Fig. 5). These strange
seaweeds live lying on the bottom in a few fathoms of water, and
the quantity which is thrown ashore shows what large colonies must
exist under the clear waters of western Connemara.

North of Clifden a wild and deeply indented coast-line leads by
Cleggan (*Claigeann*, a skull, hence a round bare hill), Ballynakill
(town of the church or wood), Letterfrack (*Leiter bhreac*, speckled
hillside) and Rinvyle towards Killary Harbour. There are deep
bays and rough head-
lands, sands and heath and
lake—a very diversified
area. A small and remote
lakelet at Renvyle has
lately been the scene of a
rather astonishing botanical discovery. *Hydrilla
verticillata* (Fig. 6)—I
don't think it has any
English name—is a little
water-plant allied to the
well-known Canadian

FIG. 5.—LITHOTHAMNION, A CALCAREOUS SEAWEED
Three-quarters natural size

Water-weed, *Elodea* (otherwise *Anacharis*), whose phenomenal spread
in rivers and canals caused something approaching a panic in England
less than a century ago. *Hydrilla* is mainly a south Asiatic plant,
occurring also in Australia, Madagascar, and east central Africa. In
Europe it was known only from Russia and Pomerania until recently,
when it was discovered growing in Esthwaite Water in Cumberland, accompanied by the Slender Naiad (likewise previously unknown in Britain, though it occurs in Ireland) and other water-
plants. In September, 1935, W. H. Pearson, one of the discoverers
of *Hydrilla* in England, happened to visit Renvyle, and found the plant
in some abundance in the little lake in this remote corner of Ireland.
Some doubt had been expressed, in view of its very discontinuous
range, as to whether the plant was truly native in Cumberland;

but no such doubt can attach to this remote Irish lakelet, and its occurrence there strengthens the case for its being indigenous also in England.

The mountains which rise north of the Oughterard–Clifden line form an almost continuous mass stretching away to Westport and Clew Bay, but for convenience we may separate those lying in Connemara (County Galway) from those which rise north of the fiord of Killary Harbour, in County Mayo. The Connemara hills form two imposing groups, the Twelve Bens (from which the Benchoona group is separated by the lovely pass of Kylemore, with its woods and lakes), and the Maam Turk range, cut off from the Twelve Bens by a broad bog-filled valley with island-studded lakes famous for their salmon-fishing. The Twelve Bens (anciently *Beanna Beóla*, the peaks of Beola) form a compact group of steep bare quartzite mountains of somewhat uniform height (2000-2400 feet). The intractable rock of which they are composed yields very little soil, and the slopes are too steep for the formation of peat; consequently bare grey rock is the prevailing feature. It is so hard that a hand-grip or foot-rest of even an inch keeps you safe on precipitous ground, and you may enjoy most exhilarating climbs over Benbaun (*Beann bán*, white peak) and Bencorr (*Beann*

FIG. 6.—*HYDRILA VERTICILLATA*,
FROM RENVYLE LOUGH
Two-thirds natural size

corr, peak of the conical hill) and Benbreen (*Beann-bruighin*, peak of the hostel). But stick to the ridges when ascending these hills, for the valleys are mostly filled with wet bog, often intersected with a network of gullies, ground very tiresome to traverse. The schists that lap round the flanks of the mountains occasionally rise high, as on the summit of Muckanaght (2153 feet), and forming as they do a much more hospitable habitat for plants than the barren quartzite, they attract the comparatively few alpine plants of the range—Mountain Meadow-rue, Purple Saxifrage, Mountain Sorrel, Mountain Sawwort, Dwarf Mountain Willow, Holly Fern, and others. The most accessible peak, and one which gives a good sample of the scenery and geology and botany of the group, is Ben Lettery (*Beann leitirigh*, peak of the wet hillside, 1904 feet) which rises directly above the main Galway–Clifden road at Ballynahinch Lake. Thence, if you wish, you can wander along high knife-edge ridges over Bengower into the heart of the range, to find a convenient descent at Derryclare or Knockpasheenmore. One glorious walk over these hills stands out especially in my memory—up over Ben Lettery, right across the range, and down again to the wooded valley of Kylemore; and I recall particularly the contrast in coming off the high naked quartzites which for hours I had been traversing, to the green oaks and blue lakes of Kylemore. It was a full and satisfying day's work.

After " the Bens ", the Maam Turk range will seem comparatively uninteresting. It has been aptly described (by H. C. Hart) as the tangled cluster of the Twelve Bens stretched out in a curved line with their tops rubbed off. From the south these mountains are imposing, high rounded bare masses of quartzite, " a zigzag series of bee-hives ". A traverse of the whole ridge from Maam Cross to Leenane provides a glorious day's walking, but the main interest will lie not in the hills themselves, but in the striking and varied scenery on either hand. I followed that route one mellow October day, and shall not soon forget the lovely tints on hill and bog. *Madhm* (Maam) means mountain pass, and *torc*, wild boar; the reference is to the gap at Maumeen, where an old track provided a short cut from western

Connemara by way of Recess and Maam village to the important passage between Loughs Mask and Corrib, by which one escapes from the barren mountain region into the grasslands of the Central Plain.

Quarries on the southern slopes of these hills—at Lisoughter and Ballynahinch, and also at Streamstown near Clifden—are the source of the well-known and beautiful stone called " Connemara Marble ", or by geologists serpentine.   This once was an ordinary limestone, such as occurs in many places among these ancient beds; but here, owing to heat and pressure and the infiltration of other substances, it has been turned into a gnarled rock of various shades of green, which polishes well, but is not suitable for out-of-doors, as the surface soon gets dull there.   At Lisoughter a mile of road will take you to the quarry, at present abandoned, where great blocks of the rock are lying about, but with surfaces so weathered that you might not immediately recognize it.

Killary Harbour (*Caol sháile*, narrow sea-inlet) provides the best example in Ireland of the true *fiord*—a submerged river-valley which has been greatly deepened by ice-action.   It is ten miles long, about half a mile wide, and attains a depth of no less than thirteen fathoms, so that even battleships can lie in it in safety; but, as is the manner of fiords, its entrance is less deeply excavated than its middle part, and requires careful navigation.   A small boat with an outboard motor would allow one easily to explore unusually picturesque ground lying on either side of the narrow rock-strewn Killary entrance.   On the north side, a flat sandy stretch with shallow lakelets and a curiously mixed flora intervenes between the Atlantic and the steep gable of Mweelrea—a lonely and fascinating place, known as Dooaghtry. On the south side, the Little Killary, a small sea-inlet of much charm, lies between the main fiord and Benchoona (*Beann chúinne*, peak of the corner?).   I wonder is the " pipe graveyard " there still?   It is forty years since I first saw it—a lonely and primitive cemetery, where it was the custom to provide clay pipes for the mourners; and these, after the funeral, were left behind, forming a very unusual decoration of the gravestones.

On the north side of Killary Harbour the grand Mweelrea group of mountains is split into three by the deep Delphi Pass and by Glenummera (*Gleann iomaire*, ridge-glen), which comes down into it from the east. There is as fine scenery here as is to be found in Ireland, and many splendid mountain walks. Motorists see but little of this region, for roads are few, and such as are creep through deep valleys. Mweelrea (*An maol riabhach*, the grey bald mountain-top) itself, the highest point (2686 feet), can be reached from the nearest road only by four miles of hard going.

The other sections of the Mweelrea mountain-mass—Sheffry to the north and Bengorm to the east—are tall fine hills, well worth the climbing. A little further eastward, across the Erriff glen, rise the Partry Mountains (*Slíabh Partraighe*, mountain of the Partraighe (a tribe)), with the Devil's Mother (2131 feet) impending over the head of Killary, and higher hills adjoining on the east. As seen from the Leenane–Westport road these mountains do not look at all exciting; but viewed from the opposite side, where Lough Mask lies spread, they are highly attractive. The range is formed of massive beds of Ordovician rocks lying nearly horizontally, but with a slight upward tilt to southward. Along their eastern side they have been much eaten into by the various forces of denudation; and by the Owenbrin River deep coombs, embosoming tarns surrounded by thousand-foot cliffs, show the effect of prolonged ice-action. Two long narrow arms of Lough Mask penetrate into the hills, and with picturesque Lough Nafooey help to make up a delightful medley of hill and dale and lake. Much of the Galway–Mayo mountain-region is but little frequented. Leenane, the natural centre, is well known to visitors, and there are hotels, large or small, cheap or dear, at Letterfrack (*Leitir fraig*, women's? wet hillside), Kylemore (*An choill mhór*, the great wood), Rinvyle (*Rinn a' mhaoil*, the point of the bare promontory), Maam (*Madhm*, a pass), and elsewhere— by no means a superfluity of them, considering the loveliness of the region.

An imposing northern outpost of this sea of hills is Croaghpatrick

(St. Patrick's rick, commonly shortened into " The Reek "), long looked on as a holy mountain. It is now the scene of a great annual pilgrimage, when thousands of people climb the stony path to render, in and around the little chapel which has in recent times been erected on the summit, homage to the patron saint of Ireland. The hill is over 2500 feet high, and the loose quartzite which forms the track is rough and slippery, so the ascent is no mean feat for the old or the infirm. Perhaps its very difficulty provides an incentive. Certain it is that remarkable scenes of courage and devotion are witnessed on Croaghpatrick on the last Sunday in July. No doubt the beautiful form of the mountain and its unique position on the very verge of Clew Bay with its myriad green islands contributed to its selection as a place of worship, for Patrick travelled far over Ireland and no doubt stood on many hilltops. While, as seen from north or south, Croaghpatrick forms a long ridge with a high central dome, see it from east or west and the shoulders become gathered together in front of or behind the main peak, so that from base to summit it forms a perfect and lovely cone. As one comes westward across the Central Plain, somewhere about Claremorris the eye is arrested by this wonderful outline, towering heavenward beyond where the long bare ridge of the Partry Mountains sinks down towards Westport—an outline comparable to that of famed Fujiyama; and one feels little surprise that both should be looked on as holy places. Their terrestrial origin, however, is widely different. Croaghpatrick is *not*, as Fujiyama is, a volcano, though, like the Sugarloaf in Wicklow and Errigal in Donegal, it is among ungeological people often believed to be so. Quartzite, of which many of our oldest mountain areas are composed, and which is a much hardened and altered form of sandstone, insoluble and intractable, tends by its superior hardness to weather out in the course of ages, and to remain while the rocks which surround it are denuded and lowered by rain and frost and wind through long periods of time; and owing to the particular manner in which quartzite disintegrates, its masses tend to assume a conical form. The fact that the disintegration produces not soil, but broken fragments and thin sand, causes these quartzite cones—as particularly in the case of Errigal—to be streaked with scree as many volcanoes are streaked with lava-flows, and helps to support the plutonic fallacy.

I remember standing on the summit of " The Reek " one Easter evening of wonderful clearness. It was dead calm. Clew Bay was like a mirror. All the mountains to north and south—Mweelrea, Sheffry, Partry, Nephin and Nephinbeg, and the distant hills of Achill, were of intensest purple, and Clare Island hung like a grey mirage across the mouth of the bay. As the sun sank towards the western ocean, it fell full on Croaghpatrick, and the shadow of the cone, stripped of its supporting shoulders, lay like a great triangle over the eastern plain, bluish against a rosy haze that covered the sunlit ground. As the sun dipped, this shadow became longer and longer, till it seemed to reach the horizon, a fascinating sight. And then abruptly the sun was gone, and I had to hasten down the stony descent to escape from the rough mountainside before darkness fell.

The particular legend which connects the patron saint of Ireland with Croaghpatrick concerns the banishment from the country of the snakes and other distasteful creatures which, it is implied, inhabited the island until his day. Like many another legend which cannot be taken literally, this one embodies an interesting scientific truth—the absence from Ireland of almost all reptiles and amphibians, including many which are frequent in Great Britain. The zoologist and geologist explain this by pointing out in the first place the un-doubted truth that Ireland and Britain not very long ago (speaking in terms of geological time) formed part of the Continent. They are as a matter of fact separated from it by very shallow seas, and an upward movement of the land or downward movement of the sea (which comes to the same thing) of quite small amount would suffice to spill the water off the shelf on which these islands stand, and leave a continuous continental land-surface. Such movements, slow and imperceptible within a human lifetime, are continually in progress on this thin cindery crust which covers the molten Earth.

Furthermore, there is plenty of evidence to show that the Irish-English land-connection broke down at some time previous to the English-French—in other words, that the Irish Sea came into being before the Straits of Dover. This allowed continued free migration of animals and plants into Britain from the Continent for some time after the door leading to Ireland had been shut. Thus, it is held, is explained the absence from Ireland of some familiar British animals and plants; they were late-comers of the general westward migration, and succeeded in crossing by land into Britain (where many of them are widely spread), but could get no further westward without passing the Irish Sea, which evidently proved a formidable barrier. So it is that Ireland has and apparently never had any Vipers or Slow-worms or Moles, nor the Common Toad nor the Crested Newt; nor among plants such widespread British species as the Needle Furze, the Sweet Milk-Vetch, Herb-Paris, Lily of the Valley and others. But we are not *quite* free of reptiles and amphibians in Ireland. There is the Common Lizard, the Common Newt (often mistaken one for the other, especially after the latter leaves its aqueous breeding-ground and takes to the land), and down in Kerry the little Natterjack Toad. The Frog is also with us, but in its case the question has been raised as to whether it is an old native or a comparatively recent introduction. Is it really one hundred per cent Irish, in the sense of having been here " always "? This question was a subject of discussion in early volumes of the *Irish Naturalist*, in which Dr. Scharff and Mr de Vismes Kane were the principal protagonists. The evidence *contra* is furnished by several old writers, whose comments on the subject are so quaint that I am tempted to quote from them. Thus Donatus, Bishop of Fiesole in the ninth century (and subsequently canonized), wrote a rhymed account of Ireland in which he says,

> Nulla venena nocent, nec serpens serpit in herba
> Nec conquesta canit garrula rana lacu,[1]

[1] Quoted by Colgan (*Triadis Thaumaturgae Acta*, p. 255, 1647) and others.

which Jack Lindsay [1] renders :

> No snakes are creeping there with venomed guile,
> No raucous frogs disturb the rustling reeds

—a fairly free translation.

Then Giraldus Cambrensis (who was secretary to Prince John, son of Henry II, when the former visited Ireland), writing in 1187, devotes a whole chapter (his chapters are very short!) of his *Topographia Hibernica* to an account of a Frog which, to the amazement of all, had been captured in Ireland. His comments are so interesting that I quote from them at some length (Bohn's translation, pp. 47-51):

[In Ireland] " there are neither snakes nor adders, toads nor frogs, tortoises nor scorpions, nor dragons. It produces, however, spiders, leeches, and lizards; but they are quite harmless. . . . It does appear very wonderful that, when any thing venomous is brought there from other lands, it never could exist in Ireland. For we read in the ancient books of the saints of that country, that sometimes, for the sake of experiment, serpents have been shipped over in brazen vessels, but were found lifeless and dead as soon as the middle of the Irish Sea was crossed. Poison also similarly conveyed was found to lose its venom, when midway on the waters, disinfected by a purer air. . . . I have also heard it said by merchants, who pursued their adventures on the ocean, that on some occasions, having unloaded their ships in an Irish port, they found toads in the bottom of the hold; and having thrown them on shore in a living state, they immediately turned on their backs and bursting their bellies died, to the astonishment of many who witnessed it. . . .

"Nevertheless, a frog was found, within my time, in the grassy meadows near Waterford, and brought to Court alive before Robert Poer, who was at the time Warden there, and many others, both English and Irish. And when numbers of both nations, and particularly the Irish, had beheld it with great astonishment, at last Duvenold, King of Ossory, a man of sense among his people and

1 *Medieval Latin Poets*, p. 78. 1934.

faithful, who happened to be present, beating his head, and having deep grief at heart, spoke thus: ' That reptile is the bearer of doleful news to Ireland '. And uttering a sort of prognostic, he further said, that it portended, without doubt, the coming of the English, their threatened conquest, and the subjugation of his own nation.

" No man, however, will venture to suppose that this reptile was ever born in Ireland; for the mud there does not, as in other countries, contain the germs from which green Frogs are bred. If that had been the case, they would have been found more frequently, and in greater numbers, both before and after the time mentioned. It may have happened that some particle of the germ, hid in the moist soil, had been exhaled into the clouds by the heat of the atmosphere, and wafted hither by the force of the winds; or perhaps, that the embryo reptile had been swept into the hollow of a descending cloud, and, being by chance deposited here, was lodged in an inhospitable and ungenial soil. But the better opinion is that the frog was brought over by accident in a ship from some neighbouring port, and being cast on shore, succeeded in subsisting and maintaining life for a time, as it is not a venomous animal."

(Giraldus appears to have accepted fully the common opinion of the time, that the sacred quality of the soil and air of Ireland made the existence of " poisonous " creatures such as toads and snakes impossible, and even caused poisons to become harmless.)

In the latter part of the seventeenth century, there was a concerted effort among Dublin students of natural history to collect information about Irish animals and plants. Thomas Molyneux, F.R.S., appears to have been the leading spirit. To Dr. Gwithers, Fellow of Trinity College, was assigned the quadrupeds: he failed to find the Frog, and apparently considering that its omission from Ireland was contrary to the scheme of things, he obtained spawn from England, which he placed in a ditch in the College Park. This, according to some, was the first successful introduction of the much-abused amphibian into Ireland, and from Trinity College it is stated to have spread all over the country.

O'Halloran, in his *History of Ireland* (1772), quotes Donatus' Latin verses mentioned above, and waxes facetious over the activities of Dr. Gwithers:

" We must here remark that we never had frogs in Ireland till the reign of King William. It is true some mighty sensible members of the Royal Society in the time of Charles II attempted to add these to the many other valuable presents sent us from England, but ineffectually; as they were of Belgic origin, it would seem they could only thrive under a Dutch Prince, and these with many other exotics were introduced at the Happy Revolution." On the other hand, Dubourdieu, in his *Statistical Survey of the County of Down*, published in 1802, states categorically that the first Frogs seen in Ireland were found near Moira, perhaps half a century before, whence some were taken to Waringstown, in the same county, and spread over the country with amazing rapidity.

The very number of these " first Frogs " makes one suspicious of the whole business, and it is desirable to turn to another avenue of approach. Can the geologists help us? If the remains of Frogs were found in undisturbed deposits which could be proved to be of great age, that evidence would be of conclusive value. So interest was keen when R. J. Ussher, excavating in the cave of Ballynamintra, reported the occurrence of bones of Frog. But they turned out to be only in the surface layer, and later on were shown to belong to mice! After a few years, further excavations, this time in the caves on Keshcorran in Sligo, revealed Frog remains deeply buried (six to eight feet down) in beds of clay, mixed with bones of animals long extinct in Ireland—Brown Bear and Wolf and Arctic Lemming. This seemed to be proof positive (at least to anyone capable of weighing scientific evidence) that the Frog was in Ireland before historic times, and that the stories of its introduction are to be discredited. But this evidence has not been fully accepted by zoologists. Frog bones are very minute, and anyone who has tried cave-digging knows how easily material from upper layers will trickle down into excavations. Until Frog remains are found embedded in stalagmite along with an ancient fauna, or other incontrovertible evidence is produced, the matter cannot be regarded as yet settled. Assuming that the Frog is an ancient native, as it well may be, it is interesting to consider how these stories of its introduction arose. It must be remembered that even a couple of centuries ago accurate observation was sadly rare, credulity rife, and natural history a subject scarcely worthy of the attention of self-respecting people. An age that believed in mermaids, and in toads entombed in solid rock, might easily get wrong about that " unpleasant but harmless animal ", the Frog. It is clear that the lover of compromise and of Patrician tradition may, if he likes, hold that in this matter everyone is right—that the Frog *was* an inhabitant of ancient Ireland; that it *was* sent to the right-about in the fifth century by our patron saint; and that Trinity College, under the aegis of William of Orange, was responsible for the reinstatement of the banished creature—a parable whose significance may be extended if one wishes far beyond the domain of zoology. If only students of animal distribution could assure us that the present range of the Frog in this country is limited to Northern Ireland and the College Park, we might all be willing to accept that solemn-eyed animal, and to forgive him his unattractive figure and disconcerting somersaults.

As a matter of fact, the most venomous by far of the few bloodthirsty monsters which Ireland produces are midges and horse-flies (for mosquitoes are rare and spasmodic, though I am told they are increasing in some of the towns—Belfast for instance). These and these alone need ever break the even tenor of his way for the wanderer. I pass by more domestic small deer, for my mind is out in the open: but in any case these latter are certainly less numerous than they used to be. The midges are always with us, but you will have noticed that at some times they are much more virulent than at others. I have seen busy parties of haymakers ordered home because they were simply losing time in a vain battle with these amazing little pests. What this variable venomosity means I do not know. Are there different kinds of midges, some more pestiferous than others? Or is it a question of one's own physiological condition?—hardly, if many people are affected simultaneously. Or is it that the midges have been already feeding on something poisonous to us?—unlikely again. As for the horse-flies, or clegs as they call them in the North, we should offer up thanks to high heaven that their season is short, for they really are a great bother. Why do they so frequently hunt in droves of half a dozen to a dozen? That has often puzzled me. And when they do, " what were the wise man's plan? " To halt, with red murder in his heart, and not move on till all his enemies are slaughtered is, I think, the course dictated by the strong instinct of self-preservation. Thank goodness, they allow themselves to be killed easily. I remember once being fairly routed by these blundering blood-suckers. It was a hot day, in a lovely tree-rimmed flowery meadow: and a little track led down to a glorious spring in the middle, of that rare bluish tint which you get only on the limestone. I was in a heroic-pastoral frame of mind, for I had had an exhilarating tramp over Blackstairs, down to Scullogue Gap and up again over Mount Leinster, and as I stooped to drink I had in mind Gilbert Murray's lovely rendering of the lines in the *Hippolytus*—

> Oh for a deep and dewy spring,
>   With runlets cold to draw and drink!
> And a great meadow blossoming,
> Long-grassed, and poplars in a ring,
>   To rest me by the brink!

Then the horse-flies arrived—not in half-dozens or dozens, but in droves, wave after wave: I never saw so many. Again and again I essayed to drink—for I was very thirsty—but each time I stooped they descended on my head in such numbers that I gave it up and fairly ran for it, wondering why Saint Patrick, instead of banishing the snakes and toads, which were all—if one may judge from those which still inhabit the neighbouring island of Great Britain—quite harmless creatures (excepting the Viper)—had not turned his attention to these misguided little pests.

Several islands lie off the South Mayo coast which are well worth a visit by those to whom the heave of the ocean is an exhilaration and not a burden. Nowadays motor boats make the passage shorter, but not smoother, and the chump-chump of the exhaust has none of the romance that attaches to the well-trimmed sail and taut sheet. Many a wild crossing I have had among these islands. I remember one from Achill Sound to Clare Island, when it was blowing a gale. Our boatman rather grudgingly agreed to take half his usual complement of passengers: but when he came out from the tail of Achillbeg into the open, he would have turned had it been possible. There was nothing for it but to carry on, and away we went under one scrap of sail, over great waves roaring in from the west. The boat rushed down into deep troughs where there was no breath of wind, and only water all round, and up again over high crests—the rollers were each several hundred yards long—where the wind half choked us, and we got a momentary wide glimpse over far-stretching angry seas to distant black foam-rimmed cliffs. Half-way across the waves threatened to comb, and one of them spilled a plentiful cascade of white frothy water over us. Down crashed our rag of sail, and we flew down wind under bare poles, while each following sea was a wall of water hovering high over our stern and threatening annihilation. Within a few seconds, as it seemed, we were half a mile to leeward, the combers had swept past, and we were able to resume our struggle towards Granuaile's Castle. Experiences like these can merit the much-abused word thrilling. There is no thought of panic, nor time for it: only a sense of intense exhilaration, coupled with thankfulness that our boatman is experienced and cool-headed: (and somewhere deep down a half-formed thought that after all we can die but once!).

Clare Island, anciently *Cliara*, which I have just mentioned, is a fascinating place. My first experience of it began weirdly. Noting that its botany was curiously unknown, my wife and I crossed over from Roonah Quay in the post-boat on an evening in July, 1903. It was dead calm, with an oily roll coming in from the west. All

PLATE XX

CROAGHMORE, CLARE ISLAND, 1520 FEET, FROM THE N.E.

the hills around were smothered in a white mist, which over the island formed an enormous arch, solid enough seemingly to walk on, and descending nearly to sea-level. We lurched slowly across in an ominous stillness, and darkness descended before it was due, as we groped our way to the little quay. Next morning, when we wished to get away to explore the island, all was dense mist and heavy rain, still without wind, and all day we fretted in our little cottage, unable to move. Late in the day the rain ceased, and a strange red glow, coming from the north-west, spread through the thinning fog. We hurried out to the north point of the island, and there, just sinking into the ocean, was a blood-red sun, lighting up dense inky clouds which brooded low over the black jagged teeth of Achill Head, rising from a black sea tinged with crimson. It was a scene fitted for Dante's *Inferno*, and if a flight of demons or of angels had passed across in that strange atmosphere it would have seemed quite appropriate, and no cause for wonder. We got to know Clare Island very well indeed during 1909–11, for the following reason. The unexpectedly interesting results arising from biological team-work on the island of Lambay near Dublin (p. 261) led to a proposal that a similar survey should be made of one of the western islands, embracing everything connected with its geology, zoology, botany and so on. Clare Island was selected, as board and lodging for working parties were possible there, and transport not too difficult—qualifications which scarcely held for the Great Blasket, a close runner-up. Clare Island had also the advantage of a diversified surface, made up of rocks of various ages, and a hill of 1520 feet dropping into the Atlantic in a grand cliff covered with alpine plants above and with great bird colonies below (Plate XX). As secretary to the committee which was formed to carry out the scheme, it fell to me to organize frequent expeditions to the island. Up to a dozen workers would spend a week or more there, or less frequently on the adjoining mainland, in order that the insular life might be compared with that on the areas from which it was presumably derived. The work grew to unexpected proportions.

For three consecutive years six or eight parties went out in spring or summer or autumn, and indeed there was no month of the twelve in which one of our collectors might not have been found investigating seaweeds or earth-worms or mosses. We ransacked the neighbouring islands too—Achill and Bofin and Turk and Caher, and others which are little more than rocks. Of the last, the most interesting was the little group of The Bills, rising steeply nine miles north-west of Clare Island, with its populous colonies of Puffins, Great Black-backed Gulls, and so on, much tamer there than their fellows on the mainland (Plate XXI). Almost every Irish naturalist took up some group, many keen workers came from England and Scotland to help us, and the chance of investigation in the west of Ireland, which to the European biologist is an area of pre-eminent interest, brought well-known men of science from Germany and Switzerland and Denmark. While the fauna and flora occupied a foremost place, opportunity was taken to investigate the history and archaeology of the island, its place-names and family names, native designations of animals and plants, climatology, geology and agriculture. Also, by the co-operation of the Fisheries department, their steamer *Helga*, specially fitted for biological research, joined in the work, and greatly enhanced the results obtained from dredging and trawling around the island. Material piled up beyond all expectation, but that undaunted body, the Royal Irish Academy, undertook the publication of the whole harvest that we gleaned, and did so at a cost of over £1000, in the form of three large volumes. The results as there shown are rather surprising, especially as regards the fauna and flora, in view of the fact that the island and adjoining areas are barren and wind-swept in comparison with the lands further east, and much of them covered by unproductive peat-bog. Of a total of 5269 animals observed—ranging from mammals down to microscopic rhizopods—no less than 1253 species were found to be hitherto unknown in Ireland, of which 343 were unrecorded also from Great Britain, and 109 new to science. Of the 3219 plants collected, from phanerogams to diatoms, 585 were new

Plate XXI

Clare Island from the Bills

to Ireland, 55 new to the British Isles, and 11 new to science. Paradoxical as it may sound, these surprising results—for the existing lists of Irish animals and plants were with reason considered in most groups tolerably complete—arose in no small measure from the limitation of area (for Clare Island covers only a little over six square miles) and its inhospitable character, for these features compelled very intensive collecting and special study of difficult or obscure groups. We were certainly fortunate in the skilled assistance which came to us so generously; 100 workers in all took part in the survey, and this number included many well-known specialists. It was a full, stimulating and interesting time. My own work in organizing and conducting, assisting in the field-work, gathering together the sixty-seven separate reports and seeing them through the press, occupied my leisure time for six years.

Inishbofin (*Inis bó finne*, the island of the white cow) and Inishturk (*Inis torc*, boar's island), which lie off the coast south of Clare Island, are seldom visited by the rambler, but are well worth a day's exploration from Cleggan or Renvyle. Inishbofin is flatter but more diversified than its neighbour, with little lakes and sandy bays to enliven its wind-shorn heather and patches of tillage, and it has a good harbour. On Inishturk the Ordovician strata form alternate ribs and hollows running across the island, so that the surface resembles corrugated iron on a large scale. It has a greater diversity of wild-flowers than either Bofin or Clare Island in relation to its size, which is much less than either (2¼ square miles), and the cliff scenery of its western coast is imposing. My wife and I spent an interesting week on the island in 1906. There is no inn there, but by the kindness of F. G. T. Gahan we secured the use of a shed belonging to the Congested Districts Board, perched on a low rock with deep water half surrounding it. In bad weather the beating of the rain on the galvanized iron roof, combined with the roar of the waves just outside the door, made a wonderful noise at night. When we arrived, after a lively passage from Renvyle, I was sent off to botanize for at least two hours, and when I returned my wife had removed from the floor a half-inch compacted layer of portland cement, herring scales, petroleum and sawdust. Then we settled down, surrounded by coils of wire, boxes of dynamite, and bags of cement, and we fried fish, baked bread and cooked bacon and eggs in one small pan over a smoky stove. In the early morning we stepped out of the door and head first into twenty feet of Atlantic water, and all day long we explored the hills and hollows and lake-lets and caves of Inishturk. It was an ideal existence, which we have repeated under varying conditions on almost every island off the coast of Ireland. But though there are cattle still on *Inis Bó Finne*, there are no Wild Boars on Inishturk, and never were.

Clew Bay (*Cuan módh*), which we now reach in our erratic peregrination, provides a startling contrast to the brown bare mountain-regions which impend over it to north and south. A tongue of the limestone of the Central Plain stretches to the sea here, producing soft outlines and a grassy surface. Further, the ice-sheet of the Glacial Period has left the lowlands filled with drumlins. These are whale-backed oblong ridges of drift, all lying parallel to the direction of the ice-flow—in this case east and west. The drum-lins here dip gently down below sea-level, producing first a series of promontories and inlets, and finally an archipelago of grassy islets, the seaward end of which is often bitten off by the waves, so that a tall cliff of drift, 50 to 100 feet in height, faces the open. In among the drumlins nestle the little towns of Newport and Westport, sheltered from ocean winds and full of tall trees and luxuriant vegetation.

On the northern side of Clew Bay the mountains begin again, high hills alternating with bare moorlands and bog-filled valleys. Over to the east is the massive dome of Nephin, looking down on Lough Conn (p. 207); then across a deep depression rises Birreen-corragh (*Birrín carrach*, rugged little pin), and further east the wild Nephinbeg range runs northward from Claggan Mountain (*Cloig-eann*, a skull, hence round bare hill), overlooking Mallaranny (*Mullach raithnighe*, summit of fern), to Slieve Car. These hills are wind-swept and desolate and inaccessible, and the going is very heavy. The mountains of the Curraun peninsula (*Corrán*, a sickle) are more attractive, though not so high, having fine cliff-ranges and many lakelets, with easy access from Mallaranny and from Achill Sound. On the plateau which caps the Curraun hills Juniper, Bear-berry and Crow-berry form a close shorn sward of alpine character.

This brings us to Achill (*Acaill*, eagle, from *aquila*), an island only in name, for the narrow passage which cuts it off from Curraun is crossed by a substantial bridge. Achill, wind-swept and bare, heavily peat-covered, with great gaunt brown mountains rising here and there, and a wild coast hammered by the Atlantic waves on all sides but the east, has a strange charm which everyone feels, but none can fully explain. Formerly you journeyed to Achill Sound by train, whence a horse-drawn vehicle ordered for the occasion jolted you nine miles through the bogs to Dugort, on the northern shore, where alone you could stay. The railway extension from Westport —one of Gerald Balfour's attempted amenities—having failed hopelessly to justify its existence, is abandoned, and you take bus from Westport to Keel, where there are now several hotels and many lodgings. From either that place or Dugort or Dooagh you explore the island, preferably—and in the most attractive parts necessarily— on foot. The ascent of Slieve More (*Sliabh mór*, great mountain, 2204 feet) from Dugort is easy, and you obtain a bird's-eye view over the whole island and a vast extent of sea and intricate coast besides. But Croaghaun (*Cruachán*, little rick, 2192 feet) in the extreme west, is the finer hill. Go up by Dooagh past Lough Acorrymore (*Loch an chorraigh mhóir*, lake of the large corrie), lying in its great coomb, to the summit, and you find yourself on the edge of a two-mile-long precipice dropping sheer into the Atlantic. Turn to the left and you descend to the far-projecting knife-edge of Achill Head (Plate XXII)—a savage place, and for the scramble to its extremity you should have nailed shoes and a good head. Or turn to the right from the summit of Croaghaun and you can visit Bunnafreeva Lough, perched on the edge of the huge cliff with another cliff overhanging it—a place so lonely and sterile and primeval that one might expect to see the *piast* or other Irish water-monster rising from the inky depths of the tarn.   Thence away over undulating shorn heath to Saddle Head, then eastward to two romantic lakes which lie close to the northern shore, and so back to Dooagh.   This last is to my mind one of the most exhilarating walks in Ireland, with its combination of mountain and ocean and short springy turf edged with tall cliffs or foam-fringed rocks.   But what is perhaps the finest view in Achill can be obtained without the expenditure of energy required for the ascent of Croaghaun.   Take the path from Dooagh (*Dumhach*, a sandbank) along the steep hillside to the lovely little sheltered sandy bay of Keem (*Caoim*, beautiful valley).   (Motors can safely go about half-way.)   And from there climb up the left-hand slope to the old coast-guard watch-house, and walk westward along the edge of the thousand-foot precipice; you will obtain changing and ever-wonderful views of the wild cliffs of Achill Head which will remain long in your memory.

All the finest parts of Achill Island lie north of a line drawn from Dugort to Dooagh—the Slievemore-Croaghaun region.   The high Meenaun cliffs to the southward look lovely from Keel (*Cael*, narrow), but save for their northern end (the Cathedral Rocks, at the extremity of Keel Strand) they are not accessible below, and their summit forms a bare stony hill—but commands a splendid prospect.   If you want less austere scenery, go to the north-east, to Valley Strand and the little lowland lakes adjoining it.   There you will find sands of reddish gold, and calm water; and the vegetation is not shorn as with a knife, while across the bay the high hills of the Nephinbeg range form a striking background.   My first acquaintance with Achill—at second-hand—came from an account which Edward Newman contributed to the *Magazine of Natural History* as the result of a visit in the year 1838—a century ago now.   Newman was a London publisher, interested in insects and especially in ferns, on which he wrote a book which is still often quoted.   It was probably the profusion of these plants in Ireland, and the hope of discovering

PLATE XXII

T. H. Mason: photo

ACHILL HEAD

something new, that brought him to this country, through which he made a long tour. He was much impressed by the rugged scenery of Achill, and waxes enthusiastic over the wild cliffs about Achill Head, and the grand precipice of Croaghaun. " It seems like a remote corner of some vast continent which has sunk for ever beneath the waves "—a not inapt description, in view of the manner in which its mountains have been shorn across by the Atlantic. Especially was he enamoured of Bunnafreeva Lough, which lies tucked in high on the Croaghaun cliffs, and is undoubtedly one of the most remarkable features of Achill: "Near the margin of the cliff a beautiful little fresh-water lake, surrounded by an amphitheatre of hills. I should think its surface was 600 feet above the sea, and its distance from the edge of the cliff scarcely 300. I doubt whether any Englishman but myself has ever seen this lone and beautiful sheet of water; its singularly round form, the depth of the basin in which it reposes, the precipitous sides of the basin, its height above the sea— all these are characters of no ordinary interest." He gossips about his favourites, the ferns, and comments on the scarcity of bird-life, but sees plenty of red-legged crows, and adds " eagles are very abundant, particularly (perhaps exclusively) *Aquila albicilla* "—that is the White-tailed Sea-eagle, now extinct in Ireland.

His comments on the housing of 1838 are of interest: " This island of Achill is more like a foreign land than any I have visited; the natives reside in huts, which a good deal resemble those of the Esquimaux Indians; they are without chimneys or windows, and the roof seems continuous with the walls; the interior is generally undivided, and is tenanted by men, women, children, pigs and poultry, and often goats and cows. These little cabins are built in what may be called loose clusters, varying from twenty to eighty in a cluster; these clusters or villages are sixteen in number, some of them are summer residences only, and are entirely deserted in the winter—others winter residences only, and deserted in summer." As to the people and their prospects: " The natives of Achill are charged with being thieves and murderers; and if I were to place full reliance on all I heard at the Settlement (this is the Protestant Mission at Dugort) they would appear to be so.   Mr Long, however, with everything constantly exposed—walls and hedges being here un-known—and living amongst a population from whom he has no power at all to defend himself, has never lost even a potato.   I do not allude to this subject politically; but bearing in mind solely the natural history of the island and its capability of improvement, I pronounce without hesitation that if goodness of soil, lowness of rent, cheapness of labour, and safety of property be recommendations —then that no spot I have seen is more likely to reward the emigrant than the Island of Achill.   Would that some unpolitical and un-sectarian philanthropists—men that took a human view of the human wants and human failings of these poor islanders would settle among them, and place in their hands the plough and the spade, teach the children to read and write, the boys to make shoes and coats, to fish, and to dig, and rake and sow, and reap, and build houses, and the girls to knit, and spin, and make gowns—use them like brothers, sisters, and children—then might this island become a centre of happiness and prosperity."   With all which one can cordially agree; but it is to be feared that the writer is sadly at fault in his estimate of the agricultural possibilities of the soaking barren peat that covers the greater part of Achill.

So much for the island in 1838.   My first glimpse of it at first hand was sixty years later, in 1898, following which, in 1904, I made a careful botanical survey of this highly interesting area.   The eagles were gone, save that an occasional itinerant Golden Eagle was reported still; but the flora was unchanged—as it still is—except that an increase in the amount of tillage, due to better drainage, tended to provide a habitat for additional colonists from the east.   The population, far larger than the meagre agriculture and spasmodic fishing could support, was maintained on American money sent home by absent sons and daughters.   Housing conditions were still very bad; Dooagh was a huddled cluster of poor thatched cabins; Keel a little better, and one or two houses were there where the warm hospitality of the family did much to mitigate the primitive conditions which confronted the occasional guest. Only at Dugort, which faces north and is somewhat remote from the beautiful western part of the island, could one find a perch which in any way recalled one's own particular cage.

Nowadays things are changed. Dugort (*Dubh ghort*, black field) has many places where the visitor can stay in comfort, instead of one only. Keel is a place of several pleasant hotels and many new houses. Dooagh is altered out of recognition, for with Government aid all the old hovels are gone, and a quite extensive village has arisen of new houses, not, as in so many places in Ireland, of design quite alien to the people and the environment. And cultivated flowers, formerly almost unknown in Achill, now deck tiny cottage gardens— Dahlias and Sweet Pea and Marigolds and Sun-flowers. There is a little more tillage too, due to continued peat-cutting and drainage. But these things have altered Achill life very little. The puppies and ducks still squabble in the village street over treasure trove. Barefoot children, "leppin' like a hare", still hunt the heifers out of the crops, and pen them into their own place with "gates" made of old cart-wheels and iron bed-ends and stools of bog-fir. The men still wear the serviceable bawneen,[1] and among at least the old women you may still see the heavy scarlet homespun skirt. In August the rye stands up white against the bogland tinged purple with heather, with an increasing golden tint as the Tufted Spikerush assumes its rich autumn colour, among patches of crimson Cotton-grass and white Mat-grass. Beyond the narrow limits of tillage and turf-cutting nothing is changed, and the mantle of heath-covered peat stretches unbroken mile after mile, as it did centuries ago, and will do centuries hence. To my mind the main charm of Achill lies in these un-changing features—the broad undulations of the treeless, roadless moorland, the tall hills, the illimitable silver sea, the savage coast-line, the booming waves, the singing wind, the smell of peat smoke and seaweed and Wild Thyme, and the soft western voices bidding you

[1] A buttonless waistcoat with sleeves, of strong home-made white flannel.

welcome or giving you God-speed. That is the Achill of spring or summer or autumn. In winter, rain, mist and storm sweep over its wide desolate bogs, the hurrying clouds hang low on the hills, the sea raves incessantly among the rocks. Frost and snow are rare visitors, but the whole island lies soaked and hopeless. " And how do you get through the winter? " asked a friend of mine. " Och, it's the grand aisy time we do be havin'," was the reply, " watching the sea rollin' in and the clouds rollin' by."

For anyone loving open-water sailing the Mayo–Galway coast offers a wonderful variety of scenery and of conditions. From the Stags (*i.e.* Stacks) of Broad Haven right round to Gorumna Island in Connemara—a distance of over 100 miles—the shore is a succession of bays and creeks, headlands and islands, of every size from Achill down to mere reefs. There are lovely deep inlets among the hills, and gigantic cliffs, little islets with ancient churches or castles, and everywhere in summer are nesting birds, widely scattered or grouped in enormous colonies. I have sailed much of these waters. The scenery is entrancing, and the heave of the open Atlantic has an exaltation about it that the choppy waters of the Irish Sea can never give. But it is no place for a fair-weather sailor. " Storms are sudden and waters deep ", and you need to watch your chart carefully to avoid sunken reefs. Landing, too, is fine sport sometimes— and re-embarkation may be more so, for a freshening wind may make difficulties. I never was marooned save for an hour or two, but once, as I have narrated above (p. 152), it looked very like a cheerless night among the grass on Caher Island.

I have always rejoiced that, along with my brothers, I learned to swim in waters that were rough, not in rivers or lakes, for it has meant to us that the sea, in all its moods, is a friend, and not an enemy. Had we been allowed, we would have bathed in every sort of weather and in all kinds of places on the wild northern coast: as it was, we often went in off the rocks when other boys of our age did not venture. To enter a rough sea is easy: the test is to get out again without hurt. We would choose a steep rock-face, and swim on our backs, face to the incoming waves, watching for a lull: then dash in on the top of a wave and, hands and feet close together, grip tight while the wave rushed down, and step up quickly into safety. With practice, we never got a scratch from the barnacles that cut like knives. It was good sport, though sometimes the fringe of foam around the rocks was a bother, as it obscured one's view to seaward. The confidence begotten of such bathing made us sceptical about places supposed to be dangerous. I have made a point of bathing wherever I heard of quicksands or things of that sort, and I never found in these places anything unusual. No doubt quicksands, dangerous to life, do exist in some spots, but it has been my luck—good or bad as you please—never to encounter one, and I still feel curious about them. But twice I have felt that I had a very good chance of being drowned, and in both cases the danger was the same—a heavy sea coming in at an angle on a sandy beach, causing a current along the shore: and some conformation that turned that current out to sea. The first time was in the north of Ireland, where a narrow reef of rocks running seaward was the trap; the other time on Fuerteventura in the Canary Islands, where heavy waves rushed over submerged banks of sand parallel to the shore into deeper water inside them, escaping seaward again through occasional channels between the banks. In each case I got into the seaward current before I knew, and realized the danger just in time: a few minutes hard swimming saved me from the chaos of broken water outside, where the rollers were meeting the swiftly flowing current. Places of that sort are really dangerous when a lively sea keeps you occupied, and you do not notice that the shore has begun suddenly to recede. There is no use trying to swim against such a seaward current: swim strongly *along* the shore and get to its edge. But if a really heavy sea is coming in on a sandy beach, the best rule is not to swim. Keep on your feet: you can have lots of fun in the broken water, and you will be safe.

From north to east of Achill lies the Barony of Erris (*Iorrus*, a peninsula), the wildest loneliest stretch of country to be found in all

Ireland. From Mallaranny you may walk for thirty miles to the
giant cliffs of North Mayo, and your foot need never leave the
heather save that twice you cross a road, fenceless, winding like a
narrow white ribbon through the endless brown bog. And if your
course lies east of Bangor (*Beannchor*, peaks) you will hardly even see
a house. If you keep to the highway, up by Carrowmore Lake
(*An cheathramha mhór*, the great quarter) to Belmullet (*Beal a'*
mhuirthid, mouth of the Mullet (peninsula)), an occasional human
habitation, and even a church, will appear, to lessen the monotony,
but as A. E. sings—

It's a lonely road through bogland to the lake at Carrowmore.

The western shore is low and broken, and the heather there often
gives place to poor pasture or tillage: but mostly the peat descends
to the sea and passes below it, so that you see thickly scattered pine-
stools standing up on the beach or out of the waves, thickly hung
with bladder-wrack, to tell of bygone forests. The northern coast
of Erris, on the other hand, is grandly precipitous, with cliffs up to
800 feet high, set with jagged promontories, deep gullies and outlying stacks, the whole forming the finest piece of cliff scenery in the
country. It is almost unknown to the visitor, for it lies far from the
highway which links Killala (*Cill Alaidh*, church of Aladh?) with
Belmullet; but little roads lead across the moorland to Portacloy
(*Port an chlaidhe*, landing place of the rampart), Porturlin (*Port*
urlainn) and Belderg (*Bél dearg*, red ford-mouth), narrow inlets in
the precipice; and from these one can traverse the whole length of
this wild coast.

The great cliff-range of North Mayo appears to have harboured
the last Golden Eagle resident in Ireland. A hundred years ago this
fine bird bred on many inland cliffs, but it steadily diminished, thanks
to " sportsmen " and gamekeepers. In 1900 Ussher and Warren
reported " a few pairs are still resident in the west, but the species
is approaching extinction ". Soon afterwards, the last eyrie was
abandoned, but stray birds were seen occasionally, and unfortunately

sometimes shot or trapped. By 1912 two birds only were known to still haunt the Irish cliffs—one on the North Mayo coast and one in Glenveagh in Donegal. The Donegal bird was trapped (by mistake) in 1926. The Mayo eagle was reported in 1930 to have been shot, but this was inaccurate, as it was seen a second time in 1930 and again in the following year. In 1935 a still rarer bird—a young White-tailed Eagle, a species once plentiful in the west, now extinct at least as a breeder—was shot on Clare Island; it was possibly of Scottish birth. One would like to hope that this is not the last that will be seen in Ireland of either of these grand creatures: but considering the reception that usually awaits them and others, it might be kinder to hope that neither eagle will again visit our country. In Scotland, under wise protection, the Golden Eagle is more than holding its own; but heaven help the bird that ventures near the " Island of Saints ".

But as a set-off against this, several other of our larger and more picturesque cliff-birds are persisting or even increasing—the Raven for instance. It has multiplied in recent years, and has nested even within a few miles of Dublin. It is seldom that you visit any Irish mountain-region without hearing its deep croak, and sometimes you may see quite a flock of them. A. D. Delap counted no less than twenty-seven at the Piper's Lake on Connor Pass not long ago, and I have watched seventeen on the cliffs of Brandon (which is also in the Dingle Peninsula), playing together with great show of tumbling and soaring. But these numbers are eclipsed by Canon Moeran's recent record (*Irish Naturalists' Journal*, vol. vi., p. 156) of fifty-six ravens together near Malinmore in Donegal.

Its delightful cousin the Chough also is holding its own well. Though occasionally seen inland, rocky coasts are the places it loves, and it may be seen in every maritime county in Ireland from Antrim round the west and south to Wexford. With its bright red legs and beak, alert movements and cheerful sharp note, its beautiful flight, and the delight it seems to take in playing in the air, it is a welcome sight wherever found; fortunately it is not a shy bird, and you may with care easily get an opportunity of making its near acquaintance. The Chough makes an excellent pet, becoming very tame; I remember an old bird on Inishmore thirty years ago that made friends with everybody; there was not a boat that came into the harbour of Kilronan of which she did not know the cabin and engine-room.

That grand bird the Peregrine Falcon also well maintains its numbers, and, like the Raven, has bred in recent times not many miles beyond the boundaries of Dublin city. Its wild *tcha-tcha-tcha* may be heard echoing from cliffs almost all over Ireland, when you disturb it as you climb the screes or crawl along the ledges. Sometimes you have the luck to come on a brood of just-fledged youngsters, which display little fear, but will flit about and perch quite close to you, so that you can admire their beautiful plumage and fierce head. Soaring around great precipices and deep mountain valleys, the Peregrine is in Ireland the master of the air. But his domination is not invariable. A few years ago, Ernest F. Clowes told a very interesting story of a combat between a Peregrine and a Raven in Ireland.[1] The Falcon was the attacker, stooping fiercely on his opponent time after time and screaming incessantly. The Raven countered his attacks by flying silently round and round in a wide circle a few feet above the ground, keenly watching his adversary. "The most wonderful thing about this fight was the way in which the Raven avoided those dashing stoops. I always regarded the Raven as a clumsy aerial performer, but the way he ' side-slipped ', the quick swerves and great cunning shown in this contest proves him to be no mean performer of aerobatics." At the fourth lightning stoop, the Raven swerved slightly to the right, and the Falcon " banked " to his left. In a flash the Raven made a vicious jab with his formidable beak, striking the tercel under the right wing. The blow was so heavy that it sent the bird fluttering to the ground. It was not killed, but soon, on being disturbed, flew feebly away. The Raven had headed for its nest as soon as the blow was struck.

[1] *Irish Naturalists' Journal*, vol. iv., pp. 15-16. 1932.
Golden Eagles nested on the Antrim coast from 1953 to 1960. The numbers of Peregrines have decreased seriously but Choughs and Ravens hold their own. Another large bird of prey, the Hen Harrier, has made a welcome re-appearance since 1950 and more than thirty pairs now breed. C.M.

Indeed, it would appear that those lords of the air, the falcons and hawks, do not always have it their own way even with the smaller fry. Father Kennedy, who for some years watched the birds on the North Bull near Dublin, narrates[1] two incidents which point in this direction: A high tide was covering the salt-marsh when a Merlin dashed down and captured a Starling from a flock. The falcon flew off with it, but the weight of the prey gradually brought the Merlin so close to the water that it had to let go. Away flew the Starling with the Merlin in hot pursuit. Three times the falcon secured the bird, but each time failed to carry it clear of the water and had to relax its grip. Finally it gave up the attempt, and the Starling flew off, apparently none the worse. The other occurrence was when a Sparrow-hawk attempted to capture a Lark, rising again and again and dashing down on it, the Lark each time giving a sudden swerve at the critical moment and thus escaping. After a long contest the Sparrow-hawk accepted defeat and went off, and immediately the Lark burst into song as though in jubilation for its narrow escape from a violent death.

It was on a barren, storm-swept, half-sandy, half-peaty flat, intersected with shallow pools, on the edge of the Atlantic, in a place that shall be nameless, that my wife and I had the most interesting ornithological adventure that has befallen us. We found ourselves suddenly among fairy-like little birds, quite unknown to us, but evidently belonging to the Plover family. The most extraordinary thing about them was that they displayed absolutely no fear of us, darting about around our feet, running over the slender water-plants which filled the pools and which, one might have thought, would scarcely have supported even a dragonfly, uttering often a small sharp cry. The back was dark slate grey, the breast white, the throat had a rufous bar on either side of a white patch. We stood astonished for a long time while they flitted and ran around us. It was only when we got back to Dublin that we found that we had stumbled on the sole Irish breeding-haunt of the Red-necked

[1] *Ibid.*, vol. v., pp. 262-263. 1935.

Phalarope, which had been discovered only the previous year. The bird is the most graceful little creature imaginable. It flies as lightly as a butterfly, and swims, as Dresser has said, like an egg-shell. "Perhaps the tamest of all our wild birds", writes Harvie-Brown. "It is utterly unsuspicious of wrong-doing on the part of the intruder on its domain, and exhibits a trusting simplicity (if I may so call it), seldom seen even in domestic fowls." A delightful account of a visit to a Scottish breeding-haunt of the Red-necked Phalarope is given by Dr. P.

FIG. 7.—RED-NECKED PHALAROPES. TWO MALES FLYING ROUND A FEMALE

Manson Bahr in the first volume of *British Birds* (pp. 202-207, 1907), with sketches made on the spot and curious details of their habits during the nesting period. One of the sketches is (by Dr. Bahr's permission) reproduced above (Fig. 7), showing two males circling round a female. "There is", says the writer, "such an infinity of grace in its every movement that we never tire watching this gem

There are now only two or three breeding pairs of Phalaropes, but since 1967 the number of these birds has increased. C.M.

of a bird." That is indeed what we also found. But we must get back to North Mayo.

For all this wild area, Belmullet is the obvious place to stay: though with a car Achill Sound, Mallaranny and Ballina are not too far away. Belmullet (*Béal an mhuirthid*, the mouth of the mullet) lies on an absurdly narrow isthmus (cut through by a canal) which separates Broad Haven on the north from the much larger and deeper bay of Blacksod on the south, and almost makes an island of The Mullet. Blacksod Bay has low and rather desolate shores on either side, but Broad Haven, though more sterile, is more attractive, as the Atlantic waves, beating into it, have carved a bolder coast-line, which outside the bay becomes very grand, as is described above. Belmullet has as a stopping-place the advantage of allowing easy access to The Mullet, that remote peninsula, half bog, half sand, full of bays and queer lakes and outlying islets; treeless, sodden, storm-swept, and everywhere pounded by the besieging sea; beautiful on a fine day, with wondrous colour over land and ocean, desolate beyond words when the Atlantic rain drives across the shelterless surface. The savage coast is guarded by two lighthouses—one on Eagle Island on the north, the other on Black Rock on the south. Between lie the two islands of Inishkea, mere reefs of rock, across which in places the waves pour in heavy weather; yet till lately each had its colony of thatched cottages, and it was only with difficulty that the people were persuaded to leave this desolate home and accept houses and land provided for them on Blacksod Bay, hard by on the mainland.

The first time I saw Broad Haven was before sunrise on a lovely morning in May many years ago, when as war correspondent I joined a landing party of a mate and two seamen from the Congested Districts Board steamer *Granuaile*. Their fell purpose was to capture and forcibly abduct a Spanish jackass which was roaming the hills "somewhere in Mayo". We landed on a stony shore where a couple of cottages gleamed white against miles of bog, and for a while I was left alone in the company of some ducks and three contemplative goats, who watched with profound attention the first sunlight gilding the cliffs of Erris Head out to the west. Goats and ducks—the most independent and also the most comical of the various creatures which in these countries man has enlisted among his little battalion of animal comrades in his fight against starvation and other ills in this strangely assorted world of ours! I have always maintained a great admiration for ducks. They understand their own business so thoroughly, and know their own minds so well. On the water, what bird sits with such perfect aplomb? Efficiency is written in its broad compact lines—none of the top-hamper of the goose or swan, none of the absurd neck-jerking of the Waterhen or Coot, which might well give them a perennial headache. No—buoyant and mobile, yet sitting well down in the saddle (so to speak), the duck gets my vote every time. The domestic bird unfortunately seldom exerts itself to fly—but what more lovely than a string of Mallard rising from a reedy lake: what accuracy in evolution, what discipline! And when they are mounted aloft, what aerial efficiency! Seagulls look as if they didn't much care whether they arrived or not—they dawdle across the sky. Rooks mostly seem tired, or else over-fed—their flight has neither energy nor enthusiasm about it. A flight of ducks compared to these is like a squadron of destroyers among a fishing fleet. And what birds build more perfect nests than Teal or Eider or Merganser—well concealed, deep and warm, even lined with down from the mother's breast? On land your duck has not the grace of a Pavlova—it rolls along like a sailor ashore (the latter does not roll so much nowadays, I think). But it looks and acts better on land than your swan, which can't help always looking " out of water ". And a duck is an intellectual bird—it can reason, to illustrate which C. B. Moffat told me a story. He watched a duck which wished to cross a rapid stream. The other bank was very steep, but there was a gap just opposite which would permit of a landing. The duck swam quickly across, but the stream carried it down some ten feet where it could not get ashore. It swam back and tried again, with the same result. Then it thought a bit, and finally waddled up the nearer bank for ten feet above its former point of departure, launched itself into the water, and struck exactly the desired landing-place.

Then as to goats. See them on some rocky place—a herd of them, of all ages—led by a grand old patriarch with huge curving horns! They fit in so naturally among heather and gnarled rock, and mount a miniature Matterhorn with such a regal king-of-the-castle air! Why the absurd head and the profusion of angles all over the body should make goats either picturesque or amusing I am not sure, but undoubtedly they are both. And like the ducks, they are wild animals, which rarely condescend to consort with us, preserving a dignified demeanour and, if treated with due respect, a certain old-world courtesy, while they watch you with wise eyes and a kind of *noli-me-tangere* expression that is in keeping with their independent attitude of mind. And as for the duck—

> And as for the duck, I think God must have smiled a bit
> Seeing those bright eyes blink on the day he fashioned it.
> And He's probably laughing still
> At the sound that came out of its bill!

I am glad to think that both of my favourites—winged and wingless—have found a champion among the latter-day poets. F. W. Harvey's verses about the ducks, indeed, of which I have purloined the last four lines above, are so excellent that I am tempted to purloin more:[1]

> From troubles of the world
> I turn to ducks,
> Beautiful comical things.
>
> .   .   .   .
>
> And ducks are soothy things
> And lovely on the lake
> When that the sunlight draws
> Thereon their pictures dim
> In colours cool.

[1] By kind permission of Messrs Ernest Benn, Ltd., 8 Bouverie Street, E.C.4.

And when beneath the pool
They dabble, and when they swim
And make their rippling rings,
O ducks are beautiful things!

But ducks are comical things:—
As comical as you.
Quack!
They waddle round, they do.
They eat all sorts of things,
And then they quack.
By barn and stable and stack
They wander at their will,
But if you go too near
They look at you through black
Small topaz-tinted eyes
And wish you ill.
Triangular and clear
They leave their curious track
In mud at the water's edge,
And there amid the sedge
And slime they gobble and peer
Saying " Quack! quack! "

.   .   .   .

And if you do not know James Stephens's poem about the goats,
you ought to! The author and Messrs Macmillan kindly allow me
to reproduce it here:

THE GOAT PATHS

The crooked paths go every way
    Upon the hill—they wind about
    Through the heather in and out
Of the quiet sunniness.
And there the goats, day after day,
    Stray in sunny quietness,
Cropping here and cropping there,
    As they pause and turn and pass,
Now a bit of heather spray,
    Now a mouthful of the grass.

In the deeper sunniness,
   In the place where nothing stirs,
Quietly in quietness,
   In the quiet of the furze,
For a time they come and lie
Staring on the roving sky.
If you approach they run away,
   They leap and stare, away they bound,
   With a sudden angry sound,
To the sunny quietude;
   Crouching down where nothing stirs
   In the silence of the furze,
Crouching down again to brood
In the sunny solitude.

If I were as wise as they
   I would stray apart and brood,
I would beat a hidden way
Through the quiet heather spray
   To a sunny solitude;
And should you come I'd run away,
   I would make an angry sound,
   I would stare and turn and bound
To the deeper quietude,
   To the place where nothing stirs
   In the silence of the furze.
In that airy quietness
   I would think as long as they;
Through the quiet sunniness
   I would stray away to brood
By a hidden beaten way
   In a sunny solitude.

I would think until I found
   Something I can never find,
Something lying on the ground,
   In the bottom of my mind.

Meanwhile the ducks which were the original cause of this
digression have launched their ships at high tide and are now well

out on Broad Haven; the goats have sauntered along the shore, and I see the sailors of the *Granuaile* returning down the mountain with the jackass captive among them. They fasten a broad canvas band round him, swim him out to the steamer, where he is jerked on board with the aid of the steam-winch—so astonished that his legs crumple under him as he is dumped on the deck. I think the Congested Districts Board had a number of these tall Spanish beasts on the west coast for a time, in an endeavour to improve the stamina of the local donkey population. There was a particularly fine animal on Clare Island, affectionately known as the " congisted ass ", which used to wander vaguely about the roads, owning no allegiance, asking no favours. The only time I ever saw it display intelligence was during a chicken-fight which happened under its nose. It watched with great interest for a minute the progress of the battle, and then emitted an ear-splitting bray that sent the combatants flying across the fence on either side of the road.

The great blanket of bog which covers Erris is broken by Carrowmore Lough, a large and bare sheet of water; to the south the ground rises into the Nephinbeg range (*Neifinn bheag*, little Nephin), with Slieve Car (*Sliabh corr*, odd mountain), 2369 feet. These mountains offer some picturesque scenery and fine walking, but the miles of wet, spongy, untrodden bog which surround them make them difficult of access. If you have a car and want to sample the biggest bog in Ireland, go north from Mallaranny to Bangor, and on east through the Glenco Pass (*Gleann cumha*) to Crossmolina (*Cros uí Mhaeilfhína*, O'Mulleeny's cross), and your drive will be one that is almost frightening in its isolation.

Indeed the Nephinbeg range of mountains is I think the very loneliest place in this country, for the hills themselves are encircled by this vast area of trackless bog. Where else even in Ireland will you find 200 square miles which is houseless and roadless —nothing but brown heather spreading as far as you can see, and rising along a kind of central back-bone into high bare hills breaking down here and there in rocky scarps, with the Atlantic winds

singing along their slopes?   I confess I find such a place not lonely
or depressing but inspiriting.   You are thrown at the same time
back upon yourself and forward against the mystery and majesty of
nature, and you may feel dimly something of your own littleness
and your own greatness: for surely man is as great as he is little:
but the littleness is actual, and the greatness largely potential.   Anyway, go up to the hills, as sages and saints have done since the beginning of the world, and you will need to be a very worldly worldling
if you fail to catch some inarticulate vision of the strange equation
in which you stand on the one side and the universe on the other.
I feel that I fail to express what is inchoately in my mind.   Perhaps
Lowell's homely rendering of similar thoughts is safer than any
attempt at more exalted language:

> Trust me, 'tis something to be cast
> Face to face with one's self at last.
> To be taken out of the fuss and strife,
> The endless clatter of plate and knife,
> The bore of books and the bores of the street,
> From the singular mess we agree to call life,
> And to be set down on one's own two feet,
> So nigh to the great warm heart of God,
> You almost seem to feel its beat,
> Down from the sunshine and up from the sod.

If you need an antidote after Erris, retreat eastward to Lough
Conn (*Loch con*, hound's lake)—still wild enough in all conscience,
but a smiling verdant place compared to The Mullet.   The lake is a
fine sheet of water, twelve miles long (including Lough Cullin, which
is merely its southern continuation).   Here we are back on the
Carboniferous limestone, whose presence accounts for softer outlines
as well as a change of flora: but close on the west the ancient metamorphic rocks prevail, and three miles from the lake-shore Nephin
(*Cnoc Néifinn*), a great dome of quartzite, rises to 2646 feet.   This is
a hill worth climbing, for it stands alone, and commands a very fine
prospect over lake and mountain and limestone plain.   Pontoon,

where a hummocky barrier of granite separates (or nearly so) Lough
Conn from Lough Cullin (*Loch cuilinn*, holly lake), makes a delightful place to sojourn.   There is shelter here; woods of native Oak
and Birch and Holly clothe the rocky slopes and the smaller islands:
and there are quiet bays full of golden granite sand, and shaded rocks
clothed with Filmy Fern and the Irish analogue of the London Pride.
Indeed, the neighbourhood of Pontoon has little of the sterility
which is associated with so much of West Mayo and Connemara,
and recalls rather the more verdant aspect of Killarney.

In our coastal peregrination we have missed several other extensive lakes which, like Lough Conn, lie along the junction of the
flat limestone of the plain with the older metamorphic rocks which
form the wild mountain and moorland area further west.   Less than
twenty miles south of Lough Conn, not far from Ballinrobe (*Baile an
Ródhba*, the town of the Robe (river)), is the delightful Lough Carra
(*Fionnloch Ceara*, fair lake of Ceara).   Its waters, derived mainly
from springs, are of a surprising pale green tint, and very clear.   The
unusual colour is enhanced by the fact that the stony shores and
bottom are coated with a white soapy deposit of lime, which reflects
the light, so that one can peer down into the clear depths, and see the
water-plants rising like slender bushes or trees from the bottom.   In
shape the lake is very irregular, with points and wooded islands
harbouring a large and interesting flora.   Out of twenty-seven
orchids known to occur in Ireland, I found no less than nineteen
about Lough Carra: and its shores form the northern limit of several
of the rare limestone plants of western Ireland, such as the Spring
Gentian and the Close-flowered Orchis.

A slow stream only a mile in length connects Lough Carra with
Lough Mask (*Loch measg*), a large open lake, ten miles long and three
to four miles broad.   The eastern bank is formed of low-lying
limestone; on the opposite shore the Maamtrasna or Partry Mountains, formed of Ordovician slates, rise from the shore to a height of
over 2200 feet.   The limestone side, facing across to the hills, is the
more diversified and interesting till one gets into the south-west

corner. Here two long narrow arms of the lake extend into the mountains. The adjoining Lough Nafooey (*Loch na feothaidh*) prolongs the lake-scenery westward for several miles, while a little to the north are a couple of grand cirques enclosing tarns which drain into the Owenbrin (*Abhainn bhroin*). This bit of country is as fine as anything that the west affords. Near the mouth of the Owenbrin turf-cutting followed by sub-aerial denudation has exposed an ancient forest of Scotch Fir over a wide flat area; the white stools, standing up in the black peat, with the blue lake behind, form a striking picture.

Lough Mask has no visible outlet, for the surplus water pours through subterranean crevices and channels under the couple of miles of land which separate it from Lough Corrib. This fact might have warned the government engineers when a good many years ago they commenced cutting a canal from lake to lake to permit of navigation from Galway to Ballinrobe. The canal was duly finished, and is there to this day, but the rock was a mere sieve, and the water when admitted at once poured through the bottom. To the exigencies of subterranean drainage is no doubt due the large rise and fall of the lake according to season—no less than six feet; and a well-marked scarp on the islands nine feet above storm-level points to a time of higher water prior to the formation of the present exits.

The chain of lakes along the western edge of the limestone is continued and concluded by Lough Corrib (*Coirib*, anciently *Loch Oirbsean*, Oirbsen's Lake), the largest of the series, twenty-seven miles long over all, extremely irregular in breadth, formed except in the north-west by solution of the limestone, and consequently very variable in depth, full of islets, reefs and deep holes. As in Lough Mask, a long narrow arm, in the north-west corner, runs far into the hills, which are formed in this place of ancient schists. The western side of the lake from Moycullen to Oughterard fringes strange country— a flat limestone tract, with stretches of bare pavement, peat bog, rough esker-ridges, limy swamps, and dense scrub mainly of Hazel, interesting for the botanist. At the southern end are large areas of very flat land, only slightly raised above water-level, and now much covered by peat—portions of the old bottom when the lake stood at a higher level. Additional evidence of this higher level is gained from the presence in these flat areas, often far from the present lake, of " mushroom-rocks "—large blocks of limestone now shaped like a toadstool. The top is umbrella-like—convex above, flat and horizontal below—and rests on a much narrower pillar of the same rock. The flat underside marks the former lake-level, above which solution of the limestone did not take place. Through the peaty flats the River Corrib, broad and slow, flows for several miles to Galway town, where it rushes down over limestone ledges to the sea. A stream of an unusual kind—the Terryland River—may be examined on the east bank of the Corrib a little above Galway. It looks like a tributary, but the water is flowing, swift and deep, *out of* the Corrib towards low limestone hills to the east. It twists for a couple of miles through flat meadow-land and then, dividing, disappears under the edge of the rising ground. I was told that at the several sink-holes the water rises and falls with the tide, but have no confirmation of this; certainly the difference of level between them and the sea at high-water is very slight.

On the lake-shores, the limestone often displays a curious form of weathering, not easy to account for. The upper surface of a horizontal slab will be densely covered with hemispherical pits with sharp confluent edges, while on the under side of the slabs the pits will be much deeper, even two or three inches in length, cylindrical, with a curved conical apex, the narrow walls which separate them having edges so sharp that one can cut one's fingers on them. Another phenomenon that invites investigation!

CHAPTER VIII

THE LAND OF NAKED LIMESTONE

(CLARE, EAST GALWAY, EAST MAYO)

IT is not altogether easy to explain why, while along the eastern side of the great Central Plain the passing away of the ice of the Glacial Period has left the limestone thickly covered with detritus, generally in the form of Boulder-clay, these deposits become thinner as one goes westward, till along the western edge of the plain, from Lough Carra in Mayo down to the Fergus estuary in Clare, a length of seventy miles, the limestone lies in many places quite devoid of covering. Its beds still rest almost everywhere horizontally, just as they were deposited as limy mud on the bottom of the Carboniferous sea millions of years ago. Long-continued aerial denudation has worn away almost everywhere in the plain the newer beds which may at one time or another have been deposited upon them, and the ice completed the process, if there was anything left to complete. If the surface of the limestone is now exposed by the removal of over-lying Glacial clay, it is seen to be smooth and polished by the passage of the ice. But where this protection is not afforded, it has been re-carved by the weather in the most interesting way. Percolating water has enlarged the parallel vertical joints which, mostly in two series more or less at right angles, everywhere traverse the horizontal beds, forming little cañons about a foot wide and often six or ten feet deep; and the flat face of the rock has suffered also, and is full of shallow solution-pans and channels and little rounded ridges. Whole solid beds of limestone have often been dissolved away, leaving only wreckage behind in the form of loose blocks. Over considerable areas even west of the Shannon and Suck a stony clay still protects the limestone, and is sometimes heavily covered with peat; but the characteristic feature of this western region is the wide expanse of bare grey rock, which attains its maximum in northern Clare, in the famous district of Burren; there the limestone, unlike its extensions in Galway and Mayo, rises into terraced hills of over 1000 feet. In the northern part of the area, where the low plain abuts on the ancient metamorphic rocks of Connemara and west Mayo, the surface of the limestone sinks gently below drainage level, resulting in the large lakes of Corrib, Mask, Carra and Conn. Possibly the more acid waters descending from the western highlands have helped to produce these lakes, by accelerating the rate of solution. But why does the Boulder-clay diminish in thickness and extent all the way from Dublin to Galway? No doubt it is connected with the fact that the main centres of dispersal of the ice-sheet lay out near the western coast. The new ice formed there would be clean and more or less free of debris, which would become more abundant in and under the ice as it slowly ground its way across the country. And out in the east, especially if the ice were melting, the mud and stones contained in it would be thrown down in increasing quantity.

The Mayo–Galway part of the area—that is, Mayo and Galway east of the line of large lakes—is a wide flat region, which has but little attraction for the visitor save for the interest that attaches to the lakes—their geology, fauna and flora. Lough Conn (p. 207) on the edge of the limestone, is a jewel in a dull setting, so far as everything east of it is concerned, and the same may be said of Lough Carra (p. 208). The larger lakes, Lough Mask and Lough Corrib, have like Conn been mentioned already (pp. 208-209). When we get to Cong (*Cunga*, a narrow river-strait), we come into a region which offers a good deal to the archaeologist. At the village itself, the underground drainage between Mask and Corrib comes to light, producing some curious effects. Standing on the narrow barrier which separates the two lakes, Cong commands an important highway between east and west. Beside the stream, on a little oasis

PLATE XXIII

ROSS ABBEY. NAVE AND TRANSEPT

among the limestone rocks, St. Fechin of Fore is stated to have founded a church in 624. Later, in the twelfth century, arose an abbey tenanted by Canons Regular of the Order of St. Augustine. To judge by what is left of it, this must have been a very beautiful building, and it is unfortunate that so little remains. Much of the land around Cong, richly wooded, is enclosed in the demesne of Ashford, and strictly preserved on account of its famous woodcock shooting. Undoubtedly the most curious feature of the neighbour-hood is the canal already mentioned (p. 209), built to provide for water traffic between the two lakes. The channel was cut through solid limestone, but the fickle rock proved to be a mere sieve, and the expensive excavation, waterless, four miles in length, still remains, a monument of engineering futility. Out in the great flat area east of Lough Corrib stand the ruins of two monasteries, unusually complete and undefaced, giving an interest to an other-wise dull region. The monastery of Ross (Plate XXIII), on the banks of the Black River a mile north-west of Headford, needs only a roof to make it again habitable. It presents an extensive range of buildings, with many beautiful architectural features, though, like most of the Irish ecclesiastical settlements, it shows little of the rich-ness of contemporary buildings in England. The abbey was erected for the Franciscans in 1351, and owes its present excellent state of preservation to the fact that after the suppression of the monasteries the monks returned to it again and again, and it was not finally abandoned until 1765. Not only are the ecclesiastical buildings intact, but you may study the arrangement of the kitchens and other domestic annexes. The whole presents a more complete picture of Irish monastic life than may be obtained at any other site in Ireland. Claregalway monastery stands by the Clare River twelve miles from Ross, and eight miles north-east of Galway. It is half a century later in date than the former, having been built by John de Cogan for the Franciscans in 1290. It had a somewhat similar history, since suppression did not mean its entire abandonment, and a small chapel still kept in repair probably points to continuous or almost continuous

According to Dr. Leask in *Irish Churches and Monastic Buildings* (Vols. II and III, 1958 and 1960) Claregalway Friary dates from about 1240 and the ruins of Ross to the closing years of the 15th century. C.M.

limited occupation during the whole of the intervening period. The buildings are more ruined than those of Ross, but much that is beautiful and interesting remains. The solid castle ruin which adjoins is one of the De Burgo strongholds, and witnessed in its day a good deal of fighting.

Far and wide over this flat region are dotted small castles which were the fortified residences of the holders of the land for several centuries, and there are also the ruins of smaller ecclesiastical establishments well worth a visit by the antiquary. This is a wide lonely country of great distances and broad skies, with few houses or trees, and endless walls of grey stone. If you want to see how lonely it can be take the new road from Galway towards Headford. After a couple of miles of hummocky limestone ground (into which the mysterious Terryland River disappears, see p. 210) you drop past the old castle and little lake at Ballindooly (*Baile an dubhlaoigh*, the town of the dark-visaged chief) and enter a stretch of six miles of road, dead level, dead straight, with neither hedges nor houses—just flat wet meadow or bog on either side, stretching away to Lough Corrib on the west, and to slightly rising ground on the east. The first time I traversed that heart-breaking thoroughfare the land was wrapped in a wet mist driving before a wind that moaned: and so, like the visitor to Castle Carabas in the *Book of Snobs* " for a mile and a half I walked—alone, and thinking of death "—save that the mile and a half was six! But on a sparkling western day all is different. Then one notices with delight the white and yellow Water-lilies in the black wayside pools, the masses of Bog-bean and Marsh St. John's-wort and Orchids in the wet ground, the lovely colours over bog and meadow, and, ever beckoning, the hills of Connemara out beyond the silver gleams that betray Lough Corrib.

If you want to explore this East Galway region, the old town of Tuam (*Tuaim dhá ghualann*, tumulus of the two shoulders) is your best centre—or Galway, if you have a car. And this is one of the regions where a car is a marked advantage, for features are few and distances long, and provided you know where to stop, you miss little even at thirty miles an hour. Tuam itself is a modest market-town, with little to suggest its long history and early importance. This importance was mainly ecclesiastical; until 1834 it was the seat of two archbishoprics, Catholic and Protestant, but by the Church Temporalities Act the latter was reduced to a bishopric and united with Killala (*Cill Alaidh*, church of Ala) and Achonry (*Achadh Chonaire*, Conary's field). The beginning of Tuam was a monastery founded by St. Jarlath in the sixth century. The present cathedral, though practically rebuilt half a century ago, retains much of the character of the older building, and hard by stands the chancel of a much more ancient church, with a very beautiful arch in the Norman style, dating from the middle of the twelfth century. The old town cross, long broken, its fragments in the possession of several people, is now again restored and complete, with its inscriptions commemorating Abbot (later Archbishop) O'Hoisin and King Turlogh O'Conor of Connacht.

A mile and a half to the north-west stands the round tower of Kilbannan (*Cill Bennán*), amid the remains of an early ecclesiastical settlement. And five miles west of Tuam rises Knockma (*Cnoc meadha*, mead hill), a limestone knob only 300 feet above the general level, but which, in this flat country, is a landmark for a thousand square miles around. From its summit you command a very wide prospect over the plain; westward the mountains of Connemara rise beyond Lough Corrib, north-westward those of Mayo, and away to the south and south-west Slieve Aughty and the hills of Burren. The top of Knockma is crowned with an amazing "modern antiquity", the work of one man, who has converted the remains of a large cashel or cairn into an elaborate stone structure of his own design. The limestone rocks of the hill harbour an outpost of the famous Burren flora, and the botanist will find here the Spring Gentian, Purple Helleborine, and so on. From Knockma you get an excellent impression of the kind of country which prevails in eastern Galway—marshy pasture, great bogs, shallow lakelets lying on white calcareous marl or on black peat, and towards Lough

Corrib increasing areas of bare grey stone, and you will note the paucity of houses and trees, and how these follow the patches of friendly drift.

If you approach Galway town (*Gaillimh*, pronounced Galliv) from Dublin by either train or car you get a rather better impression than the foregoing, for both railway and road traverse a kind of oasis, by Woodlawn and Athenry and Oranmore (*Uarán mór*, great spring) and the entrance to Galway is through tall trees. Galway was a place or at least a pass of importance from the earliest human times, for to this point converged all traffic between east and west. Lough Corrib, and at its southern end the Corrib River, interposed a continuous barrier of water nearly thirty miles in length, and only at Galway, where the river suddenly breaks down in rapids to the sea, was passage possible save by boat. The more northern route, moreover, passing between Lough Corrib and Lough Mask by way of Cong, led only into the mountains of Joyce's Country, whereas the Galway ford provided an easy and level route westward for fifty miles to the western ocean, and to all the southern shores of Connemara. Besides, Galway furnished a port sufficient for the ships of all but modern days, one of the few safe havens for a long distance along the wild Atlantic coast—a port offering easy access to the great plain to the eastward. It may have been the Magnata of Ptolemy. We learn from the *Annals of the Four Masters* that a fort was erected there by the Connacht men in 1124, which during the succeeding century was several times destroyed by the men of Munster, and as often rebuilt. In 1232 the English under Richard de Burgo arrived, drove out the O'Connors, and made Galway an English colony. Largely, no doubt, on account of its excellent position, it became a place of importance, with large sea-borne trade, a walled town which suffered much from siege and other ills in the seventeenth century. Its history has been narrated in many books. It was the advent of the railway that dealt a final blow to Galway's prosperity, by crippling its sea-borne trade and substituting Dublin as a distributing centre for the inland regions. Its walls have now disappeared, and

only one gate is left, but the town is full of remains of former prosperity—quaint old residences, and down by the harbour deserted
stores and factories. The famous Claddagh (*Cladach*, a flat stony seashore), so much extolled in sentimental guide-books, was originally an Irish fishing village outside the English town, and till lately
it showed a remarkable collection of white-washed cottages set at
random after the manner of ancient hamlets, inhabited by people
who were self-governing and retained many primitive customs.
But most of the peculiar features of the Claddagh disappeared, one
by one, to survive only in popular literature, and now that the primitive village has given way to rows of small modern houses the last
trace of special interest has gone. The thing best worth seeing in
Galway is the church of St. Nicholas, founded in 1320, a spacious
building containing a wealth of memorials of Galway history and
Galway people.

In comparison with the slow-flowing and often impure rivers
which traverse most coastal towns, the rushing Corrib, with its
limpid water and limestone rocks, is an inspiring sight. Thither
come salmon in thousands out of the sea, to ascend the rapids into
Lough Corrib and thence spread to breed throughout the lakes and
streams over a wide area. When the water is low there may be seen
from the upper bridge one of the most famous of local sights—
hundreds of great fish lying tight-packed, head to stream, waiting
for the rain that will allow them to pass up to their spawning-
grounds. Altogether Galway has a great deal of interest to offer to
the visitor, particularly on the architectural and historical side; but,
largely as a result of modern encroachment and rebuilding, these
features are not immediately obvious, and much needs to be dug out
among the back streets.

But it is especially as a gate to so much that is lovely and interesting to north and west and south that Galway is important. Instead
of its present designation—a word of uncertain origin, derived perhaps
from a woman, Galva, perhaps from the Gallaeci of Spain, perhaps
from the Gaels—it should bear a euphonious Irish name signifying

an entrance, a portal. North of Galway Bay is Connemara, whose praises I have sung already (p. 160). South of it is Burren: and no such dramatic contrast exists anywhere in the British Isles, whether of scenery or geology or vegetation, as is afforded by those two regions. If you are in a hurry—which for your own sake I hope you are not—you can glimpse this remarkable contrast by a day's motoring in each area. Another day you can take the steamer to Aran, and in the time available get the merest glance at part of the largest (and most interesting) of the three islands. But that is not the way to see any of these places: three days in each should be regarded as an absolute minimum, especially as regards Connemara, unless you are merely an abandoned and reprehensible sightseer: and for most of the time the motor should be exchanged for a pair of strong boots. The Tuam–Cong–Ross–Claregalway excursion alone demands the motor all day. As a centre for the archaeologist, whether pagan or Christian antiquities are to be viewed, Galway is equalled in Ireland only by Dublin. The latter has within easy reach New Grange, Dowth, Monasterboice, Mellifont, Glendalough: the other has Aran, Cong, Ross, Claregalway, Athenry, Kilmacduagh, Corcomroe. It is difficult to choose between them; either place offers a programme of surpassing interest.

The Aran Islands (*Ára*, a kidney) lie across the entrance of Galway Bay, and may be reached by steamer thrice a week from Galway. Although they act as a breakwater to the Atlantic rollers, the twenty-seven miles is seldom smooth, and often quite rough, which is an argument for not going and returning on the same day. There is now plenty of primitive but clean accommodation to be obtained on Inishmore (*Inis mór*, big island)—whither most pilgrims tend—and one can stay on both Inishmaan (*Inis meadhóin*, middle island) and Inisheer (*Inis thiar*, western island) also, but better by previous arrangement. The three islands are simply a reef of limestone, once a continuation of northern Clare. They are tilted downwards towards the north-east, and while that shore is quite low, the south-western side faces the Atlantic in a cliff-wall often 200 feet high, which rises at the highest point to 400 feet. A geological gap of great width chronologically, though not geographically, separates the northern end of Aran from the adjoining coast of Connemara. It is the change of rock which accompanies this gap, from limestone to granite, which to a great extent has made the Aran Islands habitable at all, for the granite has permitted of a vigorous growth of peat, which is entirely absent from the islands, and has allowed of the easy importation of an abundant supply of fuel. Not only peat, but even soil is usually missing from the Aran Islands—or was so until the islanders, stopping up with splinters the vertical joints of the limestone and spreading on it sand and seaweed brought from the shore, created by degrees a medium on which to grow their grass and potatoes and oats. The flat sheets of rock were originally strewn, as in Burren, with innumerable blocks of limestone of all sizes: this provided the ancient peoples with ample building material for their great stone forts, and the early Christian settlers for their churches and houses: and what has not been used since for domestic purposes has been built in modern times into innumerable stone walls, which both clear the fields and give protection from wind. These walls, five or six feet high and mostly only one stone thick, enclosing tiny fields of rock, are a very characteristic feature of Aran, and form difficult barriers for the uninitiated. To add a fantastic touch to the rock-landscape, numerous rounded boulders of granite, many of them of large size, brought by the ice from Connemara, have proved too tough to be broken up and removed, and some of the tiny fields look as if their walls had been built solely for the enclosure of these defiant erratics.

Apart from its peculiar topography and scenery, which alone would make a visit to the Aran Islands worth while, there are at least three features which give the place special interest—the wealth of antiquities, pagan and Christian; the remarkable flora; and the people themselves, a primitive community still preserving much of their individuality. Aran, its inhabitants and antiquities has been so often described that there is no need to go into details here: the place must be seen in order that its exceptional fascination may be appreciated. Don't *read* about Aran: go to it! Quite apart from its special interests, the wide unobstructed skies, the Atlantic foaming round the rocks, the soft air, the lovely prospect of the Connemara hills to the northward, the indefinable charm that belongs to islands and island communities, make it a place that, once visited, one never forgets. The steamer drops you in the sheltered bay of Kilronan, far from much of the more interesting ground (Inishmore is nine miles long)—hence the necessity of staying for a night or two even if you propose to visit only the largest of the three islands. Go up to the western cliff-edge and meditate on Dun Ængus, the largest of a number of great forts of dry stone, and the finest monument of its kind in Europe (Plate XXIV). It is built on the edge of a 300-foot cliff, which efficiently protects its southern and eastern sides, since the precipice is vertical or even overhanging. The semi-circular fortifications which front the landward side form three approximately concentric walls, the innermost eighteen feet high and thirteen feet thick, stepped on the inside. Outside the second wall is the remarkable *chevaux de frise*, formed of sharp stones placed on end, a kind of stone forest, designed to delay a rush of invaders. Outside this again is the ruin of a third rampart. The gigantic size and peculiar position on the cliff-edge, with the Atlantic roaring at the base of the precipice, make this great fort one of the most impressive things that Ireland can offer. And the tremendous prospect of sea and land that you obtain from it forms a fitting setting. It moved even that solid archaeologist T. J. Westropp to become lyrical: " The view from the summit of the fort is most impressive and solemn; the desolate-looking fields, ' the soil almost paved with stones ', as in 1685, fall away to the golden crescent of Kilmurvey strand, and rise up the opposite hill, past the village of Gortnagappul, to the old lighthouse near Dun Oghil. Eastward runs the long range of steep, dark headlands, and deep bays, rarely unsheeted by high-leaping spray; while beyond the huge cliff, and ' the trouble of the sea that cannot rest ', we see the ' great wall of Thomond '—

PLATE XXIV

R. Welch: photo

DUN ÆNGUS. INTERIOR AT DOORWAY

Moher—with its violet-shaded bastions. The limits of the view on clear days reach from the giant peaks of Corkaguiny in Kerry to those of Connemara; while to the south-west is only the horizon of the landless deep, whirling sea-birds, and the sparkling silver tideways." The reference to the year 1685 points to the date of the *Ogygia* of Roderic O'Flaherty, which contains (p. 175) the earliest printed description of the fort: "*Dun-ængus ingens opus Lapideum sine Cœmento tamen, quod ducentas vaccas in area contineret supra altissimam maris crepidinem è vastæ molis rupibus erectum adhuc extat in Arannâ magnâ sinus Galviensis insulâ, S. Endei incolatu, & Sanctorum multitudine postea celebri*".

Then there are other similar great cashels, plentiful remains of early Christian settlements from the sixth century *Teampull-Benen* to some of much later date, round towers, crosses, dolmens, holy wells, cloghans or bee-hive huts, castles and so on—a bewildering wealth of antiquities to find on exposed shelves of bare limestone out in the Atlantic. But the early Irish ecclesiastics appear to have rejoiced in asceticism even of a very severe kind—witness the colony which exiled themselves on the Skelligs off the Kerry coast (p. 381). Aran even flourished and became famous; pilgrims from great distances came here to study and to pray: and its very name— *Árananaomh*, or Ara of the saints—arose from the fame of the religious colonies which St. Enda founded here in the fifth century, under grant from Æ ngus, the Christian King of Munster.

The remarkable flora of Aran, embracing many rare and beautiful plants, is found mainly occupying the vertical chinks in the limestone rocks—there are few other places for plants to grow! It is an outlier of the famous vegetation of Burren, a few miles to the eastward, and discussion of it may be postponed till we reach that area, a few pages farther on (p. 225). Meanwhile we return for a little to the low limestone region of eastern Galway.

When we cross the railway at Athenry—an interesting old town, with a noble name (*Áth na Ríoch*, the ford of the kings), now a poor place, but with a massive castle ruin, a Franciscan monastery,

a Dominican monastery and a castellated town gate to bear witness
to its former importance—the amount of bare limestone begins to
increase, and continues to do so as we approach Burren.

Around here, within the area stretching from Tuam down to
Corofin (*Cora Finne*, weir of Finn) we are in the turlough region,
of which Gort is the centre. Turloughs (*turlach*, a dried-up spot)
are depressions in the surface, with subterranean drainage which,
owing to the proximity of their floors to the level of permanent
water, flood up in wet weather, forming lakes for longer or shorter
periods, the rate of their rise and fall, and the extent and duration
of their flooding, varying in different hollows, and depending on
several factors connected with the underground drainage. These
changes are often quite rapid. The turloughs are full during much
of the winter, and summer flooding is not infrequent, when a spell
of wet weather supervenes. In dry weather, some hold permanent
water on their floors; in others, a stream flows across the floor
when they are empty, appearing as a spring in the side or bottom,
and disappearing in a swallow-hole; many show no sign of water
when flooding is absent, bottom as well as sides being covered with
a green sward, a swallow-hole set among muddy rocks often
indicating the point of inflow and outflow of flood-water. The
whole drainage in much of this area is subterranean. One turlough,
Caherglassaun Lough (*Cathair Glassáin*, Glassan's town), lies at so
low a level that it is influenced by the tide in Galway Bay, three
and a half miles away, rising and falling synchronously to an extent
of several feet. The turlough area is largely bare fissured limestone
country, with many shrubs; and the most conspicuous indication
of a turlough is the abrupt cessation of all shrubby growth below a
well-marked contour. The herb vegetation, which extends from
this level to the bottom of even the deepest turlough, which may
measure as much as twenty feet, is very closely nibbled by rabbits
or sheep, and forms a dense fine green sward: the flood-water is
usually quite clear, and leaves but a slight deposit of limy mud.
These velvety swards filling the hollows among the bushy rocky

areas are very striking. Another marked feature of the turloughs is the presence of the black moss *Cinclidotus fontanaloides* on the stones and rocks. This plant can flourish under a frequency of flooding much less than that which inhibits the growth of bushes, and consequently it intrudes into the lower part of the bushy zone: the presence of the black moss, followed a few feet lower down by the cessation of bushes, is a sure sign of turlough conditions. The duration and distribution of flooding in the turloughs throughout the year cannot be determined without continued observation, but accepting the cessation of all tree-growth as a sign of frequent flooding, it is surprising how many entirely terrestrial plants descend much below this level, to places where submergence must be a much commoner occurrence. Thus Dewberry will grow up to nine feet below the bush-limit, Ribwort Plantain over twelve feet, Creeping Cinquefoil and Silverweed sixteen to seventeen feet respectively, or twenty-two and twenty-three feet below the upper limit of *Cinclidotus*. The common water-moss *Fontinalis* actually grows in the turloughs at levels higher than those at which the plants just mentioned flourish. For the student of plant-life the turloughs form a fascinating feature, and they well deserve study.[1]

Indeed, if you stay at Gort (*Gort inse Guaire*, field of Guaire's island) or Ardrahan (*Árd rathain*, height of the fort) you find yourself in a region where the solid limestone which is everywhere in evidence is really but a honeycomb, a sponge filled, below an uncertain and fluctuating level, with water. The streams are as erratic in their behaviour as the turloughs, for they are continually appearing above ground, issuing from caverns in walls of rock or from deep well-like pools, flowing for a while in one direction or another, and then vanishing again. In many places, however, especially towards Corofin, the water is held up by solid beds of limestone, and numerous lakes are the result, often fringed with a strange alternation of white calcareous marl, black peat, and grey rock.

[1] See Praeger, " The Flora of the Turloughs, a preliminary Note ", *Proc. Roy. Irish Acad.*, vol. xli., sect. B, pp. 37-45. 1932.

And there are some puzzling features such as the stumps of former pine forests rising from the lake water, although no sign is to be seen of a lower water-level in the past. This queer country continues southward through Ennis, forming a well-marked broad depression down central Clare, and slowly sinking below sea-level in the island-filled estuary of the Fergus, where it enters the Shannon —" the spacious Shenan spreading like a sea ".

West of the northern part of this lowland, opposite Ardrahan and Gort, the limestone rises abruptly into the hills of Burren (*Boireann*, great rock), famous among botanists; this high land fronts Galway Bay to the north, and to the west the Atlantic and the Aran Islands. The hills form a kind of dissected table-land, having a number of flattish summits of between 1000 and 1100 feet. But though the limestone lies here in great horizontal beds —as is very marked if one views this strange country from Galway —the hills are not scarped as at Ben Bulben, the other limestone upland of the west, but offer gently rounded outlines, with only an occasional cliff along the eastern margin. Why have we not got here a scarped table-land as in Sligo and as in the basaltic plateau of Antrim, where in both cases solid horizontal strata have produced this characteristic form of landscape? A. Farrington suggests to me that it is due to the nature of the rocks underlying the plateau. Below the basalt in the north-east are softer Secondary rocks, or else Carboniferous sandstone. The more rapid weathering of these results in the undercutting of the basalt, and consequent cliff-formation. At Ben Bulben the solid limestones are underlaid by the less resistant Calp series, with a similar result. But in Burren the hard (though soluble) beds of the Upper Limestone cover the lower grounds as well as the higher. Differential weathering is absent, so we do not get undercutting and consequent cliffs. But why these soluble beds should have been preserved at all, forming high hills in this region of heavy rainfall, while they have disappeared from off so much of the country to the eastward, is a puzzle. They are certainly suffering severely now. If they were

PLATE XXV

A HILLSIDE IN BURREN

ever covered with Glacial drift, it is vanished. If they had a friendly covering of peat—and the flora suggests that they had—it is gone likewise, and for miles the bare grey rock lies open to the sky, its surface a network of deep fissures and little drainage channels, all strewn with angular blocks large and small, the wreck of upper beds now destroyed. The hills are soil-less, treeless, waterless (Plate XXV): but in the deeper valleys there are springs, and here and there is Glacial drift and consequent farmland and native scrub of Oak and Hazel. The strangeness of this grey limestone country must be seen to be realized; it is like nothing else in Ireland or in Britain—though around Ingleborough you get similar landscape on a smaller scale. One stream, by some miracle, contrives to flow on the surface from source almost to mouth—the Caher River (*Cathair*, a stone fort), which debouches at Fanore: being so rare a phenomenon, it is appropriate that it should contain as one of its abundant plants an extremely rare Pondweed—the hybrid *Potamogeton perpygmaeus*. And this brings me to the subject of the flora of Burren, which is so remarkable, and in spring so beautiful, that it is celebrated far outside the ranks of the botanists. Throughout the whole region of the bare limestones—from eastern Mayo away down to the Shannon—this flora is found. Some of its leading members—the alpine Spring Gentian, for instance, and the Close-flowered Orchis of the Mediterranean—range from Lough Carra southward almost to Ennis. On the low limestones around Ardrahan this flora is well developed; but to see it at its maximum of profusion and beauty one must go to Burren or to Aran, during the second half of May. Its interest lies in the presence and frequent abundance of many plants elsewhere rare; and these plants display a very remarkable variety of type as regards their normal headquarters. Extremely profuse are several which are usually found on the mountains or in the far north—such as Mountain Avens, Bear-berry, Spring Gentian and several Mossy Saxifrages. With these are others of quite southern range, like the Close-flowered Orchis and the Maidenhair (Plate XXVI); and all alike grow

mixed together here right down to sea-level. Some of the former
group are here found further south (in view of their lowland
habitat) than anywhere else, while some of the latter occur nowhere
else so far north. We have, indeed, a very remarkable mixture of
northern and southern species, most of which, by a happy chance,
are also most beautiful plants. With these are others which are
very rare in the British area, like the Hoary Rock-rose and Pyramidal
Bugle: others again are conspicuous by their immense profusion,
like the Bloody Crane's-bill and Madder, Hart's-tongue and Scale
Fern. The result of the luxuriance and abundance of these is that
over miles the grey limestone is converted into a veritable rock-
garden in spring, brilliant with blossom. But how do these plants
attain such profusion on ground that is mostly bare rock? Many
live in chinks and in the rain-widened joints of the limestone, where
humus has collected; and the damp Atlantic wind, laden with mist
and showers, does the rest. Often a skin of peaty soil only an inch
thick, lying on a dry flat rock-surface, will maintain a flora of perhaps twenty species. And how is it that so mixed an assemblage
of plants—alpine and lowland, northern and southern—is found
crowded together on this queer ground? That is not so simple,
but let us consider the peculiar conditions which prevail. There is
a very damp climate—very mild also, frost being practically unknown. There is great exposure to wind, yet the rock is full of
deep chinks where complete shelter prevails. There is exceptionally
good drainage, all water sinking far down into the rock. The warm
moist air will account for the abundance of the Maidenhair: the
light soil and absence of frost help the Close-flowered Orchis to
maintain itself. The presence of alpine plants in profusion right
down to sea-level appears more puzzling, but alpine plants do not
necessarily need cold in order to be happy: indeed most of them
do not like frost, and need the warm dry covering of snow which
they get on the higher mountains; in our own gardens most do
best in a frame, where they escape the damp cold of our winters.
During spring and summer the alpines like—and on the mountains

PLATE XXVI

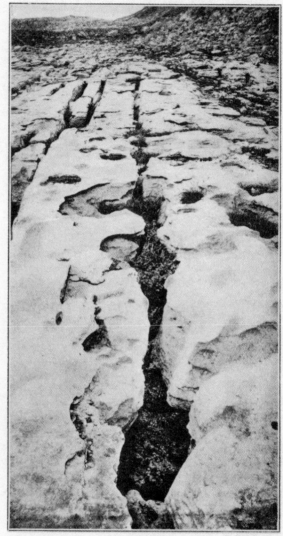

R. Welch: photo

THE MAIDENHAIR AMONG THE BURREN ROCKS

obtain—plenty of moisture combined with good drainage: this they get in perfection in Burren; and under these circumstances, the higher temperature of the warm Atlantic seaboard does not appear to incommode them in the least. If alpines attempted to descend into the lowlands in most places, the tall vegetation of summer would inevitably destroy them: but on the Burren rocks exposure and grazing and want of depth of soil combine to produce a population of low-growing plants, among which the alpines are at home. Their most obvious enemies would be the gregarious Bracken and Ling, bushes and coarse-growing grasses: these are all restrained by the factors mentioned, and the Ling also by the presence of limestone rock.

If you want to see this wonderful flower-show at its best, go, as I have said, about the middle of May or a little later. Pass through Kinvarra (*Ceann mhara*, head of the sea), with its picturesque old castle on a rock among the seaweed. When you come to Corranroe (*Cora ruadh*, red weir), take the steep hill in front of you, and visit Corcomroe abbey (*Corco Mruad*, [territory of] the descendants of Mruad), standing in an oasis of green grass among the grey limestone. Push on through Ballyvaughan (*Baile uí Bheacháin*, O'Behan's town) and stop between the old castle of Gleninagh (*Gleann eidhneach*, ivied glen) and Black Head. You can climb the rocks up to the fine cashel of Caherdoonfergus (*Cathair Donn Fergus*), and on the higher grounds you will find one or two rare plants not seen below, like the Purple Helleborine and the Wintergreen. But to appreciate fully the weirdness of this region—weirdness is perhaps the best word—you should go inland also. Take the south-western road from Kinvarra—narrow, but surface good—up through the deep rocky defile of Glencolumkille and under the cliffs of Slievecarran (*Sliabh cairn*, mountain of the cairn); take the first turn to the right, up over the ridge by Pullagh (*Pollach*, the land full of holes) and from Carran back northward to Bell Harbour, and I think you will admit that never have you been in stranger country.

There are other interests besides botany in this land of rock.

Megalithic monuments and other Bronze Age relics, as well as
Iron Age forts of stone, and such things, are there in rather surprising numbers—difficult to find among the wilderness of blocks
of similar stone, and pointing to an unexpected distribution of
population, for many of the monuments are placed high on the
bare hills of rock, not in the comparatively hospitable valleys,
where water and shelter could have been obtained.

Immediately south of the Burren hills, from Lisdoonvarna (*Lios
dúin bhearna*, fort of the fortress of the gap) on to the Shannon and
away to Killarney, the limestone dips under a broadening band of
Upper Carboniferous rocks—shales and sandstones—and the aspect
of the country alters at once.   Heavy wet soils prevail, with coarse
grass and rushes; muddy streams paved with black pebbles cut deep
gashes in the soft shale.   All the interesting plants of Burren vanish,
and you find yourself longing to be again on the rough grey rocks.
Out to the west there is one grand feature, for a broad rather bare
ridge impinges on the Atlantic at the Cliffs of Moher (*Creig Mo-
thair*) and the horizontally layered flagstones are built up for a
length of five miles into magnificent vertical cliffs, rising at their
highest point to 668 feet above the sea.   They are too steep to
support plant life, and provide few ledges whereon sea-birds can
nest or rest, which gives them a grim and savage look; and along
their base the Atlantic waves beat incessantly.   Their summit
commands a very fine view—the Aran Islands one behind the other,
the Maam Turk mountains and the Twelve Bens rising beyond the
low shore-line of Connemara, and southward a long stretch of the
Clare coast.   If you want to feel very small, go out in one of the
canvas curraghs on a day when a ground-swell is coming in from
the ocean, and get your boatman to row you along the base of
those gigantic rock-walls.   The rollers and their reflections from
the cliffs produce a troubled sea on which your boat dances like a
live thing, like a tiny cork, and the vast dark precipice above,
vertical and in places overhanging, seems to soar up to the un-
troubled sky.   It is a wonderful experience.

From this place of great cliffs and waves it is almost a relief to round Hag's Head into Liscannor Bay, at the head of which is a sandy estuary, and old castles to testify to former appreciation of the shelter which is found here. Close by is Lahinch (*Leithinse*, peninsula), with its sand-dunes and consequent golf course and hotels—a grand place if fresh air is what you are looking for. Thence Clare tails away in a wedge between the Atlantic and the Shannon for thirty-five miles to Loop Head (*Leim Chonchulainn*, Cuchullinn's leap), a wind-swept almost treeless region of rushy pasture and peat-bogs, with little attraction inland (save a few rare plants) but a fine and varied coast-line of cliffs and sands and headlands, and everywhere the boom of the Atlantic waves to keep you company. Kilkee (*Cill Choi*, Caoi's church), tucked in a deep little sandy bay, is the place to stay: and unless sylvan beauty is what you pine for, it will delight you. The ocean is here the one attraction—it and the rocks and sands, the result of its incessant battle with the land—but here it is all-sufficing. From Kilkee you can walk fifteen miles of cliff-top to Loop Head. The cliffs, on account of the rapid weathering of the shales, are almost plantless, black and forbidding: inland are miles of flattish rushy pasture, gaudy in August with masses of Purple Loosestrife and Water Ragwort: and the salt winds cause many plants of the coast to grow far from the sea. Loop Head itself, surrounded by a 200-foot cliff-wall, presents an immense garden of Sea-Pink, on which you recline at ease, picking up the landmarks to north and south of the vast expanse of ocean—on the one hand the Cliffs of Moher and the Aran Islands, and behind them the mountains of Connemara; on the other, beyond the Shannon mouth and Kerry Head, the grand outline of the Dingle Peninsula, with Brandon and Slieve Mish and all the rugged hills that lie between the two. Or if you go inland from Kilkee, a few miles takes you to the flats of Poulnasherry Bay (*Poll an oisire*, inlet of the oyster) on the Shannon side, which opens on the sheltered indented gravelly shore of the great river-estuary, a remote and lonely region. Nearby is Kilrush, whence you can take boat to Scattery Island (*Inis*

Cathaigh, Cathach's island), a mile off-shore, to visit all that is left of the monastery founded by St. Senan in the sixth century, and still a place of resort for the pious. You will find the remains of six primitive buildings, churches or hermitages, and a fine round tower.

There is much to be seen along the fifty miles of the Shannon estuary, whether one's interests are antiquarian or biological or general, and the proper way to see it is by water, which allows of exploration on either shore. With a small motor boat and head-quarters at Foynes (*Faing*, a raven) or Tarbert (*Tairbeart*, an isthmus) or Kilrush (*Cill ruis*, church of the promontory) you can have a pleasant and leisurely holiday here, in a region unknown to the tourist, but possessing much quiet beauty and all that goes with the unspoiled Irish countryside. But hotels are few, and it would be well to make sure of suitable accommodation beforehand. Camping would be the ideal plan, if only one had luck in weather. The place may become less lonely now, as these sheltered waters form the terminus of the projected Atlantic air route.

CHAPTER IX

IN THE CENTRAL PLAIN

(NORTH TIPPERARY, LEIX, OFFALY, WESTMEATH, LONGFORD, ROSCOMMON)

THE boundaries of the Central Plain are indefinite, for in all directions its continuity gets broken up as one goes outward from the middle of it—in the south by an increasing number of folds which protrude Devonian and Silurian rocks in ridges through the level-lying limestones; in east and west by masses of various older rocks; and in the north again by N.E.-S.W. folds exposing Silurians and Old Red Sandstone, as well as by overlying beds of Upper Carboniferous. The area dealt with here is the middle and most typical portion of the plain. This consists mainly of the basin of the non-tidal Shannon, and includes the greater part of it. And save for the large anticline which runs across the southern portion, exposing older rocks from Slieve Bloom to Keeper Mountain, almost the whole of it is Carboniferous Limestone, lying in horizontal beds, and seldom rising above 300 feet over sea-level. On top of the limestone is Glacial drift, usually calcareous, of varying depth, and on the drift is much calcareous moraine material, mostly in the form of esker-ridges; also immense areas of peat-bog. "We live", wrote William King a couple of hundred years ago, " in an island almost infamous for bogs". This central region is indeed the home of the red bogs or *Hochmoore*, which cover about one-tenth of the whole surface. Only in certain areas in the west is the proportion of bog higher than this, and in such cases, as in West Mayo, even though it may be lowland in situation, it is usually more of the type of mountain bog. The red bogs lie out on the plain, where the present rainfall conforms to the Irish average—about 35 to 45 inches, as compared with 60 to 70 inches average along the west coast, and 35 inches or less further eastward. The passing away of the ice left the plain covered with drift which was strewn with late-glacial material, all of which interfered greatly with the previous ill-marked drainage system. The result was much flooding, innumerable shallow lakes in which calcareous marl was formed. Many of these became eventually drained by natural causes, and the overwhelming bog spread over their surface, so that the base which the turf-cutter reaches when drainage permits him to dig the lowest stratum of peat is often white marl full of fresh-water shells. Between the bog areas is much limy marsh and peaty pasture, and where the ground rises a little, mostly as broad ridges of drift, we find tillage and good grassland. That picture belongs to the poorer and more characteristic portions of the Central Plain. In some other parts, such as Roscommon, the limestone is near the surface, and great stretches of pasture prevail; or where the drift is developed there may be large areas of farmland, with plenty of well-grown trees—which betray the direction of the prevailing wind by their bend to the eastward.

If we enter this area from that dealt with in the last chapter we cross the Shannon from Clare into the northern part of the large county of Tipperary (*Tiobraid Árann*, the spring of Ara). The crossing-place will be at Killaloe (*Cill Dálua*, St. Molua's church), twelve miles above Limerick, a commendable spot from many points of view, and one that we may make the most of here, for in our forthcoming pilgrimage over the Central Plain we shall encounter nothing like it, with its beautiful combination of mountain and lake. At Killaloe is to be seen a remarkable block of stone, the shaft of an ancient cross, which bears a Runic inscription on one side and an Ogham inscription on the other. It was observed not many years ago used as an ordinary stone in the wall around the cathedral there, and has now been moved inside the church. Runic inscriptions are extraordinarily rare in Ireland, considering the intimate if warlike relations of Scandinavia and Denmark with Ireland through several centuries. An inscription in Runic character occurs on a small strip of bronze found in Louth, now in the Dublin Museum; Carl Marstrander discovered a stone with three Runic letters on the Great Blasket not many years ago, and an obscure Rune was unearthed recently among the ruins of the Abbey of Nendrum in County Down. These are the only other examples so far known from Ireland. The Killaloe inscription, Professor Macalister says, states that " . . . [reading uncertain] carved this cross ". That is all. None of the rest of the cross has been found, and we do not know either who made it or for what purpose: probably sepulchral. The style of the lettering assigns it to about the first half of the eleventh century. The Ogham inscription on the back is a complete puzzle—as it may have been intended to be. If Macalister cannot read an Ogham no one can: and he owns himself baffled.

At Killaloe we are confronted with the most peculiar feature of that curious river, the Shannon. To appreciate this, imagine you are descending it from its source among the Cavan hills. Dropping steeply into Lough Allen (p. 134) it emerges from the hills of Arigna and Slieveanieran as a deep slow stream, and in this guise, with mazy lake-like expansions spreading over the flat land on either side, it flows on, ever broadening, into and across the Central Plain. Above Athlone it widens into Lough Ree, sixteen miles long and up to six miles broad. Below that, the country is flatter than ever, and one cannot foretell the course of the river, here only 100 feet above sea-level. Then, first on the right hand and then on the left, ranges of hills appear, steadily closing in on the Shannon as you advance. It enters the great expanse of Lough Derg, like a larger Lough Ree—a long winding area of water with arms extending on either side. The mountains close in till they seem entirely to block exit, rising high over the lake on either hand; but at Killaloe the river gives a twist, escapes through the hills, and plunges down ninety-seven feet in eighteen miles to find sea-level at Limerick. At Killaloe, Slieve Bernagh rises steeply over the river to 1746 feet, while on the other bank the Arra Mountains ascend equally abruptly to over 1500 feet. How did the river come to cut so deeply through these high grounds formed of non-soluble slates when a barrier of soluble limestone only 150 feet high keeps it from avoiding the hills altogether by turning westward into Galway Bay? For the solution of the puzzle we must look far backward to a time when the Central Plain stood much higher than it does now, so that the south-western course by Killaloe offered the easiest access to the sea. As the plain was steadily lowered by denudation, the river kept its course open by cutting through the Silurian and Devonian rocks. As the soluble rocks of the plain were removed, the insoluble slates were left standing up as hills on either hand: but still the Shannon cut down its bed correspondingly, so that it now appears like a huge dam held up by the rock-sill at Killaloe; once that is safely passed, it is free to rush down to Limerick. The actual dam is, owing to the Shannon Electricity Works, no longer at Killaloe, but further down the river at O'Briensbridge, to which point the lake is now artificially prolonged, and whence a broad canal leads to the great turbine installation at Ardnacrusha (*Árd na croise*, height of the cross) a few miles above Limerick.

The conversion of Lough Derg (*Loch Deirgeirc*, the lake of the red eye) into a huge mill-dam has fortunately not interfered with its amenities, as the amount by which the lake can be raised or lowered is not large. From the naturalist's point of view, as well as the artist's, this is fortunate, for fluctuations of water-level of more than a small amount have a disastrous effect on plant and animal life—as everyone knows who has had occasion to contrast the flora and fauna of a reservoir with those of a natural lake. All Irish biologists felt anxiety when the " Shannon Scheme " was brought forward, the botanists especially, as Lough Derg is the home of some very rare plants—noticeably the Willow-leaved Inula, which resembles a small Sunflower; it is not found in Great Britain, nor elsewhere in Ireland. It grows on the stony shores of the lake above storm-level. During recent dry summers, when the store of water had been depleted, it was much dwarfed, but there is reason to think that in normal seasons it will continue to flourish. The plant has a wide range round the northern three-quarters of the lake, ceasing only where limestone gives way to slate near the southern end. The small ungrazed islands, of which there are plenty, are the home of many interesting plants, as well as of numbers of breeding birds—gulls, terns, ducks, and so on. The southern part of the lake is the more picturesque on account of the proximity of heathery hills: you can explore it from Killaloe or Mountshannon, at both of which there are good hotels, thanks to the fishing attractions which Lough Derg offers. The northern part has flatter shores and more islands, and for the naturalist is better ground; for this portion Portumna is conveniently situated at the point where the Shannon enters the lake.

On the west side, in Scarriff Bay, a grassy island, Iniscaltra, is the site of an important early ecclesiastical settlement. It dates from the seventh century, when St. Caimin founded a monastery here, which became famous. The ruins are interesting. There is a round tower, still eighty feet high in spite of the loss of its top. There are several early churches, displaying some unusual architectural features; also a number of crosses, and incised slabs of the eighth to eleventh century. The site has been monographed by R. A. S. Macalister.[1]

To the east and north of the district last dealt with are the twin areas till lately called King's County and Queen's County, to which the earlier names of Offaly and Leix (*Laoighis*, after Lughaidh Laeighseach, a chieftain) have now been restored. Neither need detain us long. From the natural history point of view, both are typical Central Plain areas, with no special characters: for the archaeologist, only one or two widely scattered sites are worthy of attention. A few miles south of Maryborough, in Leix, is the Rock of Dunamase (*Dún Masg*, fortress of Masg), an unexpected projection of limestone in a large flat area. It is a natural fortress, and

[1] " The History and Antiquities of Inis Cealtra ", *Proc. Roy. Irish Acad.*, vol. xxxiii., sect. C, pp. 93-174, plates 7-28. 1916.

has been so used from prehistoric times. Later a strong castle was built on the rock; this was finally destroyed by the Cromwellians in 1650, and the commanding nature of the site, rather than the ruins upon it, give it a picturesque appearance. Further south the round tower at Timahoe is a notable building. Timahoe is *Teach Mochúa*, Mochua's house, after St. Mochua, who lived in the sixth century. The round tower, of less early date, is unusual in its beautiful doorway, with delicate mouldings and human heads; mostly the doorways of the round towers are of the plainest description.

The most striking physical feature of Leix and Offaly is the ridge of Slieve Bloom, which forms for many miles the boundary between them, rising in Arderin (*Árd Éirenn*, the height of Ireland) to 1733 feet, and visible on a clear day from every part of the Central Plain. Slieve Bloom and Slieve Aughty, which lies further west, are the most northern of the series of anticlines which to the southward increase in number and in elevation until only strips of limestone are left between them. All belong to the Armorican period of folding. The limestone and underlying beds were forced up into a series of east-west ridges, which the influence of the more ancient Caledonian folding changed in this region to N.E.-S.W. The Carboniferous limestone has long since been worn off the ridges and often also the underlying Old Red Sandstone, exposing a core of Silurian slates, thus—

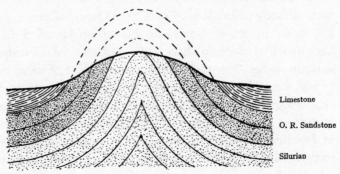

Limestone

O. R. Sandstone

Silurian

FIG. 8.—DIAGRAMMATIC SECTION ACROSS ONE OF THE CENTRAL PLAIN ANTICLINES

All that is now left of what must have been a long and lofty mountain range is the broad flat heathery ridge of Slieve Bloom, breaking down to plain level at Roscrea (*Ros Cré*, Cre's wood), and rising again to form Devil's Bit and all the hills that run thence southward to Keeper (2278 feet) near Limerick.

The mention of Slieve Bloom brings back to my memory one of the longest and wettest walks that I have had. I wished to sample that heathery ridge, in the forlorn hope of finding something interesting, so walked from Mountrath to Arderin, the highest point, getting in a gully at Glendine Gap, Welsh Poppy and Filmy Fern. Heavy rain set in, with a high wind, so I retreated to the western base of the range, and worked northward through Kinnitty: but the weather never cleared, and in mist and sheets of rain I finally recrossed the hills by a more northerly route to Mountrath. It was nothing much in the way of long-distance walking—thirty-seven miles in all, but with a lot of head wind and 2500 feet of climbing thrown in. I was never a walker like Henry Hart for instance (p. 57), and preferred a modest twenty to twenty-five miles per day, spread over twelve hours to allow plenty of time for botanizing, and continued for as many days as necessary. In the Central Plain, where there was open ground and little to detain one, I found the two-day trip a simple and productive plan—an early train to a chosen place, then fifty miles or so across country with a halt for the night in the middle, and a late train back to Dublin. That could be done on a toothbrush and a collar, and the plants collected kept fresh (with care) till one got home. It entailed also a minimum leave of absence, always an important consideration to a Civil Servant.

Offaly (*Hy Failghe*, a local tribe), formerly King's County, on the northern side of Slieve Bloom, is the most bog-covered part of the Central Plain, no less than one-fifth of its area being buried under that strange vegetable blanket. But the remainder makes up for this by being often pleasant well-farmed country, with plenty of trees and some good towns. There is not much of special interest, but out on the western edge, among the great bogs that fringe the

Shannon, some ruined churches mark the site of what was for centuries a place of European reputation. Follow the Shannon southward from Athlone for eight miles and you come to the remains of the great ecclesiastical settlement of Clonmacnois (*Clúain maccu Nóis, the plain of the sons of Nos*). Here, on a knoll known as *Árd tiprait* (the height of the well), a monastery was founded in A.D. 538 by Ciárán (Kieran) and seven followers. Ciárán had been trained at Clonard by the famous Findian, and after wandering about Ireland he chose this remote spot, dreary then as now, but desirable on account of its very austerity. The Shannon here flows through a wide bog-strewn plain, with much poor marshy land, the only feature which breaks its monotony being high esker-ridges of limestone gravel, " swelling up like mounds of emerald from the sombre bosoms of the vast bogs which stretch away like seas to the distant horizon " and often resembling abandoned railway embankments. Ciárán died a few months later, but under his successor Oenna and succeeding abbots the place grew and flourished, and became eventually a large and famous monastery. Throughout its history, which lasted for a thousand years, it appears to have suffered even more than many similar establishments in Ireland from enemies human and otherwise. Plague, fire and storm took heavy toll; but much worse were the repeated plunderings by Danes, Munstermen and finally the Anglo-Normans, which frequently wrecked the settlement, and it is difficult to understand how each time it rose from its ashes, and continued to be the home of scholars and saints, many of them men of wide reputation whose works are still extant—such as the *Annals of Tighernach* (Tighernach was abbot here) and the *Leabhar na hUidhri* or *Book of the Dun Cow* (both of the twelfth century), the *Chronicon Scotorum*, and the *Annals of Clonmacnois*. But the frequent plunderings scattered and destroyed the many objects of art—the precious vessels of gold and silver and enamel—which no doubt enriched the altars of the churches. Only a beautiful crozier remains, dug out of the ruins of the little church of St. Ciárán, and now in the National Museum. Of the town which must have

PLATE XXVII

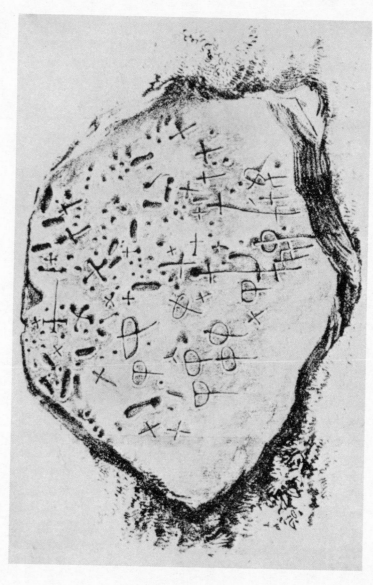

THE CLONFINLOUGH STONE
From the original lithograph by G. V. du Noyer

existed in connection with so large an establishment not a trace is left; but the churches were constructed of more permanent materials than the domestic buildings, and they, with the round towers, high crosses, and memorial slabs which still remain, form a very notable collection of monuments. There are seven churches, from feature-less early cells of small size to large buildings with richly ornamented doorways and arches; a round tower standing separately and another attached to St. Finghin's church, a very fine high cross and portions of others; two holy wells; and a great series of sepulchral slabs (over 200) covering many centuries of the monastery's existence. An incongruous adjunct to the ecclesiastical remains is the massive ruin of a castle built by the English in 1213: it was evidently destroyed by a great explosion at some subsequent date unknown, as witnessed by the huge overturned fragments.

The remains of this venerable monastery are impressive, although so much is gone for ever. The very austerity of the setting, as com-pared with the rich meadowland in which many of the old religious settlements stand, strikes the imagination; the broad Shannon flowing slowly past and the wide landscape give a sense of monastic calm: the castle ruin alone seems out of place.

At Clonfinlough (*Clúainn finn loch*, Meadow of the white lake), close by, is a large boulder of arenaceous limestone with a flat sloping face covered with strange scribings and cup-markings (Plate XXV). The scribings are unique in Ireland on account of the frequent occurrence among them of a symbol consisting of a vertical line with a little knob at the top (like a pin) and a circle across its middle part. The stone was described by Rev. James Graves as long ago as 1865, his paper being illustrated with a good drawing by G. V. Du Noyer,[1] reproduced in Plate XXVII. But its special interest was made clear only a few years ago, when the Abbé Breuil, a foremost French archaeologist, fresh from explorations of Spanish caves occupied in

---

[1] James Graves, " On a Boulder with presumed Pagan Carvings at Clonfin-lough, King's County ", *Journ. Kilkenny and S.E. Ireland Archaeol. Soc.*, N.S., vol. v., facing p. 361.

Neolithic times, came to Ireland. He showed R. A. S. Macalister his photographs of the cave paintings, and Macalister showed him in turn Du Noyer's drawing and subsequently the stone itself. Breuil recognized in its scribings, with some astonishment, an exact analogue of the Spanish drawings he had just been studying. The stone thus supplies clear evidence of a connection, hitherto unsuspected, between Spain and Central Ireland in Neolithic times. The special symbol to which reference has been made is known, by analogy with less conventionalized drawings on the Continent, to represent a man with arms akimbo.

Westmeath is a more hospitable area than Offaly, having less than half the amount of bog possessed by the latter, and more pasture. It is moreover a region of greater variety of surface, especially in the east. Here the limestone has endured minor crumplings, with the result that ridges a few hundred feet high alternate with hollows filled with pretty lakes. This lake country lies around Mullingar (*Muileann cearr*), a town which otherwise is without any special attraction. Lough Owel (*Loch Uair* (a man's name)) north of the town, fed by limestone springs, has water of a pale pellucid green, while Lough Derevaragh (*Loch dairbhreach*) close by, fed by the River Inny (*An Aoine*) flowing from Lough Sheelin (*Loch Sighleann*), through a wide bog-filled valley, is brown and peaty. These differences are reflected in the flora of the two lakes. The water of Lough Owel is indeed of quite unusual transparency. Not long ago an out-board motor engine became detached and sank in deep water. It was found a few days later—it was *seen* from a boat, lying on the bottom in fifty-one feet of water, and duly recovered.

This is a region rich in rare plants, and very attractive for the botanist. One of the best places is the " Scraw Bog ", a long narrow lake entirely covered by a floating skin of vegetation over which one can walk (or perhaps more properly wade) among a profusion of the Round-leaved Wintergreen, in Ireland found only in this neighbourhood, and other rarities. Derevaragh is a curious lake, with a broad desolate bog-fringed expansion towards the west, and in the east a long tapering arm ending in a narrow fork between steep wooded hills—a scene difficult to reconcile with the Central Plain. The whole district, from Lough Ennell up to Lough Sheelin, is pretty and interesting, with much woodland and water.

A little to the west of the Westmeath lake region the Hill of Usnagh or Uisneach rises gently to 250 feet above the surrounding undulating country, itself attaining some 600 feet above sea-level. It has a rather extensive flattish top, which was a place of importance in old days, as witnessed by the number of monuments, mostly of the nature of ring-forts and tumuli, which are scattered over it. According to ancient sources, it was the site of a royal palace and a royal cemetery in prehistoric times, and a leading place of assembly; later, in early Christian days, it was the seat of the kings of Connacht. One point is worthy of note. Though of but small elevation, the Hill of Usnagh, standing in the middle of the Central Plain, commands a singularly extensive view. From its summit, on a clear day, features belonging to no less than twenty out of the thirty-two Irish counties can be identified, and a beacon-fire lit here might be seen over one-fourth of Ireland, whence it could be readily relayed to the furthest corners. Probably this contributed materially to its early importance. Local tradition points out a large limestone erratic block on the western slope as the central point of Ireland. Dr. Macalister and I spent in 1925–30 sixteen weeks in all in excavating here on what appeared to be the two most important sites; they proved interesting but extremely puzzling. The first was Uisneach proper, on the southern spur of the hill. Here is a structure resembling a large ring-fort with two-thirds of a rather smaller one attached to its western side. Digging proved that several periods of occupation were represented, but they were difficult to disentangle. To the earliest period belonged curving ditches filled up and covered by later works of various kinds. The inside of the existing vallum showed a medley of buried house-ruins, souterrains, pavements, walls, ditches, post-holes, beds of ashes, and everywhere great quantities of bones of domestic animals. But no pottery (the absence of which is characteristic of Iron Age sites), practically no trace of permanent occupation. Great beds of ashes faced a kind of entrance at the end of an ancient road that ran to the base of the hill: and the whole place suggested elaborate ceremonials and feasts, rather than either defence or peaceful occupation.

The other monument, in the townland of Togherstown, out to the north, was in the form of two concentric earthen rings with a considerable space between them, which space was divided up by several radial walls. The interior of the inner ring was a crowded complex of walls, pavements, post-holes, flattened heaps of ashes, with two complicated souterrains—one of them with its largest chamber neatly paved with flat slabs. It appeared to have been neither a dwelling-place nor a sanctuary. Objects found in both sites, which were very few excepting the innumerable animal bones, pointed to occupation during the Iron Age—early Christian times: but to account for most of the features which both monuments displayed was quite beyond us. Everything was carefully put on record,[1] and no doubt, as knowledge grows with the excavation of other sites during years to come, the history and meaning of these perplexing remains will be made clear.

Indeed, these excavations brought home to us how little we yet know of Iron Age civilization in Ireland, even of that common object of the country-side, the ring-fort. The number of these in many districts is surprising—in Sligo for instance, where it is sometimes only a mild exaggeration to say that there is one to every field. In their simplest form they were no doubt merely cattle-pens or sheep-folds, with a palisade round the top of the bank to keep out thieves and wolves. If you dig out the ditch of an ordinary ring-fort, you find that a couple of thousand years of trampling by

[1] Macalister and Praeger, "Report on the Excavation of Uisneach", *Proc. Roy. Irish Acad.*, vol. xxxviii., sect. C, pp. 69-127, plates 3-19. 1928. *Ibid.*, "The Excavation of an ancient structure on the townland of Togherstown, County Westmeath". *Ibid.*, vol. xxxix., sect. C, pp. 54-83, plates 4-19. 1931.

grazing animals has flattened down the vallum and filled the fosse to a depth of one to two yards. If you remove the fallen material and replace it on the top of the bank the restored structure becomes quite imposing, and if you add a strong palisade along the crest it makes a formidable obstacle against enemies. Large numbers of the ring-forts were undoubtedly fortified farmsteads, and the remains of buildings are frequently still to be seen within them: but hardly one has as yet been properly examined by digging—this is work that is only now beginning. Gradually they were replaced by structures of stone and mortar—still arranged for defence—but the ring-fort type probably lingered for a long time, if one may judge by the recent appearance of the house-ruins which some of them contain. The careful digging of a hundred or so selected ring-forts will some day tell us a great deal about life in Ireland in early Christian and medieval times.

These excavations on the Hill of Usnagh have been followed recently by further work in the same area, on sites of other kinds, under the aegis of Harvard University. The summit of the hill called Knockast was found to contain a Bronze Age cemetery in which were no less than forty-three interments, a few enclosed in cists, mostly cremated and merely laid in slight hollows of the old surface.[1] Two crannogs or lake-dwellings of a later date than this have been carefully explored. One of them yielded a very fine Norse sword, a large decorated bronze sanctuary lamp of much beauty, and a unique gaming board of yew, with seven rows each of seven holes and an ornamented edge of interlacing and other patterns which indicate a Manx-Norse origin and a late tenth-century date. This crannog has been very fully examined and described.[2]

On its further side, Westmeath fronts the Shannon, which here

[1] H. O'N. Hencken and H. L. Movius, " The Cemetery Cairn of Knockast ", *Proc. Roy. Irish Acad.*, vol. xli., sect. C, pp. 232-284, plates 9-15. 1934.

[2] H. O'N. Hencken, etc., " Ballinderry Crannog No. 1 ", *Proc. Roy. Irish Acad.*, vol. xliii., sect. C, pp. 103-239, plates 13-25. 1936.

widens into Lough Ree, sixteen miles long and one to six miles broad. There is more Glacial drift around and in this lake than in the other great expansion of the Shannon, Lough Derg, with the effect that its shores and islands are less rocky and wild; this results in a less interesting and varied flora and fauna. But it has plenty of rare plants all the same, also colonies of breeding birds, and its winding shores and numerous islands may well detain the lover of nature. Athlone, at the lower end, is the place to stay if you want to explore the lake—indeed there is no other place. A motor boat makes the whole sheet of water accessible from there: otherwise you should camp, preferably on one of the small islands.

The Shannon, indeed, offers exceptional opportunities for holidays on the water, but very few avail themselves of them. Everywhere the current is slow, for the few rapids are accompanied by a short canal and a lock, and the river falls only 51 feet between Lough Allen and Lough Derg, a distance of 90 miles. There are 200 miles of waterway available—river, lake, estuary—from the Leitrim mountains to the open Atlantic. Bird life and plant life are abundant, and almost undisturbed by human influence, and much of archaeological interest is to be found along the river or within striking distance—Clonfert, Clonmacnois, Iniscaltra, and many lesser places. A more peaceful holiday cannot be imagined, for traffic on the Shannon is small, towns and villages few and far between, and there is often a broad fringe of meadow-land or brown bog from which even houses are absent. You are alone with twittering water-birds and occasional cattle that stand knee-deep in the stream, or splash behind tall groves of reeds, while grey Herons watch you from the bank, scarcely troubling to move as you drift past.

Clonfert (*Clúain ferta*, meadow of the grave), just referred to, deserves more than a passing reference, if for no other reason than that its very remoteness adds a touch of the unexpected to its interest. The place lies near the Shannon, about six miles south of Ballinasloe, in that wide region of eastern Galway which is quite unknown to

PLATE XXVIII

T. H. Mason: photo

THE DOORWAY, CLONFERT CATHEDRAL

the majority even of people devoted to rambling. Here in 558 St. Brendan founded a monastery. It survived the usual plunderings and burnings of succeeding centuries, and became the seat of a diocese, but ever maintained its pastoral isolation, and only a few houses now accompany the little cathedral. This fell into ruin, but last century saw its restoration. It is an interesting building of the twelfth century and later, famous for its very beautiful and elaborate doorway, one of the finest examples of Hiberno-Romanesque to be found in Ireland, and this door alone is worth going a long way to see (Plate XXVIII). Coming on Clonfert unexpectedly, as I did many years ago during a long day's botanizing over this lonely countryside, it was an astonishing and lovely revelation.

Athlone (*Béal átha Luain*, ford-mouth of Luan), at the southern end of Lough Ree, is a place of importance, and has always been so, for here was the only ford across the Shannon for a long distance to north and south. It stands fairly on the route from Dublin to Galway, and most of the traffic between east and west crosses the Shannon at this point. Hence the ruined fortifications, of various dates, that command the site of the ancient ford and the present bridge, which has replaced the earlier one built by Sir Henry Sydney in 1566. As a result of its strategic position, Athlone has seen more fighting than almost any other town in Ireland. Perhaps that is the reason why so little that is old now remains—only a bit of the town wall, the ruins of a couple of ancient churches, and a fragment of the castle. The antiquary stays in Athlone to visit Clonmacnois, the botanist and zoologist for Lough Ree, and the fisherman for the salmon and trout which abound in the Shannon, and especially for the may-fly fishing.

In the small county of Longford (*Longphort*, a castle or encampment) there is nothing to detain us. It is for the most part an undulating agricultural area—pleasant country, but containing little to give pause to either the naturalist or the antiquary. The mazy Lough Gowna (*Loch gamhna*, lake of the calf), on the north-eastern border, is attractive, and in the south-west Longford fronts the

Shannon, including the northern part of Lough Ree. If you climb the great Norman motte at Granard (*Granáird*) you obtain a good idea of the eastern part of the county, and from the summit (912 feet) of Carn Hill, more to the west—the highest point in Longford—on a clear day you get a wide view across its undulating expanse.

Opposite to Westmeath and Longford, the county of Roscommon (*Ros Comán*, Coman's wood) forms the west bank of the Shannon for over seventy miles—a full third of the total length of that large river. Save for that long river-front, extending from Lough Allen (p. 134) and Lough Key (p. 135) through Lough Boderg (*Loch bó deirg*, lake of the red cow) and the adjoining watery country, Lough Ree (p. 244), and on to Shannonbridge, Roscommon is decidedly dull. There are vast areas of limestone pasture grazed by sheep, their continuity only interrupted by broken-down grey walls; and for the rest the usual Central Plain mixture of peat-bog and marsh and farmland, with few trees and fewer towns or villages. If you must go to Roscommon, keep to the eastern margin, where the Shannon flows, or to the north, where, as shown elsewhere (p. 134), the lake district around Boyle (*Mainistir na búille*) is distinctly attractive. I have tramped across much of the remainder, mostly in a vain search for rare plants; and all I can say is that I hope no one else will have the foolishness to do the same, for the monotony of the scenery is equalled only by the poverty of the flora.

CHAPTER X

THE REGION OF THE PALE

(DUBLIN, KILDARE, MEATH)

IT is not known at what point or points the several legendary tribes of the early annals may have invaded Ireland, but since the days of the Norseman Dublin has been the main place of entry for friend and foe alike. Centrally situated as regards the country, with only sixty miles of sea separating it from the coast of Wales, and sheltered water on either side of the intervening channel, it has been and still remains the key to traffic between the two islands, and the natural hub of Ireland.

The situation of Dublin is one which many a city might envy—at the head of a wide bay of clean sand, with high rocky headlands guarding it on either side, and the lofty ridge of the Wicklow mountains so close that its foothills begin only a couple of miles beyond the southern suburbs. The River Liffey, which bisects the city, had originally low and marshy margins. When the Danes rowed up the river in the ninth century they occupied the first dry ground which they encountered—the knoll on which St. Andrew's church now stands, close to the foot of Grafton Street. When, 300 years later, the Normans captured the Norse town which had arisen, they chose for their stronghold a point further up—rising ground in the angle between the Liffey and its southern tributary the Poddle; and there Dublin Castle, now mainly ranges of offices, still stands. The city has spread out far to both north and south, but the southern bank still remains the site of the majority of the principal buildings.

This is not the place for a historical or topographical account of

the capital of the Irish Free State, nor am I the person to write it.
Indeed, Dublin is very fully written up already.   But a few characteristics and peculiarities may, in a freakish sort of way, be picked out—
commonplaces to the townsman, perhaps of some interest or curiosity
to the stranger who happens to stumble on these pages—and I am
one of the strangers, for I descended on (or ascended to) Dublin
nearly half a century ago from the ebullient area which encompasses
Belfast, and " home " still lies to the northward.   So long a residence
allows one to appreciate fully the many amenities of Dublin—the
pleasant human atmosphere, the stimulating environment in which
one lives, whether one's interests lie in the direction of letters or art
or music or science, or mere social enjoyment.   Belfast will be the
same some day, but, a creation of yesterday in comparison with
Dublin, it has still a long way to travel.   " I wouldn't go back for
double pay " was the way a northern exile expressed his view on
the matter, using the characteristic Belfast standard of values.   And
I recall an incident told me by the Town Clerk of Navan, which
shows a Meath man's impression of the proud city of the north.   A
young fellow had got into some minor trouble with the police,
and the question of bail arose.   " Haven't you any near relations
who would help you? " asked the magistrate.   " Haven't you any
brothers? "   " I have, indeed, Your Worship; I have three brothers
—two alive, and one in Belfast! "   For myself, I should like to continue to live in Dublin—but to be buried at Holywood.

Well then: to begin with, the visitor discovers in Dublin a
curious tendency to duplication, the origin of which often lies many
centuries back.   For instance, Dublin has two names, both Irish—
the one used by everybody, the other (*Baile Átha Cliath*, the Town
of the Hurdle Ford) used by the government.   Why the purely
Celtic name DUBLIN—*Dubh Linne*, " Black Pool ", in use for centuries, should not be good enough for official note-paper heaven
knows—apparently because it was the name used by the founders of
the city—the Danes—not that used before there was any city at all,
as was *Áth Cliath*.   But perhaps DUBLIN is after all not an Irish word.

A while ago I met a man, a civil engineer, down in Carlow, in the little hotel in Borris (where there has long hung a picture that I covet—a large print of gentlemen and ladies of the Dundreary period mounted on the original form of velocipede—a bicycle without pedals or gearing—and, straddled across these machines, propelling themselves along a fashionable promenade by a process akin to walking). He discoursed, over tea and fried trout, on local place-names. "The names of places", said he, "are of wonderful interest. It's surprising how few understand anything about what they mean. Take Dublin: how many know how it got its name? I'll tell you. Before there was e'er a bridge across the Liffey, there was a slip on each side, near the Castle, and a ferry, and beside each slip was a pub. That's how the name came—Double-inn. How many know that now?" I agreed with him that the secret was held by very few indeed.

Again, Dublin is unique so far as I know in having two cathedrals in the occupation of the same religious denomination, and none belonging to the denomination which constitutes 90 per cent of the population of the city. The reason lies far back in the religious history of the country, but a visitor from another planet could not fail to express surprise at so lop-sided a situation, whatever its origin. There are also two universities—for University College is so pre-dominant a partner in the National University of Ireland that few people in Dublin distinguish between the two: but the headquarters of the "National" are not in the imposing building in Earlsfort Terrace, but in a modest house in Merrion Square. The University of Dublin, on the other hand, is genuinely a one-college university. Where else do we find a complete university—schools, Provost's house, halls of residence, playing-fields and all—enclosed within one high iron railing and occupying the very centre of a city? The front of Trinity is the hub of Dublin. Step inside the gateway and you are among green lawns and ancient trees, set among old grey buildings, with the roar of the traffic reduced to a whisper—the most delightful contrast which Dublin affords. Our visitor will note other

pleasant features—the way it has made the most of its river, with a
road—often tree-lined—extending on either bank the whole length
of the city, and its ample squares, filled with greenery. Again, the
brick of which the houses are mostly built is not of the garish tint
found in many places, but of a soft mellow colour capable of brightening into a range of lovely tints under the variable lighting afforded
by Irish weather. The two prevailing local rocks, also—grey granite
and grey limestone—have been used with fine effect in most of the
public buildings. In the noble width of O'Connell Street (formerly
Sackville Street), as in Westmorland Street, D'Olier Street and elsewhere, you see the successful work of the Wide Streets Commission
of the late eighteenth century: but the wise example in town-
planning then set has not been maintained, and today there are points
of congestion here and there which ought to have been eased long
since and which will give increasing trouble as time goes on. Also
the speculative builder has been especially busy in recent years
spoiling the suburbs with ugly houses and ribbon-building, as in so
many towns. But these are minor defects in a fine mellow eighteenth-century city, in which the visitor often notes with surprise a
slightly foreign flavour difficult to diagnose, but no doubt in some
way due to its Danish-Norman-English-Irish history. Now I turn
to details that are more to my heart.

Undoubtedly the most interesting zoological feature that Dublin
has to offer is the Wagtail roost in O'Connell Street. Early in the
winter of 1929 a number of Pied Wagtails elected to spend the nights
in a tree, a London Plane, on the north side of Nelson Pillar (Plate
XXIX). The tree rose between sets of tramway rails, among bright
arc lights, at a place where traffic is heavy and continuous—surely a
strange choice! The unaccustomed sight led to their being harassed,
and before the end of the year the birds left. But next autumn they returned in augmented numbers, and since then have been present there
in ever-increasing quantity during the winter six months of each year,
till now they occupy three or four adjacent trees, and their number
has been estimated at about two thousand. They arrive as dusk

The Nelson Pillar was demolished in 1966 but happily the explosions did not
disturb the wagtails from their roosting habits. C.M.

PLATE XXIX

Flash-light photo by T. H. Mason

PIED WAGTAILS AT NELSON PILLAR

settles down, and leave again with morning light. Gregarious roosting is a well-known habit with Wagtails, but so large a colony in such apparently unsuitable surroundings is remarkable. " In all my birding ", writes Canon Raven, " I have come across nothing so bizarre, or, to the student, so provocative." Even when heavy periodical pruning reduced their favourite tree to half its height, they instantly left it—for just one week: and noise, lights and bustle till after midnight do not disturb them in the least.

A quaint incident in the small hours of a February morning has been described by Art O'Murnaghan: [1]

" During the course of the night there had been unusually heavy squalls of wind and sleety rain, and good-sized pools of water had been left here and there on the street. Quite near to the Parnell Monument, in the space between the last tree and a tramway standard, were several of these pools, and splashing and sporting in the water was a group of six or seven wagtails, making the most of the absence of traffic. As I passed under the ' home ' tree, which is over 200 paces nearer the General Post Office, the remainder of the colony, many hundreds in number, were roosting in the upper branches of the tree, fast asleep, and quite oblivious of the pranks of the half-dozen members of the society who had sneaked off for a bit of sport, when they should have been in their beds.

" This little event is one more item in what is surely a strange chapter of wild-bird life. A group of birds, whose natural roosting-place would be among the sedges and reeds of lonely water-courses, migrate each winter to the centre of the main street of a large and noisy city. They spend their days outside the city, where there are scores of suitable roosting-places, but at night gather in the upper branches of a couple of small plane-trees, in the midst of tramways, parked motor cars, high electric-light standards and illuminated cinemas. Then, on a nasty night half a dozen of them rouse out of their sleep, and make a night of it near two or three sleeping taxis."

[1] *Irish Naturalists' Journal,* vol. v., p. 257. 1935.

An unexpected tendency towards an urban habitat in Dublin is shown also by a group of plants which one associates rather with shady glens and the open country—namely, the Ferns. These seem out of place in the middle of a city, yet there is a Bracken growing on a damp wall opposite the Mansion House, a Male Fern in Harcourt Street, a Lady Fern and a Hart's-tongue on an area wall in Fitzwilliam Square; and till some unfortunate tidying-up was done at Leinster House, Male Fern, Broad Buckler Fern, Soft Shield Fern and Hart's-tongue flourished in the angle between it and the National Museum —all of which says something, I think, for the Dublin atmosphere. This enterprise in the matter of colonization is characteristic of the Ferns, and in Ireland a number of curious instances are on record. The Parsley Fern, in this country a very rare inhabitant of the mountains, where only a single plant occurs here and there in a remote rock-crevice, has been seen at low level on a wall of stones and sods at Bryansford and on a heap of stones in a field at Hillsborough, both in County Down; the Holly Fern, an alpine species, was found on a hedge bank at Dungannon, and at the base of a wall at Killybegs, and the Green Spleenwort at Convoy; and two ferns unknown in the wild state in Ireland, and almost unknown in cultivation, the Rigid Buckler Fern and the Forked Spleenwort, have been found, the former many years ago on a wall at Townley Hall near Drogheda, the latter on a wall over a garden at Saintfield in Down. These instances appear to show a much greater mobility among the Ferns than exists among the Flowering Plants, and there are two reasons for this—the extremely small size of the spores of Ferns as compared with the seeds of the higher plants, and the vast numbers in which they are produced. A Fern plant may produce each season not hundreds but hundreds of millions of spores, so minute and light that they penetrate everywhere, and may without exaggeration be considered a normal ingredient of atmospheric dust. I remember my delight at the success of an experiment on this feature of Fern life that I carried out as a schoolboy, after reading about spores. I boiled a sod of turf to destroy any germs that might be adhering to it, and hung it up in a room near a window, moistening it occasionally with boiled water. The nearest Ferns were in hedgerows a few hundred yards away. Within a year young plants of three kinds of Ferns developed on the peat, one of which, the Hart's-tongue, did not occur within a mile. It is the abundance and facile wind-dispersal of the spores that account for odd Fern plants in peculiar situations such as have been quoted above, and also for the very wide world-distribution which is shown by some of them and by other spore-bearing plants, such as Mosses, Liverworts and Fungi. Even among those Flowering Plants whose seeds are borne on parachutes of high efficiency, like those of the Dandelion group or the Willow-herbs, we get nothing like such freedom of dispersal.

The harbour of Dublin as such does not need notice here, but it is worth pointing out that one of the amenities of the northern suburbs is due to an unexpected result of a work intended to increase the depth of water on the bar, at the mouth of the Liffey, which for centuries had been only some six feet at low tide. About 1819, a wall one and three-quarter miles long was built from the Clontarf shore, its end reaching to the northern edge of the channel, opposite to the end of a previously constructed wall on the southern side. Shortly after its completion, sand began to collect along the back of the northern wall, a quarter of a mile or so from shore. For nearly a century this sand-bank has continued to grow, ever extending northward parallel to the coast till its further progress was stopped by the channel that runs along the Sutton shore, on the isthmus that joins the promontory of Howth to the mainland. Over three miles of low sand-dunes have resulted, with a broad sandy beach in front facing Dublin Bay, and a strip of salt-marsh along the rear, a quarter of a mile behind. A wonderful gift from the sea! On its ample extent the presence of two golf courses makes but a slight encroachment on this fine public playground, situated a short three miles from the centre of Dublin. Apart from the phenomenon of its rapid accumulation, the North Bull presents two points of interest to the naturalist. Since its only connection with the mainland is a wooden bridge at the southern end, it follows that practically the whole of its flora and fauna has arrived by either air or water. Among plants, it is noteworthy that several of the rarer Dublin species as well as a host of commoner ones are among the colonists. As to its fauna, it is now a bird sanctuary, and avian life has responded gratefully to the conditions of safety which this means. An un-expected result of protection has been that hares increased so rapidly that they threatened to devour the island, and for the sake of other inhabitants large numbers of them have had to be captured and removed!

To the geologist, the high-level shelly gravels, which the Scottish ice, coming down channel, gouged out of the sea-bed and threw down on the Dublin mountains, are of interest, matching the similar deposits found on the other side of the Irish Sea, at Moel Tryfaen in Wales. These gravels rise to 1200 feet at points on the hills south of Dublin, and from them you may pick fragments of molluscs of many kinds which once lived, or still live, in Dublin Bay. The occurrence of sea-shells in comparatively recent gravels high on the mountains was long known, and was one of the chief arguments which led geologists to postulate a submergence of at least 1400 feet in order to account for their presence. Some of these shells are of Arctic type, and the evidence of these relegates the gravels in which they occur to the Ice Age. This theory of a great submergence during Glacial times long held sway: the Boulder-clay was supposed to be material derived from melting floating ice, and the eskers were formed by marine currents. The land-ice theory which now holds the field was, as regards Ireland, founded largely on the careful work of Rev. Maxwell H. Close (1822–1903), who demonstrated the existence of former centres of ice-dispersal in western and north-western Ireland, this ice moving over the country and leaving behind scratches on the rocks, caused by included stones, and later masses of tough clay overlying these rocks and full of scratched blocks. Close's papers formed a brilliant and original contribution to a very difficult subject, still in its infancy. But as to the high-level shelly gravels, he could not account for them save by invoking a submergence of large amount in late-Glacial times. Now we have abundant evidence of a great ice-sheet moving from Scotland down the Irish Sea: where it impinged on the Irish and Welsh coasts it squeezed up the sea-bottom with its contained deposits of shells: and no doubt is entertained by present-day geologists that to this cause we owe the frequent occurrence of marine organisms in the Boulder-clay along our east coast, and even in the high-level beds, as about Dublin and Belfast.   Apart from his brilliant investigations as an amateur geologist, Maxwell Close did much useful work for his country and his native city of Dublin. For twenty-five years he was Treasurer to the Royal Irish Academy, and in that capacity forwarded in numerous ways scientific and archaeological work in Ireland.   Of a very modest and retiring nature, he was a wise helper in many directions, though his name did not appear: and to his private philanthropy many persons in need or distress owed relief from the difficulties by which they were beset.   No man was richer in

> that best portion of a good man's life,
> His little, nameless, unremembered acts
> Of kindness and of love.

I had the privilege of his friendship for the last ten years of his life, and of visiting in his company those high-level Glacial gravels which interested and puzzled him so much.   They form a kind of memorial of him such as he might have approved—standing remote, high on the hills, without enclosure or inscription.

Nor is it only on the mountains that the Ice Age has left remarkable local memorials, still very difficult to explain, despite the intensive work on Glacial phenomena carried out by two generations of geologists since Maxwell Close published his now classical researches. From the Shanganagh River south to Bray the sea has eaten into the flat, gently sloping ground that lies behind the present beach, forming a cliff of gravel, sand and clay, long known as presenting interesting and varied features.   A Sunday ramble in 1893 with W. J. Sollas (then Professor of Geology at Trinity College) led to our spending a good many winter days during the two succeeding years in examining both maritime and inland sections of the Glacial beds around the valley of the Bray River and thence to Kill-o'-the-Grange.[1] That is over forty years ago now, and geologists will recall how confused were the prevalent ideas concerning Glacial conditions and Glacial phenomena—not that the reign of confusion and obscurity over the " Glacial Nightmare " is by any means past yet. There were then many and powerful advocates of great submergence during the Ice Age, who claimed as marine deposits not only the eskers of the Central Plain but even the high-level shelly gravel alluded to above. We entered on our examination imbued with the submergence theory, and indeed at the end modified it only to the extent of claiming for Killiney " beach conditions, and the grinding and pounding of shore ice ", to explain the puzzling phenomena we were faced with. That Killiney Bay section is indeed one of the most remarkable and perplexing displays of Glacial deposits which can be found in Ireland. At the base is hard reddish or blackish Boulder-clay, variable in thickness, full of scratched blocks and pebbles of local rocks, and others from Antrim or Ailsa Craig; full too of marine molluscs, mostly broken, polished or scratched, but some complete and amazingly fresh, occasionally preserving their original bright colours or even the thin epidermis which covered the shell when the animal was alive; many of these are of northern type, and one or two are arctic forms not now living within the British area. Over this clay are beds of sand or gravel or clay contorted and twisted and laminated in a quite amazing way. The junction of these two so different deposits is most erratic. Funnels of the sands run down deep into the clay, and blocks of the Boulder-clay lie cheek by jowl with blocks of rock, high up in the sandy beds: these features, and the remarkable differences in the condition of the shells, were among the numerous things that we puzzled over. To the present-day Glacial geologist, explanations will suggest them-

[1] See *Irish Naturalist*, vols. iii.-iv. 1894-95.

selves: but forty years ago things were not so easy. We found equally puzzling sections up the Bray River to above Enniskerry, northern rocks and marine shells still persisting, as they were found to do also in the deep pits at the brickworks at Kill-o'-the-Grange. The last-mentioned place supplied some interesting fossils derived from the Antrim Chalk and Lias, not only large shells but also microscopic ones in the shape of Foraminifera (see p. 164). The Lias fossils were particularly interesting because they included not only species which belong to the Lower Lias, but others from the Middle and Upper Lias, of which beds no trace now exists in Ireland; though they are known to be present on some of the Hebridean islands. The assemblage of stones in the deposits had a strong northern facies: the rocks were largely those of the Limestone Plain, the Antrim area, and the adjoining portion of Scotland: while the animal remains pointed plainly to very cold seas. There seems now no doubt that these deposits are derived from the scooping out of the bottom of the Irish Sea by ice from the north; that they represent the muds, sands and shells that had been accumulating there for thousands of years, mixed with material torn off the adjoining land by ice-pressure: and if we postulate blocks of ice buried in this material, whose melting would cause subsequent collapse, and also frozen masses of clay deposited among the gravels or *vice versa*, we may account for many of the puzzling features of the Killiney Bay cliffs. Further than this it is unnecessary to go here. Influenced by the submergence theory, we spent an Easter holiday cycling over the Central Plain, searching the eskers for remains of marine organisms (we were by now experts in the detection of shell fragments), but the results were entirely negative. Sollas, however, published a paper [1] on the distribution of these still mysterious sinuous gravel-ridges, in which he proclaimed his complete conversion to the view that the eskers represent gravel-filled river-tunnels in a land ice-sheet, and set his face squarely against the belief that they are marine

[1] W. J. Sollas, " A Map to show the Distribution of Eskers in Ireland ", *Sci. Trans. R. Dublin Soc.*, ser. 2, vol. v., pp. 785-822, plate 69. 1896.

deposits. Further work, which might have led to more exact results, was inhibited first by Sollas's departure for the Pacific, to bore through the coral island of Funafuti; and later by his appointment in 1897 to the chair of geology at Oxford. I have regretted this, for I think we had got on tracks which a few were pursuing then, and many more have followed since, and which have done much to help towards the understanding of that most perplexing episode, the Glacial Period.

Among the foothills of south Dublin, near the hamlet of Glencullen, is the filled-up lake of Ballybetagh, from which the peat which formerly covered the lacustrine silts has been stripped off for fuel. This spot has yielded in amazing numbers remains of that splendid animal the Giant Deer or " Irish Elk "—but it is not an elk at all, and its nearest relation is the well-known Fallow Deer. This is not an exclusively Irish animal; its bones and antlers have been found as far afield as Greece, the Caucasus and Russia, but it attained finer physique in this country than anywhere else, and a much greater abundance: so it might well crown the coat of arms of Ireland as the finest and most characteristic member of our fauna, past or present. Its antlers are the most amazing thing about it— grand branching horns with a great palmate centre, and up to nine and a half feet across. When did it die out? A long time ago, measured in years. In Ireland it is not yet certain that it co-existed with man, but then we cannot be at all sure that we have yet found the oldest remains of man that may be in the country. It is older than the peat-bogs, for its antlers and bones are found not in the peat, but in and on the silty lake-deposit which often underlies the bogs. But on the Continent, where the phases of the Glacial Period are more boldly developed, it occurs in the beds belonging to the mild periods which were sandwiched between the several advances of the ice, and it lived then in company with Rhinoceros, Hippopotamus and *Elephas antiquus.* In England also it was widely spread in Palaeolithic times. When we have elucidated our Irish Glacial and early post-Glacial deposits, we shall know more about the local history of the Great Deer. Meanwhile, its occurrence suggests a whole series of conundrums: Why was it so especially abundant and vigorous in Ireland, the remotest corner of its European range? Why do its remains occur in such strange profusion here and there in the deposits of former shallow lakes (over 100 individuals have been dug out at Ballybetagh)? Why is the skull so often found separated from the skeleton? Why are male heads of much more frequent occurrence than female? Answers will no doubt come some day; indeed, there are plenty of them already, and we can take our choice, according to our fancy; but are they correct?

The question as to our finest Irish mammal is only one of a large number relating to the predecessors of the present fauna and flora that await solution. When investigation of the various deposits—peats, silts, clays, gravels and so on—which have accumulated during and since the Glacial Period has been carried out, we may hope to know a great deal as to the date and manner of the incoming of the animals and plants which now inhabit Ireland; not only that, but a flood of light will be thrown on early human history, of which much still remains still uncertain. It is satisfactory to feel assured that this work is now in full progress (see p. 163).

The coast of the Dublin area is formed mostly of Carboniferous limestone and Silurian slates, which show on low rocky shores alternating with stretches of sand. But disturbances of early date have produced some bolder features. To both north and south of Dublin Bay fragments of the old Cambrian floor of the country protrude, forming the Hill of Howth and Bray Head. It is the presence of quartzite, that intractable rock, which causes these two sentinels of Dublin to stand up so boldly. On Bray Head you can see plainly how the quartzite ribs stand out bare and rugged, while the intervening slaty beds underlie bracken-filled hollows. And further inland the cones of the Great and the Little Sugar-loaf again proclaim the resistance of the quartzite to any form of denudation.

Howth (Danish *Hoved*, a head) is a more isolated patch of

Cambrian rock than Bray Head—a mere worn-down knob of slate
and quartzite, the mud and sand of a very ancient sea. On its landward side you may see the Carboniferous limestone—the limy mud
of a long subsequent sea—lapping up against the older rocks; around
the other sides the waves have eaten into the land, producing the
cliffy scenery that is so well known to Dubliners. Howth was still
an island within early human history; the sand-spit that joins it to
the mainland at Sutton is a sea-beach raised above wave-level in
Neolithic times. As I first knew Howth, half a century ago, it was
a delightful old-world place. Even round its rock-bound margin
houses were few, and one could wander at will along its grassy
slopes and over its broad heathery top. Now houses and bungalows,
most of them inartistic eyesores quite out of keeping with their
setting, encroach more and more on the open spaces; along the
southern shore, with its superb view across Dublin bay, the greed
of land-owners confines the visitor to a narrow muddy track between
high barbed-wire fences. But much of the plateau-like top, where
in late summer the Heather and Gorse form one of the loveliest
sights in Ireland, is mercifully still unspoiled, and free to the weary
town-dweller—how long will it remain so? Howth is full of varied
interest—ancient churches and prehistoric monuments, rare flowers
(it has the largest flora for its size of any area in Ireland), shelly
gravels plastered by the ice of the Glacial Period against the steep
seaward slopes, nesting gulls, obscure fossils in the ancient rocks (the
oldest fossils in the country) and prospects both to north and south
that are unsurpassed in Ireland. Would that so unique a national
inheritance—what remains unspoiled of it—might yet be saved
as a breathing-place for the increasing thousands of Dublin's
population.

The island called Ireland's Eye, on the north side of Howth,
furnishes a curious case of name-corruption. Its old name was
Inis Éreann, island of Eire or Eira, who was a woman. The Danes
substituted the termination *öe*, island, for the Irish *inis*: subsequently
Éreann (of Eire) was mistaken for *Éireann* (of Ireland) and Eire's

island became Ireland's Eye. This islet is very picturesque, with high cliffs on one side, and rocks and sand elsewhere around its Bracken-covered surface. An ancient church, and a granite martello tower erected to repel Napoleonic landings, are emblematic of the monuments found all over Ireland, representing piety and war.

Looking north from Howth, the eye is caught by the dark rocky profile of Lambay (*not* Lambay Island, for the last syllable already signifies " island ", being the Danish *öe*, variously mutilated as in Dalkey, Saltee, Anglesea and Ireland's Eye). Lambay is a delightful island, especially interesting on account of its origin, for it is the stump of a little ancient volcano. It was away back in Ordovician times that lavas, of the type called andesitic, broke through the crust and poured out over an area which may have been considerably larger than they occupy now (the island is only about a square mile in extent). Probably the far-reaching Carboniferous sea afterwards engulfed it, and spread over it the limestones that are so extensively developed in Ireland; but if so all trace of them is now worn off, and except for a small patch of Old Red Sandstone of the familiar conglomeratic type the whole island represents the product of the volcanic phase. Like Howth, it is scarped round three sides by the sea, with picturesque cliffs and stacks, and only in the east does it slope down to a beach. And as on Howth, the central part is high (to 418 feet) and covered with Heather and Bracken.

I got to know Lambay very well during the years 1904-10. Cecil Baring, as he was then, came to the National Library seeking information concerning his new possession. He told me how in Munich in 1903 (I think) he and his wife saw in *The Field* an advertisement " Irish Island for Sale ", and how they promptly bought it and set about making habitable its old castle, which was probably the fortress recorded as being there in 1467, already modified to suit more modern requirements. Under the guiding hand of Sir Edward Lutyens, it was converted into a very delightful medieval-modern residence. A couple of cottages upon the hill

were also set in order, and there or in the castle my wife and I spent
many a delightful holiday.   I think the Barings would willingly
have spent their lives on the island, for they became intensely
interested in everything it contained: but continuous sojourn
did not last long.   After a few years business affairs in London
intervened.   Then Mrs Baring died, and was interred on the island
she loved so much; and more recently her husband has been buried
beside her.   Shortly after he took possession of Lambay, I suggested
to him that a detailed study of its natural productions—animal,
vegetable and mineral—would be interesting, and might have important scientific results.   He accepted the suggestion at once.
Workers in various branches of natural science were enlisted, and
during 1905 and 1906 twenty naturalists in all stayed on Lambay,
some of them several times, as the guests of Mr and Mrs Baring, and
ransacked the island from end to end.   Considering its small size
and the uniformity of prevailing conditions, the results were rather
surprising.   Five of the smaller animals found—three worms, a mite
and a bristletail—proved to be new to science; twelve other animals
were new to the Britannic fauna; and between eighty and ninety
animals and plants were hitherto unrecorded from Ireland.[1]   It was
the unexpected success of this intensive study of a limited area that
led to the carrying out a few years later of a similar undertaking on
a much larger scale—the Clare Island Survey (p. 185), which added
very largely to our knowledge of the fauna and flora of Ireland.

Lambay fortunately remains in possession of the Baring family,
and the present Lord Revelstoke continues his father's policy of preserving the island as a sanctuary for animal and plant inhabitants.
Under protection, the great colonies of breeding sea-birds have
increased, and in many cases spread from the cliffs to the grassy
slopes, where you have to pick your steps among innumerable nests.
Rarer birds like the Peregrine and Raven are unmolested there, and
the Fulmar Petrel is a recent arrival; the Great Grey Seals, always a

[1] " Contributions to the Natural History of Lambay ", *Irish Naturalist*, vol.
xvi., pp. 1-112, plates 1-25.   1907.

PLATE XXX

EASTERN COAST OF LAMBAY

fascinating feature of Lambay life, bask on the rocks and breed in the caves. Once I stalked a group of them there on a flat tidal rock until I lay among them, and could count every bristle and hair on their mastiff-like faces; they watched me closely, but never stirred. And we had delightful adventures with white baby seals, quite devoid of fear, which bumped against the boat and let us stroke them, while a watchful mother swam continuously and silently round.

The flora of the county of Dublin is attractive, and is large in view of the small size of the area. This is due mainly to the varied nature of the materials of which it is built up—sea sands, clays, limestones, slates, granites, the last rising to 2473 feet on the Wicklow boundary. Of the various habitats for plants, lowland bog and lake alone are missing in Dublin, and the absence of the latter is compensated by flower-fringed canals. In addition to a large native flora, Dublin is exceptionally rich in alien plants which have established themselves there; some, like the silver-leaved Cineraria of the Dalkey cliffs, to the enhancement of natural beauty. That knowledge of Dublin plants is so complete and so accessible is due to the work of Nathaniel Colgan (1851–1919). The home county had always been a playground of Dublin botanists, but Colgan systematized and greatly enlarged our knowledge, and his *Flora of the County Dublin*, published in 1904, will long remain the final court of appeal on matters relating to local plants.

Fate had decreed for Colgan a singularly uneventful career, for at the age of twenty he obtained by examination a clerkship in the Dublin Metropolitan Police Court, and there he remained till he retired under the age limit, forty-five years later. But his restless enquiring mind was not trammelled by the monotony of a dull Civil Service post. Holidays were spent in foreign travel with stimulating companions, of whom C. F. d'Arcy, the present Archbishop of Armagh, was the chief, and he contributed many literary articles to Dublin magazines. His interest in botany developed about 1880, and under the influence of A. G. More he settled down to a detailed examination of the flora of his native county, with the eminently

A supplement to Colgan's *Flora* was published in 1961 by the National Museum. C.M.

satisfactory results already named: his *Flora* is a work of singular completeness and accuracy. But before it was finished another heavy task was imposed on him. Under the will of his leader A. G. More, who died in 1895, the work of completing and publishing the second edition of *Cybele Hibernica* fell on Colgan and his friend Scully. It proved a laborious task: how successfully it was accomplished is known to every Irish botanist. Later Colgan deserted Flowering Plants in favour of conchology. He lived no longer in Dublin now, but by the sea at Sandycove, and perhaps that influenced him in changing from botany to zoology. Shore-collecting and dredging replaced floral field-work, and especially among the nudibranchs he advanced our knowledge materially. He was still busily engaged on this study when he died.

Colgan was a man of wide and varied accomplishments, of excellent literary taste, with an unusually critical cast of mind and keenness of observation. He called himself a sceptic, by which he meant an instinctive demanding of proof in many cases where others were content to accept things at their face value. " But *is* it? " was his frequent question, and many an entertaining discussion ensued. A very shy man, he worked for years almost unknown to his fellow-scientists. Finally, connection with the Dublin Naturalists' Field Club brought him in contact with other biologists, and when he undertook the marine mollusca in connection with the Clare Island Survey, the jolly parties in whose company he worked broke down the last of his reserve, and his talent and humour became known to all of us.

His friend Primate D'Arcy wrote of him: " He was the most lovable of companions. His keen intellect, wonderfully wide reading, subtle irony, and felicity of expression threw light on everything, and made the commonest experiences enjoyable. He ought to have been a great man, famous in the world. It was only his strange self-suppression and too great modesty which prevented it. He was not easy to know, but the knowledge was well worth having."

If Nathaniel Colgan had done no other work, we ought to be grateful to him for his masterly clearing-up of the muddle—the many muddles, indeed—concerning the Shamrock, accepted everywhere as the national emblem of Ireland. And as I do not think that his enquiries in this field are well known, I recapitulate them here. He became interested first in the question of what actually is the plant or plants, for there are several, worn on St. Patrick's Day; and in 1892 and 1893 he made a kind of census, inviting from every county in Ireland specimens of " true Shamrock " for identification. Of the results of this enquiry, I shall deal presently. He then became involved in the past history of the Shamrock, and instituted a laborious survey of the literature of the subject: this led him far afield, and produced a wealth of curious legend and fact, which was communicated to the Royal Society of Antiquaries of Ireland.[1] In this paper, he arranged the references chronologically, and began each with a date and a heading; if I quote these only, adding the work cited, the reader will get an epitomized view of the history of the Shamrock in literature:

1570. A Flemish botanist records that the Irish freebooters eat cakes made of the Meadow Trefoil (Matthias Lobel, *Stirpium Adversaria Nova*, p. 380).

1571. The Shamrock appears by name for the first time in English literature, and is said to be used as food by the Irish (Edmond Campion, *Historie of Ireland*).

1578. An English rhymester detests the wilde Shamrocke manners of the Irish wood kernes (John Derricke, *Image of Ireland with a Discoverie of Wood Kerne*).

1586. Stanihurst asserts that the Irish term Water Cresses, Shamrocks (Holinshed, *Chronicles*).

1595 *circa*. The Irish feed on Sham-rokes when reduced to starvation in the Munster wars (Edmund Spenser, *View of the Present State of Ireland*).

1597. An Elizabethan herbalist records that the Meadow Trefoil is called Shamrockes by the Irish (John Gerard, *Herball*).

[1] *Journ. R.S.A.I.*, vol. xxvi., pp. 211-226, 349-361. 1896.

1599. The herbe Shamrocke being of a sharp taste is willingly eaten by the wild Irish (Fynes Moryson, *Itinerary*).

1611–1630. The Shamrogh or Shamroote becomes established (in English literature) as a staple food-stuff for the Irish (John Speed, *Theatre of the Empire of Great Britain*; George Wither, *Abuses, Stript and Whipt*; John Taylor, *All the Works of John Taylor the Water Poet*).

1638. The Earl of Antrim proposes to feed with Shamrocks an Irish army of 8000 men (Thomas Wentworth, Earl of Stafford, *Letters*).

1654. An antiquarian writer makes mention of the Meadow Trefoil as a food of the ancient Irish (Sir James Ware, *De Hibernia*).

1680. An Oxford physician attributes the strength and agility of the Irish to their Shamrock diet (Henry Mundy, *Commentarii de Aëre vitali, Esculentis ac Potulentis*).

1681. The Shamrock badge makes its first appearance in literature (Thomas Dinely, *Journal*).

1682. The Shamrock is used as a summer food by the Irish in the rocky districts of the County Clare (Sir Henry Piers, *Chorographical Description of the County of Westmeath*).

1689. The Shamrock is firmly established as an emblem of Ireland and the Irish (James Farewell, *The Irish Hudibras*).

1699. " Their Shamrug is the Common Clover " (Edward Llwyd, Letter to Tancred Robinson, in *Phil. Trans.*, vol. xxvii., p. 503. 1712).

1727. The Trinity legend of the Shamrock makes its first appearance in literature (Caleb Threlkeld, *Synopsis Stirpium Hibernicarum*).

1737. The Irish make bread from the honey-scented flowers of the Purple Clover (Linnaeus, *Flora Lapponica*).

1772. The Shamrock food supplanted by the Potato (John Rutty, *Natural History of the County of Dublin*).

1830. The Wood-Sorrel Theory of the Shamrock is propounded (James Ebenezer Bicheno, in *Journ. Roy. Inst. Gt. Britain*, vol. i.).

Each of Colgan's headings quoted above is followed by the relevant passage from the work in question, and by comments and notes, often of much interest, for which his original paper must be consulted. He himself sums up the whole matter as follows:

" For almost a century after its first appearance in literature the Shamrock presents itself solely as a bread-stuff or food-herb of the Irish, probably so used only in times of famine or scarcity of corn.

" The Shamrock thus used as food was one or other, or, perhaps, both of the Meadow Clovers or Trefoils, *Trifolium pratense* (Purple Clover) and *T. repens* (White Clover) of modern botanists.

"There is no reason to believe that this Shamrock food was used at any date later than 1682.

"The Shamrock badge, or emblem, makes its first appearance in literature in the year 1681.

"The Wood-Sorrel (*Oxalis Acetosella*) was not at any period used in Ireland as a badge or emblem, nor did it ever serve as a food with the Irish in the same sense as the Meadow Trefoil."

And so it would appear that the word Shamrock cannot be traced back beyond 1571, and the Irish form *Seamróg* (a diminutive of *Seamar*, clover) is not known earlier than 1707. The older Irish manuscripts are silent, as are the numerous lives of St. Patrick and other early sources, concerning the attractive legend which connects Ireland's patron saint with her national emblem—and the Shamrock as an Irish emblem dates back no further than 1681. The only early reference is not to *seamróg* but to *scoithshemrach*, which would seem to have been some kind of clover. This word, in the contracted form *scothemrach*, appears in the well-known fourteenth-century MS. the *Leabhar Breac*: and as the incident in connection with which it is mentioned is interesting, I transcribe it (from Colgan), as a slight compensation for the loss of the Patrician legend:

"One day Saint Sciuthin was walking on the sea, when he met Saint Barré, of Cork, who was in a ship. 'Why do you walk on the sea?' said Barré. 'It is not the sea,' answered Sciuthin, 'but a plain, flowery, shamrocked' (*scothemrach*, perhaps better rendered clovery); and he picked up a purple flower (or, perhaps, a handsome flower), and cast it to Barré in the ship, and said: 'Why does a ship swim on the plain?' Then Barré put down his hand into the sea, and took a salmon thereout, and cast it to Sciuthin."

Colgan's earlier papers [1] on the Shamrock were concerned only with the identity of the plant which nowadays is worn on 17th March, St. Patrick's day, as the national badge; for, as is well known,

[1] *Irish Naturalist*, vols. i.-ii. 1892–93.

there is more than one claimant to the title " true Shamrock ". He approached the enquiry by the only reliable method: he collected, or got collected, about St. Patrick's day in 1892, specimens of "true Shamrock " from different parts of Ireland, and planted them, and when they blossomed identified them; as a result, six counties voted for the yellow-flowered Lesser Trefoil, *Trifolium minus*, three for the White Clover, *T. repens*, and two for both. Not content with this partial result, in 1893 he circularized people in all parts of Ireland (today we would have done it by wireless S O S) and received plants from twenty Irish counties; these, grown and identified, reversed the previous decision, giving 19 votes for White Clover, 12 for Lesser Trefoil, 2 for Purple Clover, and 2 for Spotted Medick. The plants were all collected by persons who prided themselves on knowing " true Shamrock ", and though the two leading plants bear a close resemblance early in the season, it may be assumed that in all cases the choice was deliberate. But a previous enquiry by James Britten gave eight more votes for the Lesser Trefoil, making 20 for it as against 16 for the White Clover: so honours are fairly even as between these two plants, while Purple Clover and Medick are entirely out of the running: and it may be noted that the Wood-Sorrel has not a single supporter. By " true Shamrock " any Irishman means the plant that St. Patrick is reputed to have used in his demonstration of the Trinity: so the census indicates the plant to which the legend is locally attached. But the selection holds good only around the month of March. Anywhere in the country you will be told that the Shamrock never flowers: in other words, once St. Patrick's day is past, no further notice is taken of the plant. You will also learn that the Shamrock will not grow in an alien soil—though all the Irish claimants are as common over much of western Europe as they are here. Passing over these statements, which do not help to identify the plant, you find that the actual diagnosis leads to a clover with small neat leaves—a condition always fulfilled by the Lesser Trefoil, but requiring starved specimens of the White Clover. Show any countryman a *flowering* specimen of either, and he will scout the idea of its being, or ever having been, " the dear little, sweet little Shamrock of Ireland ".

Colgan's excellent *Flora of County Dublin* recalls the work of a distant predecessor, Caleb Threlkeld, who almost two hundred years before wrote what purported to be a list of the plants of Ireland— and it was the first of its kind—but which was mainly a flora of the metropolitan area.[1]   The author was a medical missionary, a native of Cumberland, M.A. of Glasgow, M.D. of Edinburgh, who lived long in Dublin, and eventually died there.   He was a good botanist, and well versed in the works of his contemporaries.   But he was more than that—a man of independent and vigorous mind, with strong views on many subjects: and his comments on current opinions and contemporary life give his *Synopsis* a quite peculiar interest.   Like others of his generation, he was a firm believer in the efficacy of herbs: indeed, he adhered clearly to the cheerful doctrine that every plant, even if it were not created specially for that purpose, was useful in the cure of human distresses: and almost every species in his list of some 300 has one or up to half a dozen ailments appended to it, from freckles and fevers to hysterics and "heterogeneous humours", which its proper application will relieve. But one turns from this thaumaturgy to the more personal side of his writing, from which I cannot resist excerpting a few paragraphs.

Caleb has no doubt as to the importance of botanical study: " The Science of *Botany* being not only generally useful, but even absolutely necessary to us Mortals, emboldens me to present the ensuing small Treatise to Your Grace, who is so eminently noted, as a benevolent Patron of Mankind in general.   It was upon Account of this extensive Usefulness, that some great Kings, and mighty Princes (as *Lysimachus, Gentius, Mithridates,* &c.) by their personal Knowledge of Plants, and others, (as the renowned *Cyrus,* who had the Honour to be called by his *Name* by the evangelical Prophet,

---

[1] *Synopsis Stirpium Hibernicarum Alphabetice Dispositarum.   Sive Commentatio de Plantis Indigenis praesertim Dublinensibus instituta . . . Auctore Caleb Threlkeld,* M.D.   Dublin, MDCCXXVII.

above a hundred Years before he was born) have countenanced, encouraged and even practised *Horticulture* and *Agriculture*; and as Botanick Studies have a native Tendency to the Support, Comfort, and Delight of Mankind, with this View it is, that I have laid this Essay upon *Irish* Plants at Your Grace's feet." (From the Dedication to the Archbishop of Armagh.) And this from the Preface: " Many Generations of Men are come and gone from this Earth, since the Formation of *Adam* out of it, yet the Earth itself with its verdant Furniture abideth for ever. . . . So that although we are not the same Nation of Men, who dwelt here a thousand years ago, yet the spontaneous Plants are the same they were in the times of the *Danes* and *Brian Boro*, and in my opinion it had been more Benefit to Mankind to have made stricter Inquiries into the natural Growth of the Soil; (the Beauty of which while it allures our Eyes, and even captivates our Senses, raises in us the most exalted Idea of the Magnificence of the great Creator) than to have trifled away Pains and Time, in amusing us with fabulous Stories concerning the Generations of Men preceding us, whose almost endless Genealogies are often fallacious and dubious, and where they are certain, of very little Importance to us in civil Affairs, not that I blame laudable Searches into Antiquity, but I give the preference to these durable and succouring Studies."

He is very emphatic as to witchcraft and such things, which nevertheless he takes seriously: under *Antirrhinum*, the Snapdragon, we read: " There are many frivolous Superstitious Fables which are reported of the Power of this Plant, and some others against Spectres, Charms and Witchcraft. The only true Remedy against such Abominations, as spring from Observers of Times, Inchanters, Witches, Charmers, Consulters with familiar Spirits, Wizards and Necromancers, is to hearken to that Prophet the Lord *Jesus Christ*, before whose faithful Ministers Satan falleth as Lightning from Heaven." Of the divining rod he is merely contemptuous, writing under *Corylus* (Hazel): " That a divining Rod of this Wood should be used to find out Metalls, is owing to the Impostures of *Satan*, whose design is to abuse the Creatures with vain Amusements under the old Colour of Knowledge more than is fit for Men ". He would not have approved of some modern fashions: under *Verbascum* (Mullein) he remarks: " The woolly Leaves . . . are said to dye the Hair yellowish, if that can answer any valuable End: For the Hair of the Head, and its natural Colour, is the Work of God, and if so, all Abuse of it is unlawful by consequence ". He is much concerned, indeed, with God and the Devil: " The Fruit of the Bramble is reputed infamous, for causing sore Heads; whence it comes to pass that to scare Children from eating of them, some call them *Scald-berries*; but I look on this as a vulgar Error, and that after Michaelmas the D——l casts his Club over them, which is a Fable: For the Earth is the Lord's, and the Fulness thereof ". Occasionally he allows politics to intrude: " Those who would give to the *Spaniards* the Honour of intrencing this useful Root, called *Potato*, give me leave to call designing Parracides, who stirred up the misled Zeal of the People of this Kingdom to cast off the *English* Government, which is the greatest Mercy they ever enjoyed, for it freed them from foreign Insults, and domestick Slaughter of one Sept or Clan against another, and united them to a powerful and just People; so that for the future I hope they will not only acquiesce, but praise him by whom Kings Reign, for our Gracious Sovereign King *George*: to ascribe the Honour of the *English* Industry to the effeminate *Spaniards*, cannot be passed over without a Remark which I hope will offend no body ". When he deals with botanical matters he is mostly accurate: "*Dodder* is opening and cleansing, accounted good to purge Meloncholy, and against the Itch; it is a Nompareil having no Leaves, but red Threads, and after it has fastened its Claspers, or small Tendrils up on a Plant, as Line, Thyme, Netle, Madder, or such like; it quits the Root, and like a coshering Parasite lives upon anothers Trencher, and like an ungrateful Guest first starves, and then kills its Entertainer: For which Reason irreligious Clowns curse it by the Name of *Hell-weed*, and *Devil's-gutts* in Sussex; however it is a good bathing herb for meloncholy People ".

One likes to think of the good doctor, in wig and knee-breeches, sitting in his house in Mark's-Alley, with the learned works of Tournefort, How, Ray, Merrett and Gerard before him, inditing these comments and reflections—the last he was destined to publish, for he died, a comparatively young man, in the spring of the year following the appearance of the " piquant medley of herbal and homily " which constitutes his book.

The adjoining counties of Kildare and Meath are naturally associated with Dublin, for at all times they gave a free outlet from the metropolis towards west and north, and shared with Dublin a fertile soil and early agricultural prosperity. Wicklow, on the south, was in a different category—a mountainous region, inhabited by the restless O'Byrnes and O'Tooles, who long gave trouble to townsman and countryman alike. Modern Dublin has something for which to thank those turbulent glen-folk; but for them and their like we should not have been able to boast the finest mountain thoroughfare in the kingdom—the Military Road, which traverses the whole length of the Wicklow mountain-chain, now rising high, now dropping into the valleys. Other more picturesque mountain-roads there are, as in Kerry, which, intent on crossing a high ridge or chain, ascend a glen on one side, pass over a rocky col, and descend a glen on the other. But where else do you find a road which follows the axis of a mountain-chain for forty miles, and where for a dozen miles at a stretch the heather fringe by the road-side never ceases? It was the lingering unrest consequent on the 1798 rebellion that caused the English government to construct this thoroughfare, tapping the heads of the deep glens and allowing of rapid military movement; so we may be grateful to the marauding Wicklow tribes for one of the important amenities of Dublin. But what has become of the warlike O'Tooles? O'Byrnes (now more frequently Byrnes) we have always with us; in Dublin we meet them at every street corner: but O'Toole is a much rarer name.

Wicklow still forms a great physical barrier on the southern flank of Dublin. Railway and road creep southward along the coast towards Wexford; but the main traffic goes westward into Kildare, and thence spreads itself over the southern half of Ireland. Kildare is a varied area. The east and south are mostly foot-hill country of the Wicklow highlands—a ridgy Ordovician tract, fertile and well populated, while the north-west pertains to the Central Plain, with bog and limy soils. The antiquary can see much in day trips from Dublin. Kildare itself (*Cill dara*, church of the oak), now little more than a village, is a place with a long and distinguished history from its foundation by St. Brigid about 490, a place of European reputation for learning and piety through-out the middle ages, finally battered to pieces during the wars of the seventeenth century. The cathedral, erected on the site of older churches in 1229, has practically been rebuilt, and the lofty round tower, 105 feet high, has been adorned with a ridiculous battle-mented top: but its doorway, unusual in being richly ornamented with chevron and zigzag mouldings, is fortunately intact. Kildare has many other objects of antiquity of various ages, including (in the north-east) some pillar-stones of unusual height—long needles of granite—associated with interments of the Bronze Age: but I shall content myself with referring to the only site with which I have more than a visiting acquaintance.

On the eastern edge of the county, at Colbinstown near Ballitore (*Bél átha a' tuair*, ford-mouth of the bleach-green) is the puzzling cemetery of Killeen Cormac (*Cillín Cormaic*, Cormac's church [yard]), on which a good deal has been written in attempts to identify it with the burial-place of Cormac, King of Munster, or with a certain church founded by St. Palladius. The site presents an irregular low mound, crowded with graves old and new, and surrounded at its base by a much disturbed kerb of large slabs of the local Ordovician grit. Outside this is a kind of circular plat-form raised four or five feet above the level of the surrounding field, and retained by a modern circular wall of about the same height. There are no graves or gravestones on the raised ring—they are all on the mound inside the kerb; the latest of them are of quite modern date, but among these are early cross-slabs and pillar-stones. And of special interest is the fact that several of the pillar-stones bear inscriptions in Ogham characters, which projects the date of the first use of the place as a cemetery back at least as far as the earliest days of Irish Christianity. It was in the hope that excavation might throw light on the origin and history of Killeen Cormac that Dr. Macalister asked me to join him in an investigation of the site in 1929; with Ruby Murray to help us and my wife as commissariat officer we spent a pleasant and fruitful Easter week there. We were specially interested in the Oghams, of which Macalister has made a study for many years, for though very rare in this part of Ireland (they attain their maximum in Kerry and Cork), no less than three were known at Killeen Cormac. For most people, I think, a mystery hangs over this curious form of writing: certainly until that week I was ignorant concerning it, but by the time our work was complete a good deal had been learned. Though our excavations were strictly limited by the profusion of graves of recent date, we dug up four more Ogham stones—one of them a fragment of a grand pillar-stone, which may have stood ten feet high. Killeen Cormac, indeed, proved to be quite an Ogham museum, isolated, and peculiar on account of its continuous use as a cemetery down to the present day. Something of what I learned during that spring week I give here, for the benefit of others who may know as little about early Irish inscriptions as I did.

Though evidence may be adduced for supposing that some sort of primitive writing existed in Ireland in pre-Christian times, the first definite examples appear in the earliest inscriptions in Ogham character, dating from about the fourth century A.D. The majority of the Ogham inscriptions are about fifth to seventh century, and they die out again a couple of centuries later. (The cursive Latin script, as employed throughout the Roman Empire, was introduced into Ireland at about the same time as the appearance of Ogham, in the fourth century, and with the spread of Christianity in Ireland attained a wide vogue in manuscripts. This, changing very little through the centuries, has remained in Ireland associated with the native language, and is what is now commonly called Irish character, while in other connections it has developed into the writing which we use today.) But to return to Ogham. The letters employed are based on a cumbrous but simple plan. Draw a straight line and make short strokes on either side of it or across it, and you get the principle. One to five strokes above the line give you five letters; the same below the line five more; the same across the line, an additional five (these strokes being all at right angles to the base line); five other strokes across the line, but at an angle to it, give you still another five letters; these twenty, with a few other symbols of less simple form, make up the alphabet (Fig. 9). The cumbrousness of the Ogham character prevented its ever being used for ordinary writing purposes, but it was much employed

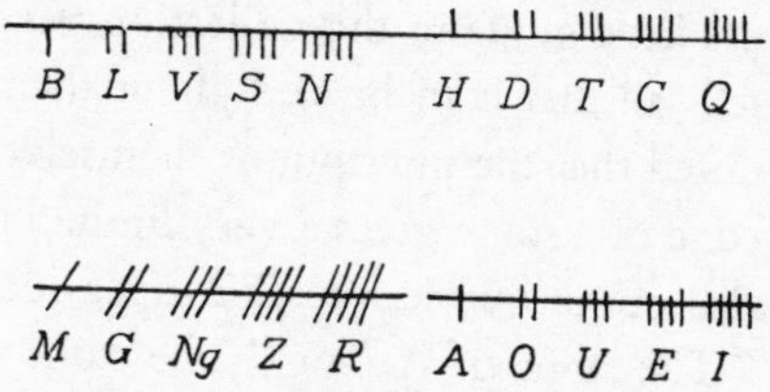

FIG. 9.—THE OGHAM ALPHABET

on memorial stones, the stem-line being usually a sharp edge of a squarish elongated block. The art of writing in Ogham was never completely lost, and down to the beginning of the nineteenth century it was used on occasion by peasant scholars. In view of what has been said above, the reading of Ogham inscriptions would seem to be a simple matter: but several circumstances combine to make it often the reverse. Firstly, the words used, especially the personal names, are of an archaic type, preserving the forms current several centuries earlier, before the beginning of manuscript, and therefore unfamiliar; secondly, the spacing of the letters in the inscriptions is often irregular, rendering difficult the separation of the words (which, as has been said, are often of obscure form); and again, weather and casualties of various sorts have frequently made the inscriptions now very difficult to decipher—some have nearly vanished owing to decay of the stone; others have been deliberately obliterated, in whole or part. All of which means that we need not be surprised if the readings of different scholars vary, or if their transliterations include blanks and queries.

To us in Ireland the most interesting point about Ogham is that it originated here and has always been essentially an Irish form of writing. Inscriptions still exist in the country to the number of at least 300, and they occur in almost all Irish counties, though very irregularly scattered. They have been found also in Cornwall, Devon, Wales, Isle of Man and Scotland, no doubt the result of Irish colonization: but they are unknown on the Continent. The National Museum in Dublin contains a representative series, and the little guide to this collection, recently written by Dr. Macalister, tells all that is to be said about them and their history. It will be noted that the inscriptions themselves are of necessity short, for the edge of a stone gives a very limited field, and even a single word in this cumbrous script takes up a lot of room. The usual form is " The stone of A." or " The stone of A. son of B.", etc. This is shortened by omitting " The stone ", but preserving the genitive to indicate its omission. So we get simply the name (say) *Garagni*; or *Caginati maqi Vobaraci*, the second word being the genitive of *mac*, son.

From this digression I return to Killeen Cormac. Our examination made certain things clear, such as: the site is not an ancient dun or tumulus, but a natural mound of Glacial gravel; there is no indication that it contains a sepulchral chamber; nor is there any trace of a church, though a squarish hollow on top of the mound is suggestive. Many of the memorial stones were lying prostrate, some completely buried. We found (and in most cases re-erected) nine uninscribed pillar-stones, seven pillar stones with Ogham inscriptions, and seven inscribed pillar-stones or slabs of early Christian type.[1] This tidying-up has added materially to the

[1] Macalister and Praeger, "Report on Excavation recently conducted in Killeen Cormac, Co. Kildare", *Proc. Roy. Irish Acad.*, vol. xxxviii., sect. C, pp. 247-261, plates 26-30. 1929.

interest of a cemetery of unique character. Two of the stones deserve special mention: one shows in addition to an Ogham inscription another in well-cut Roman capitals, the only Roman inscription of so early date known in Ireland: the other bears in relief a head of Christ of primitive workmanship and clearly of very early period.

Meath (*Midhe*, middle [province]) is a grand county—large, fertile, well wooded, well populated. It is the finest cattle country to be found in Ireland, and nearly three-quarters of its surface is occupied by its famous pasturage. On the other hand peat-bog is rare, and lakes are absent save along the west and north-west margins. The Boyne (*Bonouinda* of Ptolemy) and its tributaries, spreading like a fan, permeate the whole area, and the Boyne river-basin is almost coincident with the county. The principal towns lie on the river, and most of the biological and archaeological interest of Meath, as well as most of its scenic beauty, are associated with the course of the Boyne. The county has a short but attractive coast-line fronting the Irish Sea, with much to interest the biologist. The estuary which runs thence for four miles to Drogheda is interesting also. At that place the stream has cut a gorge 200 feet deep, resulting in steep streets and a lofty railway bridge. The town is actually in Louth, but as it is the natural gateway of Meath it will be included here. Drogheda is picturesque, and a fine town gate, and the tower of the old Dominican Abbey, both conspicuously placed, enhance this effect. The town had the tempestuous career which was the fate of every place in Ireland that was worth fighting for, its crowning agony having been in 1641, when it was stormed by Cromwell, its fall being followed by deeds of unparalleled ferocity. From early times the place was of importance, for the ford here (Drogheda = *Droichead-átha*, pronounced Drohed-aha— the bridge of the ford) lay on the main coastwise thoroughfare between north and south, and it and the " Pass of the North " through the mountains beyond Dundalk constituted the crucial points on this route; to the present-day traveller from Dublin to

Belfast they still form the two most notable features. No river in Ireland offers a combination of scenic beauty and historical interest to compare with the Boyne. From Navan, where it is joined by its almost equally large tributary the Blackwater, the river traverses a richly wooded valley which in places is gorge-like, as where the limestone protrudes on either bank at Beauparc (Plate XXXI). There has been a local squeeze here in old days, and the rock is sharply folded—a rare feature in this formation in Ireland. Above Navan both the Boyne and Blackwater are more open. The upper-most reaches of the Boyne lie in flattish boggy Central Plain country far to the south; the Blackwater, flowing south-east from the wood-encircled Lough Ramor, crosses undulating Silurian country, and is an attractive stream throughout. Wilde's *Boyne and Blackwater*, a book long out of print, does full justice to the interest—archaeo-logical especially—of the Meath area.

On the north side of the Boyne six miles or so above Drogheda, on raised ground overlooking the river, is *Brúgh-na-Bóinne*, the royal cemetery of Ireland in the Bronze Age, of which the leading monu-ment, the immense tumulus of Newgrange, is the finest thing of its kind in western Europe—a great cairn of stones, nearly a hundred yards in diameter at the base and some fifty feet in height to its flattish top. The sloping edge is or was sustained by a continuous kerb of great flat slabs set on end, and at some distance outside this rises what remains of a ring of great standing stones, each many tons in weight. On the south side a passage formed of large upright blocks roofed with others, over sixty feet long, leads to a grand chamber made subcruciform by three recesses, and roofed with overlapping blocks and a final keystone twenty feet above the floor. A large number of the stones bear incised markings, often of very bold design and deeply cut. These are in the form of spirals, lozenges and many other forms, such as are often found on Bronze Age memorials. There is no need to enter here into details of this stupendous monument, but it is interesting to discuss some of its less obvious features. This is a grazing country, and for many

An abridged edition of Wilde's *Boyne and Blackwater*, illustrated with the original woodcuts, was published in 1949. C.M.

PLATE XXXI

R. Welch: photo

THE BOYNE AT BEAUPARC

centuries cattle roamed freely about and over the mound. The consequent tramping is mainly responsible for its present external condition. We find that the kerb of slabs four to six feet high inside which the great mound of loose stones was once contained, is now buried to its upper edge by stones which have slid down from above. That even the upper edge of the kerb-slabs can be seen at all is due to a retaining wall some five feet high built on top of it in recent times to prevent further slipping. A few years ago the Office of Public Works, in which the monument is vested, excavated along the base of the kerb for about a third of its circumference: Dr. Macalister and I were privileged to take part in this work, which was under the direction of H. G. Leask, officer in charge of ancient monuments. We had to sink a trench for six feet through loose stones to reach the base of the kerb, and it was evident that all the sloping ground between the kerb and the flat surrounding field was made of material that belonged to the mound. The original mound sloped upwards from the top of the kerb: to restore it to its pristine form all the material now supported by the modern retaining wall built on the top of the kerb, and all the slope outside the kerb, would have to be restored to the top of the mound. This material is of such quantity that its replacement would make the mound much more conical and much higher than it is at present—a most imposing structure; and this great cone would rise not from the top of a flattish slope as at present, but from level ground running in to the base of the kerb, thus adding a further six feet or so to its height.

One or two other interesting points came to light. Many of the buried stones of the kerb bear incised ornament resembling the forms found in the chamber, but smaller and lightly cut—trivial, indeed, in comparison with the bolder scribings of the interior stones. Next, the stones of the kerb towards the north of the mound have in many cases fallen outwards, and it cannot be seen whether any of these is inscribed—it will be remembered that one of the most remarkable of the scribed stones of Newgrange is a kerbstone which is fallen, but under which an excavation has been made which allows examination of the rich ornament on what had been its upright face. Then again we were struck with the great quantity, among the ordinary field stones of which the mound is composed, of two extraneous elements. There were thousands of bits of white quartz—angular pieces some inches in diameter. The sharpness of their edges suggested that they had been quarried, and their quantity (we saw at least twenty tons in a limited excavation) negatived the idea that, like most of the stones, they had been obtained near the site. There is no quartz in the limestone rocks that extend south of the Boyne; they had been brought apparently from the Silurian area that stretches northward, and in which rocks veins of quartz occur. And again, we found about a thousand rounded boulders of granite, egg-shaped or globular, from about half a foot to a foot in diameter. Granite is not found anywhere in this neighbourhood, though there is a considerable area of this rock on both sides of Carlingford Lough. But the rounded form of these granite boulders points to prolonged wave-action on an exposed beach; the only place where such conditions prevail is on the shore of County Down about Kilkeel and Annalong. There can be little doubt that both the white quartz and the round granite boulders had some religious or mystical significance, and that they were brought here from a distance. White stones are a characteristic accompaniment of Bronze Age interments, and rounded pebbles of other rocks are also sometimes found: but the amount and size of these offerings—if such they were—at Newgrange have no parallel in Ireland.

Nor is Newgrange all that *Brúgh-na-bóinne* has to offer. There is the smaller but still imposing tumulus of Dowth (*Duthaidh*) less than a mile away, with many similar sculptured stones; also that of Knowth (*Cnodhbha*)—at present closed: and several small earthen cairns that have never been excavated. There is still much to be done in the scientific exploration of this imposing mausoleum.

Meath is rich also in Christian remains, as would be expected in so favoured an area; but these are well known, and I need not indulge in platitudes concerning them—Mellifont, Monasterboice

Excavations at Knowth and Newgrange are in progress. Recent books are, *Newgrange* by S. P. O'Riordain and Glyn Daniel (1964) and a paperback *Guide to Newgrange* by Claire O'Kelly (1967). C.M.

(*Mainistir Buite*, Buite's monastery), Kells (*Ceanannus*, head residence, modified to Kenlis), Trim (*Áth truim*, ford of the elder-trees) are names that to the antiquary connote abbeys, churches, high crosses, castles, round towers. All are easy to reach and interesting to visit, and lie in pleasant and picturesque surroundings. Then on Slievena-Calliagh, away out to the west near Oldcastle, there is a second remarkable Bronze Age cemetery—more than a score of cairns of stone on a windy hill, containing burial chambers showing rock-scribings of the characteristic forms, and often identical with those of Newgrange. When they were excavated in 1867-68 they yielded many fragments of pottery and human bones, sea-shells, pieces of flint, rounded pebbles, and other accompaniments of Bronze Age sepulture. Unfortunately the place is much exposed to the weather, and some of the carvings have suffered: but it remains a museum of the curious art of the Bronze Age.

A site of another kind, and one of foremost importance in early Irish history, is Tara, near Kilmessan in central Meath. I wonder did anyone ever leave Tara without a sense of disappointment? Of the long and surpassing importance of this royal residence and city there is no doubt: it was the centre and pulse of Ireland for two thousand years; but very few sites of so great interest have so little to show—a low broad swelling hill, commanding a wide prospect: and about its summit a few raths and mounds and other earthworks, and an odd pillar-stone: that is all—save a hideous modern statue of St. Patrick. In this cattle country earthen structures suffer badly: fifteen hundred years of trampling will deprive them of much of their imposing appearance, and leave them flattened and featureless. Then the finding here of two torques of gold in 1810 had a disastrous effect, in giving apparent confirmation to the widespread idea that ancient remains are associated with buried treasure: in consequence, human destruction was added to that caused by the cattle. And as if this was not enough, enthusiasts quite recently were allowed to dig there, searching for the Ark of the Covenant—causing further confusion! Fortunately, such desecration has at last been made illegal, and all archaeological excavation is now under strict control. But what Tara was must not be judged from what Tara is. No doubt buildings of wood formed the main feature of the place, and they may have been of noble proportions. Of these no trace remains—though it may be hoped that careful excavation will eventually reveal their foundations, in the shape of post-holes now filled with material recognizably different from the surrounding clay. The best thing that Tara offers to the present-day pilgrim is the truly regal prospect that lies around that open windy hill-top. From this, indeed, it derives its name, for Tara is a form of *Temhair*, a view-point or *Aussichtspunkt*. To north, west and south stretch the fertile lands of Meath, and beyond them on a clear day you can fix points all over the Central Plain, situated in half a score of counties. With that panorama before you, the mounds and earthen rings seem but an insignificant cenotaph. So you may—and should—go to Tara and dream of its past glories—founding your dreams on what is definitely known about it, not on the romances, old and new, which are associated with it; but what you find there, except the view, will provide no stimulus to your dreaming.

CHAPTER XI

THE WICKLOW HIGHLANDS

My brevity as regards Wicklow does not arise from lack of appreciation. That lovely region of mountain and lake has given me so many days of delight that it would be easy to succumb to the temptation of lingering over the beauty of each hill and valley from Enniskerry to Shillelagh. But as it is known intimately to many, and has been much written about already, my personal tribute to its more obvious interests may be taken for granted. It is a compact area. You can, if you wish, see most of the best of Wicklow in a day's motoring, if that can be called " seeing "—down by The Scalp (*Scealp*, a chasm or cleft), Enniskerry (*Áth na scarbhe*, the ford of the rough crossing), Glencree (*Gleann cruidhe*, glen of cattle), Lough Bray (*Lough breagh?*, lake of the hill), Sally Gap, Glenmacnass (*Gleann luig an easa*, glen of the hollow of the waterfall) to Glendalough; and back by Glenmalure (*Gleann maoil úghra*, glen of the lover of skirmishes), Aughavannagh (*Achadh meadhonach*, middle field), Donard (*Dún árd*, high fort), Hollywood Glen and the Slade of Saggart (*Slad*, a stream in a mountain valley; Saggart = tassagard, originally *teach Sacra*, Sacra's house): but that would be only to insult a lovely region. Like any other area of beauty and interest, it needs leisure and study if one is to understand it and enjoy it, and the proper way to see Wicklow is to walk it. The motorist will get glimpses of the scenery, but of the *causes* of the scenery, which is far more interesting, he will gather no hint. Yet Wicklow is particularly attractive from this point of view. Firstly, its topography and scenery are very directly dependent on its geology, which is striking and simple. After the thick masses of slaty rocks of the Ordovician period had been laid down in an ancient sea, a mass of molten granite rose up below them, and forced them into a broad and elongated dome running in a south-westerly direction. The granite slowly cooled and consolidated, and the forces of denudation played upon the slaty covering till it became largely stripped off, remaining as a fringe lapping round the granite core, which forms a long range of mountains—the greatest area of granite in Ireland, and greater than any in Great Britain. The continued sculpturing action of rain and frost and streams, and of ice during the Glacial Period, has left the country as we see it now. The massive granite has weathered characteristically into broad domes, while the surrounding schists have assumed more varied outlines, forming rocky foothills with deep glens, especially on the eastern side of the chain. The frequent lakes usually represent hollows scooped out by the ice, now filled with water. Another legacy of the ice is the overflow channels or " dry gaps " which are specially well developed around the flanks of the hills. These illustrate in a very interesting way the conditions prevailing as the Glacial climate began to ameliorate. The hills tended to get melted out while the ice-blanket, several thousands of feet thick, still lay heavily over the lowlands. The streams descending the newly freed valleys found themselves dammed; lakes were formed, with the hills for sides and the ice for front, and these rose till the water escaped laterally along the ice-edge. These torrents, flowing *along* the hill-sides, cut deeply into the ridges which restrained them, and we find their tracks still, rocky gorges cut across the ridges where these were lowest. Two very fine examples are The Scalp and the Glen of the Downs, one on either side of the lake which at the time of their formation occupied the middle part of the valley of the Bray River. Piperstown Glen, at the back of Montpelier Hill, is a notable example, showing a higher level than the overflow channels just mentioned; it discharged the water which collected against the ice around Killakee (*Coill a' chaeich*, blind man's wood), and we can still see the delta of gravel which it deposited as it entered the adjoining lake which filled Glenasmole (*Gleann na smól*, valley of the thrushes). These temporary lakes often got much silted up owing to the turbid torrents which foamed down into them from the hills, and the material which accumulated in them now forms little plateaux along their margins at about the ancient water-level, and high above the valley-bottom, which in some cases has been since re-excavated. In Glenasmole this phenomenon is notably displayed. Indeed, even the casual visitor cannot but observe these features and others that tell of the enormous influence that the Ice Age had in moulding the surface into the form which it now displays: while to the trained eye of the geologist the impress left by the Glacial Period is everywhere.

At the northern end of Wicklow, about Bray, a peculiarly picturesque feature is introduced by the weathering out of hard quartzites which are included in a limited area of Cambrian rocks which here occupy the surface. The quartzite, which is simply ancient sand greatly altered by heat and pressure, is interbedded with slates, which have been removed, leaving the harder material standing boldly up, and tending to weather into cones, as is the manner of quartzite. Denudation has thus given us the Great Sugarloaf and Little Sugarloaf and the bold escarpment of Bray Head. It is long since local imagination first saw in the Great Sugarloaf an ancient volcano, and picturesque fables like this die hard, for one often hears still this explanation of its peculiar shape: but there is nothing volcanic about it. If you want romance you should search the slaty rocks which alternate with the quartzite bands on Bray Head. If you are lucky—that is, if you know how and where to look—you will find fan-like markings which represent the very oldest animals known from our country. What kind of lowly creatures these were is not certain, and indeed the question as to whether they really belong to the animal kingdom has long been argued over, and can scarcely be said to be yet universally accepted; but the finding more recently of less problematical fossils—a Holothurian and a probable Trilobite—in the same beds strengthens the probability of their organic origin. In many other places Cambrian rocks have yielded well-preserved animal remains that tell us much about the life of that exceedingly remote time, but these and a few other faint markings on the rocks are all that Ireland can show.

The name " Wicklow " conjures up to enthusiasts the vision of an Irish Golconda, for a considerable quantity of gold was obtained a century and more ago by washing the gravel about Croghan Kinsella and the Gold Mines River which descends from it. Perhaps £200,000 would be a fair estimate of the value of the precious metal so obtained by the combined efforts of the government and numerous and often illicit local prospectors. Efforts to discover a rich motherlode from which this gold may have come have failed, and it seems probable that the metal is widely and very sparsely distributed in a thin band overlying the solid rock and that the local concentration of gold on which the miners worked has been now exhausted. It must be remembered that Ireland is quite exceptionally rich in gold ornaments of early periods. The famous collection of the Royal Irish Academy in the National Museum in Dublin contains over 500 objects of gold, all found in Ireland and most of them belonging to the Bronze Age, and many of these are of large size. The " Great Clare find ", made by workmen in a cutting during the construction of the Limerick and Ennis railway in 1854, consisted of hundreds of gold objects, of which the net value of the metal, at present prices, must have been in the neighbourhood of £10,000: unfortunately most of the ornaments were sold and melted down, but those which eventually reached the National Museum make an imposing display there. It has been reasonably suggested that this gold came from Wicklow, the only place in the country from which the metal has been obtained in more than very minute quantities. But whatever the source, it appears unlikely that a fortune awaits some lucky prospector. The so-called Wicklow " Gold Rush " of 1935 may have been justifiable as a political stunt, but otherwise it was imbued with a mixture of comedy and pathos such as is frequently found in Irish affairs. For there still lingers here a deep-seated conviction that Ireland is a country flowing with milk and honey in a

Analysis of the metal in the ancient gold ornaments has established the probability that the gold was not native. C.M.

Gold may still be found in some Wicklow rivers but it is estimated that panning would not yield an income of more than about £2 a week to a prospector. The mineralogical sense, and that only sinister influences prevent our land being an El Dorado bristling with pit-heads and dumps and the tall chimneys of chemical works.   Until late years our failure to develop the mineral wealth that fairly bubbled under every county was of course due to the jealousy and tyranny of an alien government. Now that we govern ourselves, the reasons for Ireland's not being another Lancashire are not so obvious, and intense mental concentration may suggest even to the enthusiast that this is possibly due to an over-estimate of our mineral wealth, not to any human influences, good or bad.   This, indeed, is the mere naked truth.   A century ago, the mining of coal and iron and copper in Ireland could pay its way—though not much more;   nowadays, with cheap transport distributing the products of the richest mineral areas in the world, we have in this country very little that is worth working, whether it be gold or coal or copper or lead;   and the vision of a Black Country replacing the pastures of the Central Plain or the heather of Wicklow or the pleasant fields of Kilkenny or Tyrone must be left to the dreamers.

There is only one mineral with which Ireland is abundantly endowed, and that is peat;   and if digging in the ground (other than agricultural!) ever produces wealth for this island, it is from peat and peat products that that wealth will come.   The time is not yet; but each £100 devoted to peat research may ultimately prove of more value to Ireland than each £1000 spent in chasing round after gold and copper and iron and coal.   In the former case we shall be building up towards a tolerably certain future;   but the other will remain to a great extent the melancholy process of

> Dropping buckets into empty wells
> And growing old in drawing nothing up.[1]

An unfortunate result of the presence of ancient gold in Ireland has been that for many centuries past it has been connected with

---

[1] The foregoing was written at the time of the " Gold Rush " and " Copper Boom " of 1935.

future for other kinds of mining is very much brighter than was believed in Praeger's day and there have been important developments in recent years. The value of ores exported in 1968 is of the order of £9 million and this figure may increase rapidly for future years. **C.M.**

ancient tombs, and innumerable tumuli and cairns, mostly of the Bronze Age, have been wrecked in the hope of the discovery of objects made of the precious metal. This digging has been quite futile, and has resulted only in the destruction of much that might have been of high archaeological importance. The burial customs of the people of the Irish Bronze Age, to which period our prehistoric gold belongs, did not at least usually include the interment of precious objects along with the ashes or bodies of deceased chiefs. It is possible, as Dr. Macalister suggests, that some interments contained objects of value, and that, the tradition of these having been handed down, they were rifled at subsequent periods when the sanctity which guarded them was no longer potent. As it is, I believe there are only three recorded instances in which any object of gold has been found in an ancient tomb in Ireland. A large number of undisturbed Bronze Age graves, of various types, has in recent years been carefully examined by expert excavators in this country, but in none of them has gold or other objects of intrinsic value ever been found. The grave goods, indeed, are singularly meagre, in comparison with the contents of tombs of many other races or other periods—a few beads, objects of stone, shells and such things are all that accompanied the funeral urns. Most of the golden ornaments, of which hundreds still exist, and of which a much larger number must have been sold by their finders and melted down, have been discovered not in tombs, but in every kind of unlikely place, where at some time they had been concealed or lost. Two remarkable cases occurred recently. In Burren (north Clare) the dog of a young fellow, Pat Connolan, started a rabbit, which took refuge among some limestone rocks. Peering into crevices to see where it had gone, Connolan saw something shining. He drew it out, a large thin curved object of yellow metal, and took it home. His uncle declared it to be brass-work off an old coffin, and advised him that it was unlucky to have such a thing about the house, so he pitched it into a nearby bush. A couple of years later, District Justice Gleeson, when rabbit-shooting, happened to pass that way, and conversation

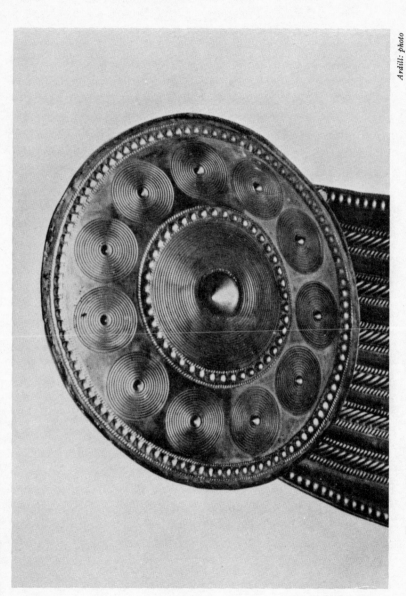

THE BURREN GOLD GORGET, SHOWING A TERMINAL DISC AND PORTION OF THE LUNULE

Natural size

Ardill: photo

turned on the occurrence of antiquities of one kind or another. Connolan called to mind the curious brass ornament: he grubbed in the bush, found it there still, and handed the astonished magistrate the finest gold gorget ever found in Ireland—a truly magnificent object, dating from about 700 B.C., of great size, and quite perfect. To either end of the richly embossed lunule a large concave gold disk, tooled with a series of fine concentric circles, was fastened with gold wire (Plate XXXII). The wire itself was a marvel of skill— little thicker than sewing-cotton, and twisted as finely and closely as thread, so as to increase its holding power. In its great size (more than a foot across) and weight (over half a pound), in the profusion and richness of its beautifully executed ornament, and the excellence of its condition, this Clare gorget is a truly astonishing relic of the Bronze Age. It is to be seen now in the National Museum, the pride of the wonderful collection of prehistoric gold. Not long afterwards, the schoolmaster at the village of Balla in Mayo, giving a lesson on the early history of Ireland, showed his pupils a picture of a fibula—a curved stem with two greatly expanded ends, probably often used as a cloak-fastener between two buttonholes, and a frequent form of gold ornament in Ireland. Up went the hand of an urchin of eleven—" Please, sir, I've got one of those." " Indeed? Where did you get it? " " I found it in the bog. I'm using it to play with." " Well, bring it with you tomorrow and let me see it." Next morning the child produced a gold fibula in perfect condition and of astonishing size, measuring nearly half a foot across. The find-place (*fundort*, as Dr. Mahr would call it), was, as I am told by Professor O'Riordan, a boggy field over which were strewn those burned broken stones so common on prehistoric living-sites, which indicate the boiling of water by dropping hot stones from the embers into earthenware pots which themselves could not stand the direct heat of the fire. This object is also in the National Museum, and it and the last form the most notable accessions which have been made for many years to the great collection of prehistoric objects of gold.

The flora of Wicklow is large, and contains many interesting plants, but it is noteworthy that very few of them are to be correlated with the mountainous character of the terrain. The rarest plants are largely natives of the seashore, members of an eastern group which attains its maximum on the gravelly coast that characterizes Wicklow and Wexford—several rare clovers and so on. The mountain flora is distinctly poor: a character which it shares with the other conspicuous eastern mass of high ground, the Mourne Mountains in Down. The mountain flora of Europe decreases as one comes westward, chiefly no doubt on account of diminution in the amount of elevated ground. The exposure on the Irish west coast acts in the same way as does the harsher climate of northern Europe, reducing the elevation necessary for the growth of alpine plants. In eastern Ireland the mountains apparently fail in two respects as a favourable habitat for this interesting section of the flora—they are not high enough, nor do they participate to the necessary extent in suitable climatic conditions: so as compared with the Welsh hills or the Lake District, the alpine flora shows a marked drop in Wicklow and Down, and a certain recovery on the mountains of the west, and especially of the north-west.

Recent researches have revealed the presence in Wicklow of representatives of both the Hiberno-Lusitanian and the Hiberno-American plant-groups (p. 360), formerly looked on as practically confined to the western side of Ireland (Waterford to Donegal). The Pyrenean Saxifrage formerly known as London Pride has been found on Lugnaquilla and on the adjoining mountain of Connavalla, and the North American rush formerly called *Juncus tenuis* (but now *Juncus macer*) has a wider distribution. This eastern extension of peculiar western groups is matched in the north by the occurrence about Lough Neagh of the Lady's-Tresses called *Spiranthes stricta*, a very fragrant orchid, and of the sea-grass *Glyceria Foucaudii* around Strangford Lough—the former a North American, the latter a Mediterranean species.

Where Wicklow is mentioned one naturally thinks of Glendalough (*Gleann dá locha*, the glen of the two lakes), foremost of the many lovely Wicklow valleys both in scenic beauty and archaeological interest. Here a comparatively small stream had in the course of time cut a valley in the hills, the upper portion through the granite of the central mass, the lower part through the schists which flank it. The ice of the Glacial Period scooped out the valley, especially in the lower part, where it left a deep trough, much deeper than the outlet, with precipitous sides. A small lateral stream has thrown a little delta across the middle of the trough, so that there are now two lakes separated by a low barrier. Further down than the Lower Lake the ice in its retreat left a larger moraine athwart the valley, which is still a conspicuous feature, close by the Royal Hotel. The Upper Lake is much the longer and deeper, and on its southern side the mountain drops into it in a wild precipice of slaty rocks. It was here, on a little shelf approachable only by water, that an oratory and cell were built for St. Kevin, who lived in the valley as a hermit, and was buried there in A.D. 618. The site of this earliest church may still be seen, occupied by remains of a later date. The settlement founded by St. Kevin grew and flourished and became famous until six other churches arose on sites lower down the valley. On the moraine a small stone-roofed church was built at an early period, and later a round tower 140 feet high, also the Cathedral of what was now a diocesan see and of a city which the Danes thought worth plundering on a number of occasions in the eleventh and twelfth centuries. The round tower still rises high above the trees on the moraine in the middle of the valley, imparting to it a sense of peace and sanctity: and the little churches, some of which have beautiful carved ornament, are many of them in a good state of preservation, and are carefully conserved. The surrounding steep mountain slopes are wooded, with native Oak or with planted Pine, looking down on the lakes and the green valley-bottom; and the whole is singularly impressive and beautiful. The first time I saw Glendalough heavy clouds hung on all the higher Wicklow hills; and as at length we turned out of sunny Glenmacnass and faced the entrance of the Glen of the Two Lakes, it seemed like a black cave under the level dark canopy. To see it to best advantage one should have a bright day, for then the colouring, especially around the Upper Lake, is indescribably beautiful: but under no conditions does it fail to be impressive.

You can set foot on the heather six miles from the centre of Dublin, and save for crossing two roads, not leave it till you drop down on Aughrim, thirty miles to the southward as the crow flies, keeping all the while along the granite backbone of Wicklow. Or if you take the Military Road, it will lead you along the range to the same place by a more picturesque route, past Lough Bray and Glenmacnass waterfall, rising twice to 1600 feet and dropping into deep valleys, giving you views of Glenasmole and Glencree and the upper Liffey and Glendalough and Glenmalure—all places to be not glanced at, but explored at leisure, for they are lovely and interesting. This route, it will be noticed, leads you along the eastern slope of the chain; and it is true that most of the picturesque ground, including all the lakes, lies on this side. The Wicklow lakes are especially lovely; indeed, if you plan a tour so as to include them, without thought of other features—Lough Bray (*Loch breagh*?, lake of the hill), Lough Tay (*Loch tua*?, silent lake) otherwise Luggela (*Lug a' lagha*, the hollow of the hill), Lough Dan (*Loch Donn*?), Lough Ouler (*Loch iolar*?, eagles' lake), Lough Nahanagan (*Loch na h'anachaine*?, lake of the calamity), the Glendalough lakes and the tarns on Lugnaquilla (*Lug na coille* (or *gcoileach*), hollow of the wood (or grouse)) you will have seen the best of Wicklow. Few cities have at their door so wondrous a playground as has Dublin, in this as yet unspoiled region.

Like most Irish waters, the lakes of Wicklow (barring one that has trout which squeak), possess each a *piast*, a gigantic water-snake with a horse's head or water-horse with a snake's body (whichever you prefer), ever present though seldom seen, but even still vividly alive in legend. Here is a story concerning one of these creatures, told to my sister some years ago by an old man on the shores of Lough Nahanagan:

" In ould days there was livin' in the County Down a poor woman that was a cripple. The power of her legs was gone from her intirely, an' she could har'ly put a foot under her. Well, there come to thim parts a wise man that was a doctor, and he gev out that he could cure all manner of disaises. So the woman sent for him an' asked could he cure her lame legs. ' There's no cure for you,' sez he, 'but wan, and I go bail it's too hard for you.' 'Tell me what it is,' sez she, ' whether or no.' ' Well,' says he, ' away in the County Wicklow there's a lake among the hills. It goes by the name of Loch Nahanagan. If you can get there, and wash your legs in the water of that lake, you'll be cured.'

" At first the poor sowl thought this was intirely impossible. ' But still an' all,' says she, ' I'd be better dead than livin' this way; so with God's help I'll try it.' An' she set out. Sometimes in a horse-cart, and sometimes in an ass-cart, or maybe in a boat, wan way an' another she travelled south, an' after a long, long while she found herself among the wild mountains of the County Wicklow. An' the people there was good to her, an' two strong lads put her in a chair, an' they carried her up over the heather to Loch Nahanagan. An' they set the chair down in the lake a short piece off the bank, so she could wash her legs quite handy, and there they left her, well content to be at her journey's end.

" Now, at the bottom of this lake there was livin' a terrible monster called a water-horse. An' when the water-horse heard a splashin' an' dashin' goin' on overhead, he gets in a towerin' rage an' up he comes to see who darred make free with his property. The poor woman was sittin' as aisy as you plaize, washin' her legs an' watchin' to see thim growin' straight an' strong, when she heard a noise, an' lookin' roun' her here she sees the frightful beast risin' out of the middle of the lake with his eyes rowlin' an' his tail lashin' out behin'. When he saw the woman he let a roar like a bull an' made wan rush at her. But, my dear! did she wait for him? In wan minute she was out of the chair, an' through the water, an' up the bank, an' over the mountain like a hare! An' she never

stopped nor stayed till she sat down by her own fireside in
the County of Down. An' the legs of her were cured from that
out."

In the richly wooded valley of the Bray River stands the old
house of Fassaroe, which to naturalists will ever be associated with
Richard Manliffe Barrington (1849–1915), zoologist, botanist,
traveller, climber, and to those who had the privilege of knowing
him one of the most delightful and inspiring of men. Trained for
the bar, he preferred the profession of land valuer, which kept him
much in the open air and frequently on the move: but his duties
did not prevent extensive travelling and biological exploring. He
was intensely interested in both animals (particularly birds) and
plants. In pursuit of rare birds he visited all the western islands from
the Shetlands to the Blaskets, as well as North Rona, Rockall and
St. Kilda; and his reports on the flora of Tory Island, Lough Erne,
Ben Bulben, Lough Ree and the Blaskets are familiar to every Irish
botanist. He went further afield too, and, a highly expert alpinist,
climbed many of the loftiest Swiss peaks, and carried out a remarkable walk across the Rocky Mountains, having plenty of adventure,
for no danger or discomfort or hardship deterred him from what he
set out to do. Among zoologists he is especially remembered for
his persistent work, carried out for a long period, on the migration
of birds as shown by observations at Irish lighthouses. The good
offices of the keepers round the coast were enlisted year after year,
innumerable observations were tabulated, and thousands of specimens examined. A great collection was built up out of the birds
received from lighthouses and lightships, which eventually contained
no less than eighteen species not known previously as Irish visitors;
this collection is now in the National Museum, and a large volume
enshrines the classified results of the lighthouse observations. These,
together with many notes and papers in various zoological and
botanical periodicals, form the memorial of an active, useful and
happy life.[1]

[1] *Irish Naturalist*, vol. xxiv., pp. 193-206, portrait. 1915.

CHAPTER XII

THE SOUTH-EAST

(Wexford, Kilkenny, Carlow, South Tipperary, Waterford)

South-eastern Ireland—a vague term, but sufficient for present needs—is a fertile region, watered by large rivers, finely wooded, with a low coast-line, frequently sandy for long stretches. There is none of the excitement of Connemara or Kerry about it: but if sylvan beauty, noble architectural remains, lovely river scenery, and in the west high mountains, can compensate, then Kilkenny and Wexford and Waterford deserve ample treatment here, for they are by no means well known, and are worth knowing. The modelling of the area is influenced by the great variety of rocks which occur within it: but there is one leading feature which deserves exposition. It concerns the trio of rivers—the Suir, the Nore and the Barrow—which, rising at different points on the great rock-fold of Slieve Bloom and Devil's-bit in the Central Plain, converge at Waterford and discharge through the fine inlet of Waterford Haven, which is their submerged valley. If you look at an orographical map, or for the matter of that if you follow their courses on foot or otherwise, they appear to run uphill, for the ground on their lower stretches is much higher than it is in their upper reaches. After descending from their mountain sources they meander southward over a plain of limestone through the flattest of flat valleys; and then enter an area of more elevated ground formed of non-calcareous rocks, through which they cut deep gorges, and flow through them at an accelerated pace to the sea. It is the change of rock which gives the key to the puzzle, and the faster decay of the soluble limestone in comparison with that of the slate and so on which form the ground further south. Long ago the limestone plain stood much higher than it does now: the other rocks were higher too, but not so high as the limestone, so that the ancient rivers flowed southward over a sloping surface. The limestone has been greatly lowered; the others not so much so save where the rivers were actually cutting; and hence the curious present topography. These gorges, especially on the Nore and Barrow, are very beautiful, with high precipitous wooded banks. They are at their best around the point where the two streams join, and thence up to Inistioge and Graiguenamanagh: and no river scenery that Ireland can offer excels them. This south-eastern river system, also, is the home of two interesting wild-flowers not found elsewhere in this country—the Nettle-leaved Bell-flower and the Meadow Saffron or *Colchicum*, often called Autumn Crocus. The first haunts woods and copses, the second damp pastures; and both are widespread here.

In Kilkenny, at Kiltorcan (*Cill torcán*), south of Thomastown, the Old Red Sandstone rock has yielded a galaxy of fossil plants of high interest and in an excellent state of preservation. The rock was quarried for road-metal, and as you tramped along you could pick up on the highway fragments of very ancient ferns and other extinct vegetable forms. These plants are among the earliest relics of past vegetation found in Ireland—older than the abundant plant remains from which the Carboniferous Period takes its name, and which by their accumulation have produced the principal deposits of coal. The vegetation which clothed the land in Old Red Sandstone times was very different from that which occupies it now. The flowering plants, such as the trees, herbs, grasses, which dominate the world today, were then all unknown. Instead there were forests and glades of plants lower in the scale of life, most of which, though still present on the Earth, now hold a subordinate place—club-mosses, and horsetails, and ferns. Many of these grew to tree-like proportions, and the fine fern called *Archaeopteris hibernica* (that is, " Irish Ancient-fern "), which is especially abundant at Kiltorcan,

bore grand fronds many feet long and two feet or more wide;
Figure 10, taken from W. H. Baily's original drawing in the

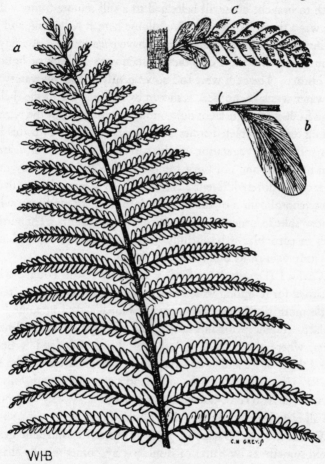

FIG. 10.—*Archaeopteris hibernica*
About ⅟₇ natural size.   From the original figure by W. H. Baily in
Memoirs, Geological Survey of Ireland

Memoirs of the Geological Survey, shows what it looked like.   An
attempt to depict the forest landscape of those remote times at
Kiltorcan forms the frontispiece of G. H. Kinahan's *Manual of the*

Geology of Ireland. And in these woods none of our familiar types of animals were found—no mammals browsed, no birds flitted from branch to branch: these all belonged to a still remote future. But there was a fine relative of the woodlouse here at Kiltorcan, and the remains of other invertebrate animals have been found. A study of the sandstones and the fossils they contain casts a gleam of light on their history. The beds were laid down gently in shallow water: and that water was lake, not sea, as shown by the presence of the shell of a large fresh-water mussel of quite modern aspect, and of the remains of strange armour-plated fishes of fresh-water type. Into this lake fragments of the vegetation of the surrounding land were carried down by rivers, and got buried under further layers of sandy mud, so that over a dozen different plants have been preserved to us, thanks to slow consolidation of the material into the hard sandstone which we now split in order to obtain these ancient fossils. The *Archaeopteris* in particular is beautifully preserved, and we can still trace every tiny vein of its much-divided fronds.

Wexford (Danish *Weis fiord*) is a highly fertile county which has earned for it among its lovers the name of the Garden of Ireland (a title more justifiable than those occasionally seen in some " demoniaco-seraphic penman's latest piece of graphic " in local newspapers, where Bray becomes " the Brighton of Ireland ", Belfast " the Athens of Ireland ", and Bangor in County Down " the Irish Lido "). It is a pleasing area, sufficiently diversified with hills and rivers. The Irish coast-line is here at its flattest. Rocky and mostly bold all round the north, west and south of the country, it presents, in Wexford, as in Wicklow, great stretches of sand and gravel, backed sometimes by banks of Boulder-clay, sometimes by shallow inlets of the sea. These lonely shores are a paradise for sea-birds, and some plants very rare in Ireland, such as the Sea Stock and the Sea Cudweed (Plate XXXIII), have here their headquarters.

For some reason not immediately obvious, the people of the region lying behind the lonely shores of south Wexford retained until quite lately much of a life bygone elsewhere, and still to some

PLATE XXXIII

R. Welch: photo

SEA CUDWEED AT LADY'S ISLAND LAKE

extent retain it; this appears in their customs and also in their language. Of their curious dialect a good deal has been written. Under grant from Henry II, this area was " settled " by Strongbow and other Anglo-Normans. In other words, they cleared out the existing farming population, and installed their own followers instead. It is the language that these settlers spoke which has persisted: some Irish got mixed into it by degrees, and even a century ago it was a difficult speech for ordinary English-speaking folk to understand. Here is an example, from General Vallancey's *Memoir*: [1]

> Fade teil thee zo lournagh, co Jone, zo knagge.
> Th' weithest all curcagh, wafur, an cornee.
> Lidge w'ous ana milagh, tis gay an louthee,
> Huck nigher, y' art scuddeen; fartoo zo hachee.[2]

And here is a more recent example, from *Paddy Coghlan's Wedding*, given by Kathleen A. Browne; [3] it will be noticed how much nearer to modern English it comes:

> A vidler hay shudled wi' hade to a vall
> An smithered hays videl, bow, strings an al;
> A pipere vel bak lik own in a smote
> An a cat at a big-peeps an a taal o hays cote.[4]

I do not know how far this dialect and some curious customs which accompanied it now survive, but there is little doubt that whatever may be left in the quiet country-side will not long withstand the combined attack of motor cars, gramophones and " wireless ".

[1] Charles Vallancey, " Memoir of the Language, Manners and Customs of an Anglo-Saxon Colony settled in the Baronies of Forth and Bargee ", *Trans. Roy. Irish Acad.*, vol. ii., part 3, p. 36. 1788.

[2] What ails you so melancholy, quoth John, so cross,
You seem all snappish, uneasy and fretful:
Lie with us on the clover, 'tis fair and sheltered;
Come nearer, you're rubbing your back, why so ill tempered.

[3] *Journ. Roy. Soc. Antiquaries Ireland*, vol. lvii., p. 127. 1927.

[4] The fidler he staggered with his head to the wall,
And smashed his fiddle, bow, strings and all;
The piper fell back like one well smitten,
And the cat ate his bag-pipes and the tail of his coat.

The older invaders, of a thousand years ago, the Norsemen, used the word " fiord " in a wider sense than that in which we employ it nowadays, for the inlet from which town and county of Wexford derive their name is an extensive mud-filled arm of the sea, suitable for the Northmen's shallow ships, but fitted for steamers only of small draught. Its naturally wide entrance is almost closed by a long tongue of gravel and sand, as is the way of most of the inlets in this area. Sediment from the River Slaney, which debouches into its upper end, tends to decrease the available depth of water. It is therefore from Rosslare, a few miles to the southward, not from Wexford, that traffic with the coast of Wales, here only fifty miles distant, is now maintained. But at Rosslare there is no natural harbour, and a long breakwater shelters the passenger steamer for Fishguard. A little south of that again, Carnsore Point (Carns *öre* (Danish), the sandy point of the carn) forms the marked south-eastern angle of Ireland: and by way of corner-stone, a little patch of granite, an outlier from the great granite mass of the Leinster Chain, forms the extreme point and holds at bay the ravages of the sea.

That the sea has encroached far on the land all along this east coast seems evident from the great banks of sand and gravel that lie some miles out at intervals all the way from Dublin Bay to Carnsore Point, and represent the wreck of a land made of Glacial drift. These banks have been moulded by the tides so that they form narrow north-south ridges, and wave-action maintains their crests at a very uniform depth of one to two fathoms, while the surrounding water is deep enough to float the largest vessel. These curious shoals are most nearly matched by the Goodwin Sands on the coast of Kent. Lightships on their seaward side warn vessels off, for the banks are a mere death-trap. If a ship grounds, the tide digs a deep hole on the down-stream side, into which the vessel topples, and in a surprisingly short time she disappears completely. On many older maps these banks were correctly shown by dotted areas. Then some map-maker drew them with a firm line, making islands of them, and thus they appear in many later sixteenth-century publications, owing to the copying which was in vogue then as now: presently the error was noticed, and in the seventeenth century they became sand-banks again.

A low north-south ridge ten miles west of Carnsore strikes the coast at Crossfarnoge or Forlorn Point (*Cros fearnóg*, the cross of the alders)—the English name appropriate in view of the wide stretches of lonely shore to right and left—and is continued seaward in the Saltees (Salt-*öe* (Danish), Salt island) two little islands lying three and four miles out to sea. The larger and more distant, the Great Saltee, is one of the most populous and interesting breeding-grounds of sea-birds to be found in Ireland. The island rises from a boulder-beach on the north side over a rough grassy surface overlying Boulder-clay, to a height of about 200 feet, where it breaks down in a rocky scarp to a sea which is often turbulent, for the island lies fully open to south-west gales sweeping in from the Atlantic. Part of the Great Saltee used to be farmed (it is still grazed), and the dilapidated farm-house affords the only shelter from the elements. The area of tillage can still be traced, but it is now fully occupied by native plants, including great quantities of luxuriant Wild Hyacinths, while the seaward parts are gardens of Sea-Pink, Sea Campion and Scurvy-grass. The rabbits keep the grassy parts as smooth as a tennis-court, which leaves the more room for the plants which they do not nibble. Now that tillage is no longer carried on, and that protection is afforded to the birds during the close season (when alone they are there), these have increased rapidly, and their great colonies form a wonderful sight in the month of June. On a recent visit a careful observer estimated the number of birds in the water on the lee side of the Great Saltee at two millions! The leading species of the avian population is the Herring Gull, which breeds in thousands along the crest of the island and on the rocky slopes. It is much too abundant, indeed, in view of its relentless depredations on the eggs and young of the other birds. Great and Lesser Black-backed Gulls and Kittiwakes are there in much smaller numbers;

Guillemots and Razorbills are of course present in crowds, and there are far-stretching Puffin villages on the earthy slopes, quite bare of vegetation, owing to the tramping of the inhabitants of the innumerable burrows. There are large Cormorant colonies also. An interesting new-comer is the Fulmar Petrel, which was found nesting, for the first time in Ireland, in Donegal in 1910. This fine bird was once known as almost exclusively an arctic breeder, St. Kilda being the only exception. Then in 1839 it was seen breeding on the Faröes, and it continued to spread. The year 1878 found it in Shetland, and 1891 in Orkney. By 1898 it had reached the Scottish mainland (Cape Wrath) since when it has expanded its British breeding-haunts far down the coasts, and has even reached Yorkshire. Now it breeds also in Antrim, Dublin, Wexford on the eastern side of Ireland, and in Donegal, Mayo, Galway, Clare and Kerry on the western, and is no doubt spreading still. As it lays only one egg, and does not breed twice in a year, its rapid spread indicates unusual success in the rearing of its young. The Gannet is another new-comer to Wexford. It was long known to nest, in Ireland, only on the Little Skellig in Kerry; then it spread to the Bull Rock in Cork; and now for some years one or two pairs have bred on the Great Saltee. Choughs are there too, and those strange birds the Manx Shearwaters. These make their nests in holes or under stones, and the males and females take turns at sitting on the eggs, the birds " off duty " spending the day far out at sea, and only returning after darkness has fallen, when they fly about the island uttering an extraordinary cry which I have heard likened to that which might emanate from a cross between a mad cock and a donkey. On Lambay we used frequently to try to see these birds, but though their wild call was uttered close over our heads it was always just too dark to get a glimpse of them. But it is as well that they are so coy, because at close quarters they have an awkward habit of ejecting an evil-smelling oil unexpectedly, which may make you rue your attempt to make near acquaintance. An aristocratic inhabitant of the Saltees is the Peregrine Falcon, which nested for

From 1950 to 1963 Great Saltee was manned in spring and autumn for the observation of migrating birds. A number of species were added to the Irish list and many, previously believed to be rare vagrants, were found to be regular visitors.

many seasons on the large island: perhaps the pair which had their home there did not like crowds, or the great increase of the plebeian Herring Gull, for they have now shifted their eyrie to the Little Saltee, a mile to the north-east. For years now the Civic Guards stationed at Kilmore Quay on the adjoining mainland have been good friends to the birds, being vigilant in preventing egg-taking or shooting during the breeding season, with the pleasing result that the islands are in fact a sanctuary. And the protection against disturb-ance afforded them has made the birds delightfully tame. On two occasions I have sidled up to a Guillemot and stroked its back before it darted away in arrow-like flight.

I made the acquaintance of the wonderful avifauna of the Saltees during a pleasant week in 1913, as one of a party of zoologists and botanists. The bird-men were desirous of studying the night-life of this populous city, so we disclaimed the clock and all its works, and came and went as suited us, by day or by night, sleeping on a wisp of hay on the floor of the farm-house (and getting plenty of fresh air, since half of the roof was gone) or out among the bracken on the hill-side. A loaf and a cold ham stood at all hours on a table in the corner, and on the fire was a boiling kettle. I recall one nocturnal vigil when, scattered along the ridge of the island, we endeavoured to determine the main colony of the Manx Shear-waters: but their weird cries did not help us, for they seemed to come from everywhere at once. Three of our party of six, I re-member—R. J. Ussher, Canon Lett, De Vismes Kane—were over seventy years of age: a good testimonial to the health-giving qualities of outdoor hobbies. An advantage of our rough quarters was the readiness with which we forsook our beds of hay to spend what is the best part of the day—the early morning hours—in the open. Unless we had been out during the night the brightening light would be a trumpet-call, to which some of us at least would respond with alacrity, and from the top of the cliffs would welcome the sun as he rose over the horizon where Wales lay sleeping.

This question of early rising is mostly a difficult one, especially

Other bird observatories have since been established around the coast. The Fulmar now nests on sea cliffs in all four provinces. c.m.

in Ireland. To the lover of nature the earliest hours of the day are perhaps the most entrancing: but so few of us can enjoy them. The only dawns that are familiar to the majority are the late, grey, chilly half-lights of winter, as different from the triumphant dawns of May and June as night is from day. Our whole plan of life—bed at eleven, hot water at eight, and no meal between say 7.30 P.M. and 8.30 A.M.—renders difficult any display of activity in the early hours of the long days. An afternoon siesta would solve the problem of too little sleep: but it is but few who can achieve that within the North European time-table. And the number of people whose minds refuse to work at four o'clock in the morning with the alertness which they command at nine is considerable.

> What if the lark does carol in the skies,
> Soaring beyond the sight to find him out;
> Wherefore am I to rise at such a fly?
>   I'm not a trout.
>
> An early riser Mr Gray has drawn,
> Who used to haste the dewy grass among
> " To meet the sun upon the upland lawn "—
>   Well—he died young.

So sang Thomas Hood, and most of our town-bred mechanical-minded friends, models of punctuality and propriety and prosperity and all the other " p's ", will endorse the sentiment. Knock them up before summer sunrise, or let them make a bed of the heather for a night, and they will not have the mental energy to see and hear as they would during orthodox hours. The loss is theirs, for those first hours have an enchantment about them. And this magic begins early:

> At two o'clock in the morning, if you open your window and listen,
>   You will hear the feet of the wind that is going to call the sun,
> And the trees in the shadow rustle and the trees in the moonlight
>   glisten,
> And though it is deep, dark night, you feel that the night is done.

So says Rudyard Kipling. And that first stirring of the sleeping

Earth, before the earliest bird ventures on a tentative chirrup, is a thing that is felt rather than heard or seen. Then comes the gradual greyness of dawn, and the waking-up of all the birds (I am thinking now of spring and summer), and at length the curious pause of expectancy before the growing gold in the north-east bursts into that first spot of fire which means the sun. The most wonderful sunrise I ever saw was not in Ireland, but high up on Teneriffe, where we had slept at 6000 feet in a gigantic shattered crater of black and purple cliffs, and white, yellow, orange and scarlet volcanic muds. And though I have described it elsewhere,[1] I feel impelled to repeat what I wrote on the spot.

"I awake in the small hours. The moon has set; the stars blaze and scintillate in a sky of blue-black velvet, the jagged peaks above us ghostly and pale against it. The silence is almost frightening. Suddenly a green meteor dashes down the sky. Does one really hear the swish of it; or is that fancy? It bursts and vanishes, leaving a fading path behind; one is again alone with the cliffs and the innumerable pin-point suns. A long silence. Then a startling wild cry, which re-echoes from the rocks, like no cry one has ever heard before. What is it? Bird? Beast? Or some elemental being in this dead home of terrestrial convulsions. It comes not again. Only once or twice the crash of a falling rock. . . . When we wake the east is paling, down behind the black cinder cone. It is bitterly cold. We stumble up the rough hillside and crouch in blankets to watch the sun rise. The light grows rapidly. Below us, spreading to an infinitely far horizon, is a smooth ocean of cloud, dove-grey, delicately corrugated. At its distant edge, straight as if drawn with a ruler, is the dawn. First a yellow flush, soon a vivid rainbow of colour in horizontal bands—red lowest, then orange, yellow, green, blue, broadening and brightening. Suddenly all the cliffs and peaks around flush vivid rose-pink, and then with a blinding flash the sun is up, quivering, pouring lambent waves of gold across the valley. The effect on the cloud-ocean is almost immediate. Great billows

[1] *Beyond Soundings*. Dublin, 1930.

arise, water-spouts of vapour writhe high into the air. Floods of glowing white mist advance and flow round the edges of the black cone; they submerge our valley, rise higher, break, wreath round the dark crags far above, catch the light again and ascend as snowy clouds into the blue. The sun breaks through again, white now, not gold. Day is here, and with it we remember our chilled bodies, and that it is not yet five o'clock. Hot coffee is clearly indicated. Then off for a long morning's climbing among gigantic cliffs, returning with floral spoils when once more the heat and glare become unbearable."

The Irish atmosphere, I am afraid, tends to keep us in bed in the early hours, and this is especially true of the warm humid south-west. I remember in Cork some years ago expressing surprise that there was no breakfast-car on the early train to Dublin. "What would be the use of that?" rejoined my host: "who would get up for that train when there's a later one?" The atmosphere, indeed, accounts for much of the difference between north and south. Even still when I go to Belfast I find myself ready to rise an hour earlier than in Dublin—and as for Cork! In theory I have been away over the hills in the dawn a thousand times, and have watched a thousand summer sunrises; but in practice the number has dwindled sadly. Many of the early mornings that materialised remain among my treasured memories. On Rathlin once we were marooned by a sudden storm. The wind died down as quickly as it had arisen, and after midnight we were able to leave for the mainland. It had fallen dead calm, with a long oily swell on which a scrap of moon flickered. As we cleared the island the light on the Mull flashed out, to be joined by others on Inishowen and on distant Inishtrahull: and these kept us company till the first faint gleam of dawn appeared over Kintire. Ghostly gulls began to flit past noiselessly, and black porpoises broke the surface, which now showed grey flashes reflected from the eastern sky. The high basaltic cliffs of Bengore Head suddenly glowed orange as the sun rose, while those of Fair Head were deep in shadow. Hurrying Puffins from the great Rathlin colonies flew straight as arrows over the crests of the smooth rollers, and Gannets suddenly appeared in the sky above, snow-white, leisurely quartering the gleaming sea and dropping like plummets close to the boat. Now it was full day, and active bird-life was everywhere. It was quite strange when we stepped ashore at Bally-castle, to find the town still plunged in sleep.

I remember a different morning in autumn, when I left Glenda-lough at daybreak to push a bicycle up to Wicklow Gap, and ride it thence to Dublin to breakfast with a friend arriving by the mail-boat. All the creatures of the hills seemed to have come down from the dew-drenched heather to rest or sleep on the road: not only the domestic sheep, but Hares and Stoats and Foxes; and it must have been a Badger that I saw whisking out of sight round a boulder. There was white mist streeling across the pass, and the roads were fringed with drooping flowers and spider-webs hung with tiny drops so that they gleamed like silver filigree. All the way from Laragh to Togher not a human being was seen: the beasts and birds and I had the mountains all to ourselves. I felt that it was I who was an intruder into their hills.

On the other hand my mind goes back to a farm-house on the Sligo coast, and on being knocked up at four in the morning to breakfast on whisky and cold potatoes prior to embarking in a rough sea and heavy rain to sail to Inishmurray in a wet and leaky boat. Another non-idyllic morning was spent in Kildare. I had arrived after dark in a small town that shall be nameless, seeking a lodging between two days' botanizing. The only hotel that I found was not appetizing. I do not know whether my restlessness was due to imagination or to something more definite, but sleep came reluctantly and went prematurely. So when it was daylight I prowled till I found stale bread and some milk; then left money on the hall table and escaped through a window. Midday found me twelve miles away, in the large railway gravel-pit at the Curragh, which I had long intended to examine. Then a great thunder-storm came up. The only shelter was afforded by a line of loaded trucks standing derelict on a siding. I made myself comfortable, lying at full length under one of them—and went fast asleep. Presently a locomotive came through the storm and took the trucks away to Thurles; but I slept on, while the rain continued to come down in sheets. When I woke it was late in the afternoon and the sun was shining. All of which shows the advantage of sleeping by night and waking by day, in contradiction to what I have just been preaching.

The camper has opportunities for pre-prandial delights such as I have sung; but I cannot find that he is inclined to rise earlier than other people, and if he does, a cup of hot tea may appeal to him more than a tramp over wet grass. These musings apply, of course, to our own latitude and our own climate—Atlantic conditions. Go eastward a few hundred miles, and in Germany or Austria or Switzerland you will find it easy to start off for a day's outing at five in the morning, just like everyone else.

But to return to the Saltees. I shall always associate the great bird-city there with that stalwart ornithologist and loyal friend R. J. Ussher, for that was the last time I was in the field with him—he died a few months later at the age of seventy-two, at his home at Cappagh in County Waterford, still in the midst of zoological research. Ussher was delicate in his early years, and ill-health interfered with both school and college work: several winters were spent on the Mediterranean with his mother and a tutor. Egg-collecting was his first natural history hobby, and to that futile and objectionable pursuit he was devoted during the greater part of his life, bequeathing finally an immense collection of eggs to the National Museum. However, this activity led him to explore every part of Ireland where rare birds might breed, and he took an increasing interest in the birds themselves, and became a highly skilled ornithologist. Possessing leisure, enthusiasm and knowledge, and being unwearying as a correspondent, he was in a very favourable position for amassing material relating to the native avifauna, and fortunately he was impelled to publish what he knew. In 1900 appeared *The*

Birds of Ireland, still our chief source of reference on all avian matters. Though the name of Robert Warren appears along with Ussher's on the title-page, the full brunt of the work fell on the latter.

As early as 1879 he had begun to take an interest in the fossil animals found in cave deposits; this interest was stimulated by Professor Leith Adams, with whom he undertook important cave excavations in Waterford in the following years. These resulted in the finding of remains of Bear, Reindeer, Irish Elk and other extinct mammals. Of his later laborious cave-work in conjunction with Scharff and others I have written on another page (p. 328).

Ussher had an interesting and charming personality. With a gentle and timid manner he combined a large degree of fearlessness, as when he descended on a rope many of the loftiest precipices in Ireland to reach the nests of Peregrines or Ravens. Not robust, though of burly proportions, he was indifferent to discomfort, and much of both his cave-work and his ornithology were carried out under conditions sufficiently trying. Deeply religious, he took a warm and practical interest in church affairs; and as a resident landlord he was punctilious in his public duties as Deputy Lieutenant, Grand Juror and High Sheriff. I am tempted to repeat two anecdotes which illustrate his many-sided character. Hearing of a breeding-place of the Sandwich Tern on an island in Rathroeen Lough near Ballina, he hastened thither. He failed to find a boat upon the lough, so stripped and swam to the island. On landing, he found that the colony was situated behind a high fringe of nettles. Undeterred, he waded through the stinging plants and reached his objective! On another occasion, Robin Dillon (afterwards Lord Clonbrock), a keen entomologist, was staying under his hospitable roof. When Sunday came, the visitor, preferring a day in the open to the rigid Sabbath of Cappagh, went off with net and sandwiches, returning late, hungry and muddy, when he thought that religious observances would be over. His host opened the door for him: "Supper is over: but you are just in time for prayers", he said.

The present standard reference is *Ireland's Birds* by Robert F. Ruttledge, published in 1966. C.M.

Beyond the narrow limestone promontory of Hook Head we come at once on Waterford Harbour, the broad and deep sunken valley through which the Suir, Nore and Barrow discharge their waters. Spenser in his *Faerie Queene* has pleasant things to say of all these rivers:

> . . . the gentle Shure that making way
> By sweet Clonmell, adornes rich Waterford.

> . . . the stubborn Newre, whose waters gray
> By fair Kilkenny and Rossponte boord.

> . . . the goodly Barrow, which doth hoord
> Great heapes of Salmons in his deepe bosome.

And they well deserve his praise, for their courses lead to Waterford Haven through very lovely scenery.

Waterford itself stands on the edge of the Suir, seventeen miles up from the sea, and beyond a series of sharp river-bends; but only half that distance separates it from Tramore, with its cliffs and sands facing open water. Waterford City offers little of special interest to the visitor. It is well planned, with some fine buildings. Reginald's Tower, built by Reginald the Dane in 1003 (for the place was a Norse stronghold in old days, and the " ford " in its name is " fiord "), which stands on the edge of the quays, is the most striking of several towers and other remains which tell of Norse or Anglo-Norman occupation. The immediate neighbourhood also, though picturesque along the river, offers nothing requiring comment. But the geologist will be interested in the rock-section immediately behind the railway station, where inclined beds of purple conglomerates of the Old Red Sandstone series are seen resting on the vertical edges of folded grey Ordovician slates, making a very striking picture. A beautiful and characteristic panorama of local river scenery is obtained by ascending the hill above Cheek Point (*Pointe na sighe*, point of the fairies), at the junction of the Suir and Barrow—winding rivers, fine demesnes, rich woods, with the beautiful ruin of Dunbrody Abbey rising on the eastern bank. Along the lower courses of all three rivers there is much scenery of this kind, English rather than what one usually associates with Ireland, but quite characteristic of the river-valleys on the east side of Ireland—Lagan, Boyne, Liffey, Slaney, the south-eastern streams, Blackwater and Lee. Go up by boat with the flood from Cheek Point past New Ross to St. Mullins on the Barrow, or Inistioge (*Inis Teóc*, Teoc's island) on the Nore (where tidal influence ceases), through the wooded gorges to which reference has already been made (p. 295), and you will see some very picturesque ground. On the Barrow you can continue (by canal) right up to Dublin if you desire. It is well worth penetrating all three river-valleys for some distance beyond the " top of the tide ". On the west side of the Barrow above St. Mullins the clear-cut cone of Brandon Mountain (not to be confused with the Kerry Brandon) rises from the river-bank to 1694 feet. Here we are back on the granite of the Leinster Chain, and near its southern termination: this southern part of the granite mass is mostly low-lying, unlike the great uplands which it forms in Wicklow. The heathery slopes of Brandon give an added charm to the little town of Graiguenamanagh, nestling by the river at its foot. On the other (Carlow) side of the Barrow, a few miles away, a high ridge of granite rises, which culminates in Blackstairs (2409 feet) and Mount Leinster (2610 feet), and which on its eastern slope looks down on County Wexford. A traverse of this ridge from White Mountain to the Nine-stones gives a very fine day's walking: in the middle you must descend to 630 feet at Scullogue Gap (*scológ*, a small farmer), where the main road from Enniscorthy to Bagenalstown slips through the long barrier of high ground. Here, I was told by local people, the young bloods of both counties used to meet annually at a kind of fair, where trials of strength often resulted in broken heads. The name *Nine-stones* no doubt refers to some megalithic monument, but I do not know that it is there now. Instead, some " person or persons unknown " have placed by the wayside nine pieces of granite of no striking appearance. This spot

is the summit of a road—still traversable by a careful motorist—
which crosses the northern shoulder of Mount Leinster at over 1600
feet, and commands on a clear day a wider view than can be seen
from a car almost anywhere in Ireland.   Further north, at Bagenalstown and Carlow, the plateau of the Kilkenny coal-field drops in a
steep slope to the Barrow on the western side of the river, while the
eastern bank flattens down: and from here up, the river becomes
much less interesting.   The small county of Carlow, indeed, offers
few features except for the beautiful course of the Nore through
Bagenalstown, Borris and Graiguenamanagh on its western edge,
the smaller Slaney passing through Tullow and Newtownbarry in the
east—extremely pretty in parts—and the high Mount Leinster ridge
further south.   The name of the county is a puzzle.   Carlow, earlier
Catherlogh, signifies *four lakes*, or *quadruple lake*, but it is one of the
few counties in Ireland that is absolutely devoid of lacustrine amenities.   Tradition indicates that these lakes were former expansions of
the Barrow, but the nature of the ground lends no support to this
view.

If we follow up the Nore above its tidal limit at Inistioge—a very
pretty place—we pass Thomastown and Bennettsbridge and arrive at
Kilkenny (*Cill Chainnich*, St. Canice's church), an ancient and historic
city, full of interest to the antiquary.   As early as 1172, Richard de
Clare (Strongbow), to whom the Kingdom of Leinster had been
granted, erected a stronghold here.   His only daughter was given
in marriage to William le Mareschal, who built or rebuilt the castle
which has grown into the present imposing pile rising over the Nore,
and long occupied by the Ormonde family.   St. Canice's cathedral
is an attractive building, which suffered severely at various times
on account of frequent wars.   Thus we read of the Cromwellians:
" The Cathedral Church of Saint Kenny, they have utterly defaced,
and ruined, thrown down all the roof of it, taken away *five* great and
goodly bells, broken down all the windows, and carried away every
bit of the glass, and all the doors of it, that hogs might come, and
root, and the dogs gnaw the bones of the dead ".   This was by no

means the only catastrophe, yet the cathedral has at various times been lovingly restored, and is a very beautiful and interesting church, full of medieval monuments. The city was a place of importance for a long period. Parliaments were held here during the fourteenth and fifteenth centuries, and many momentous decisions were taken on the banks of the Nore. The picturesque old bridge which crossed the river under the shadow of the castle is gone, having recently made room for a less beautiful but more commodious structure. But the streets, often narrow, still recall the old town with their frequent ancient churches and fragments of other buildings of early date decked with Wallflower and Red Valerian and Wall Pellitory.

The rock in the vicinity of Kilkenny is a fine hard Carboniferous limestone, full of fossils, which polishes black, and has long been used for fireplaces and other ornamental work: the abundance in it of large white shells (brachiopods) especially, gives it an unusual appearance; there is also a grey limestone, crammed with the broken stems and arms of sea-lilies (encrinites) which is rather fascinating. I can remember poring, as a child, over a polished slab of this in a way that I never pored over any book.

Six miles north of Kilkenny, on elevated ground overlooking the Dinin River, is situated the Cave of Dunmore, anciently *Derc ferna* (the cave of alders). This is not one of the most extensive or remarkable of Irish caverns, but its wide entrance has been open and accessible since prehistoric times, and it has a very long literary history, with many quaint or interesting touches, from which it may be permissible to quote, as they illustrate the reactions of many generations of men to what was long an object of mystery or curiosity. Probably the earliest reference is that contained in the Irish Triads, very ancient verses which enumerate, among proverbs and wise sayings, three of the most remarkable natural or artificial objects in Erin; there it is stated that the three " dark places " of Ireland are *Uam Chnogba, Uam Slangae, Derce Ferna*. Again, in the *Annals of the Four Masters*, compiled from ancient sources by Michael O'Clery and his colleagues in the Abbey of Donegal in 1632-36 (see p. 49), we read, under date Anno Christi 928:

"Godfrey, grandson of Imhar, with the foreigners of Ath-Cliath (*i.e.* the Danes of Dublin) demolished and plundered Dearc Fearna, where one thousand persons were killed in this year, as is stated in this quatrain:

"Nine hundred years without sorrow, twenty-eight it has been proved,
Since Christ came to our relief, to the plundering of Dearc Ferna."

Another early reference occurs in Broccan's poem in the *Book of Leinster*—*Ro shaltair for in luchtigern i ndorus derci Ferna*: the full passage as translated reads:

Aithbel, she was a jewel of a woman, mother of Ercoil, the wife of
    Midgna,
Who killed the ten Fomorians in the strand of Tonn Chlidna,
Who burned the seven wild men in the glen at Sliabh Eibhlenn,
Who scattered the black fleet against which the men of Ireland failed,
Who hunted the red hag that she drowned in the midst of the
    Barrow,
Who trampled on the luchthigern in the door of Derc Ferna.

The *luchthigern* (lord of the mice) referred to was a sort of gigantic cat which inhabited the Cave of Dunmore, and of whose prowess wonderful tales are told: the tussle between it and the Amazonian Aithbel would have been a hero-fight worth seeing.

We pass on somewhat abruptly to the staid eighteenth century, and from tradition to the printed page and appreciative observation. In 1709 Dr. Thomas Molyneux, well known for his discourse on the "Irish Elk" in the *Philosophical Transactions* of the Royal Society of London, visited the cave, and wrote an account of it in his journal. He was much struck with the "dreadfull Romantick appearance" of the entrance; and describes how "from the top the water distilling in a 1000 places, and trickling down the sides, was petrified, so that the inside of ye Cave is almost entirely covered with the petrified substance". He mentions a colony of rabbits in that part called the

Rabbit Burrow (they are gone now, though the name remains); and describes the bottom of the Well, and that part of the cave beyond the Rabbit Burrow, as being " full of human bones, especially the well, in which there are several skulls "—the first reference to the abundant human remains which so exercised the minds of later writers. Much more thrilling is the account given in *A Tour through Ireland, in several Entertaining Letters* . . . (Dublin, 1746), which was the work of " two English gentlemen ". I am tempted to give a somewhat long quotation. They found the approach to the cave guarded by " a monstrous Flight of different Species of Birds, whose Numbers darken the Air as you come near the Mouth, and their different Voices seemed to tell us that we were going to view something extraordinary. . . . When you enter the Mouth, a sudden Chilness seizes all parts of the body, and a Dimness surrounded our lights, as if the Place were filled with a thick Fog. . . . Our Faces, through this Gloom, looked as if we were a Collection of Ghosts, and the Lights in our Hands seemed as if we were making a visit to the infernal Shades. . . . The Shining of the petrified water (for I think we may justly call it so) forms so many different Objects, that it is not unpleasing; and by the Help of a little Imagination, we might make out Organ pipes, Pillars, Cilinders, Pyramids inverted, and ten thousand various Things in Art. . . . In several Places were Skulls and human Bones, as it were set in the crystalline Substance. . . . We were informed that two miles from the Mouth was a Well of Wonders; but indeed, my Lord, none of us had Curiosity or Courage enough to travel so far. . . . When we came out, we thought we had abandoned the Regions of the Dead, to draw the Air of Paradise. They tell you many romantick Legends of this Cave." And so on and so on. Few of the visitors are so impressionable as these: some are quite the reverse, like Thomas Campbell (1778). He began the descent to the cave's mouth, but finding it " damp and slippery " returned, and held the horses while his servant explored the cavern. " Even beauties too highly extolled, before you see them, seldom answer your expectations. I will not, however, rank this among beautiful objects, for to me it had nothing to recommend it. . . . Do not, however, imagine that I lost my day with this bawble." Later we come to scientific descriptions and observations, especially by A. W. Foot and E. T. Hardman, both of the Geological Survey of Ireland: and imagination ceases to influence the explorers. As a matter of fact, the highly picturesque entrance is the most romantic part of the cavern—a very wide arch, hung with a green curtain of Ivy and a profusion of Hart's-tongues, under which one descends by a steep slope, which represents the fallen roof of the continuation of the high entrance chamber. From its extremity you climb to the left, through steep and narrow funnels, to find two passages running in opposite directions, sometimes small, sometimes opening out into chambers of noble dimensions, with floors concealed by great fallen blocks of rock. In both branches human bones occur in abundance, especially about " the Well ", in which there is still clear water; they represent persons of both sexes and of all ages, and there can be little doubt that they belong to the victims of the Viking raid in the year 928: many of them are now encrusted with or enclosed in crystalline stalagmite. Elsewhere the stalagmite forms some striking features, such as the beautiful pillar known as the Market Cross. The cave is well worth visiting, but go prepared for a scramble, and with plenty of candles.

The Kilkenny coal-field, lying between the Nore and the Barrow, is a feature chiefly of geological interest. It forms a plateau with sides descending steeply east and west into the valleys of the rivers named, and is a remnant of Coal-measures which formerly covered much of the surface of Ireland; the Kilkenny beds now make a kind of island, resting on the older limestone, which has been laid bare on every side by their removal due to long-continued denudation. The coal-seams which they contain are not noteworthy for either their quantity or their quality, but the coal has for centuries been used locally, and during 1914–18 was mined more extensively.

A mile south of Thomastown (mentioned a few pages back) and
These coalfields and others nearby continue to yield mainly anthracite. Conventional mining is decreasing but is being replaced by the open-cast system. C.M.

PLATE XXXIV

T. H. Mason: photo

HOLYCROSS ABBEY.   EAST WINDOW AND CHANCEL

ten miles south of Kilkenny, in a well-watered nook near the Nore, the ruins of Jerpoint Abbey (*Seiriopuin*, Jerry's bridge) stand, a beautiful building in a beautiful setting.   The founder and date of foundation are uncertain; the architecture points to the twelfth and thirteenth centuries, and carved monuments in stone carry its history on to the beginning of the sixteenth century.   The delicate carving of the cloisters, with every slender column of different design—a characteristic feature of good Irish work—will be noted, and the fine central tower.

Out in the plain, thirty miles or more west of Jerpoint, stands the Rock of Cashel, famed for the wealth of ecclesiastical remains, mostly in the Hiberno-romanesque style of architecture, that are crowded upon it.   The rock itself is interesting, being a sharply folded mass of limestone with steep or cliffy sides rising from level ground.   So remarkable a site has naturally been in human occupation for a long time.   The name Cashel (*Caiseal*, stone fort) refers to an ancient stronghold on the rock, erected by a King of Munster in the fifth century.   Later a town sprang up at its foot; Cashel became the seat of an archbishopric, and was created a city by Charles I.   The medieval buildings crowded on the summit include the cathedral, the lovely church called Cormac's Chapel, a lofty round tower and an ancient cross—not to mention a conspicuous modern cross which is quite out of place and should not remain there.   The buildings are full of architectural interest, and Cormac's Chapel is very beautiful and indeed unique.   On low ground close by stand the ruins of Hore Abbey, and in the town the Dominican priory is of considerable interest.   There is nothing like Cashel anywhere in Ireland, and it must be seen, not read about: the visitor will not be disappointed, however far he has travelled to see it.   Indeed, he will need to have time to spare when in this neighbourhood, for only ten miles to the northward, on the edge of the River Suir, close to Thurles, stands another beautiful building, the Cistercian abbey of Holycross (Plate XXXIV), one of the most elaborate of its kind in Ireland. It was founded in 1182 by Donall O'Brien, King of Thomond, and

Most of the ruins on Cashel are Gothic. Cormac's Chapel is the only Romanesque building. c.m.

was long a place of pilgrimage owing to its possession of a portion of the true cross, which was given by Pope Pascal II to Donough O'Brien, grandson of King Brian Boru. This remained for centuries in the beautiful abbey, in a shrine of gold and jewels, which is now preserved in the Ursuline Convent in Cork. The abbey ruins are very extensive, and " abound in elaborate detail of such exquisite feature as to deserve very careful attention ".

One cannot write of this area of south-central Ireland without mention of such notable architectural monuments as Cashel, Holycross, Jerpoint, but I confess to feeling awkward in touching a subject which—to my great loss—I have never studied: and so, having paid homage to them, I turn with a certain feeling of relief to three noble natural monuments whose proximity adds beauty to the wide view obtained from the Rock of Cashel or the square tower of Holycross—the mountain-groups of the Galtees, the Comeraghs and Knockmealdown. If you come up the Suir valley from Waterford, by road or rail, you soon see high hills rising in front to both north and south. On the right is Slievenaman (*Sliabh na mban*, mountain of the women, 2564 feet), a broad isolated dome, a conspicuous landmark from all the plain to the northward. The prospect from its summit is one of great extent and much beauty, with a diversity of mountain and valley, river and wood: but except for the view, it has not much to offer to the climber save a fine walk. But the hills on the left, the Comeraghs (*Comaraigh*, place of confluences), with their southern continuation the Monavullagh Mountains, are in a different category, and are among the most interesting in Ireland. They form a plateau (highest point 2609 feet) of Old Red Sandstone rocks—conglomerates and grits, or in more popular words pudding-stones and slaty rocks, mostly purple in colour, and lying almost horizontally. Such plateau structure tends to break down round the margins into steep cliffs, and the Comeraghs are no exception. During the Glacial Period, ice and snow, collecting in the glens, scooped out their heads with a peculiar clawing action which resulted in a precipice at the valley-top and often along its sides, with a deep hollow below, which subsequently formed a lake. The material thus excavated was dumped across the valley further down, damming in the lake and forming a chaos of great blocks of rock and finer material, through which the stream now pursues an often devious course. These well-known Glacial phenomena—the coomb with its dark tarn and wilderness of moraine—are especially well displayed in the Comeraghs. The finest example is Coomshingaun (*Cúm seangán*, glen of the ants, though why so called it is not easy to guess, unless it is that one feels like an ant, crawling among the great blocks of rock on the moraines, under the shadow of those gigantic cliffs). It is situated on the east side of the range, and less than a mile from the main road from Carrick-on-Suir to Dungarvan, and should on no account be missed by anyone who finds himself in the neighbourhood. The entrance to the coomb forms a conspicuous feature from the thoroughfare. Turn off where the stream which comes out of the valley foams down (where there is a cottage with a hospitable tea-pot), and a rough path will take you right up to the tarn. Or start half a mile further south, at the highest point of the road, and take to the heather there—bearing to the right, for if you keep too high you will find yourself on the top of the cliff that fringes the coomb. The valley-bottom for the last half-mile is all moraine, spread wave beyond wave—great mounds and blocks of purple rock, full of white water-worn pebbles of quartz which represent the wreck of much more ancient rocks, whose fragments formed stony beaches fringing the ancient lakes of Devonian times. The little stream runs sometimes underground, sometimes in loops and little cascades on the surface, and leads you to the edge of the tarn, lying a thousand feet or more above sea-level, with another thousand feet of almost vertical cliff towering from its upper end. You cannot go all round the tarn, unless you are prepared to either swim or climb, for at one point the cliff descends for a short distance straight into deep water; but if you keep along the south shore, which is also the more picturesque, till you come near this barrier, and then turn your back on the lake, a gully will take you right to the top after a steep but not difficult climb. The coomb and tarn are so beautiful from above that the scramble is well worth while. Then on the top you can keep to the north, round the head of the corrie, and down easy slopes to the lower end of the lake. But just before the steep slope replaces the cliff, on a spur which you pass, note a megalithic structure in a very unusual situation—a number of rough slabs of coarse conglomerate on end, close together. It probably represents a sepulchral monument of the Bronze Age, and is surely the only one in the country placed in so elevated and wild a situation.

There are other corries and tarns in the Comeraghs besides Coomshingaun, and lofty cliff-ranges; the area furnishes very fine walking and climbing, with Dungarvan or Clonmel or Carrick-on-Suir as a base. Scenery and geology are the best things that these mountains offer to the naturalist. In plants the range is rather poor, considering the large amount of elevated and precipitous ground. A number of alpine species cling to the cliffs, but they are of the more widespread kinds. The best plant of the hills is *Saxifraga spathularis*, till recently confused with the London Pride of gardens, which, ranging from Kerry north along the coast to Donegal, finds a home also on the Comeraghs and the near-by Galtees, and on the Wicklow Mountains. On the Comeraghs it is abundant in Coomshingaun and other places—a neat smallish form—ranging from 500 to 2200 feet.

The Galtees (*Sliabh na gcoillteadh*, mountain of the woods), lying twenty miles N.N.W. of the Comeraghs, offer a contrast to the latter group in that they form not a table-land but a high ridge, with conical peaks which attain in Galtymore 3015 feet. You get a fine view of them from the Cork train as you go past Limerick Junction and Emly (*Imleach*, swampy place) with the much lower ridge of Slievenamuck in front; between it and the Galtees lies the fertile Vale of Aherlow (*Eatharlach*, a valley), sheltered and beautifully situated. Rising abruptly as they do from the plain of Tipperary, with high grassy peaks and deep gullies, the Galtees form a very imposing group. A great fold in the rocks has caused the Old Red Sandstone to protrude through its covering of Carboniferous Limestone, and the Silurian rocks to protrude in their turn through the Old Red Sandstone; so the higher grounds are formed of conglomerates and slates. As in the Comeraghs, there are some fine corries with high precipitous cirques looking down on dark deep tarns: but the glens that lead to them are longer and deeper than in the former range. The ridge runs east and west, rising rather abruptly at the eastern end from the valley of the Suir at Caher (*Cathair*, a stone fort), and subsiding into a wide area of foothills north of Mitchelstown, at both of which places one may stay comfortably. The tarns all drain northward, but there are some fine glens on the southern side also. A walk along the saw-like crest of the ridge, between the two towns named, means fifteen miles of mountain ground—a magnificent but somewhat formidable day's work. The ordinary person will find it enough to cross the range by way of one of the tarns and one of the peaks—and have a car to drop him in the morning and pick him up on the opposite side in the evening. In that case Lough Curra (*Loch Corra*? Corra's lake), lying at 1850 feet, may be selected, as being the easiest to reach of the several tarns, and as offering besides the most interesting flora. You ascend by a stream which debouches into the Vale of Aherlow at Newtown, and subsequently cross the ridge at about 2500 feet, to descend a long glen past Galtee Castle. But Lough Curra is overhung by a gigantic cliff which descends sheer into the water—a thousand-foot wall of rock—and a detour is necessary to gain the summit of the ridge, where you can, if you like, make a dash of a mile to the east to gain Dawson's Table, or Galtymore, the highest point of the range. If you long for savage grandeur, make for Lough Diheen (*Daibhche*, a tub or vat); it lies at 1800 feet a little to the east. You get the impression there of quite recent Glacial action, owing to the sparseness of the vegetation, the bare savageness of the cliffs, and the great moraine below the tarn. On the day I was at that place the clouds hung low, the black water reflected the bare black cliffs—for there was no breath of wind: no plant grew in its waters, and even its shores were mere bare rock and waste. I think I never saw a more lifeless or gloomier place in Ireland. Very different was a day when I crossed the ridge by Lough Muskry (*Muscraighe Chuirc*, the name of the surrounding territory), all sunlight and sparkle, in which the lake joined, in spite of its huge surrounding cliffs: while the alpine plants on the ledges were in abundant bloom—good broad solid ledges too, along which you could walk without fear, gathering Mossy Saxifrages (of which there are several in the Galtees, inviting further investigation) and other mountain plants. The alpine flora of the Galtees, which is fairly rich in comparison with that of other Irish mountain regions, is concentrated on these high cliff-ranges over the tarns. The rarest plant which occurs is the Alpine Rock Cress, of which a small colony was discovered by H. C. Hart above Lough Curra.

After the grand range of the Galtees, the third of the local mountain groups, Knockmealdown (*Cnoc Maoildomhnaigh*, Maoldomhnach's hill), lying between Caher and the Blackwater, cuts a rather poor figure. Seen from the north, across the valley of the Suir, it forms a very fine upstanding row of peaks, rising to 2609 feet: but this is merely clever window-dressing. There is nothing except this single row of summits—no lakes or corries or deep glens or cliffs; very little bare rock: and so, while they furnish fine walking, the zoologist or botanist will find these hills somewhat monotonous. But they possess one valuable asset—a main road which crosses the ridge at its centre, at an elevation of 1114 feet. The motorist and cyclist, to whom all but the skirts of the Galtees and Comeraghs are denied, can breast the ridge and obtain magnificent views to north and south.

Should you find yourself in the neighbourhood of the Galtees, the opportunity should be taken to visit Mitchelstown Cave, the most extensive and complicated cavern to be found in Ireland. There are actually two separate caves close together. They lie in the limestone trough which intervenes between the Galtees and Knockmealdown, and are readily accessible from the Caher–Mitchelstown road. The " Old Cave " has been known for a long time. It was in it that the Earl of Desmond took refuge after his futile rebellion in 1601, and here he was made prisoner by the White Knight of Kerry. It was long a place of resort for refugees and later for tourists, and it would still rank as a notable " curiosity " but for the discovery during quarrying of the " New Cave " in 1833. This proved, as by degrees it was explored, to include a singularly complicated series of passages and chambers. It was not till 1908 that, as a result of a week's work by C. A. Hill, H. Brodrick, A. Rule and myself, complete plans of both caverns were published.[1] The map of the cave which we made is shown in a reduced and simplified form in Fig. 11.

For visiting such a cave as this, a few precautions must be taken, for the world which one enters is totally different from anything that one encounters above ground. First, wear a suit of strong overalls —ordinary clothes get torn and dirty; also a hat well padded against sharp projections. Next, bring plenty of candles (which, on account of the climbing and squeezing required, are better than any breakable lamp); also a coil of rope for steep places. Then, unless the guide is with you, have a large ball of string and lay it out as you go, so that you may find your way back: between the darkness and the labyrinthine nature of the passages—not to mention frequent climbing up and down—it is impossible to recognize the route as you return, and a compass does not help. In a complicated cave you are working in three dimensions; sometimes one passage passes over or under another, sometimes the passages anastomose in a confusing way; and as there is altogether a mile and three-quarters of passages at Mitchelstown, it will be evident that both care and endurance are required. The annexed sketch-plan, though in only two dimensions, will show how curiously complicated a cave can be.

The subterranean landscape is very strange: it cannot be described, and must be seen—the yellowish or greyish tint that prevails, the encrustation of stalagmite or of mud that is everywhere, the extra-

[1] *Proc. Roy. Irish Acad.*, vol. xxvii., sect. B, pp. 235-268, plates 14-17.

ordinary irregularity of the passages—now so narrow or low that a man can scarcely crawl through, now expanding into noble chambers with lofty roofs lost in the darkness overhead, now rising vertically, so that you must climb, with a candle stuck in your hat; now descending in so steep a slope that it cannot be negotiated without a rope. An extract from an " Itinerary " of part of Mitchelstown Cave, as given in the paper quoted, will exemplify: " Next ensues a longer crawl on hands and knees, the roof being only 2 feet high, and you emerge into the Scotsman's Cave. Here there is active stalactite-formation, with water dripping from the roof. Leaving this chamber by climbing up high on the right, two crawls over slopes of stalagmite must be negotiated, when O'Callaghan's Cave is reached. You have then to squeeze through a narrow crack between fallen boulders and take to the left, up a slope into a low bedding-cave. Again up to the left, over a second slope, and another squeeze through an overhanging rock-curtain leads to a second bedding-cave, where you negotiate a drop of 7 feet over a huge jammed boulder. The way then leads downwards, and you enter a level passage, across three gaps in the floor, the Crevasses, and, descending a bank of stalagmite, find yourself at the entrances to the Labyrinth. These entrances are three in number, and lead into a complicated system of passages at various levels, which are remarkable for their abundance of fine stalactites and stalagmites. Leaving the Labyrinth on the right, you enter Brogden's Cave, which is a long straight passage 10 feet high, enriched by many beautiful formations. One little alcove on the left-hand side, known as the Chapel, is particularly worthy of notice. It is fringed on either side with beautiful curtains of crystalline stalagmite." And so on. The most remarkable feature of all limestone caves is the deposited carbonate of lime, given up by the evaporating water which percolates or once percolated through the soluble limestone. The remarkable forms which this takes, depending from above or rising from the floor, must be seen to be believed—pillars, bosses, curtains, of beautiful or fantastic form; the material itself is often snowy

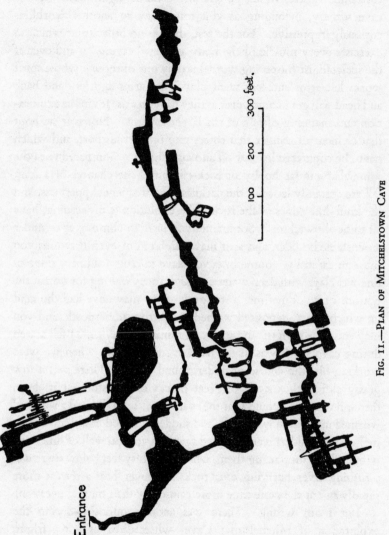

Fig. 11.—Plan of Mitchelstown Cave

crystalline calcite, which glitters in the candle-light. This strange cave scenery, belonging as you might say to another world, is curiously impressive. For the rest, there is no other sport which so exercises every muscle of the body as does " caving ": and even if the speleologist (imposing word!) is only one of those " whose spirit works lest arms and legs want play ", his arms and legs and back and head will get as much play as they have any use for in the exploration and mapping of one of the larger caverns. Nor is it without that element of danger that enters into most true sport, and which has to be countered by caution and experience. Compared with the somewhat similar hobby of rock-climbing, the chances of a long fall are certainly less, but the darkness, the frequent slipperiness, and the knife-like edges of the rocks where solution is proceeding, have all to be allowed for. Sometimes you have to climb over or under an unstable boulder, and as it may weigh ten or even fifty tons you must go carefully. Sometimes you have to cross a slippery slope of fine wet clay, with deep water or rough rocks waiting for you at the bottom of it: sometimes a stalagmite floor may have had the sand on which it was deposited washed away from underneath, and you may crash through it: and so on. I think the only time I felt scared during cave work was in the Marble Arch region, when we were working out the course of underground rivers. There was a low grassy cliff with a slope of great blocks of limestone at its base, through which we could hear the roar of water. I donned a rope and wormed my way downwards, and suddenly found emptiness below me. The boulders were jammed against a vertical wall of limestone with nothing supporting them, while some fifty feet below there was a rushing river hurrying over rocks. I never beat a retreat more rapidly and at the same time more cautiously than on that occasion.

But I am wrong. There was another episode—during the exploration of Mitchelstown Cave—when *all* of us got a fright, though we would not admit it at the time. We had just finished the mapping of this labyrinthine cavern, and were resting in its furthest gallery—the Victoria Cave, nearly a mile from the entrance.

Suddenly through the utter stillness came a long dull roar. What was it? The only possible explanation seemed to be a fall of roof somewhere, and each of us thought of all the low passages where any collapse would signify indefinite or permanent imprisonment. We soon started back; no obstruction appeared; and after an hour we saw with relief the first greenish glimmer of daylight. The explanation came when the plan and section of the cavern were laid out to scale. The ground overhead falls towards the Victoria Cave, which has only some forty feet of rock between it and the surface, and just over that cave a road passes. What we had heard was the rumble of some vehicle—probably an innocent bread-cart—on the thoroughfare above.

Among the curiosities of the limestone caves are " cave-pearls " and " anemolites ". The first are hard pebble-like accretions which form around small nuclei such as grains of sand where water drips into a little pool. The water-drops tend to turn the nuclei over and over as carbonate of lime is deposited on them, so that eventually hard nodules are formed with concentric structure, and up to half an inch in diameter. Anemolite is the name given to stalactites which are formed in a draught; the motion of the air, by producing unequal evaporation, causes the stalactites to grow, not straight down, but at an angle, which is sometimes very marked. Even in the deepest caves the air is not still; in limestone caverns it is always fresh and pure.

Another interesting point about these deep caves is that they harbour a special cave fauna—animals which live in them habitually, and are not found anywhere else. About the cave-mouths you get some creatures that belong to the open, but seek the caverns for shelter—such as spiders; or in the case of bats to spend therein the hours of daylight. Further in are others which can live in the darkness but are also found in the open. Finally we come on the true troglodytes—certain insects, mostly wingless (spring-tails); small, for there is not food enough to support any but minute creatures; white or pale-coloured, in accordance with their surroundings; and blind, since eyes would be of no use to them. Such creatures are to be found even in the innermost recesses of Mitchelstown Cave, and are never seen except in deep caverns; they feed on minute vegetable debris presumably washed in by water, which they find in the cave earth or elsewhere, and live, one would say, a singularly uneventful existence. But how do they get from cave to cave? Some of the Mitchelstown troglodytes occur also in Dunmore (p. 313): some in caves on the Continent. Here is another of the ten thousand zoological puzzles.

But when cave fauna is spoken of a quite different collection of animals is usually intended. The smaller, drier caves were in early times the favourite home both of early man and also of many animals now extinct, especially beasts of prey, such as bears and wolves. And as the latter dragged into the caves the creatures on which they preyed—entire if small, in pieces if large—it follows that the caves became museums of the life of past times—the more so because the incrustations of stalagmite or the layers of clay which formed on their floors owing to percolating water or to streams tended to bury and so preserve the remains, and to produce a stratigraphical sequence corresponding to their chronological succession. Hence it comes that cave deposits form one of the richest quarries from which the history of the past can be hewn—man and his weapons and implements on the one hand, animals from Mammoths down to mice on the other. In Ireland little had been done in this important branch of historical and zoological research until lately—the caves of Knockninny in Fermanagh, and Shandon and Ballynamintra in Waterford. The animal remains obtained from these were reexamined by Dr. Forsyth Major in 1899, and his report made clear the desirability of further exploration; the Royal Irish Academy, ever ready to assist scientific investigation, advanced the necessary funds and appointed a committee to carry out the work—R. F. Scharff, G. Coffey, G. A. J. Cole, R. J. Ussher and myself: and the row of caves which forms a conspicuous feature of the limestone cliff on the steep western side of Keshcorran in Sligo was chosen for the first excavation. The work of superintendence fell on R. J. Ussher. Cave work of this kind is an exact science. The material must be taken out layer by layer, minutely examined, and every fragment of human or organic origin carefully labelled and preserved for determination. When it is remembered that the excavation has actually to be done by artificial light, and that the material handled is often not laid down in continuous or horizontal strata, and may be full of boulders fallen from the roof, and other obstacles, it will be clear that the digging of a cave requires much skill and patience. As a result of the work at Keshcorran, that interesting small animal the Arctic Lemming was added to the Irish fauna; with it in the lower older layers remains of Reindeer, Wolf and Bear (in quantity)—all now extinct—were obtained, together with many other animals still living in Ireland, while from the upper layers came evidence of human occupation from about the tenth century A.D. onward—articles of bronze, iron, stone and bone, charcoal, and bones of many domestic animals.

In 1902-3-4, aided by both the Academy and the British Association, extensive investigations were made in the caverns of County Clare, the practical work being again undertaken by R. J. Ussher. He sent up to the National Museum no less than 70,000 bones obtained in the Newhall, Barntick and Edenvale caves. The gigantic task of identifying this collection fell almost entirely on Dr. Scharff. Included were bones of the African Wild Cat, unknown hitherto in Europe, Irish Elk, Arctic Lemming, and most of the animals of Keshcorran, with some additional ones. In 1903-6 Ussher worked at the great cavern at Castle Pook (the goblin's castle) near Doneraile in Cork, unearthing vast quantities of Bear, Reindeer and Spotted Hyaena—the last unknown hitherto in Ireland. There were plenty of bones of Mammoth and Irish Elk, gnawed by Hyaenas and Bears: and among smaller animals found, the Norwegian Lemming was new to Ireland.[1] Some further work on Irish

[1] Full reports on all this cave work have been published by the Royal Irish Academy.

cavern deposits has been done since, but what has been said will show the nature of the task and the results that may be expected.

To return to the Waterford coast. At Tramore (*An tráigh mhór*, the great strand) it is broken by a deep bay, with a line of steep dunes backed by salt-marsh running out from the high western side and nearly cutting the bay in two. This is the home of some rare seaside plants, such as Asparagus. East of it, at the entrance of Waterford Harbour, is Dunmore (*An dún mhór*, the great fort), a charming fishing-village much recalling those of Devonshire, with its steep red rocks and little sheltered harbour: but like Devon, its beauty will soon be spoiled by modern villas, the natural result of rapid road transport, for Waterford is only ten miles away. West of Tramore there is twenty miles of almost unbroken cliff and precipitous slope tenanted by sea-birds and a wealth of wild-flowers, with small villages nestling in gaps of the rocky wall, where streams enter the sea. Then we reach Dungarvan Harbour, which is the sunken end of a long limestone trough which comes east almost from the Kerry boundary, and which by its solution has captured the Blackwater, which follows it as far as Cappoquin, and then surprisingly turns abruptly southward to follow a much older deep north-and-south cut through high beds of Old Red Sandstone to enter the ocean at Youghal. So Dungarvan, situated at the head of its bay, has only a small river to boast of, coming down from the Comeraghs close by on the north: as in the case of Tramore, its bay is split transversely by a straight narrow ridge of sand very curiously placed.

Another stretch of bold coast brings us past Ardmore (*An áird mhór*, the great height) to Youghal (*Eóchaill*, yew wood) and the mouth of the Blackwater. Ardmore is worth pausing at if antiquarian interest is an attraction: for here is a group of remains that points to an important centre in early Christian times. There is a lofty round tower, divided by string-courses into five sections—an unusual feature; a cathedral of mixed architecture: a very ancient oratory; a thirteenth-century church, and some Ogham inscriptions. And on the beach, covered at high tide, is a crannog or lake-dwelling

—pardon the apparent hibernicism. The piles which enclose it are sunk a few feet into a thick bed of peat, and were formerly covered by a storm-beach, now washed away. Clearly the peat-bog grew at a time when the land stood somewhat higher than at present. Then probably at the back of a storm-beach a lagoon formed in which the crannog was built; and the beach has shifted inwards until now the lake-dwelling is on the foreshore.

I have lingered over the Waterford coast, because it is known to very few, and is well worthy of being known better. Those who love the maritime scenery of Devonshire will find here an Irish analogue: a high coast—mostly of volcanic rocks it is true, but with Old Red Sandstone at either end—flowery slopes, lofty cliffs and stacks and pinnacled islets with colonies of sea-birds of many kinds, as well as Choughs, Peregrines, Ravens; and an illimitable glittering sea extending to the southward. You can follow the shore tolerably closely by road, but walking along the breezy cliff-top is the way to enjoy it properly. There are not many places at which to stay—Dunmore, Tramore, Dungarvan and Youghal, and no doubt a few private houses between—but that is one of its charms, for it keeps it unchanged and unspoiled.

Mention of the Waterford coast will recall to the naturalist that tragic bird the Great Auk or Gairfowl, now extinct for nearly a century, of which the last specimen certainly seen in the British Isles was captured in Waterford Harbour in May, 1834. The story of that lonely bird has often been told—how a fisherman saw it, exhausted and half-starved: so hungry indeed that it came close to the boat to receive sprats which were thrown to it: how it was captured with the aid of a landing-net, and remained in captivity with various owners for some four months, living chiefly on potatoes mashed in milk, and on fish. The skin, mounted and presented by Dr. Burkitt, may be seen in the Zoological Museum of Trinity College, Dublin—a large, tall bird, much resembling its smaller cousin the Razorbill, and not unlike a Penguin in its erect posture and rudimentary wings, quite useless for flying. Up till a

couple of centuries ago the Great Auk was abundant on many parts
of both the eastern and western coasts of the North Atlantic. That
it was a frequent article of food with the older peoples is shown by
the presence of its bones in kitchen middens in Denmark, Great
Britain and in Ireland (Waterford, Clare, Donegal, Antrim). The
number of bones obtained from the Irish coastal settlements would
appear to indicate that breeding-places were hard by, for the bird,
though helpless on land, was a powerful swimmer and diver, and not
easily captured or killed. But that rapacious creature, man, one of
the few that kills for the love of killing, ranging far and wide,
invaded its haunts, and the birds were doomed. We may read
appalling accounts of the slaughter of the auks in the pages of
Hakluyt; and much more recently too, as on Funk Island near
Newfoundland (in the journal of Aaron Thomas of H.M.S. *Boston*,
1794, quoted by Lady Blake in the *Victoria Quarterly*, August, 1889,
and transcribed by R. J. Ussher in *Irish Naturalist*, January, 1899).
The details are too terrible to repeat, but the method of obtaining
fresh eggs was ingenious: " The quantity of birds (Great Auks)
which resort to this island is beyond . . . belief. . . . As soon as
you put your foot on shore you meet with such thousands of them
that you cannot find a place for your feet, and they are so lazy
that they will not attempt to move out of your way. . . . If you go
to the Funks, you pursue the following rule: you drive, knock, and
shove the poor penguins in heaps! you then scrape all the eggs in
lumps, in the same manner as you would heaps of apples in an
orchard; numbers of these eggs being dropped some time, are stale
and useless. But you have cleared a space of ground . . . you retire
for a day or two . . . at the end of which time you will find plenty
of eggs, fresh for certain, on the place which you before had
cleared." Although the ruthless destruction of the birds and eggs
was already prohibited at that date (1794), the helpless creatures
steadily diminished at the hands of their enemy, man, like the Bison
in America. The final diminution and disappearance of the bird
appears to have been somewhat sudden, for there is no doubt that

a second specimen was procured on the Waterford coast at about
the same time as the other: then in 1844 one was reported as washed
ashore on the Cork coast, and in the following year two birds
believed to have been Gairfowl were seen on Belfast Lough. By
the middle of the nineteenth century the Great Auk was gone for
ever. So far as Ireland is concerned, the only specimen that remains
to show us the appearance of this curious bird is the young female
in Trinity College Museum. Mr Grieve (appropriate name!) has
given a melancholy inventory of the known relics of this once
abundant creature—about 80 skins, about 24 skeletons, some 70 eggs,
a couple of physiological preparations, and a large number of
detached bones. *Sic transit gloria alcae.* We may recall " the last
of the Gairfowl " as little Tom (in *The Water Babies*) found her
standing erect on the Allalonestone, the last of an ancient race, " a
very grand old lady, full three feet high, and bolt upright, like some
old Highland chieftainess ". " It is quite refreshing nowadays to
see anything without wings ", she told him. " They must all have
wings, forsooth, now, every new upstart kind of bird, and fly.
What can they want with flying, and raising themselves above their
proper station in life? In the days of my ancestors no birds ever
thought of having wings, and did very well without; and now they
all laugh at me because I keep to the good old fashion. Why, the
very marrocks and dovekies have got wings, the vulgar creatures,
and poor little ones enough they are; and my own cousins, too, the
razor-bills, who are gentle-folk born, and ought to know better
than to ape their inferiors." The old Gairfowl may have got a
little astray as regards her pedigree: but such amiable inaccuracies,
one may think, have not been altogether confined to birds.

   That gorge of the Blackwater below Cappoquin is associated in
the minds of those who are interested in either birds or will-o'-the-
wisps (strange that these should have a common meeting-ground!)
with the curious question of luminous owls. It was R. J. Ussher
who persuaded Miss Mildred Dobbs to write down[1] her very

---

[1] *Irish Naturalist*, 1911, p. 124.

interesting observations regarding these mysterious fowls—if such they be. The ferryman at Villierstown, an ex-gamekeeper, first drew her attention to them, saying that he saw birds there at night-time which gave out light. On watching, she and her sister saw them on a number of occasions, and remembered that they had often seen these lights before, but had not realized the difficulty of accounting for them. Let us have her own words: " The first time I saw them myself was one winter evening at dusk; the ferryman, just as I was stepping into the boat, pointed down the river, saying, ' There are two of the birds now,' and I saw a couple of the lights moving along the hillside towards Headborough between it and Strancally, a point a mile in a straight line from where I stood. They moved irregularly, sometimes disappearing, sometimes nearly stationary, then moving rapidly. Even though the ferryman evidently was in earnest when he said they were birds, I should have doubted their being anything but the light from a trap or bicycle being driven along the Strancally drive and disappearing and appearing between the trees; but one light turned and went rapidly back, past Strancally, crossed the river (which is quite 200 yards at that point), keeping about 60 feet above it, and in a few seconds began going along the opposite hillside and then after a minute disappeared." Again—" I and my two sisters were on the ferry slip one evening at the end of last December, about $2\frac{1}{2}$ hours after sunset; the night was dark but we could see the course of the river and shape of the hills about. We lingered a moment to see if any birds were visible. We saw a light flash up on the left across the river, half-way up the hillside; it was reflected brightly in the river, the night being perfectly calm. It disappeared at once and I remarked that ' it must have been a cottage door opened '. Then a moment later it came again in the same place but went up with a swoop to nearly the top of the hill, a rise of some 100 feet in a few seconds, and then moved rapidly to the right, got dimmer and disappeared; it appeared again beating backwards and forwards along the hillside with long swoops, but was not so brilliant. At the same time a light appeared down the river and it looked as though someone were carrying a lantern and walking along the top of the embankment towards us and about a half mile away. It was difficult to see if this was moving much or not, but it seemed to be coming nearer and to go out over the river once or twice, and then disappeared. A few minutes later we saw it again much nearer, a quarter of a mile off, and it gave the impression of moving rapidly towards us and about three feet from the ground; it came to within 100 yards and then the bird turned and the light vanished for a moment, and we saw it again out over the fields to the right, 200 yards away and pretty high up. . . . Now when I see a light I stop to observe it, and if I see it suddenly swoop out over the river or travel in half a minute from the bottom to the top of a hill 400 feet high (and sometimes even high in the air above it, as I have seen on occasions), I know it is a bird and not a man with a lantern. The most remarkable fact that strikes me each time I see one is the quality of the light. I expected to see a white phosphorescent light, not the reddish yellow it is; when the bird swoops up it seems to flash out brighter and not so red, but this may be a delusion, the bird moves so quick." Thus far Miss Dobbs. Confirmation of her statement comes from Rev. W. H. Rennison, a local resident, who records exactly similar phenomena from the same stretch of river.

What does it mean? In *The Times* for December, 1907, there was an interesting correspondence relating to a supposed luminous owl that was seen on a number of evenings in that month in Norfolk. A local gamekeeper declared that he had once shot one of these moving lights and that it proved to be a " poor old half-starved Barn Owl ". A Shropshire correspondent stated that he had known a pair of Barn Owls of which one or both had the gift of luminosity, but only when in poor condition. So there seems good evidence for the supposition that the Barn Owl at least may be luminous, in certain circumstances. C. B. Moffat, in commenting on Miss Dobbs' communication, points out that J. E. Harting, in his *Recreations of a Naturalist*, quotes evidence of the existence of luminous spots on the

Great Blue Heron of the United States. Writing in a subsequent volume of the *Irish Naturalist*, Pastor Lindner draws attention to a case where green paint-like smears on the feathers of a young Mediterranean Cormorant were found to be growths of a lowly plant, an alga of the *Ulvaceae* group: the inference being that it might be that the light was due to some other micro-organisms, in this case luminous.

The matter is very puzzling, and perhaps the most remarkable feature is the brightnesss of the light emitted, which was clearly visible at the distance of a mile. One thinks of the somewhat similar phenomenon—so far as light is concerned—of will-o'-the-wisp, about which there appears to have been much exaggeration and romancing; but it is clear from what I have quoted that the crossing of the river and the soarings of these mysterious Blackwater lights are not compatible with any explanation along these lines. Here is a great chance for a patient investigator.

CHAPTER XIII

FROM CORK TO LIMERICK

THIS area, the county of Limerick and the middle and eastern parts of the large county of Cork, is not far short of 3000 square miles. It consists mostly of peaceful and unexciting agricultural country, with a good deal of upland ground in Cork, especially along the south bank of the Blackwater, but very little that can be called mountain, and what there is has no special interest. Lakes are practically absent. Below Mallow the River Blackwater flows through a picturesque and well-wooded valley. Biologically this district possesses a certain interest, for it forms a kind of threshold to the fascinating region which adjoins on the south-west. Quite a number of the rare plants which one associates with Kerry and its geological and biological continuation West Cork, spread in diminishing numbers into eastern Cork and Limerick; and—if we know where to look—we can find "London Pride",[1] Giant Butterwort, Irish Spurge (often common) and Yellow Bartsia. These diminish eastward, showing that we are here passing out of their main stronghold. Interest within the area centres round the city of Cork and the Atlantic seaboard on the one hand, and the city of Limerick and its fine river on the other. With these two places as centres the visitor can easily reach all the spots best worth seeing, whatever his interests may be.

The Lee rises among high mountains far westward on the boundary of Kerry, above Gouganebarra, where glaciers have scooped an enormous cliff-fringed hollow containing a green alluvial flat and a deep lake; a small island in which was chosen by

[1] See p. 360.

St. Fin Barre, near the close of the sixth century, as a religious retreat. The saint's special mission here, according to tradition, was the extermination of the last Irish dragon, which had apparently been overlooked by St. Patrick. Be that as it may, a special sanctity attaches to the place, and a modern chapel is the most conspicuous feature of Fin Barre's island, now connected to the mainland by a short causeway just beyond the hotel. The saint subsequently migrated from the source of the Lee to its seaward end, where he founded a monastery which became the nucleus out of which the city of Cork arose. His name is suitably commemorated in the tall Protestant Cathedral there, which is dedicated to him.

But we must descend the Lee in more leisurely fashion than this. Foaming down from Gouganebarra it passes down a fine valley between hills (with the precipitous Glacial overflow channel known as the Pass of Keimaneigh (*Céim an fhíaidh*, the pass of the deer) on the right, through which runs the road from Macroom (*Magh cromtha*, sloping field) to Glengarriff (*Gleann garbh*, rugged glen). The Lee, running east, slows down to enter Lough Allua (*Loch lua*), a pretty winding lake four miles in length, with hills on either side thick with gorse and heather. The mountains are now left behind. Above Macroom, where the stream runs through flat meadows, it spreads out, dividing and rejoining again and again, among trees and bushes, forming a delightful combination of wood and clear swift water—a very curious feature, and unique in Ireland. The place is suitably called The Gearagh (*Gaertha*, a woodland along a river) and is well worth exploring in one of the flat-bottomed boats which are in use for this purpose. Below Macroom the Lee offers nothing to detain us till we reach Cork (*Corcach*, a marsh), twenty miles further on. Here, at sea-level, the river divides, forming a flat island over a mile long, with hilly ground on either hand. It was at the lower end of the island that Cork arose, where the river begins to widen into its estuary—

> The spreading Lee, that like an Island fayre
> Encloseth Corke with his divided flood.

The Gearagh has been sadly reduced in size following the flooding of the valley as a reservoir for generating stations downstream. C.M.

The city has long since outgrown its island, and streets now climb up the slopes on all sides. It lies in a deep hollow, into which the railway from Dublin descends nearly 500 feet by means of sharp curves, a gradient sometimes as steep as 1 in 60, and a tunnel three quarters of a mile long—an unusual form of approach to a city for a main line. The seaward approach is equally erratic—a fifteen-mile zigzag channel through waters sometimes broad, sometimes very narrow. The peculiar topography around Cork is a result of the underlying rocky structure. The east-and-west crumpling to which Ireland was subjected after the Carboniferous limestone had been laid down is here strongly in evidence. The north-and-south pressure which produced this folding made itself felt especially in Cork and Kerry, the rocks being thrown into a series of crests and hollows. The limestone got by degrees worn off the crests, so that a series of parallel bands resulted, the limestone of the downfolds alternating with the slates of the Old Red Sandstone which had underlain the upfolds. For a while, following much denudation, the local rivers flowed across a southward-sloping plain thus constituted, of broad alternating bands of slate and limestone. But the more rapid decay of the soluble limestone caused the formation of ever-deepening east-west valleys, which eventually tapped the north-south drainage. The streams were thus diverted from their former courses and sent eastward, to discharge into the ocean through whatever gaps they could find, cut by the more ancient north-south rivers through the ridges of Old Red slates. Thus we get the peculiar courses of the Suir, Blackwater, Lee and Bandon River. At Cork much solution of the bands of limestone has occurred, allowing the sea to spread far over the land between the Old Red ridges (Fig. 12). So on entering from the ocean we pass northward through a high narrow gateway into the broad expanse of Cobh (Queenstown) Harbour (*Cóbh chorcaighe*, the Cove of Cork), excavated in the limestone down to the underlying Carboniferous slate. Then a second ridge of slates is encountered, through which a narrow channel with high shores takes us past Monkstown and Passage West into Lough

Mahon, where a broad limestone depression extending eastward to Youghal is occupied, almost from Cork to Middleton, half by sea and half by low land. This is the bottom of the long limestone valley down which the Lee flows, and we traverse it westward for a few miles to Cork, with a third rib of Old Red forming a high slope on the northern bank. Through a narrow gap in this ridge the

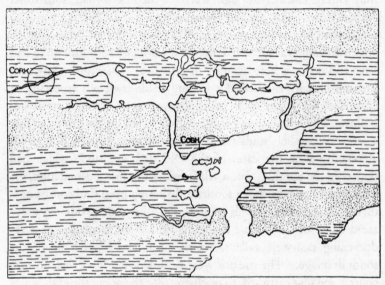

FIG. 12.—GEOLOGICAL SKETCH-MAP OF CORK HARBOUR
Limestone shown by horizontal lines, Old Red Sandstone by dots
Scale 4 miles to 1 inch

railway and road to Dublin escape towards the north, to climb over a much higher ridge beyond, in order to reach Mallow and the Blackwater. The region between Cork and the ocean is, then, an archipelagic area, often richly wooded, with many villages and large residences—a picturesque and fertile region, very attractive, and quite unlike anything else in the country.

The shore-line west of Cobh Harbour is high and rocky, with little sunken river-valleys excavated in the Carboniferous slate, allowing the sea to enter in long slender arms—a bold and very varied coast, often cliff-bound. The longest of the submerged river-valleys is that through which the Bandon River reaches the sea. Near its mouth the old town of Kinsale (*Ceannsáile*, head of the tide), long a place of naval and military importance, rises street above street on the northern bank. A sharp bend in the stream provides perfect shelter here, but for modern shipping the harbour has long since become inadequate, and the place which once accommodated ships of the line—hostile Spanish ones for ten weeks in 1601!—is now a populous rendezvous of the herring-fleets. Kinsale's ancient walls are gone, and forts which subsequently defended it are in ruins. On the west side of the river-mouth the Old Head of Kinsale, familiar to transatlantic travellers, forms a long cliff-bound projection—a place commanding on a clear day a great prospect of the Cork coast to left and right.

East of Cobh Harbour the Atlantic coast is less broken up. The little village of Ballycottin, with its hotels tucked in below the hill out of the westerly winds, and its tall rockstack surmounted by a lighthouse, is a fine open place, close to the ocean, yet well sheltered. Further east, beyond Knockadoon Point (*Cnoc a' dúin*, the hill of the fort), also with a satellite islet, we come to the old town of Youghal (*Eóchaill*, yew wood), at the narrow mouth of the Blackwater. Youghal is, like Kinsale, a place with a great deal of historic interest clinging to it, but without much now to show for it. It is associated with such names as Walter Raleigh, Richard Boyle, Oliver Cromwell; and the pleasant house in which Raleigh lived as chief magistrate is still inhabited. The main attraction of Youghal now is the fine sandy beach on the south side, which is the cause of a recent eruption of villas and bungalows.

These small ports of the south coast—Baltimore (*Baile an tighe mhóir*, town of the big house), Kinsale, Youghal, Dungarvan (*Dún Garbháin*, Garvan's fortress)—have a long history, mostly of fighting between English and Irish; and their tales of Spanish and even Algerian invasions or raids show what importance attached to them, and how their story was influenced by the open sea-passage that stretched from their portals to the Peninsula and the Mediterranean.

This Cork coast—Cobh, Glandore (*Cuan dor*), Berehaven—brings back one of the most interesting experiences I have had, when in 1888 I was privileged to be one of an expedition sent out by the Royal Irish Academy to explore the deep waters off the south-west of Ireland. Here the Continental Shelf narrows, and the 1000-fathom line is only about 150 miles distant from the coast of Kerry. Stimulated by the remarkable results obtained by recent similar expeditions in various parts of the world, which had revealed for the first time the rich and remarkable fauna of the deep sea, A. C. Haddon, then Professor of Zoology in the Royal College of Science for Ireland, induced the Academy to finance exploration of the ocean lying west of Ireland. Expeditions undertaken in 1885 and 1886 had limited their operations to the deeper waters of the Shelf. It was proposed in 1888 to attempt dredging and trawling further out, where the water was over a mile deep. The introduction of steel-wire rope for dredging, and thin steel wire for sounding, had made these operations much simpler than when hemp had been employed. The sea-going tug *Flying Falcon* was chartered for the venture. The leader on this as on previous occasions was that remarkable man, W. S. Green, of whom more anon, and also on board were C. B. (afterwards Sir Charles) Ball, W. F. de V. Kane and J. Hewitt Poole of Dublin, John Day of Cork, and Joseph Wright and myself of Belfast. We left Cobh on 27th May, and after some preliminary work, had a successful haul in 345 fathoms two days later. Steaming westward, a sounding in the afternoon showed 1080 fathoms. The sounder came up with its tube choked with *Globigerina* ooze. This is a pasty cream-coloured material, widely spread on the ocean floor, consisting of the shells of microscopical creatures which live in the waters above, especially Foraminifera (see p. 164), among which the genus *Globigerina* is largely represented. This was the ground we had come for, and an Agassiz trawl was sent down with 1270 fathoms of wire rope. Then we drifted slowly on, and at the end of

an hour began hauling in. It took another hour to get the mile and
a half of rope safely wound, but at last the trawl appeared, and in its
net a variety of strange and beautiful animals, which we examined
with delight, and safely preserved. That night a gale came up, and
we had to make all steam for Valencia, but it passed, and the boat's
head was turned westward again. At midday, in a very heavy sea,
the Agassiz trawl—which has the advantage over the beam trawl
that it has no upper or lower side, but works either way up—was shot
in 750 fathoms with excellent success, for it came up with a splendid
catch of marvellous creatures. There were great sea-slugs, red,
purple and green; beautiful corals, numerous sea-urchins with long
slender spines; a great variety of starfishes of many shapes and of
all colours, including one like a raw beefsteak, which belonged to a
new genus; strange fishes, and many other forms of life. This and
the previous hauls provided a fine display of the nature of the fauna
which lives in complete darkness on the sea-floor a mile or more
below the surface. The display of brilliant colours was especially
noticeable, for what is the use of colour in absolute darkness? Yet
purple, scarlet, orange, brilliant green were all there, in the brightest
tints. Then there was *Brissinga*, a lovely starfish that shivers and
falls to pieces as it comes aboard; *Dorocidaris*, a sea-urchin with
great spines a couple of inches long and as thick as a slate pencil:
another sea-urchin which has discarded a limy covering, and is
simply a soft bag; *Cassidaria tyrrhena*, a large handsome univalve
mollusc of Mediterranean habitat, only once before taken off the
Irish coast; and so on and so on. By the time all these treasures had
been safely bottled it was blowing so hard that it was deemed wise to
run for shelter, and we had a very bad night of it. Before Berehaven
was reached, the starboard paddle-box was smashed, and the cook's
galley stove in and wrecked. I remember that when at last grey
dawn gladdened our sleepless eyes, Green's face, ghastly white under
a sou'-wester, appeared at the cabin door. He looked round at the
wreckage strewn on the floor, but all he said was, " It has just occurred
to me that if the hippopotamus had been shown his photograph

before he was created, he would have been able to suggest some important improvements!" The trivial incident was quite characteristic of the man. He bore any hardship with a laugh, and no emergency disturbed his whimsical good humour. On this occasion he had had a heavy fall the evening before, and was in great pain; but at midnight he had gone to the bridge to help the captain with the wheel (for we had sailed short-handed) and there he stuck till we reached land. It blew hard for two days, and we remained at anchor repairing damage, and doing some trawling in shelter. Then there was a rise of glass and we started off again, but we had got no further than the Bull Rock when another gale came down, and we had to run for it and to abandon further attempts to reach deep water. We dredged and trawled a bit around Baltimore, and then reluctantly headed for Cork. But we came near never reaching it, for a dense fog engulfed us, and while crawling through it we found ourselves faced with the cutwater of a White Star liner, at what seemed only a few yards distance. Our captain whirled the wheel hard to starboard, and the liner did the same; I saw Green glance round, counting the life-belts. But before we got clear a becalmed fishing-boat was seen, right in the new path of the liner, her skipper tooting frantically on a horn to attract attention. We had steam, while the fishing-boat had none: so the liner swung back and right down on us. We fairly scraped by her; though she was going dead slow, she passed us like a railway train. We had a glimpse of her high bridge with the captain gazing down at us, of a few frightened passengers on her decks; and in a moment she was again lost in the fog, and her booming horn sounded fainter and fainter; we were left wondering whether the incident had occupied one second or one hour. We entered Cobh Harbour next morning.

This was my first meeting with that remarkable personality, William Spotswood Green; he was again our leader in the two expeditions to Rockall in 1896 (p. 44) and after that I had for many years the privilege of his friendship. Born at Youghal in 1847, he went in due course to Trinity College, Dublin, and entered the church. But from childhood, love of the sea and of adventure and exploration were a ruling passion. Appointed rector of Carrigaline near Cork in 1878, all the time he could spare from his duties was spent on the water, or in mountaineering in Switzerland or Norway. There was little about fishes and fisheries that he did not know, and he became an expert climber. Never robust, he was advised not to spend the winter of 1881–82 in Ireland, and when he discovered that Mount Cook (12,349 feet), the highest of the New Zealand Alps, had never been climbed and that its ascent was considered impracticable, he naturally went out and climbed it. "I hold", he wrote, "that the essence of all true sport consists in the pleasurable feelings experienced when natural difficulties, whatever they may be, are overcome by skill. The greater the difficulty, the greater the adventure, and the greater the pleasure in conquering it." He was a believer in J. K. Stephen's principle:

> To find out what you cannot do,
>   And then to go and do it:
> There lies the golden rule: but few
> I ever found above the ground,
>   Except myself, who knew it.

How arduous and dangerous a task he set himself when he confronted Mount Cook one learns from the book he wrote about it.[1] His companions were two picked guides from Grindelwald; and the ascent from and descent to their final camp occupied sixty-two hours. For on the way down the weather broke; they were overtaken by darkness and compelled to spend a whole night 10,000 feet up and 5000 feet above the mean limit of perpetual snow, on a ledge so small and narrow that sitting down, or even shifting six inches from where they stood, was impossible. But there, at least, they were protected from the falling massess of ice which a rapid thaw and heavy rain were bringing down on all sides. It was an amazing feat of endurance, and one can imagine their relief when about 5.30 in the morning it was light enough to allow them to begin again cutting

[1] W. S. Green, *The High Alps of New Zealand*. Macmillan, 1883.

steps down the ice slope. A little later he tried tropical forests for a change, but got only fever and ague out of them. So when opportunity served, finding that the Selkirk peaks in British Columbia were very little known, and that the just completed Canadian Pacific Railway gave easy access to them, he went off with his cousin Henry Swanzy and did some fine exploratory work, surveying and mapping among high mountains and huge glaciers.[1] Between times he carried on his marine investigations in Ireland, and was leader of three deep-sea dredging expeditions between 1885 and 1888, and maintained his clerical duties as rector of Carrigaline; but as Stephen Gwynn has said, the only ecclesiastical post he would have really liked would have been that of chaplain on board a pirate ship.

In 1890 he left his parish to become Inspector of Fisheries, and during that and the following year gave much of his time to the survey of fishing-grounds undertaken by the Royal Dublin Society, which was carried out mainly under the leadership of E. W. L. Holt and A. C. Haddon. In 1892 he was appointed to the Congested Districts Board, which gave him opportunities for much useful work in the west, and he found time to lead in 1896 the expedition to Rockall, of which I have written on a previous page (44); but official work in the Fisheries Office in Dublin absorbed more and more of his time. I used to think of him in his room in Kildare Place as a kind of shorn Samson. Sometimes I met him going home with a bundle of papers over which he must spend the evening —some wretched dispute relative to poaching, or fishing rights, or a wrangle with the English Treasury over expenditure. Slow routine and a red-tapish atmosphere must have chafed that ardent spirit, but the conviction that he was helping the fishing people carried him on, and he was an almost over-conscientious officer in his imprisonment. He had satisfied the two chief desires of his life: he had explored the high mountain-snows of two continents, and also the depths of the ocean. It must have been a delight to him to retire, in 1914, to West Cove in Kerry, on the edge of the rocky Atlantic coast that

1 W. S. Green, *Among the Selkirk Glaciers*. Macmillan, 1890.

he knew and loved so well; there he died five years later. He might well have written for himself R. L. Stevenson's lines:

> This be the verse you grave for me:
> *Here he lies where he longed to be;*
> *Home is the sailor, home from sea,*
> *And the hunter home from the hill.*

I am very grateful to W. S. Green for the glimpse which, by his kindness, I obtained on that dredging expedition of the fauna of the deep sea. No matter from what angle you approach it, the question of the sea and its inhabitants is fascinating. The whole economy of the ocean is so different from that of the land. In both spheres all life is dependent on the green chlorophyll-possessing plant, which alone has the power of making organic food-material—whether for itself or for the innumerable robbers which prey upon it—out of air and water. On land the green plant is a conspicuous and abundant feature, and the relations between it and the animal are often direct, most of the largest beasts and many of the smaller ones deriving the whole of their sustenance from it. But things are different in the ocean, for the larger sea-plants form a zone on our shores so narrow as to be altogether negligible in the oceanic food-supply; the immense food-store of the sea is located on the surface and in the upper layers of water, in the form of countless millions of microscopic floating plants, the diatoms and desmids. These are devoured by hordes of minute crustacea and other animals, which in turn form the food-supply of larger creatures, both fishes and invertebrates, and so on up to the largest of the creatures of the ocean. The original source of all sea-food is thus seen to be in the upper waters: thence it passes down either through the migrations of animals or by the sedimentation of dead matter, till it reaches at length the creatures which live on the sea-floor in total darkness a mile or two miles or more below. It is the sun's energy that gives to the chlorophyll-containing diatom its life-giving food-value. Through how many intermediate links in the form of carnivorous creatures may not this energy have passed before it reaches finally the sedentary creatures on the floor of the ocean, to enable them in turn to sustain life under the strange conditions of their existence?

And what of the sea-beasts themselves? Beauty, grotesqueness, savagery are all represented among them on a scale unknown among terrestrial creatures, and the gardens of the sea far surpass those of the land in brilliance of colouring and variety of form. It is easy nowadays to be transported into these mysterious regions. When I was young I had to be contented with Wyville Thomson's *Depths of the Sea* as the sole key to unlock the fairyland of the ocean. But now, in the wonderful books of William Beebe and others one may pass " the ivory gate and golden " into a very strange and beautiful new world.

The Blackwater, which rises in Kerry, eighty-five miles from its mouth, is the largest and most striking example of the river-capture by east-and-west limestone valleys which has been mentioned above (p. 339). It cuts right across the ancient line of drainage, and diverts many of the streams of northern Cork, discharging into the sea on the borders of Waterford far to the eastward. Its limestone valley through Mallow, Fermoy, and Lismore is very beautiful, richly wooded and with hills on either side. At Cappoquin (*Ceapach Chuinn*, Conn's plot of land) it deserts this valley (which runs on eastward to strike the sea at Dungarvan), and turns abruptly southward through a gorge of more ancient date across one of the Old Red Sandstone ridges, to enter the ocean through a narrow high gateway at Youghal.

Fermoy (*Feara muighe*, men of the plain) was the scene in 1930 of an Irish battle quite different from any of those which are recorded as having shaken the country through the centuries—one in which Starlings were the invaders, and Rooks the defenders. The episode, which has been described by W. M. Abbott,[1] is one which reflects creditably on the capacity in the domain of military tactics of the Rook, which one is rather inclined to look on as a stupid noisy bird. The field of battle was the tops of two groups of tall trees, one in

[1] *Irish Naturalists' Journal*, vol. iii., pp. 191-192. 1931.

Fermoy and one on an island in the Blackwater below Fermoy bridge. Both of these places were used for nesting in spring, and for roosting in winter, by the Rooks, which congregated nightly to the number of several hundreds, accompanied by friendly Jackdaws. A mile and a half away, in a wood of young conifers, Starlings had a great roost, and each winter evening flocks estimated at 10,000 or 12,000 passed thither over the town of Fermoy. On the evening of 2nd November, however, after the Rooks had retired for the night, the homing Starlings hesitated, wheeled round and round over the town for a while, and then suddenly poured down into the Rooks' dormitories. The Rooks protested vigorously and noisily, rising and flying round wildly, but the Starlings merely returned the owners' bad language and refused to budge. After some hours of recrimination things became quiet. Each night for a week exactly the same thing happened, but on 9th November there was a surprise. Until the arrival of the Starlings everything was quiet, but when the intruders appeared, up rose not the usual Rook population of some 300, but a black mass estimated at 1500 to 2000 birds, with tremendous cawing. They did not attack the Starlings, but hovered, densely packed, a few feet above the tree-tops. Four times the horde of Starlings poured down, four times the Rooks rose and renewed their dense barrage. The Starlings in the end admitted defeat and made off to their own pine-wood. One section of the Starlings held on till 11th November, when they also were finally defeated by the same tactics. The Rooks were taking no chances, and remained in abnormal numbers until 14th November, when they gradually reduced their garrison till the population was again normal. The Starlings made no further attempt, and eventually left the neighbourhood altogether. The most remarkable thing about the incident was, as Mr Abbott says, the deliberate summoning and arrival of reinforcements on the part of the Rooks, and the clever form of passive resistance by which they vanquished their smaller but vigorous and aggressive cousins. In a general rough-and-tumble, numbers of the Starlings could have slipped through, but the dense stratum of Rooks prevented this effectually, and the Starlings were completely out-manœuvred without a blow being struck. But how did the Rooks arrange for large reinforcements, and how did they think out and maintain their clever ruse?

The County of Limerick abuts on Cork along a tract of ground mostly high but quite devoid of any special interest—heathery hills, not steep enough to be picturesque, nor high enough to be exciting, with a gap at Charleville, allowing the Dublin–Cork railway to get through. I spent three days tramping this region once, botanizing, but it yielded nothing—except the satisfaction that comes of long days spent in fresh open country, in itself no small thing. But further north, Lough Gur, Limerick's only lake, is a place of much and varied interest. It lies three miles north of Bruff, among limestone hills. Drainage has reduced its size, and its two castles no longer stand on islands as formerly; the lowering of the water years ago also exposed some lake-dwellings, while all around is a wealth of monuments of earlier periods—many stone circles, stone alignments, dolmens, gallauns, raths. The finest circle, fifty-six yards across, is peculiar in that it is erected on the inside slope of a great earthen vallum of ring-fort appearance. Numbers of weapons of stone and bronze have been found in the vicinity, and it is clear that the place was one of great importance in early days. Botanically, also, Lough Gur is interesting. One of its abundant plants is the Golden Dock, now almost extinct in Ireland; and in its waters the Hornwort and other uncommon species flourish. Close by is a bog which has yielded many antlers of the Great Deer or "Irish Elk". Except for Lough Gur, Limerick offers little of interest until one approaches the Shannon, which forms the whole northern boundary of the county.

Adare (*Áth dara*, the ford of the oak), on the river Maigue, while never a place of civil importance, was a notable ecclesiastical centre, with three friaries grouped near the great fourteenth-century castle of the Fitzgeralds (Plate XXXV). The friaries in two cases have been converted to modern use; White Abbey, the Trinitarian friary,

Plate XXXV

T. H. Mason: photo

Desmond Castle and Franciscan Friary, Adare

for a while a ball-alley, is now the Roman Catholic church; the Augustinian building is the Protestant church; the Franciscan friary, much the most beautiful of the three, has, like the others, had the advantage of being under the care of the Earls of Dunraven, whose seat, Adare Manor, close by, is one of the handsomest residences in Ireland. Adare is indeed an architectural museum, and has besides attractions for the naturalist in its river and rich woods: and the presence of an excellent inn make it an interesting and pleasant place in which to sojourn.

Limerick city (*Luimneach*, a barren spot of land) was a Danish foundation, like so many of the Irish seaports. Ascending the Shannon estuary as far as the tide flowed, these invaders found here an island on the eastern bank formed by a narrow by-pass from the main stream. Here arose what is still called the English Town, now the older part, housing the castle and other relics of its stormy subsequent history. From this cramped site the town has spread southward, well laid out along the river, with quays and docks at its lower end: and here all its diverging lines of railway, five in number, are brought into a single station—a piece of sound planning which other Irish cities may well envy. There is plenty of historical interest in Limerick, for which see the usual guide-books: the open-air visitor will find much of attraction about the river-front. There is a large rise and fall of tide here, and flood, with its deep water extending the length of the town, is very different from ebb, when much of the bed of the Shannon is exposed, and the river rushes swiftly through banks of gravel and reefs of rock. Muddy gravels here are the home of at least one very rare plant. This is the Three-angled Bullrush, unknown elsewhere in Ireland, and in Great Britain confined to a few river-estuaries in southern England. At Limerick, between the bridges, it forms tall dark groves, much resembling those of the Common Bullrush. The estuarine habitat which it affects in Britain and Ireland affords a good illustration of the law that towards the limit of its range a plant often becomes very faddy—if one may use the term—as to the kind of place in which it will grow. On the

Continent, where the species is frequent, it is found not only in brackish water around the coasts, but in Central Europe, along the edges of rivers and lakes: whereas in these western islands its few stations are in estuaries only. But if you follow the old canal from Limerick to where it strikes the Shannon a mile away, you will see the plant growing again, quite dwarfed, it is true, in the swiftly-flowing river well above the point to which even spring-tides rise.

A little above Limerick the tail-race from the Shannon Electricity Works—still commonly called the " Shannon Scheme ", though it is an accomplished fact of some years' standing—comes in as a broad canal, and above this the volume of water in the river is sadly diminished, especially during summer. At Castleconnell, formerly famous for its salmon-fishing, the limestone steps over which the water used to foam are mostly dry, but here and on to O'Briens-bridge, where is situated the dam which allows the river to be diverted to Ardnacrusha, the banks are picturesque and interesting.

Below Limerick the Shannon assumes at once estuarine form, with muddy foreshores fringed with tall reeds (among which the Three-angled Bullrush mentioned above is conspicuous); seven miles down it begins to widen, and ten miles further on the broad Fergus estuary, choked with islands and mud-banks, opens on the north. Opposite to this, on the Limerick side, a narrow tidal creek leads up to Askeaton. This is an attractive place. There are the remains of a noble Franciscan abbey, and of a great castle built in 1199. The wide area of bare limestone, through which the River Deel has cut a deep trench, recalls the remarkable similar tracts in Clare and eastern Galway: and it is, indeed, a southward extension of this driftless, soilless country (p. 211). But the peculiar vegetation which makes the naked limestones of such unusual interest further north dies out southward. About Ennis some of the characteristic plants, such as the Spring Gentian, still persist; but at Askeaton the only representative of the rarer species is the Salzburg Eyebright. This, along with plenty of Madder, Squinancy-wort, Scale Fern, etc., growing in the crevices of the limestone, recall the wonderful flora of Burren: but it is only an insipid make-believe, not the genuine thing.

A little further west, at Foynes and Newcastle, the limestone passes under shales of Upper Carboniferous age, which inland rise into bare heathery uplands running down into Kerry; and the incoming of sporadic patches of Giant Butterwort and Irish Spurge show that we have finally left the flora of the Central Plain for the fascinating vegetation of the South-west.

CHAPTER XIV

THE KERRY HIGHLANDS

(KERRY AND WEST CORK)

So far as the singular beauty and interest of the South-west are concerned, " Kerry " does not very correctly specify the area which is so widely known and so much visited. If you want to see the whole of it, you must begin outside Kerry, about Roaring-water Bay in West Cork, and work northward till you reach Tralee Bay, where you may desist. That measures only forty miles in a straight line: but if you followed the coast, zigzagging around the great Devonian promontories and the deep intervening inlets, the distance would be close on five hundred miles—and what a glorious walk that would be! The western extremity of the county of Cork would thus be included, for it is part and parcel of this lovely region of mountain and ocean; on the other hand, the northern part of Kerry would be omitted, for there you enter a tract of quite different aspect and of very little interest. The much-advertised tourist region occupies all the middle part of the area just defined, and includes many names to conjure with—Glengarriff, Kenmare, Parknasilla, Waterville, Valencia, Killarney—all but the last situated on the coast. But it does not include perhaps the most interesting region of all—the Dingle Peninsula in the north. That, like the southern end of the district, beyond Bantry Bay, as yet hears but seldom the accents of London or New York. The whole area is a sea of mountains, with ocean inlets cutting thirty miles into the hills—deep clear Atlantic water dividing rugged masses of green and purple slates.

The story which geology tells as to how Kerry got its present

form is interesting, and for the benefit of non-geologists I shall try
to tell it in non-geological language. Towards the close of Carboniferous times—that is, after the familiar grey limestone which
covers so much of Ireland and the beds of sandstone and shale which
succeeded it were laid down on an ancient sea-bottom, but long
before the beginning of the Mesozoic period, when the New Red
Sandstone and white Chalk were formed—the crust of the Earth in
Ireland and beyond it was subjected to intense lateral squeezing from
a north-south direction. This forced it into a series of great east-
west folds, thousands of feet high from base to summit—the Carboniferous beds on top, and below them and following their ridges
and hollows the massive strata of Devonian time, and other deeper-
buried systems. A series of pieces of corrugated iron laid one over
the other will illustrate what happened. For reasons which need
not be probed, the folding was developed particularly conspicuously
in the Cork–Kerry area. Later deposits (if any) which may have
been laid down on this folded rock-surface during the immense
period of time intervening between then and now have vanished,
and what we see is the result of this ancient crumpling, now greatly
modified by the effect of millions of years' exposure to sun and frost,
rain and rivers. The limestone has been mostly worn away, and
removed in solution into the sea; it remains only at the bottoms of the
troughs, the present valleys: while the more resistant slates, carved
into a wilderness of mountains, still tower up, forming long rugged
heathery ridges. A sinking of the land has enhanced the effect by
allowing the sea to flow far up the troughs. That the ridges were
formerly longer is shown by the high craggy islands that lie off their
extremities, and continue their direction out into the Atlantic.

Of course this is a wet region: situated as it is, it could not be
otherwise. On Mangerton in 1903, 141 inches of rain were recorded!
But that was a *tour de force* on the part of nature. The annual average
sinks to 40 in favoured places, and you need not reckon on more than
60 inches except in valleys deep among the hills. I have not had
more soakings in Kerry than elsewhere in Ireland, and indeed on two

occasions work was impeded by heat and drought. It is alarming
to learn that the most persistently wet place is at Gearhameen near
Killarney (the focus of holiday life), where for seventeen years the
precipitation averaged over 87 inches; but Gearhameen is beyond
the extremity of the Upper Lake, well out of the way; at Killarney
town the score has dropped to 55. By way of compensation for the
heavy rainfall, the same cause which produces it—the warm ocean
which encircles Kerry—is the reason of the high and uniform
temperature which prevails there. The effect of this is seen especially
in local gardens where great Tree-ferns, and Daturas with hanging
bell-shaped blossoms a foot long, flourish in the open, and Bamboos
and Mesembryanthemums of many kinds, as well as a host of other
plants seldom seen out of doors so far north in Europe, grow in rank
profusion.

At the southern end of this land of great mountain promontories,
in West Cork, you find yourself in a little-known and tourist-free
region of much charm. You stay on Sherkin Island (*Inis Oircín*,
little pig's island), or Cape Clear Island, at Schull (*Scoil*, a school)
or far out at Crookhaven: and you walk and boat and fish and lounge
and bathe, and enjoy the glorious air and sea; towns and trams and
telephones seem like bad dreams, or like fugitive glimpses of an
earlier and inferior existence. A meandering railway penetrates to
Schull, and roads are as good as you could expect them to be in so
lonely a country. All is furzy heath and rocky knolls, little fields
and white cottages and illimitable sea, foam-rimmed where it meets
the land, its horizon broken only by the fantastic fragment of rock
crowned by a tall lighthouse which is the famous Fastnet.

Tucked in a sheltered nook of the stormy cliffy coast that extends
eastward from Cape Clear is Lough Ine, a spot which on account of
its scenic beauty, its topography and its remarkable fauna deserves
consideration. Lough Ine is a rectangular piece of water about a
quarter of a square mile in area, connected with the sea by a narrowing channel two-thirds of a mile long, which at its entrance to the
lough is only a stone-throw wide, with a sill of rock across it which

prevents the water of Lough Ine ever dropping below about half-tide level. Through this constriction the ebb and flow rush with great velocity. As no streams of any size flow into it, the water in Lough Ine is of salinity almost as high as that of the Atlantic outside, and beautifully clear. A remarkable feature is its unexpected depth. Along the western shore (where also the ground rises steeply into wooded hills), the slope below water amounts almost to a submarine cliff, and over more than half its area soundings indicate no less than fifteen to twenty-four fathoms. The explanation of this deep square depression is not easy, and I have sent the hat round among my geological friends without receiving any helpful contribution.

The clear sheltered lake, fed by pure Atlantic water entering at one corner during the upper half of each tide, resembles a gigantic marine aquarium, and the peculiar conditions of life have remarkable repercussions on the fauna and flora. Many forms common on the surrounding shores are absent or very rare in the lough—for instance, the great brown oar-weeds that are so familiar a sight at low water; their place is taken by beds of whitish encrusting coralline seaweeds. On the other hand, many animals and some plants grow to quite unusual dimensions. The fauna is characterized by a remarkable abundance and variety of species, particularly of sedentary and sessile species: for instance, the beautiful Purple Sea-urchin *Paracentrotus lividus*, of which twenty adult specimens, besides smaller ones, may be counted on each square foot over quite extensive areas, most of them wearing on the top of the spines a parasol, in the shape of an empty *Anomia* shell; *Anomia* itself, the Pearly Oyster, is likewise enormously abundant, and innumerable smaller creatures more beautiful than these—echinoderms, polyzoons, tunicates, coelenterates, sponges and so on, many of brilliant colour and beautiful form. To lean over the side of a boat and view the bottom with a " water-telescope " is like peeping into a strange calcareous sort of fairyland. Perhaps the queerest feature of this queer place is the occurrence even under only a few feet of water of animals mostly found in deepish or quite deep sea—various starfishes, the coral

Caryophyllia smithii, the brachiopod *Crania anomala*, the crinoid *Antedon bifida*, and that little white cousin of the Common Mussel, *Lima hians*, which can flit about through the water like a marine butterfly. Lough Ine is worth visiting at any time, but if you happen to go there in summer, when Professor Renouf and his students are at work investigating the lough and its myriad inhabitants, you may have an opportunity of seeing and understanding much more than you otherwise would.[1]

Crossing from the east the first of the many mountain-ridges that in this region run out into the ocean like a shark's teeth, we come to Bantry (*Beann traighe*, the race of Beann), a market-town busy in the very leisurely way which means busyness in the south-west of Ireland; and we pass on round the indented head of lovely Bantry Bay to Glengarriff, consisting of several large hotels and a few other houses. It stands at the extremity of a fairy-like island-studded bay, facing full south, very sheltered, almost frostless in winter, seldom too hot in summer (though the midges may be pesky), embowered in native oak-woods and semi-tropical shrubs. A fine centre, too, for the explorer, for roads lead in many directions through the mountains and along the coast. But best of all is it to penetrate on foot into the wild region of hill and cliff and lake lying just west of Glengarriff; not built on such a massive or lofty scale as Macgillycuddy's Reeks. but surpassing them for variety and sheer beauty. Enter this enchanted region by way of Barley Lake or the Adrigole glen, with strong boots and a raincoat to exorcise the demons of air and water, and I would wish to be with you in body, as I shall be in spirit. If you are not a walker, encircle the area by motor—down the edge of Bantry Bay, across the hills by the new Healy Pass Road, or on by Berehaven, up the Kenmare River, with endless mountains facing you across the water, and back to Glengarriff by the thousand-foot climb that takes you through the tunnel at Turner's Rock—sixty miles or so, of which there is not one which you would like to

[1] For a preliminary account of "Lough Ine and its Biology", by Renouf, see *Journal of Ecology*, vol. xix., pp. 410-438, plates 23-26, 3 maps. 1931.

Most of the research work at Lough Ine is now under the control of the University of Bristol. c.m.

miss, and a good road all the way—good, that is, for those who do not forget that they are in the heart of Kerry, and not on the tarred highways of more sophisticated areas.

Kenmare (*Ceann mara*, head of the sea), aptly named, at the head of the so-called Kenmare River (which is a mountain-fringed sea-inlet thirty miles long), is in my estimation the finest centre in Kerry whether for walking, cycling or motoring. All the higher hills of the south-west, excepting those on the isolated Dingle Peninsula, are grouped around it—the Caha range (*Ceatha*, a shower—the showery hills), Knockboy and its neighbours, Mangerton, the Reeks, Mullagh-anattin, and many other summits of over 2000 feet, and from Kenmare roads lead into them and through them in every direction. Kenmare is actually nearer to that gem of Killarney, the Upper Lake, if you walk by the old road, than is Killarney itself. And the railway company helps to keep the holiday crowd away from Kenmare by making you spend an hour and a quarter over the last twenty miles— a curious policy, in view of the fact that it owns large hotels at Kenmare and Parknasilla (*Páirc na sailleach*, park of the willows), which one might assume it is anxious to fill. But who travels by rail nowadays, anyway?

It is not necessary to patronize the reader by advising him to go here or there if he is at Kenmare. Of the five main roads that radiate from it, all pass through miles of lovely scenery, and lead to other places of equal beauty. The only dull road is the first half-dozen miles of that which leads south-west to Parknasilla and Water-ville, and who will grudge an uneventful introduction to a journey which leads to such places? Begin quietly, by climbing Boughil (*Buachaill*, a boy), bathing in Inchiquin Lough, scrambling about the falls on the Roughty River (*O'Ruachtan*, a family name) above Morley's Bridge, and you will be tuned for longer raids into this inexhaustible unspoiled wilderness of hill and lake.

Now that we have reached the heart of Kerry, it is meet that something should be said about the vegetation that lends an additional charm to the physical beauties of the region. Kerry is a Mecca not only for the British but for the European botanist, on account of the many rare and interesting plants which grow, often in great abundance, on its hills and in its glens and lakes. These are of all kinds—trees and herbs, ferns, mosses, liverworts. Their special interest, apart from the great beauty of some of them, lies in this—that they are rare in or more often absent from Great Britain and the central parts of the Continent, and that they belong, not to the multitude of plants which migrated from middle Europe across England to Ireland in past times and have settled down over both islands, but either to countries far to the south of Ireland—Spain and the Mediterranean region—or to distant North America. Research has proved abundantly that they are not human introductions, but have migrated by natural means. These groups have their Irish headquarters in Kerry, and some in Connemara, whence some continue northward, especially to Donegal. A few of the southern species have colonized south-western England on their way from the Spanish area to Ireland; while a few of the Americans are found sparingly in Scotland, or north-western Europe. What are these plants? One of the finest of them is the Strawberry-tree, *Arbutus*, which gives character to the Killarney woods by its glossy leaves, Lily-of-the-Valley blossoms, and prickly scarlet fruit. Then there is the Saxifrage which till lately was considered to be the " London Pride " of English gardens, but is now known to be an allied plant found in the Spanish peninsula, spread along the Irish western and southern coasts and also in Wicklow; and the Kidney-leaved Saxifrage, which attains its main Irish development in the south-west. There is the Large-flowered Butterwort, which covers the hills and bogs of Kerry and West Cork, bearing a rosette of shining yellow leaves, and in May a cluster of great deep purple violet-like flowers. The Irish Spurge, too, so common in the south-west, and spread sparingly as far as Donegal, is a southerner. And there are other southern plants in western Ireland which do not grow in Kerry, but farther north, the most striking being three species of Heath which are referred to in the pages dealing with Connemara (p. 169). The

PLATE XXXVI

T. H. Mason: photo

THE REEKS FROM BALLAGHOSHEEN PASS

American ingredients in the Irish flora are fewer and not so conspicuous, but they include a highly fragrant Orchid—a species of Lady's-Tresses, found in Europe only in south-west Ireland—and another closely allied to it, confined to the Lough Neagh basin and a single place in west Scotland. Another remarkable plant is the Pipewort, spread from Cork to Donegal, occurring also in west Scotland, and next in North America; and there is the Canadian Blue-eyed Grass—an iris rather than a grass—widespread in the west of Ireland. It is specially significant that the members of these Hiberno-Iberian and Hiberno-American groups are not altogether limited to the vegetable kingdom: some animals show just the same peculiar distribution. Perhaps the most famous is the Spotted Slug of Kerry, elsewhere confined to Spain and Portugal: and there is a number of others, including molluscs, beetles, false-scorpions, woodlice and earthworms, found in Ireland, and elsewhere only in the Pyrenean or Mediterranean regions. One animal form, a freshwater sponge, widespread in Ireland and found also in western Scotland, belongs elsewhere exclusively to North America, and reinforces the American group. One could fill a book with discussion of the many problems raised by the presence in Ireland of these animals and plants—the date of their arrival, the manner and the route by which they travelled, and the meaning of their curious distribution: but here we may be content with a recognition of their presence and of their peculiar interest.

The Large-flowered Butterwort, or Bog Violet, as it is often called (though it is not related to the violet group) which decks the bogs and rocks over thousands of acres in Kerry, deserves special mention. " No one ", wrote Dr. Scully, " who has seen its groups of deep violet flowers—sometimes over an inch in diameter—on the black dripping rocks of Connor Hill, or on the boggy roadsides between Killarney and Kenmare, will deny its claim to be considered the most beautiful member of the Irish flora ". The contrast between the rich tint of the blossoms and the bright yellow-green of its plump rosettes of leaves, which rosettes may be nine inches across, enhances its loveliness: and its abundance over wide areas is surprising in contrast to the usual rather sparse distribution of the several other species of Butterwort. Nor is its beauty the only point of interest which it offers, for it is one of those few plants which have developed the remarkable habit of supplementing their food-supply with an animal diet. It may be noted in passing that most of the plants which are in part carnivorous (none of the higher plants is wholly so) are inhabitants of bogs or other places where food-materials are not readily available: so we may fairly trace the origin of this curious habit to hunger. If you examine with a lens one of the tongue-shaped shining leaves of the Butterwort, you will notice that it is all studded with curious little mushroom-shaped structures. Under a low power of the microscope you will see the details of these, and you will note also a multitude of other protuberances, only slightly raised above the general surface. Both kinds are minute and abundant; they number together about 25,000 to the square centimetre (about one-seventh of a square inch) and on an average plant there may be half a million of them. Both series are glands, which have a very peculiar function. They pour out a colourless secretion which covers the leaf, and which by its stickinesss tends to hold small insects or other creatures that may alight on it. Should the glands be disturbed by drops of rain, or grains of sand, or other inorganic materials, nothing happens. But should any nitrogenous material, such as the body of an insect, come in contact with them, they begin to discharge an acid fluid similar to the gastric juice of animals, and like it having a high dissolving power, so that the animal substances are brought into solution; they are then absorbed by the plant. When this process of digestion is complete the glands resume their emission of mucilage only. The leaf-edges themselves, which are slightly inflexed, are sensitive, and if an insect alights near the margin, the leaf slowly curls inwards, bringing fresh glands in contact with the prey, and thus hastening its absorption. The similarity in the powers of this digestive excretion of the Butterwort to that of animals has been known for a long time, and it has been and still is employed, as in Scandinavia and Switzerland, for " renneting " milk, in lieu of the usual rennet obtained from the digestive organs of calves.

The Sundew or *Drosera*, of which three species occur on our bogs, supplies a still more remarkable example of the carnivorous habit. The small leaves are hairy—" all whiskery like a bee's leg ", as a Connemara man described it to me—and these are not ordinary hairs but sensitive tentacles which not only secrete both glutinous and digestive juices as in the Butterwort, but are extraordinarily responsive even to almost microscopical quantities of animal substances, closing in on the food one by one till the leaf is like a shut fist. They are much more efficient hunters than are the Butterworts; if you examine their leaves you will find plenty of trapped animals—and not only little ones, but sometimes a small dragon-fly, or even a wasp which, if its wings get caught, cannot free itself, and comes to a miserable end.

The Large-flowered Butterwort has a characteristic distribution —Ireland, western France, Spain, Portugal and the Alps. Most of the Irish plants of the same geographical group (see p. 360), very old residents here, conservative as to their habitats, are rather strictly limited in range. But this Butterwort, while its natural area is well-defined, has shown on occasion an unusual willingness to expand its empire. John Ralfs planted a few roots on Tremethick moor in Cornwall, where it increased amazingly till enthusiastic collectors got to know of it, and nearly exterminated it. Plants were then transferred to Trangle moor and the neighbourhood of the Land's End where, according to Davey's *Flora of Cornwall*, they " multiplied with marvellous speed ". Now, to the true naturalist, and especially to the student of geographical distribution, this whole episode is a rather shocking story—the introduction of the plant even more than its extermination, as I shall try to explain. The planting of attractive flowers in wild ground where they do not grow naturally may appear at first sight an innocent and commendable activity. But it is not long ago since the Royal Horticultural Society in Dublin had to protest against a leaflet exhorting people to " beautify the country-side " and offering seeds for the purpose: and in England a President of the Linnean Society and others have protested vigorously against similar suggestions which will be still in the minds of nature-lovers on the British side of the Channel. Why? For this reason: the present natural distribution of plants and animals is a matter of high interest and importance to all students of nature, for it is the heritage of a long past. We see in this present arrangement the result not only of far-extended competition, but of past climates and different distributions of land and sea: and the vicissitudes of the plants and lowly animals throughout the ages have an important bearing on the past migrations and history of man himself. Since geographical botany and geographical zoology became exact sciences, the greatest naturalists of their day—Charles Darwin, Alfred Russel Wallace, Humboldt, Sir William Hooker, and others—have based far-reaching conclusions as to the past on observed present distribution. Any interference with this precious heritage, this priceless document which is furnished by our indigenous plants and animals, is therefore unwarranted and deplorable. The inevitable changes which arise from man's activities—unintentional introduction of foreign seeds and so on in the practice of agriculture and commerce—make the interpretation of present distribution sufficiently difficult. May we be spared the additional confusion caused by the activities of well-meaning but misdirected folk who would, by their " beautifying ", confuse still further these important issues!

There is another jewel in the Kerry crown, an animal unique, known only there, a resplendent creature called the Carrabuncle. It is true that it has never been seen by the cold critical eye of science, but Matthew Arnold reminds us through the mouth of Empedocles that " much may still exist that is not yet believed." The Carra-buncle is mentioned in Charles Smith's *Antient and Present State of the County of Kerry*, published in 1756, as having been seen in the Killarney Lakes—but he erroneously assumed that the name he heard belonged not to an animal but to the familiar precious stone. Henry

Hart, when exploring the Kerry mountains in 1883, came on its track again, this time on Brandon. He learned that its home was in Lough Veagh (*Loch betha*, birch lake) where the people gather fresh-water mussels for the pearls which some of them contain. " These come off an enormous animal called the Carrabuncle, which is often seen glittering like silver in the water at night. This animal has gold and jewels and precious stones hanging to it, and shells galore; the inside of the shells shines with gold." Five years later, Nathaniel Colgan happened on Hart's informant, when climbing on Brandon, and obtained further particulars.[1] The true home of the Carrabuncle, it appears, is Lough Geal (*Loch geal*, shining lake), not Lough Veagh. His informant had never seen it, but if you could only catch it you would get some things of great value that follow after it. The postman and the publican, interviewed by Colgan, confirmed the fact of the Carrabuncle's existence. But it is seen, it would appear, only once in seven years, and then it lights up the whole lake.

I have been five times at Lough Geal, but was unlucky as to date, for I saw nothing, and the lake was mostly inky black, with heavy clouds hanging on the dark cliffs which impend above it. But a very interesting side issue to the legend, as yet unexplained, pointed out by Colgan, arises from the reference by Alfred Russel Wallace in his *Travels on the Amazon and Rio Negro*, to the Carbunculo, a mythical animal of the Upper Amazon and Peru. Colgan was puzzled as to the connection (if any) between the Irish and the South American creature. The probable explanation of the presence of the name in these two widely separated areas lies in the fact that both regions were in intimate connection with Spain. A. Farrington tells me that till recently fishermen from the Peninsula brought to southern Ireland cargoes of salted cod obtained on the Newfoundland banks, which went in Cork by the name of *bockalow*, which is clearly the Spanish *bacallao* (Portuguese *bacalhao*), cod or ling—I well remember the horrible stuff we ate with unwelcome frequency in

[1] See *Irish Naturalist*, vol. xxiii., p. 59. 1914.

the Canary Islands under that name. It would seem that Carra-buncle corresponds similarly to the Spanish Carbunculo, meaning the precious stone we call carbuncle—though how the word came to be applied either in Ireland or on the Amazon to a water-monster is not clear.

The floral beauty and interest of Kerry in the springtime I have endeavoured to describe in *The Botanist in Ireland*, and I can best pay tribute to it now by repeating what I wrote then: for the sake of non-botanical readers, I have substituted English plant-names for the Latin ones there used:

" To see the peculiar flora of Kerry in its most characteristic aspect the time to visit the area is not the usual holiday period of July and August, beloved of botanists, but the month of May and early June. Then the Large-flowered Butterwort, the glory of Kerry, is at its best, its great purple blossoms nodding in the wind over hundreds of square miles of bog and rocky mountain. ' Lon-don Pride ' and the Kidney-leaved Saxifrage are in full bloom too, decking the rocks, woods and glens with their slender red stems starred with white flowers. The Irish Spurge is at its loveliest stage, just attaining full growth, and forming luscious clusters of greenish gold along the streams and in all the rough pasture land. By the end of June it will be wholly green, with tubercled fruit and a straggling habit. The Royal Fern also is at its loveliest, golden brown, its strong shuttlecocks of fronds half expanded, with loose rags of brown fluff clinging to their straight smooth glaucous stems; it lines the streambanks and fences everywhere, and lights up the brown bogs. Alone among the rare species, the Arbutus is not at its best. Growth is only just beginning, the old leaves are yellowing and falling, and the half-grown fruit, so beautiful at a later stage, is still inconspicuous.

" Everywhere Gorse is blazing, with Broom following close behind. In the woods the delicate green of the young Birch con-trasts with the old gold of the Oak and the grey-green of the Willows; the Holly, though full of flower, looking very dark in comparison. The shaggy young stems of the Male Fern add again a touch of golden brown, while half-expanded Lady Ferns and Bree's Fern are full green. The two species of Filmy Fern are still in excellent condition, *H. tunbridgense* separating itself at once from its ally by its bluish-green tint, and the broader rounded tip of its tiny fronds.

" In the lakes there is as yet little life. The Water Lobelia alone is sending flower-stems up towards the light. The Awl-wort, Shore-weed and Pipewort are still dormant, the curiously persistent old fruit-stems of the last lying criss-cross like straws on the fresh green mats of foliage.

" By the sea, the white sheets of Scurvy-grass have already passed away, but the rocks are bright with Sea-Pink and Sea-Campion, often in remarkable profusion, while the dunes are decorated with thousands of the yellow and blue flowers of the Sand-hill Pansy."

To the botanist, Kerry will always stand associated with the name of Reginald William Scully (1858-1935), who gave us a book upon its plants which is the most complete account yet written of the botany of any Irish area. Scully was a doctor, but the presence of private means rendered unnecessary the adjunct of a practice, and while he remained a helpful member of his profession, he was able, under the incentive of A. G. More, to carry out during nearly thirty years a very complete botanical survey of this large and mountainous area, during which he added considerably to our knowledge of its vegetation. His *Flora of County Kerry*, published in 1916, forms a fitting memorial to an earnest and methodical worker, and a man whose old-world courtesy and scientific modesty lent to his companionship a special charm.

I am going to indulge in a grumble about Killarney—not about the lovely region of mountain and lake, but about the town which is its focus and gateway. It is all wrong; but indeed the wrongnesses are mostly its misfortune, not its fault. In the first place, it stands in the wrong place—on flat ground, with a lake two miles wide and five miles in length cutting you off from the paradise on

its southern side—for to west, north, and east, the district around
Killarney is quite dull. Nor does the town stand by the lake-shore,
but over a mile inland, with the high walls and dense trees of
Kenmare demesne preventing for several miles even a glimpse of
lake or mountain. The road which leads down to Lough Lene
(*Loch Léin*)—the only one—offers to the visitor a mile and a half of
flat straight dull thoroughfare, with flat fields on one side and a high
wall on the other. It takes you to the cramped confines of the fine
old ruin of Ross Castle, on the edge of the water: if you attempt
to go to right or left—" Sixpence, please! " The other roads leading from Killarney are dull too, especially the western one. The
Kenmare road is somewhat better from the start, but you go four
miles before the lovely wooded hills begin. Fortunately some of the
hotels are well out on this side. The town itself is unattractive,
devoid of the amenities which one associates with a great tourist
centre as found in other countries: and while the principal streets
are neat, the outskirts cannot claim exemption from a recent comment on the Irish provincial town: " its most striking feature is its
ruined buildings in various stages of decay. A decorative *motif* is
supplied commonly by the display on suitable walls of rival political
slogans." It is just because I am an enthusiast as regards the beauty
and interest of Ireland that I make these comments. Much-
advertised Killarney, seen every year by thousands of visitors, should
be in the forefront of effort to show a fair and smiling face to the
strangers whom Ireland attracts to her shores from all parts of the
world. As to those unfortunate topographical features which
Killarney cannot help, they are by no means without compensations.
If the beautifully wooded demesne were not reserved and "Sixpence,
please ", no doubt it would be bare agricultural land, with notices
regarding trespass and barriers of barbed wire. And the four miles
of road that intervene between the town and the Arbutus woods of
the hills mitigate the enthusiasm of the crowds of invaders who
otherwise might litter them with paper and cartons and broken
glass, harry the wild flowers, and carve their names upon the trees.

So you will understand why, for my own part, I prefer to sojourn at quiet Kenmare, far from the madding crowd, and thence cross the mountain-ridge to the Upper Lake, entering the Killarney fairyland at its least frequented part (Plate XXXVII). But if you stay at one of the excellent hotels well outside Killarney town, you will be in lovely scenery all the time, and the Kenmare road will lead you into the heart of the hills. If you are motoring, of course, you can afford to stop anywhere, for ten minutes will take you through the unexciting immediate environs of Killarney. And if you turn your back on the dull country north of the Lower Lake, what a lovely region lies before you! To the south the huge mass of Mangerton (*Mangartagh*, mountain of long grass?), with its enormous lake-filled cirque called the Devil's Punch-bowl. Close by, between Mangerton and Stoompa, is the Horse's Glen, long and deep, with three lakes between its rocky walls, and a grand cirque above the highest of them. It takes a big day's work to explore those two great coombs, and you must go on foot. A day for each of them will not be found excessive even by a vigorous climber. It is the remote tarn of the Devil's Punch-bowl that supplies Killarney with its excellent water—"The grandest water in Ireland, sorr", a local enthusiast told me; "Just a drop of John Jameson in it and it will go down your throat like a torchlight procession, and warm the nails in your boots, begob!" To the south-west, beyond Torc Mountain (*Torc*, a boar) is the valley in which lies the Upper Lake. It has been excavated so deeply by ice in old days, that its floor is level for five miles into the mountains, so visitors to the Gap of Dunloe are rowed down the slow stream that occupies the valley-bottom, and on across the Lower Lake. This valley is for the botanist and zoologist the special attraction of Killarney—very sheltered, excessively humid, filled with luxuriant native woods of Oak, Arbutus, Birch, Holly and Mountain-Ash, under which the Saxifrages, Filmy Ferns and other interesting plants for which Killarney is famous run riot among a profusion of mosses and liverworts of extraordinary luxuriance and often of extreme rarity. And a feature that adds to the beauty and interest of these woods is this: they are not confined within bounds, like most that we know, but run up the hills to their natural limits, where exposure makes them halt; and we see the tree-edge fluctuating up and down along the mountain-sides between 600 and 800 feet according to the amount of shelter afforded by the conformation of the ground to the gales of winter. West of this unique valley rise the tall hills of the Purple Mountain group, with Tomies Mountain, densely wooded below, descending steeply into the waters of the Lower Lake; and beyond Purple Mountain, across the deep gash of the Gap of Dunloe, the Reeks tower up above everything else. It is a wonderful bit of country.

If you want to experience to the full the enchantment of Killarney get out on the lake on a calm evening (having contrived to leave your garrulous boatman behind), and watch the changing effects of light and shade on the towering hills and the water and the woods as sunset approaches. If you have been lucky, and have got a day of that indefinable astonishing Killarney atmosphere, you will admit that in your life you have never seen anything more lovely. But to be rowed about (fortunately motor boats are still almost unknown) one of a party of eight, with a running commentary such as " Look now, there's the Elephant Island, right forninst ye. Do ye see his trunk, and his little eye. But he won't touch you, sorr. There was once a giant . . . "—that keeps you firmly pinned down to earth, when you might be away in whatever sort of Elysium the enchant-ment makes for you.

Like the large lakes of the west, Lough Lene (or the Lower Lake) is excavated out of the Carboniferous limestone where it abuts on older insoluble rocks. The Killarney side and also Muckross Lake have limestone shores—a hard splintery rock; while on the opposite side the Old Red Sandstone rises from the water and up to the mountain-tops. On Ross Island the limestone is curiously fretted, forming jagged shores, and in the bay east of it fantastic islets of honeycombed rock impart a peculiar character to this part of the lake. Ross Island itself, scarcely an island but rather a penin-

PLATE XXXVII

R. Welch: photo

THE UPPER LAKE AND THE REEKS, KILLARNEY

sula, is a delightful jungle of a place—part swamp, with great groves of six-foot Royal Ferns, part jagged rock with Arbutus and Yew and rare forms of White Beam, part planted, with gigantic trees of many kinds; it would be well-nigh impenetrable but for the avenues which traverse it from end to end.

Macgillicuddy's Reeks (*i.e.* Ricks), the highest mountains in Ireland (Carrantual, *Corrán tuathail*, an inverted reaping-hook (from its outline) is 3414 feet), are not so conspicuous from Killarney as their proximity and height would lead one to expect, for Purple Mountain and Tomies Mountain, separated from " The Reeks " by the deep Gap of Dunloe, rise between, screening them somewhat effectually. But from other sides, and especially from the north, they tower up boldly, a close-set group of sharp peaks, overtopping all the hills around (Plate XXXVI). They are thus cut off from Killarney by both water and mountain. The Reeks are best approached from the north-west—from Caragh Lake and Glencar; on that side a driving road passes within three miles of the summit of Carrantual at a height of 545 feet, and the track that runs up the Caragh River over to Cummeenduff takes you both closer and higher. The orthodox way of ascending Carrantual from Killarney is to drive to Gaddagh bridge, six miles west of Lough Lene, and ascend the Gaddagh River and on up the wild Hag's Glen. The slopes are steep and often grassy, with so much precipitous ground that you must choose your route carefully; and there are dark tarns lying in cliff-walled coombs of green and purple slates, and knife-edge *arêtes* above—altogether an inspiring place for the mountaineer. The walk along the main ridge, from above the Gap of Dunloe forms, in the estimation of the late H. C. Hart, who was a very competent judge, " the grandest bit of mountaineering to be met with in Ireland ". The Gap of Dunloe, which cuts the Reeks off from their natural continuation on the north, is a deep Glacial overflow channel, formed by a torrent when the ice lay piled so high on the lower grounds around that this was the easiest point of escape for the marginal streams. But one can scarcely view it in peace on account of the cloud of human gadflies which infests it, attracted thither by the stream of tourists passing through it on Killarney's favourite lake-and-mountain excursion.

Then there is lovely Caragh Lake (*Loch carthach*, rocky lake) to the west (Plate I), and the fine Mullaghanattin mountain-group to the south-west, with Parknasilla and the Kenmare River beyond, and further west the steep Drung Hill group looking down on Bantry Bay; and beyond that, at the seaward end of the great promontory, Derrynane and Waterville and Valencia—names that recall, to the haunter of Kerry, memories of mountain and lake and ocean of infinite variety. But they must be seen to be realised, and the inadequacy of writing about them becomes quickly obvious. We must linger a moment over Staigue Fort (*Stéidhg*, a stripe (of land)), the most remarkable prehistoric monument in Kerry. It stands about a mile from the sea near West Cove beyond Sneem (*Snaidhm*, a knot). A great circular wall of dry masonry, eighteen feet in height, and many yards in thickness, encloses an area about eighty-eight feet in diameter. Narrow platforms run round the interior side of the wall, with flights of steps joining them. A single tunnelled doorway, flat-headed, with sloping jambs, gives entrance. History and tradition are alike silent as to its origin; the name, Staigue Fort, conveys nothing. One of its most remarkable characters is its perfect condition; for the similar cashel called the Grianan of Aileach was much dilapidated before its restoration, and that at Narin is in a ruinous state. But Staigue Fort stands there untouched by time, silent, imposing, mysterious.

For Kerry north of Killarney there is little to be said. Interest stops abruptly at Lough Lene, save for one most notable exception—the Dingle Peninsula, of which more anon. Geology is at the root of the change, for the Old Red Sandstone rocks which have given us the noble scenery of southern Kerry are here superseded by soft shales of the Coal-measure series, with a fringe of limestone along the shore. The result is flattish ground occupied by rushy pasture, or low broad hills smothered in peat bog. The bold Dingle Peninsula forms a kind of western island on the edge of this

Coal-measure area, and, excepting it, dull country stretches all the way from Killarney north to the Shannon. I once spent three days along the estuary of the sluggish Cashen River (*Casán*, a path, *i.e.* navigable) in a vain search for the rare Three-angled Bullrush, *Scirpus triqueter*, reported to have been gathered there, and elsewhere in Ireland known only on the Shannon about Limerick. Hour after hour I concentrated my gaze on the fringe of muddy vegetation at the base of the dyke which restrains the Cashen from flooding the flat rushy fields on either side; and I can remember with what longing my eyes turned towards the glorious outline of Slieve Mish (*Sliabh Mis*, mountain of Mis, daughter of Mureda) and Brandon, towering to the southward, and running far to the west out into the ocean. But for the botanist the muddy Cashen offers an ample compensation, for it is one of only two places in Ireland where the rare Dwarf Spike-rush, *Scirpus nanus*, is found—the other being Arklow. This is a tiny slender grass-like plant, only an inch high, creeping through the sandy mud and forming a thin green sward; often entirely covered by fresh deposits of mud, but waiting patiently till change of tide or wind again exposes it to the light of day. It is so rare that it is almost worth pilgriming to that dreary tract to gloat on its very insignificance. Should the tide be up when you get there, or should the plant be concealed by semi-liquid mud, you can still find it, for the search for food by many water-birds results in its being plucked up and drifted ashore, where it often forms a fringe at high-water mark.

It was on peat-covered hills near Gneevgullia, out to the north-east of Killarney, that there occurred, three days after the Christmas of 1896, an extensive bog-burst that attracted much attention on account of the tragic circumstances accompanying it, a family of eight persons, their home, and their live-stock, having been carried away and buried. These bog-bursts or bog-slides are not very uncommon in Ireland, on account of the great prevalence of peat-bogs in the country. In certain conditions, the lower layers of a bog may become so highly charged with water that under the pressure of the superincumbent mass they gush out at the lowest point of the floor, dragging the wreck of the more solid upper layers after them. If the bog be large and deep, a great flood of semi-liquid matter may be ejected: and should the slope below the point of ejection be steep, a devastating torrent may result. Unwise turf-cutting, by producing a high face without due preliminary draining, has been frequently the cause of these accidents. It was so in the fatal Kerry case; the face of the turf-cutting gave way, and a vast mass of peat and water precipitated itself down the valley, the flood ceasing only when it entered the Lower Lake of Killarney, fourteen miles distant. When the flow finally died down, about a week after the outburst, a great saucer-shaped depression, at its deepest no less than forty-five feet below the former slightly convex surface, showed the amount of the extruded material. This, with the abundant stumps of pine which it had contained, was spread for miles over the lands below, the width of the covering varying according to the slope of the valley-sides. " The flood has left behind it, in the upper portion of the valley," says a contemporary account, " a deposit of peat averaging three feet in thickness, here as everywhere contrasted by its black colour with the grassland or other surface on which it rests. Its compact convex margin, like that of outpoured oatmeal porridge, often two feet in height, serves equally well to define it; so that it was an easy task to determine and map the high-water level of the flood. The surface of the deposit was everywhere broken by great roots and trunks of Scotch Fir, which, in their enormous numbers, bore convincing testimony to the evisceration which the bog had undergone. The appearance of this sea of black peat, with its protruding stumps of black trees, was a sight melancholy in the extreme."[1] The evacuated area showed a depression three-quarters of a mile long and broad; the upper crust had broken away along a series of concentric cracks as the lower layers rushed out, and thousands of floes

[1] R. Ll. Praeger and W. J. Sollas, "Report of the Committee . . . to investigate the recent Bog-flow in Kerry", *Sci. Proc. Royal Dublin Soc.*, N.S., vol. viii., pp. 475-508, plates 17-19. 1897.

a yard or more thick went careering down the valley, to be stranded here and there; the centre of the area of movement was swept bare down to the gravelly drift on which the bog had rested; near the edges, the heather-covered floes still lay about, getting more numerous and closer together till the margin of the firm bog was reached, where the cracks could be seen in all incipient stages. I had ample opportunities for studying this disastrous bog-burst, for I was one of a small party, headed by W. J. Sollas, who a few days after the occurrence hurried down from Dublin to investigate on behalf of the Royal Dublin Society. It was dark cold weather, the Reeks were white with snow, the district a rather desolate one, and I well remember the feeling of depression with which we gazed at that black slimy mass stretching down the valley, somewhere in which lay entombed the bodies of Cornelius Donnelly, his wife, and his six children. Other bog-bursts, old and recent, I have visited, but none so devastating as that of Knocknageeha.

These bog-slides being rare and unexpected occurrences, and somewhat mysterious and terrifying to the local people, it follows that exaggeration hangs around them, and that newspaper accounts, often the only source of information available, are often wildly inaccurate. This was exemplified in 1906. The Dublin press of 20th June of that year contained exciting details of a bog-burst in Offaly on the previous day, which sent Professor Seymour and me scurrying down to Ballycumber the next morning. Four acres of bog had been " torn up and scattered as if by an explosion ", while a man narrowly escaped being buried. The people in terror had driven their cattle off the adjoining land, and abandoned the dwellings which lay nearest the scene, while the bog " kept heaving in all directions ". In the train, we read in the morning papers the names of twelve tenant-farmers who had had their lands covered by the bog-stuff; heavy rains had made the situation critical, for the swiftly flowing Brosna River passed within thirty yards of where the bog now rested, and any further movement would choke the stream and flood large areas of crops. Tramping out of Ballycumber under a scorching sun, laden with cameras and other implements of the chase, we therefore hoped to catch the bog-slide in the very act, *flagrante delicto*. As we approached the scene of the disaster, enquiries from a passing girl only elicited a smile and a "Never heard of it". Further enquiries were more successful, and we were directed to a spot where several men were peacefully cutting and stacking turf, aided by a donkey and a pony. There was no destroyed fuel or crops, nor ground covered by outbursts of peaty matter; nor was there any interruption of the tranquil life in the cottages whose chimneys peacefully smoked some few hundred yards distant. The "swiftly flowing Brosna", little more than a stagnant ditch, was nearly a mile away. Eating our lunches on a dry bank in the middle of the "explosion", we heard from one of the heroes of the tragedy his account of the affair. It was the usual story—the bog had not been drained in advance of the cutting, and the cut face consequently slipped forward by about thirty feet, covering the cut-away part. All was over in ten minutes, and some of the men engaged in saving their peat did not even leave their work. Is it any wonder that one becomes sceptical regarding local reports of these and other unfamiliar occurrences of the country-side?

There are records of at least twenty or twenty-five bog-slides in Ireland, dating from the beginning of the eighteenth century, and others have certainly occurred even within that period. As regards the extruded material, all trace of it soon vanishes, for when it has dried it makes excellent fuel, sometimes at the people's very doors! But the characteristic saucer-like depression in the bog may last long, and several times, tramping the Irish hills, I have come across the site of an unrecorded burst, often visible at a distance by the more abundant growth of Ling, which rejoices in the better drainage which it finds there.

When Professor Sollas and I looked into the question of bog-slides in 1896, we found that more occurrences of the sort appeared to have been recorded from Ireland than from all the rest of the world. They are certainly an especially Irish phenomenon; we

have a kind of "corner" in bog-slides, and it behoves us to make the
most of them. It is satisfactory, then, to find that such as have
occurred in the last forty years have been duly investigated and
reported on. The actual proximate cause of bog-slides is not always
obvious, and no doubt differs in different cases. They happen mostly
during the winter half of the year, as might be expected. Springs
under a bog, increasing the liquidity of the interior, may be responsible: heavy rain, by increasing the weight of the cover, may prove
the "last straw"; seismic movement has also been suggested.
Mostly the envelope would retain the semi-fluid mass were that
envelope continuous: but turf-cutting or sometimes a natural scarp
often provides a line of weakness. I remember George Francis
Fitzgerald accounting for the large number of local bog-flows by
the suggestion that the frequency of political tremors in Ireland
shook the bogs down the mountain-sides; but he thought that a
grave objection to this theory lay in the fact that only three had been
recorded from Ulster!

Tralee (*Tráigh Li*, Li's strand) is a name to conjure with, not on
account of attractions in the town itself, but because it is the gate to
one of the loveliest regions of Kerry. In the town there is one thing
worth seeing—the new county building, for the stone which has
been used in its construction is the most effective material that I have
seen in any Irish structure. It is a local sandstone from the Old Red
strata, of many beautiful shades of warm brown, red and yellow, no
two adjacent stones the same, and all blending into a lovely whole.
So far as I am aware, this singularly pleasing material has not as yet
been used in any other public building in Ireland, and it is to be
hoped that it will become better known.

Out to the west of the dull North Kerry country which extends
north and east of Tralee lies the last and in some ways the finest of
the great mountain-promontories—the Dingle Peninsula. This
differs from the others particularly in that its high east-and-west
backbone turns suddenly northward and, rising to 3127 feet in the
grand mountain of Brandon, drops into the ocean in a gigantic

precipice. At the landward end of the peninsula, the ridge of Slieve Mish (*Sliabh meissi*, mountain of the phantoms, 2796 feet) rises over the town of Tralee. Were it not eclipsed by the loftier and wilder mountains to the westward, Slieve Mish would rank as a very fine group of hills. On a spur at the western end, at an elevation of 2050 feet, is the remarkable prehistoric fortress of Caherconree (*Cathair Conraoi*, Cú Raoi's town), a promontory fort with a mountain precipice instead of the usual maritime cliff guarding two sides of it, and a massive wall, now much ruined, enclosing its triangular area on the third side. The site is a commanding one, overlooking a wide stretch of the wild country which lies to the west. There a wilderness of high hills and coombs and tarns extends, terminating in Brandon; while beyond, a lower storm-swept stretch continues to Slea Head and Sybil Head. Further still, the Blasket Islands, the tops of submerged mountains, raise their lofty and fantastic forms far above the ocean. The town of Dingle (*Daingean*, a stronghold) is the natural centre for this district, but the southern slopes of the mountains are smooth and dull compared with the northern, and the lover of either scenery or climbing will prefer the hamlet of Cloghane (*Clochán*, stepping stones), with its comfortable little inn. There he is strategically placed, with Beenoskee and the other central hills on one hand, and the grand crags of Brandon towering close on the other. Brandon is to my mind the finest mountain in Ireland—a huge mass, eight miles long from Brandon Point to the pass above Kilmalkedar, and five miles broad, deeply sculptured on the eastern side into spurs and valleys. A grand coomb runs up from near Cloghane, much resembling the famous one on Snowdon —a deep transverse gash extending almost from base to summit of the mountain, with a huge cliff occupying the left-hand side, while the bottom presents a series of rock-steps one above the other, each occupied by a clear lake. In the upper part the bare rock seems so newly modelled by the ice, that one might imagine the Glacial Period was only just passed away. On the western side, Brandon offers a steep unbroken slope, and its ascent from there is straightforward—and uninteresting; but if one approaches it from the Cloghane side, the widespread cliff-ranges give little choice, and you follow the old path up the coomb. As climbers sometimes get wrong here, the way being by no means evident, a hint may be useful. From Cloghane take the road which turns right, out of the Dingle Road a little beyond the chapel, and follow it for half a mile. Then bear a little to the right up the hill, aiming for either the bottom or the top of a dark line on the crest of the low lip of the coomb. This dark line is the heather on a wild moraine, better avoided. Either route brings you into the coomb, near Lough Cruttia. Up the coomb you cannot go wrong till you get near the top. Keep to the left then, up a very steep grassy slope close to the base of the cliff, where you will notice the remains of the old zigzag pilgrims' road (for Brandon is a holy mountain), and you will emerge from the coomb upon the smooth reverse slope a short distance north of the summit. The view of the wild western end of the peninsula, framed in an immense expanse of ocean, with the Blasket Islands beyond Mount Eagle, is a thing to be remembered. When you turn back, be careful not to miss the little nick on the right by which you commence the descent into the coomb; but if you want a longer walk, keep on northward along the ridge and over Knocka-bristee, and see the grand precipice which falls to the northern sea, and so home by Brandon village. Or you can come down from the summit by Brandon Peak, keeping the great cliff on your left, and past Gearhane to the low grounds.

Brandon is a very wet place, and the summit is often enveloped in cloud for days at a time—in winter for weeks—yet I have always had luck there; bad mist only once in half a dozen visits, and once deterrent rain. I remember a whole week during which the summit stood up bathed in sunshine all day, while at night the black peaks rose clear against the starlit sky, looking extraordinarily near.

Beyond Brandon lies a very remote area, approachable by only a single road—that which passes through Dingle—wind-swept and sodden, and yet surprisingly rich in monuments of antiquity, both pagan and Christian. Along the southern slopes of Eagle Mountain, and extending from Ventry Harbour (*Fionn tráigh*, white strand) to Dunmore Head (*Dún mór*, great fort), is the largest collection of prehistoric dwellings to be found in Ireland. The area has been monographed by R. A. S. Macalister.[1] He catalogues altogether 501 objects of antiquity, of which 414 are the remains of cloghans, or bee-hive dwellings, built singly or in groups. There are also 19 souterrains, and numerous raths, rock-shelters, promontory forts (Dunbeg being a very fine example), standing stones, sculptured stones, sculptured crosses. He believes the fortified headlands to be the earliest of the galaxy, and pre-Christian in date; following them came a long period of occupation extending well down to the Middle Ages. Nor does this surprising colony stand alone. Not far away is the early stone-roofed Oratory of Gallerus, the interesting twelfth-century church of Kilmalkedar, and a number of other monuments; the whole making this remote place one of the most attractive for the antiquary which can be found in the country.

The Blasket Islands (*Na Blascaoid*) form an interesting and romantic excursion from Dunquin, under Mount Eagle. In summer weather you land easily on the Great Blasket, but the others are more difficult of approach, and I never succeeded in getting ashore on Inishtooskert or Inishvickillane. The Great Blasket forms a ridge four miles long, half a mile wide, and nearly a thousand feet high along its knife-like backbone. Human settlement is confined to a cluster of cottages at its broader end, facing the land: and one finds there even a little cultivation of potatoes and oats. Elsewhere the exposure is tremendous. It is the only island of the group which is inhabited, except for the light-keepers on the Tearaght; and to philologists it is a prized sanctuary of the Irish language, a place of pilgrimage for students of the ancient tongue. Hence one is able to stay there, if fish and potatoes are deemed a sufficient diet. The views from its lofty ridge

---

[1] " On an Ancient Settlement in the south-west of the Barony of Corkaguiney, County of Kerry ", *Trans. Roy. Irish Acad.*, vol. xxxi., pp. 209-344, plates 17-25. 1899.

Great Blasket was evacuated in the 1950's and its only present-day inhabitants are a few men who spend the summer there, fishing and tending the sheep. C.M.

over tne rugged Kerry coast, the precipitous adjoining islands and the illimitable ocean on three sides, are unforgettable things. At the same time, I confess when I recall the Blaskets I mostly think of snails! When I botanized there one of the party was A. W. Stelfox of the National Museum, who was investigating the Mollusca. The island children, consumed with curiosity, followed us about, and watched with astonishment the collecting of box-snails and slugs. Presently we went home to our usual dinner of one herring and potatoes. When we emerged again, a deputation was waiting for us—half the children of the island, bearing cans, boxes, saucers, cloth caps and what-not all full of crawling molluscs, which, they told us, a penny or two might add to our possessions. It was difficult to explain to them that only certain rarer kinds were sought for; when they realized that their labour had been in vain, the whole of their spoils was emptied at our feet, and for the rest of our stay the cottage, inside and out, was alive with these interesting but unwelcome animals which, with misdirected energy, penetrated to every corner, and wrote their slimy autographs on wall and floor and ceiling.

A more difficult sea-trip is that which has the Skelligs (*Sceilig*, sea-rock), twenty miles to the southward of the Blaskets, as its objective. They lie well out to sea, across six miles of open ocean—eight if you go from Valencia, the usual starting-place. They are one of the few places in Ireland which, to my sorrow, I have not succeeded in reaching. Thrice I waited about Valencia for a good day, but the sea continued to run high, and landing was declared impossible, though it was midsummer. I suppose it is salutary that some of one's desires in this world should remain unfulfilled, even if they are as modest as this one. There are two rocks here, of lovely outline, towering like cathedrals. The larger, the Great Skellig, rises to 714 feet, and clinging to the cliff like swallows' nests are the huddled houses of anchorites of old days. There are six small clochans or stone huts; the little oratory of St. Michael, in which alone mortar was used; three other small oratories and several crosses, the whole enclosed in a cashel of dry stone (Plate XXXVIII).

In the chinks of the anchorites' huts, Stormy Petrels now build their nests. What sense of devotion or of penance could have inspired such an existence—to be lashed by storms, confined to a few yards of carved-out paths on the cliff, living on God knows what, cut off for weeks or months at a time by miles of angry water from the mainland and from all human succour. Today, the keepers in the comfortable lighthouse buildings below have a life which few would envy them: but imagine the existence of those hermits of early Christian times!

The Little Skellig, on the other hand, is tenanted in summer by thousands of Gannets, which have here one of their rare breeding colonies—grand birds, six feet or more across the wings, familiar to the seaside holiday-maker who watches their slow deliberate flight and their headlong dive as they shoot like arrows into the blue water. Like many birds, shy during the rest of the year, they know little fear when they are sitting on their eggs or tending their young, and you walk among them so far as the steep rocks will allow. For their nesting material they rely mainly on what they can find floating in the sea. Instead of grass, seaweed is used (*Fucus* and *Ascophyllum*): and they seem to have a fancy for anything unusual which they may discover. A. D. Delap tells me of strings of onions, blue castor-oil bottles, and a child's tin clockwork steamer, carefully built into their nests. But the myriad Gannets by no means monopolize the steep rocks of the Little Skellig. Fulmars are there too, and Stormy Petrels, and all the other birds of the coastal breeding-colonies; it is a populous city, dependent for everything on the stormy ocean that surrounds it. As to inhabitants of these rocks other than birds, the Great Skellig supplies an interesting problem. No less than thirteen species of mollusca live there—nine kinds of snails and four of slugs; and many of these are species which on the mainland affect native habitats—rocks and deep glens and so on—and are not found about the habitations of man nor in gardens nor fields. So they are very unlikely to have arrived in the lighthouse boat among vegetables or other imports, or to have come with the old monks in past days.

Plate XXXVIII

T. H. Mason: photo

On the Great Skellig, showing bee-hive cell, St. Michael's Church, and the Little Skellig

It is likewise highly improbable that they have been conveyed by water, or by flying creatures such as birds; which drives us to the theory that they have been there since the rock, now isolated by six miles of rough and deep water, was portion of the mainland—which also seems unlikely. But this is only one of ten thousand little problems which confront us if we keep our eyes open and our minds alert, and which we cannot answer—at least in the present state of our knowledge. And there is no use in guessing.

> O, I wad like to ken—to the beggar-wife says I—
> The reason o' the cause an' the wherefore o' the why,
> Wi' mony another riddle brings the tear into my e'e
> —" *It's gey an' easy speirin* ", says the beggar-wife to me.[1]

And now our peregrination through Ireland is completed. We began appropriately with the wild landscape of Inishowen, and end with the wilder landscape of the Blaskets. Not that the really characteristic Ireland lies in these areas of mountain and sea: rather is it to be found in the wide bogs and pastures of the Central Plain. But the Atlantic fringe, with its tall brown hills, its tattered coast-line and its snowy foam, is the region to which one's errant thoughts recurrently stray, and which remains a lodestar to people of many lands—a magic region which, once viewed by the stranger, rests for ever in his memory.

·   ·   ·   ·   ·

I said at the beginning that I had no intention of writing a guide-book to Ireland: and no one would be so rash as to describe by that name these desultory chapters. If my reader fails to find reference to some place in which, or in associations of which, he may be interested, I can only retort that he was warned; that I have done what I said I would, and roamed at random.

Another point: I can hear a reader—I assume that I shall have at least one—grumbling that human interests have not received in these pages the respect which is their due: that I have written of the rocks and flowers, birds and beasts, and paid scant homage to the towns

[1] Robert Louis Stevenson.

and the myriad fellow-creatures who live or have lived in them. I seem to find that human activities, past and present, and all that belongs to them, are not in need of exploitation in yet another of the many books which profess to be descriptive of Ireland, in contrast to the claims of the land and the landscape, and all that goes to make them. Both have, or should have, a deep significance to all thinking people, and I should like our education to be so arranged that a person of ordinary intelligence would find as much to interest him in the ground he walks on, the air he breathes, the myriad lower creatures, large and small, which share the earth with him, as in the present activities of populous human hives, or in the memorials of bygone piety or warfare which are everywhere with us—strange how in Ireland these divide the visible past between them. But since there are twenty books which treat of history and archaeology or the present outward symbols of human life for one that ventures to draw attention to the varied interests of man's natural environment, I am impenitent as to my choice.

But the study of nature in the open needs contemplation and quiet, and these become increasingly difficult to obtain. Hurry and noise are the keynotes of today, and where these prevail we need never hope to lure the fairies from their hiding-places. Perhaps I have arrived at the stage of old-fogydom, for I recall the more leisurely, deliberate, spacious days of Queen Victoria, the courteous quakerish naturalists who taught me truths that lie at the bottom of all true science, and I confess that I look back on the general attitude of those times, and of those old-fashioned exponents of man's relation to the universe, with a deep affection. One was encouraged to *think* in those days; but how many young people of today do not prefer the noble sentiment of the *Rejected Addresses*—

> Thinking is but an idle waste of thought,
> And nought is everything, and everything is nought!

The present time is one of rush and clatter, of fuss and noise and glare: and I fancy I see repercussions of all this or of the new mentality which has produced it, and which it has produced, in the strange literature and art and music of the day. My medieval mind will not rise to modern heights. I frankly confess to preferring Mozart to Ravel, Constable to the cubists, Browning to James Joyce: and I have a sneaking fellow-feeling with a writer in *Punch* a few years ago:

> What with *Gertrude*, *Ep*, and *Ein*,
> When I hear the name of *Stein*,
> I go creepy down the spine.
>
> .   .   .   .   .
>
> What with *Gertrude*, *Ein*, and *Ep*,
> Life and Art are out of step,
> Are we then down-hearted? Yep!

All of which merely shows that I have lived my life and said my say, and that it now remains to bow and retire.

But to revert to Ireland and my praise of it: that at least is not to be set aside, for beauty—whatever that may be—is everlasting, in whatever manifestation, and its worship can never be out of season. And Ireland is a very lovely country. Indeed, there is only one thing wrong with it, and that is that the people that are in it have not the common-sense to live in peace with one another and with their neighbours. Past events and political theory are allowed to bulk much too large in our mental make-up, and the result is dissatisfaction, unrest, and occasionally shocking violence. That "frontier", which is a festering sore in Ireland's present economy, was the noble gift of an English Government—but Ireland brought it on herself. "Well, now", said a Connemara man to me, "politics is the divil itself": and in this country that is only too true. If St. Patrick had banished from Ireland politics, instead of snakes, he would have conferred a far greater boon, and this lovely land would have had peace and charity, as well as faith and hope.

I do not think that, where countries are concerned, beauty can be considered a comparative term. All countries are beautiful, each in its several ways. But how can one contrast the beauty of Holland with the beauty of Norway? To the patriot, the loveliest country is—or should be—that in which he was born and in which he has lived, for it has given to him the very foundation of his being. And to minds well balanced there is no danger that the beauties of other lands will make us depreciate the charms of our own. That is a common experience. I believe, on the contrary, that foreign travel leads to a truer estimate and appreciation of one's own land— I am thinking of natural features, not of sociological and such-like affairs, in which many countries could teach us in Ireland a good deal. " I did not know what my own house was like ", says Father Keegan in *John Bull's Other Island*, " because I had never been outside it." It may be that some of the over-praise (as well as under-praise) of Ireland that occasionally offends one's sense of proportion has come from persons so circumstanced. If this book is held to have been guilty of over-praise, at least it is not due to that fault. I have wandered about Europe from Lapland to the Aegean Sea: but have always returned with fresh appreciation of my own land. I think that is as it should be.

INDEX

THE WAY THAT I WENT

After more than twenty-five years *The Way That I Went* remains the finest guide to the Irish countryside. Perhaps the reason is that it was written not as a guide book but rather as an outstanding man's memories of a land which he had known intimately for seventy years.

The book is concerned in the main with the topography of Ireland. A quarter of a century does little to alter the appearance of vegetation, mountains and ruins and there are not many changes to be made in Praeger's account. In a few cases further research has rendered his ideas obsolete. There have been interesting fluctuations in the numbers of some bird species, and industrial developments have changed the face of the land to some extent. Footnotes have been supplied by Christopher Moriarty to bring the book up to date in these respects, and a few modern references have been included.